National Life and Character
in the Mirror of Early
English Literature

T0371322

National Life and Character in the Mirror of Early English Literature

BY

EDMUND DALE, M.A., D.Lit.

Cambridge:
at the University Press
1907

CAMBRIDGE UNIVERSITY PRESS
Cambridge, New York, Melbourne, Madrid, Cape Town,
Singapore, São Paulo, Delhi, Mexico City

Cambridge University Press
The Edinburgh Building, Cambridge CB2 8RU, UK

Published in the United States of America by Cambridge University Press, New York

www.cambridge.org
Information on this title: www.cambridge.org/9781107680180

First published 1907
First paperback edition 2013

A catalogue record for this publication is available from the British Library

ISBN 978-1-107-68018-0 Paperback

PREFACE.

THE remote origin of this book was a Paper on the Influence of the School of York read before a society of which the writer was a member some six years ago. From this small beginning sprang the idea of a work on the Inner Life, Thought and Influence of the Early English Church, which came to nothing. The next stage, two years later, was a contemplated thesis on the development of the Anglo-Saxon conscience, but under the direction and advice of Mr A. J. Wyatt, M.A., this became *The Development of the National Character and Social Life as reflected in Early English Literature*. After the completion of this stage occasional intervals of leisure during the last two years have been given to preparation for publication, the present title being finally adopted. To Mr Wyatt the writer is greatly indebted for many excellent hints and searching criticism. Mr Wyatt has also most kindly read the proofs, and the book has greatly benefited by his assistance in the final revision.

The writer's thanks are also due to the learned Master of Peterhouse, Dr A. W. Ward, who has suggested several improvements in the arrangement of the matter and other details.

Acknowledgment must be made of the help afforded by many works upon the literature of the period, chief among which were Mr Stopford Brooke's *History of Early English Literature*, Professor Ten Brink's *Early English Literature*, M. Jusserand's *Literary History of the English People* and *English Wayfaring Life*, Dr Courthope's *History of English*

Poetry, vol. I., Professor Morley's *English Writers*, vols. I.—IV., Professor Ker's *Epic and Romance*, Professor Lounsbury's *Studies in Chaucer*, and Dr A. W. Ward's *Chaucer* in the English Men of Letters Series. These authorities laid the primary foundations for the later work of research.

The idea of the book is that by pricking in, as it were, literary illustrations upon the background of history a study of the period might gain in interest and definition. The writer has tried to keep his modernisations as close as possible to the originals, his primary purpose being to give reproductions which should be at the same time faithful and clear. The marginal references are regarded as an essential part of the book, without which its value in the eyes of the scholar would be diminished, as they practically remove the whole from the domain of pure imaginative fiction to the sure ground of a literary and historic reflection of real life and character. It is hoped that they will be found to give just sufficient direction to the sources of the material without being in themselves unwieldy.

As to the views and opinions expressed, the writer would emphasise the point that it is, in the main, the literature which speaks, and not himself. Though it is almost impossible to be perfectly unbiased or impartial where one's own nation is concerned, still he has ever had before him the ideal of a faithful representation of life and truth. Perhaps he has slipped occasionally, perhaps frequently, and so can only plead that his work has had far more influence upon him than he has had upon the book.

E. D.

January, 1907.

CONTENTS.

SYNOPSIS.

INTRODUCTION.

Purpose—Method—Material.

CHAPTER I.

THE ENGLISHMAN OF THE CONQUEST.

Development of life and character—The invaders and their songs—
The *Beowulf* and *Widsith*—Character of the invaders—Early continental
life, warfare and migrations—Offa and the Angles—Raids and feuds
—Fight at Finnsburg—Cynewulf and Cyneheard—Alfred's law " Of
Feuds "—Hrothgar and Ingeld—The Geats and Sweons, and the Fight
in Ravens' Wood—Revenge—Composition.

The sea—Raids over sea — Britain— The invasion— Hengist and
Horsa—Conquest of Kent—Treachery—Conquest of Sussex—Kingdoms
of Wessex and Northumbria founded—Fall of Bath—Uriconium—
Lament of Llywarch Hen—Fall of Chester—Complétion of conquest—
A battle—Mutilation, treachery, hatred—The school of war—The hero—
Beowulf, Offa, Ælfwine—Character of Beowulf—The age of Beowulf;
contrasts.

The king, earls, thegns — Relations between lord and thegn —
Affection—Widsith, Hrothgar, Beowulf—Faithfulness—Beowulf and his
thegns—Andreas and his followers—Beowulf and Wiglaf—Beowulf's
death—Consequences of unfaithfulness—Separation—The freeman—
Liberty—The serfs and slaves—Captured Welsh and English slaves.

The settlement — The hall — The township — Occupations — Pastures
—Sport—Racing—Sentinels—The mark—Evil spirits—Charms—Good
spirits—Hospitality in the settlement—Beowulf at Heorot—Responsi-
bilities of the host—Banquet at Heorot; hoards and treasures—Etiquette
—Strife—Drunkenness—The gleeman and his mission—Home and kin
—The English woman, heroine and peace-weaver—Her faults—Marriage
customs—Conjugal affection; *Husband's Message* and *Wife's Complaint*
—Brutality—Chastity—Punishment of the unchaste—Women and war
—Love for children—Changes due to migration and settlement.

Wyrd and fatalism—*Lament of Deor*—The warrior's death; the funeral pyre—Burial—Passing out to sea; Scyld—The mystery of life—The Sparrow in the Hall—Immortality—Ancestor and nature worship —Deities and their abode—Religion; sacrifices—The *Eddas*—The story of Balder.

CHAPTER II.

THE ADVENT AND INFLUENCE OF
CHRISTIANITY.   PAGE 61

Nature of Teutonic Christianity—The Celtic Church of Wales—Welsh aloofness—Admiration of Rome—Prestige of the Empire—Landing of St Augustine; conversion in Kent—Conversion in the north; Cefi — Eadwine's influence — The kingdom of heaven — Opposition — Blending of the old and new faiths—Christianity itself modified.

Teaching of charity and humanity—Morality benefited—austere views of marriage—Against drunkenness—Christianity upon the battlefield—Against violence and slaughter—Practice of Christian virtues.

Conference at Whitby; Rome or Iona, Wilfrid—Roman organisation; divine right of kings—Pilgrimages to Rome—Influence for evil—Pope and king; Wilfrid's appeal.

The monastic schools and the new learning—Educational life at York—Books and libraries—Theology; the end of all learning—Christian craftsmanship—Famous scholars—Missionaries—Benedict Biscop and his pictures—Influence of pictures upon the English imagination—Story of Drihtelm—Influence of Benedict—Bede—His death—Tenderness—Change in the heroic ideal—The contemplative life; Cuthbert; asceticism—The supernatural—Asceticism and the miraculous—Corruption in some monasteries. .

Cædmon and his song—The blending of old and new in his verse—The three elements in Old English poetry; scriptural, traditional, Teutonic—God and Satan—Satan cast into hell—Hell—Parallels with *Beowulf* and other heathen poems—Adam and Eve; the Fall—Consciousness of sin—Pity for the fallen—Other Teutonic modifications.

The poets—Parallels between the *Beowulf* and Christian poems—Hrothgar's Christian speech—Wyrd changed by Christianity—Thanks offered to God—Misfortune a mark of God's anger.

The school of Cynewulf—Life and conversion—Wider Christian reading—Influence of outer world preserves English spirit—Disasters in the north; resultant change of character—Cynewulf's conversion—His prayers—The *Dream of the Rood*—Christ to the host of the lost —Life simile; heaven—Cynewulf the poet of the Cross—Expansions from Gregory and use of Balder myth—Use of Latin hymns and Roman ritual; Joseph and Mary—Stern uncompromising opposition to adversaries of the faith; emotional excitability—God alone knows whither the soul passes—Eagerness for death—The age of zealous enthusiasm.

CHAPTER III.

THE DISCONCERTING FACTORS. PAGE 124

The blight—Despair—Need of leaders—Struggle for supremacy—
Ecgberht's ideal—Coming of the Danes—Sense of impending doom;
omens and prodigies—Danish attacks—Ferocity—Ecgberht's death—
War of occupation—Dissensions in the north; the school of York
dispersed, Peterborough burned—Warfare general—The lessons of
failure.

Edmund of East Anglia—Alfred the Great, his age and character
—Athelney; Alfred and Guthrum—Plans for defence; the new navy—
Its first exploit—Consolidation—Relations with Rome; thank-offerings
—Alfred's labours; laws—Translations—Education at his court and
schools—Work—Edward the Elder; education of his sons and daughters.

Song of the Battle of Brunanburg—Edgar and his policy—Recrudescence of violence—Decadence—Dunstan—Opposition to monastic
despotism—Edgar and monasticism—Monks and canons—The end of
the world—Developing reason.

Murder of Edward; accession of Ethelred—Battle of Maldon—
Fading of the heroic age and its song—Tribute and treachery—Character
of Ethelred—Defence disorganised—Treacherous massacres of Danes—
Martyrdom of Ælfeah—Wulfstan's *Sermon to the English*—Edmund
Ironside—Cnut; his popularity—Weakness of his sons.

Edward the Confessor and his chief nobles—Contact with Normandy;
Eustace at Dover—Edward's death; the claimants to the throne—
Harold's oath—Repudiation and preparations for invasion and defence
—Stamford Bridge—The fleet fails to defend the coast; William lands
in the south—Preparations for battle at Senlac; the oath and the monk
—The night before the battle—The Norman advance—Assault upon
the hill—Stratagem of pretended flight—Defeat—Resignation.

CHAPTER IV.

THE BLENDING OF THE RACES. PAGE 177

The Norman-French—Their character in history—Life and character
of the age in the *chansons*—The warrior—Death of Roland—The
Norman ideal—William I; his readiness, cleverness and example—Contemporary estimate of his character—*Doomsday Book*—His followers—
Normans supreme in England—Subsequent discord.

Reign of Stephen—Turbulent factions; civil war, barons, bishops
and people—Norman romance; Saxon sadness—Saxon record of the
reign—Degenerate churchmen.

The French England—French influence—Literatures French, English,
Latin—Increasing contact—Clergy and minstrels—Soldiers—Outlaws—
Barons and people against king and favourites—Common hero worship—
The two temperaments; *Owl and Nightingale*—Change to a brighter life
—The romance a step towards the Renaissance—A romantic age—Celtic

influence—Provençal influence; courtoisie—Influence of Crusades—Taste—Greek romances—Advance of knightly ideal—The age impressionable.

Home life; the castle—wife and family—morning mass and matins—Hunting party—Maying—Castle grounds—Indoor occupations—Evening—Dinner—Social intercourse and entertainment; music—Chess—Accomplishments—Qualities of the peerless knight—Gawain and Chaucer's Knight—The peerless lady—The gallant—Story of William II—The ladies—Tales round the hearth—*Florice and Blancheflour*—*Aucassin and Nicolette*—Immorality—The vanity of the world—The jongleur and his entertainment—His tales—*Richard Cœur de Lion*—Bedchambers—Happenings in the night—Unrest.

Departure of sons from home—Journey—Court and king—Contrast of the Charlemagne of the *Roland* with the Charlemagne of *Huon of Bordeaux*—The Charlemagne of the romances—King Mark of Cornwall; decay of the kingly ideal—Warnings against misuse of kingship—Life at court.

Call to Crusade—Dubbing knights; tournaments and ordeals—The judgment of God—The combat—Effect upon spectators—Banquet after tournament—Scenes of cruelty after ordeal—Historical examples—Women burnt or scourged—Embarkation for the Holy Land—The friends of God—Fighting and slaying—Saracens confounded with Jews—Riches of the Orient—Conscience forbids further slaughter—Humour—Jests—Return.

Christ the lover for the desolate—Religious appeal to womanhood—Convent life—Surreptitious contact with the world; the Sacristan Nun—The Church and celibacy—The papacy—Self-confidence in thought; Berengarius—Influence of Arabic learning; Abelard—Roger Bacon.

Satire—*Roman de Renart*—Satires against the clergy—Burnellus.

The universities—Poor scholars and free education—English theology; a topical sermon—The friars.

Life and food of the poor—Poor maids—Amusements of the poor—Miracle and Mystery Plays—Sunday—Ordeal by fire or water—Voice of the people—How poor men rose in life—The workers in the cities—The Jews educate the English in finance and commerce.

CHAPTER V.

THE RESULTANT NATION.   PAGE 255

The new life—Rise of middle and lower classes—Problems of the age—The new national career—The English language in the ascendant—English writings and translations—French ceases to be taught in the schools—Scoffing at Frenchmen—Insularity increased.

Conquests—The war with France—Sea-power—A sea-fight—Boasting of Cressy—The English archer—His value increasing—Effect upon the yeomanry and peasantry—Rise in importance of artisan and merchant-trader—Enthusiasm wanes—King and Commons—Weak kingship and discord.

Spirit of the Renaissance and political liberty—The gentleman known by his deeds, not birth—Feudal system undermined—The Renaissance and the beautiful in life—The age of desire.

Trade—The shipmen—Jealousy of the alien—Competition—The master-craftsmen—The London apprentice—Countryman's visit to London—Roguery of small traders—Pedlars.

Credulity and superstition—Extremes of character—The stains against the brightening background—The new era of kindness and conscience.

Decay of tournaments—Extravagance in dress—the toilet—Correspondence between dress, manners and character.

Satires on women—On wives—Reaction—Good women—Cressida and love—Lovers—Wedding—Marriage—Parental instinct—Correction of children—Morality.

Pleasures of the table—Hospitality—Bedrooms—Inns—Taverns—Gambling and brawling.

Life and conscience in Chaucer and Langland—Unsanitary conditions and disease—Physicians—Distress in the country; influx to the towns—The peasant and his rights—The Ploughman—Cry of the poor—Peace against Wrong—Poor men's sons—Poor and the law—Inferior types—Wastrels, impostors and hunger—Rebellion of the peasantry—Influence of Wycliffe's teaching.

Life on the roads; rogues and vagabonds; minstrels in disrepute—Free life of the countryside.

Pilgrims—Hermits—Fanatics, hypocrites, sceptics—The reformer's satire—Holy Church—Her teaching and ordinances—Religious thought—The papacy—Pope Holy—Sins of clerks—The friars—Their methods—Their immorality—Their wealth—Scandal connected with their deaths—The pardoners—The deceit perceived—Young clerks—The Clerk of Oxford—Langland and the Reformation—Wycliffe—The Parson.

"Ex ejusdem creaturae seminibus et primordialibus causis totius seculi tempus naturali cursu peragitur, ubi Pater usque nunc operatur, et Filius, ubi etiam corvos pascit et lilia vestit Deus."

BEDE, *De Natura Rerum*, 700 A.D.

"Nature, the Vicar of the Almighty Lord."

CHAUCER, *Parlement of Foules*, 1381 A.D.

"Nor do I so forget God as to adore the name of Nature; which I define not, with the Schools, to be the principle of motion and rest, but that straight and regular line, that settled and constant course, the Wisdom of God hath ordained the actions of His creatures, according to their several kinds....In brief, all things are artificial; for Nature is the Art of God."

SIR THOMAS BROWNE, *Religio Medici*, 1635 A.D.

INTRODUCTION.

THE purpose of this study is to examine and set forth the ever-developing character of the Englishman in the successive ages of his early career, until modern life begins, together with the corresponding development of political and social life which determines and, at the same time, is determined by it; "to hold, as 't were, the mirror up to nature," as the centuries pass by; "to show virtue her own feature, scorn her own image, and the very age and body of the time his form and pressure."

The method employed will be, as far as it is possible, to permit the Englishman to speak for himself, while we use his words as self-revelations of his life and thought and character. Thus one may hope to minimise the errors which arise from fallacious reasonings and biassed judgments, and to attain more closely to scientific accuracy and truthfulness.

So for the material for our work we turn to the literature in which each age has left us a reflection of itself, remembering that no literature is merely fortuitous or accidental, but springs from the very heart of the nation in which it lives; that a true poet is never independent and self-contained in his art, but derives his inspiration from the great movements of his time, paints his pictures from the men and the life he sees about him, and is encouraged and uplifted by the sympathies of those whose hearts leap at his words because he has sounded the depths of their humanity. A literature is but the means by which the aspirations and ideals of a nation find expression in an abiding form.

CHAPTER I.

[To about 650 A.D.]

THE ENGLISHMAN OF THE CONQUEST.

WHEN our forefathers were passing from the Continent
to the invasion and settlement of Britain they were making
neither the first nor the last of their many migrations.
Already many marks of past experience had been impressed
upon the race; already the mighty and mysterious forces of
nature had left their influence upon both life and character.
For the inner man grows, changes and developes as does the
outward man; and in the inner life, as in the outer, there are
always the first faint cries of new births to blend with the
voices of the living and the last sighs of the dying. There is
always a continual development of character and social life
from age to age, as we all come from the past with its lesson
towards the future with its hope. Each successive age in the
history of the development of man incorporates into itself
the substance of the ages past, shapes that substance as the
pressure of circumstance or environment demands, and at its
close leaves its own composite deposit of experience for the
making of the ages yet to be. In one long unbroken chain
of many links the development of mankind goes on throughout all time, its end Eternity. No race, no age, depends
upon itself alone. Born of the past, yet plastic to the
present, ever changing towards the future, the Englishman
first stepped out upon these shores from the bosom of his
keel.

In the ranks of the invading hosts were many who could
touch the harp with skilful fingers while they chanted the
Beowulf, 2106. rude melodies which the warrior loved, blending recitals of
the stirring deeds of the past with softer and more mournful
memories of the old homeland beyond the sea. There was

always some sympathetic chord in the Englishman's rugged nature to vibrate in unison with either strain.   Chiefs and warriors, heroes and commoners alike, could weave their spells upon the strings, hoarding up in their breasts the *Beowulf,* *Widsith,* 1. treasures of song and story which, in the days of their youth, Bede, *H. E.* they had heard the gleeman sing.   Many there were who IV. 24. could themselves frame new songs and shape the story of the present into verse for the gleeman of the future to recall in after days; and it seems that thus the story of their invasion was first handed down.   While the long, black ships passed across the lonely seas, or lay hidden in some quiet creek, the plaintive notes would often while away the period *Rhyme Song* of inactivity.   As the host advanced into battle, the wild *Gnomic V.* notes of the war-song rose high above the din; and, when *(Ex.)* 170. the victory was won and the excited warriors sat down to *Beowulf,* 496, 868, 1063. feast and to play, the harp was brought forth to exult in impassioned strains over the ancestral honours of the race.

One of the earliest of these old songs is the *Lay of Beowulf* which seems to have had a long and regular growth, out of the myths and legends of remote antiquity, among the Continental tribes.   This poem, whatever its date may be, affords a typical example of Old English song in the heathen days, and reflects, with accuracy and completeness, the life and thought, the manners, customs and character of our early ancestors.   Their aspirations and beliefs, their passions and affections, their feuds and warfaring expeditions, their battles and conquests, their songs and banquets after victory, are here clearly reflected, to stand out as self-revelations of a primitive and warlike people.   Another poem, of like or even greater antiquity, is the *Song of Widsith*, the wandering gleeman; and there are many echoes of such old songs scattered throughout Old English poetry.   From this material, which the English tribes brought with them from the Continent, we best learn to know their past history and character.

We see that the invaders are just emerging from a state of chaos, already grouping themselves into warrior tribes, and acknowledging the tribal ties for their own preservation.   The family is no longer the unit in the social organism; life is no longer distinctly nomadic.   That they have but recently left such a state may be seen in the strong claims which the ties of blood relationship still impose, and in their restless, roving habits. But they have not yet grouped themselves into settled states or nations with distinguishing characteristics or clearly defined territories. Their character is, correspondingly, in an almost chaotic condition ; elements of good intermingle inextricably with elements of evil. In the same type, even in the same being, all the traits of utter barbarism, all the selfish instincts and mad impulses of the savage, blend with the higher qualities of a nobler humanity. Passionate cravings, insatiate lust, brutal ferocity, treachery, revengefulness, unreliability, improvidence, childishness, everywhere lie side by side with staunchest devotion, loyalty, self-sacrifice, heroism, wisdom, caution ; and often the accidents of circumstance, or the wayward fancies of the moment, decide which rises uppermost. Such is the deposit of the past, such the material from which the future Englishman is to be evolved.

When we turn to examine the antecedents of these men we begin to understand how their condition may be accounted for. The Continental life depicted in the poems is essentially migratory and chaotic, the strenuous life of the warrior in a state of continual unrest. Many tribes, accustomed to the freedom and license of a roving life, are seen packed together in North-West Europe, always increasing in numbers, and ever assailed by a steady pressure upon all sides. Behind them, from the east, press the Huns ; in front, to the west and south, even as far as the Saxon Shore of Britain, the Latin race attempts to bar their progress. Frequently we hear of the exceeding fecundity of the race, and how, in consequence, it is the custom for chosen bands to emigrate in order to relieve the pressure. Against the ever-increasing restraint the tribes struggle violently, each seeking to preserve its own liberty. They passionately refuse to surrender the old life to the new circumstances. A movement in one quarter transmits itself, with increasing turmoil, through every tribe, and agitates in turn each particle of the seething mass of humanity.

In the *Widsith* some of the tribes are seen slowly moving westwards, pressed from the east by the Hunnish hordes of Attila, and fighting for their lives. "Full often there war ceased not, when the army of the Hræds with sharp swords

Alfred's Metra, I. I.

Will. of Malmes. I. I. Layamon's *Brut* 13854. Wace's *Brut*, etc.

Widsith, 119.

about the woods of Vistula was forced to defend their old
ancestral seat against Attila's hordes." In another quarter, 127.
"full often from the troop flew the whistling shaft and the
yelling spear against the grim folk, where Wudga and Hama,
chieftains adorned with gold, sought to avenge their warriors
and their wives." For generation after generation in their
migration to the west they must have fought so often with
all the fierceness which despair alone could give that the lust
of strife had entered into their blood, and the excitement of
the fray had become almost a necessity. They had so often
encouraged each other with loud cries to harden their hearts
and to sell their lives dearly in defence of all they loved that
now they begin to enter into battle with the wildest songs
upon their lips and the intensity of ferocious delight in their
eyes. They struggle continuously for the supremacy among
themselves; and in this connection is to be found the first
mention in our literature of the Angles and their land, a
continental England not yet deserted for the fields and woods
of Britain. Offa, the first great king and national hero, a
half historic, half mythic personage, stands out as the conquering warrior; and his people are already winning the
mastery over their neighbours: "Offa ruled the Angles,
Alewih the Danes. Of all those men Alewih was the 35.
proudest, yet over Offa he never proved his valour; but
Offa, first of men, while yet a youth, won the greatest of
the kingdoms. None, at his age, won greater renown than
he. With his single sword at Fîfel-Dor he extended his
borders against the Myrgings; Angles and Swæfs thenceforth held sway as Offa won it."

Great chiefs, like Scyld, rise upon the earth and grow in *Beowulf*, 4.
power; they deprive many tribes of their mead-seats, and
force their neighbours to obey them and to pay tribute. Like
Hygelac, who "for pride endured woe, feud with the Frisians," 1205
they make raids and carry off much booty, protecting under [c. 512 A.D.].
the banner the spoil they have taken, and in its defence
falling in the war-rush beneath the shield, dead through
"the drinking of the swords." And when a famous chief 2355.
lies dead the attacks of old-time enemies upon his unpro- 2913.
tected country are but to be expected. In the might of 2923.
3000.
spears and swords lies the sole protection against the horrors 1770.
of war; and often does the warrior experience "the iron- 3117.

shower" when the storm of arrows driven by the bowstrings smites upon the shield-wall.

Often was the warrior, by the fierce onrush of his foes under cover of night, roused from sleep to cry aloud to his men to arm quickly to fight for their lives. So, in the hall, a good war-troop would always retire to rest with their shields by their heads, and with their helmets, corslets and

1243. spears on a bench above them. "Such was their custom that they should always be prepared for war, both at home and on foray, as their lord had need." Then would the hall ring again with the din of battle and the challenges of attackers and defenders. Thus it happened at Finnsburg where Finn the Frisian treacherously surprised Hnæf the Dane, his guest and the brother of his wife.

The Fight at Finnsburg [follg. Grein and Bugge].

The warriors are sleeping in the hall; outside, the full moon is shining; it is near the dawn when men sleep most heavily. From without comes the sound of a stealthy rush,

5. and there is a flicker of flame. The chief, stirred by fore-boding fears, awakes and listens. Is it the dawn that so lights up the hall? He hears the ring of mail corslets, the rattle of spears, the clatter of shaft on shield, the arrows singing about the doors. It is no dawn; the roof is ablaze;

10. and he is up on his feet with a loud cry: "Awake now, warriors mine! Meet the rush of the foe! Be ready to strike! Forget not your fame! Be brave in heart!" The warriors leap up at his call, seize their swords, and hasten to defend the doors. Sigeferth and Eaha are first to the one; Ordlâf, Gûthlâf and Hengest first to the other. All is tumult and confusion beneath the reek of the smoke and the crack-ling flame; hard it is to discern friend from foe. Above the uproar a fierce voice is heard without, crying aloud to know who holds the door; and a challenge rings out boldly:

24. "Sigeferth is my name. I am chief of the Secga, a rover widely known. Many woes, many hard battles, have I borne. Here is appointed thee whatsoever thou willest to seek of me." So a fight to the death begins within the walls; the hall-floor rings again with the din; the swords flash in the light of the flames as though all Finnsburg were full of fire.

For five days the fight continues, and then Hnæf's corslet is broken, his helmet cloven, and he receives a mortal wound.

But his followers under Hengest hold their own, and slay *Beowulf*, 1070. many of their assailants, including Finn's son. Finn himself is forced to come to terms, and to make rich gifts as the price of peace. Yet, when the winter has passed, Hengest again renews the strife, and is himself slain, leaving the feud for Gûthlâf and Ôslâf to carry through. Finally Finn's hall is taken and he and his followers slain. Then the avengers depart, leading with them Hildeburh, Finn's wife, and a great booty.

There is a somewhat similar story of feud and surprise attack in the *Anglo-Saxon Chronicle* which shows that the character of the English was not transformed in this respect by the migration across the sea. Sigeberht, an under king of *A.-S. Chron.* Wessex, for wrong-doing, was deprived of his kingdom, with 755 A.D. the exception of Hampshire, by Cynewulf and the West Saxon Witan. Soon afterwards he slew Cumbra, his oldest "ealdorman," and for that deed was banished into the Forest of Andred. There a herdsman stabbed him to death, and so avenged Cumbra. But Sigeberht had a brother, Cyneheard, who took up the feud with Cynewulf. Hearing that the king was in the company of a woman at Merton with but a little troop to protect him, Cyneheard came upon him there and surrounded the bower before the king's followers found him. When the king perceived this he posted himself at the door and nobly defended himself until he caught sight of the atheling, when he rushed out and severely wounded him ; and they were all fighting against the king until they had slain him. By this time, hearing the cries of the woman, the king's thegns became aware of the tumult, and ran thither, each as he was ready. And the atheling offered them money and life, and none of them would take it, but they went on fighting until they all fell, except one British hostage, and he was sorely wounded. In the morning the king's thegns who were left behind heard what had happened and rode to the town to avenge their lord. Bribes they indignantly refused : they would never follow the murderer of their king. So they kept on fighting about the gates until they got within and slew the atheling and the men who were with him, all save one, and he was often wounded.

So largely are such attacks a feature of the life of the Teutonic peoples that, in Alfred's days, the laws take

Laws of
Alfred, No. 42.
"Of Feuds,"
A.-S. Laws,
Thorpe, p. 40.

cognisance of them, but can only prescribe regulations to
check the wanton shedding of blood. If a man know his
foe to be home-staying he is not to fight before he has
demanded justice of him. If he is strong enough to besiege
him he must not attack him for seven days, if his foe remain
within. If after seven days his foe will surrender and deliver
up his weapons he is to be kept safe for thirty days, and
notice must be given to his kinsmen and friends. If he flee
to a church for sanctuary the sanctity of the church is to be
observed. If the man is not strong enough to besiege his
foe, he must ride to the "ealdorman" and beg aid of him, and
if the "ealdorman" will not aid him he must ride to the king
before he fights. If the foe will not surrender then he may
be attacked ; but if he be willing to surrender, and any one
after that attack him, the assailant must pay "wer" (blood-
money) and "wite" (fine), and forfeit his family rights. But
a man may fight in his lord's defence without penalty, and
so may the lord fight for his man. In the same manner
a man may fight for his born kinsman if he be attacked
wrongfully, except against his lord, which is not allowed.

Beowulf, 2025.

To settle a feud was always an exceedingly difficult
matter, as we learn from the lips of Beowulf. He tells of a
feud between Hrothgar the Dane and Froda the Heathobard,
in which the latter had been slain. To settle it, Hrothgar had
given his daughter in marriage to Ingeld, the dead man's son,
and Beowulf prophesies what the end will be. A Danish
thegn will come with the bride among the Heathobards
wearing a well-known sword, a spoil of battle, and some
fierce old warrior, who remembers the strife, will see it. He
will say to the young chief: "Canst thou not, my friend,
recognise the sword, the dear iron, which thy father bore to
battle on his last foray, when the Danes slew him? Now,
here, a son of I know not who of those slayers, exulting in
his trappings, walks the floor, boasts of the slaying, and bears
the treasure which by right thou should'st possess." So he
will remind him constantly with bitter words until occasion
offers, and then the Dane will sleep, bloodstained and lifeless. Then oaths will be broken, and murderous hates again
well up. And it came to pass even as Beowulf had said,
for in the *Widsith* we read that Ingeld afterwards led his

Widsith, 45.

Heathobards in battle array to Heorot, but his host was

overthrown and cut to pieces by Hrothgar and his nephew Hrothulf.

We hear of many such long-protracted feuds in the story of Beowulf, the most noteworthy being that which is connected with the hero's line. Ohthere and Onela, sons of *Beowulf*, 1923. Ongentheow, king of the Swedes, raid the lands of Hæthcyn, king of the Geats, Beowulf's uncle. Hæthcyn revenges himself by a raid against Ongentheow, whose wife, the mother of Ohthere and Onela, he bears away with him. But Ongentheow, old and terrible, pursues and slays the sea-king, and rescues his wife. He follows up the remnant of the leaderless Geats, his mortal enemies ; and they escape with difficulty into Ravens' Wood. Here he surrounds with his host those spared by the sword, now in a pitiable condition, weary with wounds. " Woe oft he promised the 2938. wretched band, the whole night long ; he said that on the morrow he would slay them with the edge of the sword ; some should hang on the gallows-tree for sport to the birds." But at dawn horns and trumpets are heard ; and the sore-hearted ones have hope of rescue. Hygelac, Hæthcyn's brother, with his army, is near at hand, and is following up the blood-stained track to the assistance of his distressed comrades. " The blood-trace of Swedes and Geats, 2947. the deadly onslaught of warriors, was widely visible, how the folk with each other carried on the feud." Ongentheow fears to meet him ; " he trusted not in resistance, that he could withstand the sea-men, from the sea-farers protect his treasure, his children and bride." He flees with his followers to a fastness in the heights, and takes refuge in an earthen fort. Hygelac follows close behind. Ongentheow's banner is captured ; the Geats storm the ramparts, and pour into the enclosure. The old warrior stands grimly at bay ; the swords of the Geats on every side bar the way of escape. Eofor and Wulf, two young warriors, brothers, single him out. Wulf, son of Wonred, strikes fiercely at him, and from the stroke the blood spurts in streams from beneath his grizzled hair. Yet all undaunted, though his wound is mortal, the stout old king returns the blow with interest. He cleaves Wulf's helmet, and fells him to the ground, all bloody, unable to strike another blow, though he struggles to rise in spite of the pain of his wound. But Eofor breaks through Ongentheow's guard, smiting over the rim of his shield with his broad sword ; and the king, the shepherd of his people, falls. Even his foes admire him, and speak well of him, because he is brave. The fort is won; Wulf's companions bind up his wound, and raise him to his feet; while Eofor strips the body of Ongentheow of its trappings, the iron corslet, the hard hilted sword, and the helmet, and bears them in triumph to Hygelac, who, before all the host, promises him a magnificent reward for his valour.

So ends the fight in Ravens' Wood, but not the feud. 2382. When Hygelac is dead Eanmund and Eadgils, Ongentheow's grandsons, having rebelled against Ohthere their father, come into the land of the Geats, and Heardred, Hygelac's son, is slain by Eanmund. Weohstan in turn takes up the feud against them, and slays Eanmund; and Eadgils returns home. 2397. Long afterwards he again raids the Geats, and is slain by Beowulf. Thenceforth, while Beowulf lives, the feud is quiescent, for his prowess is well-known ; but when he is dead all expect the feud to break out afresh. "That is the 3000. feud and the enmity, the deadly hostility of men, because of which I expect that the Swedes will attack us when they hear that our lord is dead," says he who tells the tale : " I 2923. expect not at all from the Swedes either peace or good faith."

The passion for revenge was one of the most prominent characteristics of the Teuton, and almost partook of the nature of a religious duty. When Beowulf attempts to assuage the grief of Hrothgar for the loss of his friend and follower Æschere, and gives him the best consolation that he knows, 1385. " Sorrow not, wise one," he says; " better it is for every one to avenge his friend than to mourn much. All of us must come to the end of this life; let him who is able gain glory before his death ; that is best in the end for the warrior dead. Arise, warden of the kingdom, let us hasten on the track of the slayer; I promise thee she shall not escape, go where she will. This day do thou bear patiently all thy woes, as I expect of thee." The old man leapt up at once, comforted by his words, and we hear no more of passionate grief for Æschere. Vengeance was then the best antidote for sorrow ; for was it not the delight of the gods themselves?

Practically, the principle of revenge lay at the root of the social life of the Teutons, affording as it did the only check in lawless times upon the passions of violent men. It was undoubtedly the sole preventive of anarchy in the social organism, the most powerful restraint against crime. Among our ancestors it was held to be one of the chief of the accepted rights of the individual; and as such had its recognised legal status, since the right of an offended person to avenge himself upon the offender was allowed by law a money equivalent, the "bôt" or "wer-geld," composition or blood-money. In Alfred's Laws we find quoted: "If any one thrust out another's eye, let him give his own for it; tooth for tooth, hand for hand, foot for foot, burning for burning, wound for wound, stripe for stripe[1];" but by degrees the custom had grown up that the injured person might sell his right for a price, if he chose to do so. At first he was not bound to forgo his revenge, but by the end of the eighth century it had come to be generally recognised that the payment settled by law must be accepted. To refuse it threw the onus of the wrong upon the refuser. But the killing of his own brother by Hæthcyn, though accidental, was a "fee-less fight" that could not thus be atoned for; and treason was likewise "bôt-leas," admitting of no composition. "The English race, after they had received the faith of Christ,...ordained that secular lords with their leave, might, without sin, take for almost every misdeed, for the first offence, the money 'bôt' which they then ordained; except in cases of treason against a lord, to which they dared not assign any mercy....He who plots against his lord's life, let him be liable in his life to him, and in all that he has."

This system of composition is frequently met with in the *Beowulf*. "Afterwards I settled the feud with a fee," says Hrothgar, "I sent to the Wylfings old treasures; he swore oaths to me." And a further development of the system is seen when Hrothgar, as being responsible for the safety of the guests under his roof, pays the blood-money for Beowulf's thegn, Hondscio, whom Grendel has slain.

The existence of such a custom has its own moral significance. It shows that the barbarian is emerging from that primitive condition in which the passion for slaughter is ever uppermost. Here at last is a remedy for the violent shedding of blood upon the slightest pretext, the first foundation of a

Marginal notes:
Laws of Alfred, 19. *A.-S. Laws*, Thorpe, p. 22.

Beowulf, 2442.

Laws of Alfred, 49. *A.-S. Laws*, Thorpe, p. 26.

p. 29.

Beowulf, 469.

1055.

---

[1] Exodus xxi. 24, Deuteronomy xix. 21.

definite legal system, which will develope with the development of civilisation. Further, the offender, by paying the blood-money, practically confessed his offence, recognised it to be a wrong against the individual offended and a crime against society, and proffered reparation. The receiver, on his side, practically promised to forgive and forget, and became reconciled to the one who had injured him. With Alfred, as we have already seen, composition and mercy are *Supra*, p. 11. synonymous. Though an element of compulsion may have been involved, still the system stands as a mark of social and moral progress.

Sometimes the Teuton could forgive freely in smaller matters, though rarely or never in greater. Beowulf, the magnanimous hero, when about to proceed upon his second 1466, 1489. quest, remembers not the taunts of the envious Hunferth. He accepts from him the loan of a far-famed sword, and arranges that in case of death his own sword shall be given to his former detractor. And so we happen upon a brighter, kindlier side of the Teutonic character.

When our literature opens, these barbarian tribes have reached the extreme verge of the land; the line of least resistance now lies across the sea, and any further progress must be in that direction. To the dweller by the coast the ocean appeared to be the mightiest of superhuman beings, a sea-giant of terrible and awe-inspiring aspect, living and passionate as man himself, a raging personality[1]. There was something in its nature, in its restless, heaving motion[2], akin to his own character, which at first terrified and afterwards irresistibly attracted him. An exultant joy, a passionate triumph, possessed him when first he succeeded in overcoming the terrors of the wind and storm; and the call of the sea came to be ever-present in his ears, luring him on. We may hear it in the words of the Seafarer: "Why crash *Seafarer*, 33. together now the thoughts of my heart, that I myself should try the high-tossed streams, the salt waves' tumult? Incessantly the desire of my heart exhorts me to go forth 50. that I far hence should seek a foreign strand....All things, to him who thinks upon the ocean waves afar to sail, spur on

---

[1] Cf. "Fîfel," "Eagor," "Geofon," "Gârsecg."

[2] Cf. "ýða geswing," "ýð-gebland," "ýð-gewealc," "ýð-gewin": the swinging, the surging, the rolling, the strife of the waves.

the eager-hearted to the voyage....My thought now hovers
o'er my breast, and speeds above the sea-flood, then yet 58.
again, hungry and greedy, comes back to me, calls as it flies
alone, and irresistibly whets me on to the sea, o'er the
expanse of the heaped-up ocean." None can escape the
spell; all earthly joys, harp and treasure and woman's love,
fade before it; "he ever has longing who once sets out upon 47.
the sea."

So the Teuton puts out his "wood-bound" vessel to the
sea, and with foamy neck like a bird it races before the wind *Beowulf,* 204,
across the ocean, braving the dangers of the high-tossed 216, 535.
waves. Mightily does he pride himself on his ship, his sea- *Andreas,* 241,
manship and his prowess on the deep. He wages war upon 266, 273, 274,
the whale, the walrus and the seal, even in the coldest 370, 440, 489,
weather, when the north wind blows and the waves rise 511.
high, while the darkening night descends upon the sea. He
hears the cordage rattling in the storm, wet with the spray
of the billows which beat upon the bulwarks; and, for the
moment, the water-terror rises from the deep and chills his
heart, as he fights with hands benumbed and frozen to keep
the stem to the waves which threaten to overwhelm him. He
keeps his watch by night upon the prow, while his bark drives *Seafarer,* 6.
on beneath storm-beaten cliffs; his feet are bound in icy
fetters by the frost; icicles hang about him; the hail flies by
in showers. Instead of the joyous laughter of men, nothing 18.
he hears but the booming of the sea, the wild swan's song,
the soughing of the seal, and the sea-mew's scream. "There 10.
Care sighed hot about my heart, and Hunger within tore out
the breast of me, sea-weary." It is always the hardship of
the life upon which he dwells, because he has mastered it,
fighting his battle alone in the solitude of the sea. Such is
the strong man's sport. "Strong is the test to him who long *Andreas,* 313.
explores the deep sea-road."

He now carries on his raids and feuds across the sounds
and narrow seas, sailing with demoniacal laughter and savage *Riddle,*
yells into the open bays and river mouths, eager to pillage XXXIV.
and burn and slay. He is already a sea-king and knows his
strength.

In larger and still larger numbers the hosts make ready *Andreas,* 235.
to cross the sea, on invasion or foray bent. The warriors *Elene,* 225.
 Beowulf, 210,
come marching down at dawn to the sandy beach, stepping 1890.

over the shingle, eager for the expedition and blithe of heart.
The wide-bosomed ships stand ready by the shore, their
high-beaked stems pointing landwards and resting on the
beach. The crews climb on board, bearing with them their
equipment; the ships are pushed off, and one after another,
amid the cheers of the folk, put out to sea under oar and sail,
with the shields ranged in line along the bulwarks. Then,
with swelling sails, the foamy keels speed on their course
till the cliffs of the land they seek rise glistening on the
horizon, till the goal is reached. A shelving beach is chosen;
the vessels are run ashore and made fast with anchors, while
the warriors prepare to disembark. They form in battle
array upon the shore, making a brave show of weapons and
armour, and with their banner at their head. Then, leaving
a guard for the protection of the fleet, they march inland to
meet the foe they have chosen to attack.

Gildas, *Six
O. E. Chron.*
pp. 300—310.

Each year the radius of their operations lengthens, until
at last they discover the island of Britain, with its spacious
plains and pleasant hills, its cultivated fields and rich pastures,
its lucid fountains and abundant rivers, a great contrast to the
homes whence they have come. Its inhabitants, "groaning in
amazement" under the cruelty of the Picts and Scots, and
weakened still further by domestic feuds, at first seek alliance
with the roving bands. But the alliance does not endure
for long, and soon the struggle begins for possession of the
island. Here is a home for the superfluous population of
many a continental tribe; and the invaders come "like
wolves into the sheep-fold" in ever-increasing hosts.

A.-S. Chron.

In the *Anglo-Saxon Chronicle* we have a collection of
brief records, partly compiled from still earlier records,
dealing with the invasion and conquest of Britain by the
Angles, Saxons and Jutes[1]. From its pages can be formed
a complete idea of the nature of the invasion and of the
violence of the invaders. We read how, in the year 449 A.D.,
Hengist and Horsa, two roving chieftains, came to Britain,
and, at the invitation of Wyrtgeorn, king of Kent, landed
at Ebbsfleet to aid the Britons against their foes, and how
afterwards they turned and fought against them. Hengist,

Nennius,
Sect. 37.

with all the craftiness and penetration of the typical barbarian leader, had speedily grasped the situation, and at

[1] Geatas? Frisians?

once took measures to augment his forces, summoning fresh
bands from the fatherland to divide the spoil.

In 455 a great battle was fought at Aylesford, in which
Horsa was slain after an impetuous onset which scattered the   *Hen. of Hunt.*
troops opposed to him like dust before the wind, and Hengist   Bk. II.
with difficulty escaped defeat.   In another battle in 457   *A.-S. Chron.*
the new-comers slew four thousand men, and the Britons[1]
abandoned Kent, and with great fear fled to London.   In
465 they slew twelve Welsh chieftains.   In 473 they fought
and took so much booty that it could not be reckoned, and
the Welsh fled the English like fire.   Like a conflagration
the slaughter spread from the eastern to the western sea.
The Britons lost heart, and offered feeble opposition to the   Gildas, *Six*
"fierce and impious whelps from the lair of the barbarian   *O. E. Chron.*
lioness, whom they dreaded more than death itself."   Fire   p. 310.
and sword devastated the land.   The towns were laid waste,   *Hen. of Hunt.*
churches and houses were levelled to the ground, the priests   Bk. II.
were everywhere slain before the altars, and the people
perished, without respect of persons, so that there were not
left any to bury the bodies of the fallen.   Some in despair fled
over sea.   Some hid in the woods and mountain strongholds,
fearing for their lives, and suffering the horrors of extreme
privation.   Those who were captured in the mountains were
at once massacred ; those who were driven by famine and
exhaustion to surrender were either butchered or enslaved.
"There was hardly a grape or ear of corn to be seen where   Gildas, *Six*
the husbandman had turned his back."   *O. E. Chron.*
                                                                  p. 312.
It is said that three hundred of the British chiefs and   Nennius,
nobles were treacherously massacred in the height of the   Sect. 46.
struggle.   Hengist proposed a truce, and offered peace and
friendship as a stratagem to get them into his power.   All
unsuspicious, the Britons came to a banquet and sat unarmed,
each with a Saxon at his side.   When inflamed with wine
and mead, Hengist's followers, at a loud cry from their chief,
drew forth the knives which they had concealed about them,
and each struck down the guest who sat beside him.   Such
was the outcome of Wyrtgeorn's invitation to those who were
stronger than he.   Fierce, warlike, determined, crafty, greedy
of booty, greedy of slaughter, they had proved themselves
terrible guests.

---

[1] Or, as the English called them, Wealas, Welsh, i.e. foreigners.

The monks who in after years compiled these records in the seclusion of the cloisters seemed well satisfied with the prowess of their ancestors. This tale of battle and bloodshed, of conquest and booty, they long remembered. The martial spirit, which even the austerities of the monastic life could not entirely quench, long lived on, and nearly eight hundred years later we have an English priest describing these invaders as "the fairest men that ever came here," and representing the British king as saying in tones of admiration that he had never before seen such as they. Their imposing stature and immense strength, together with their skill, resolution and coolness in the fight, greatly impressed their adversaries, and went far to make their conquests all the more secure.

Layamon,
Brut 13797,
13831.

Hen. of Hunt.
Ant. Lib.
pp. 44, 54, 51.

In 477, under the leadership of Ælla the Saxon, a second group of invading bands landed on the southern coast. They slew many Welsh, and drove some in flight into the wood which was called Andredesleah. In 491 they besieged Andredescester, but the defence was long and obstinate. The Britons swarmed like wasps upon the flanks of the besiegers, who were continually harassed with ambuscades by day and sallies by night; but nothing could save the stronghold. The more the Saxons were assailed the more vigorously they pressed the siege. At last, exhausted by famine, the defenders were overwhelmed, and all, with their women and children, were slain with the sword, none escaping. In their rage at the stubborn defence and their own heavy loss the Saxons completely destroyed the city.

A.-S. Chron.
Hen. of Hunt.
p. 45.

Another band of Saxons under Cerdic landed further to the west in 495, advanced inland in the face of strong opposition, and laid the foundations of the kingdom of Wessex. In the north, in 547, Ida the Angle founded the kingdom of Northumbria, and won from the Welsh the title of "the flame-bearer." In 577 the Saxons fought with the Britons at Deorham, slaying three kings, Coinmal, Condidan and Farinmail, and then capturing the three great fortified cities, Gloucester, Cirencester and Bath, thereby inserting a wedge between the Britons of the midlands and those of the south-west. Bath they left behind them in ruins after slaughtering the defenders. Gildas, who was born about the time of the destruction of the city, describes such a scene as there took place: How the columns were beaten to the ground by

A.-S. Chron.

v. Ruined
Burg.
Gildas, *Hist.*
Six O. E. Chr.
pp. 313, 311.

stroke upon stroke of the battering-ram; how the inhabitants
with their bishops and priests were routed, while the sword
gleamed, and the crackling flame spread round them on
every side; how the ruins of lofty towers and walls lay in
the midst of the streets, with here and there a holy altar
overthrown; how mangled and blood-stained bodies lay
unburied amidst the debris, exposed to the ravenings of the
wild beasts and birds of prey, a pitiable spectacle. Then the *A.-S. Chron.*
Saxons advanced with fire and sword up the Severn valley
as far as Uriconium by the Wrekin, and afterwards (584) to
Fethanleag (Faddiley) in Cheshire, whence they returned
raging under heavy loss but victorious. Cutha, one of their
kings, had been slain, and part of their host put to flight,
but Ceawlin, their other king, had turned defeat into victory,
and had taken many towns and a great booty.

The fate of Uriconium was very like that of Bath.
Cyndyllan, the Welsh chieftain, was slain in the battle, and
we have the mournful tale of the burning of his home and
the massacre of his family. "The hall of Cyndyllan is dark *Heroic Elegies*
to-night, without fire, without bed—I must weep awhile and *of Llywarch*
then be silent. Except God doth, who will endue me with *Hen*, Owen,
patience? Gloomy seems its roof, since the sweet smile of p. 77.
humanity is no more. The hall of Cyndyllan is without love
this night, since he owns it no more—without its lord, without
the company, without the circling feasts, without fire, without
songs. Tears afflict the cheeks—without fire, without family!
It pierces me to see it, roofless, fireless. My chief is dead,
and I alive myself! The hall of Cyndyllan is an open waste
this night, the seat of chill grief—without the men, without the
women. The hall of Cyndyllan is silent to-night—Great, Merciful God, what shall I do?" is the Lament of Llywarch Hen.

> "The eagle of Eli I hear this night.
> He is bloody; I will not dare him.   p. 81.
> He is in the wood; heavy is my load of grief.
>
> .   .   .   .
>
> The White Town between Tren and Trodwyd!   p. 87.
> More common was the broken shield
> Coming from battle than the evening ox.
> The White Town between Tren and Traval!
> More common was the blood
> On the surface of the grass than the ploughed fallow."

Such was the price the vanquished were called upon to pay.

In 613, by his victory at Chester, Æthelfrith of Northumbria broke the power of the Britons in the north, though
not without great loss in his own army. Here again there
was a great slaughter of the fugitives, and more than two
thousand of the monks of Bangor Iscoed were slain. " If they
cry to their God against us," said Æthelfrith, "verily they
also fight against us, although they do not carry arms." The
invaders seem to have always been most severe upon the
British priests.

The two successes at Bath and Chester show that the
strategy of the English was of no mean order. With these
two places in their hands, and the surrounding districts
strongly held, they had gained possession of the keys to
both north and south, and were enabled to deal with the
British in detail.

Quite a typical record is that of the year 597 : " Here
Ceolwulf began to rule among the West Saxons, and ever
he fought and made war either against the Angles or the
Welsh or the Picts or the Scots." By this date the invading
tribes have begun to fight with each other, so far has the
conquest progressed. By the middle of the next century the
subjugation of Britain is almost complete. There is the great
battle at Pen (658) in which the doggedness of the Saxons
gained the day. At the first attack they began to give
ground, but dreading flight more than death and standing
upon their defence they at last wore down the enemy. The
strength of the Britons melted away like snow, until they
turned their backs upon the Saxons and fled from Pen even
to Pedred, and incurable was the wound inflicted that day
upon the British race. With this exception the fighting is
now mainly confined to the struggle between the Northumbrians and the Mercians in which the Welsh take part
as the allies of the latter people.

The whole story of the invasion and conquest is a record
of violence and desperate savagery in which the elemental
passions of warlike men ruled unchecked. Horde after horde
swarmed from oversea to the great harrying and spoliation,
"reddening the sun with smoke, and earth with blood,"
continually gaining ground, ever pressing further and further
into the heart of the country. Yet, as the literature of the
losing side will show, the contest was by no means always

Marginal notes:

Bede, *Hist. Eccl.* II. 2.

A.-S. *Chron.*

Hen. *of Hunt.* Bk. II.

one-sided; and, naturally, the stouter the opposition the greater the ferocity on either side. In the *Gododin* we have the story of the battle of Cattraeth (c. 570) which is said to have lasted for the space of a week, and in which hundreds perished in one short hour. After fighting for three days the Welsh had the advantage and refused a proffered truce. Then victory veered round to the side of the invaders, and, in the end, of 363 Welsh chieftains but three escaped with their lives. "Mead in the hall cost us dear," sighs the bard. We read, too, of the desperate valour of the Welsh Owain, hot in pursuit, giving no quarter, mowing down the foe like grass; and of the terrible Urien before whom quailed in fear the trembling Saxon, "who with fair hair wet and forehead bloody is carried away on his bier." And there are some who tell of a series of disastrous defeats inflicted upon the Saxons, culminating in the battle of Mount Badon (c. 520) by which the advance was checked for a while, and would have us believe that there is historical foundation for the legends which glorify the fame of Arthur and his Table Round. Henry of Huntingdon says that at this period there were many battles in which sometimes the one side, sometimes the other, were victorious, but that the more the Saxons were defeated the more they reinforced their depleted forces by sending invitations to the warriors of all the neighbouring parts of the Continent. So in the end the ferocity and dogged pertinacity of the invaders, which so often converted a battle well-nigh lost into a victory won, prevailed, and the conquest became an accomplished fact.

Gododin.

Taliesin.

Hen. of Hunt.
Bk. II.
Geof. of Mon.
Bk. IX. cc. 1—
5.
Nennius,
Sect. 50.
Hen. of Hunt.
p. 49.

From various passages in Early English literature we can picture for ourselves the invading host advancing into battle, fighting and pursuing. News is brought to the camp that the enemy is near; the horn sounds for battle; and at the signal the eager-hearted warriors, with their war-shirts of ring-mail already covering back and breast, firmly secure the clasps of their helmets, seize their weapons, and leap to their places in the ranks, forming in compact array under the banners of their chiefs. The war-whoop is up-raised, and the march begins. Some of the warriors are on horseback, some on foot, and all are well armed. Their uplifted spears seem like a bristling wood; their harness gleams; their shields and bucklers glitter in the sun. At the

Andreas, 1203.
Genesis, 445.
Exodus, 191,
320, 200, 157.

head of the host rides the king, his standard before him.   In
170. front and on the flanks mounted scouts ride to and fro to
mark the position of the foe.   With banners waving, horns
and trumpets sounding, and armour clashing, they prepare
for the attack.   The mounted men leap from their horses;
252. and the leader, with shield upraised, springs before his men,
exhorting them to bear themselves well in the coming
conflict.   They greet him with a shout; the war-song rises;

Maldon, 22,
62, 108.
Exodus, 236.

the clashing of spear upon shield resounds.   He gives orders
for the conduct of the battle, and takes his place in the
van, surrounded by his choicest fighters.   The troops draw
together in close array, presenting to the foe an impenetrable
wall of shields, and the order to advance is given.   Spears

Genesis, 2062,
1991.
Judith, 220.
Elene, 108.

and arrows fly through the air, smiting upon helmet, shield
and armour; and many a fighter falls.   Then, with a loud
war-cry, the onset is made.   Host hurtles against host;
furiously the standards are dashed together and borne down.
Spears and shields are broken; helmets are cloven, and
corslets shorn in pieces; the shield-wall is broken through.
Now the long swords are snatched from the sheaths;

Hen. of Hunt.
Bk. II.

battle-axes rise and fall, making terrible wounds, as warrior
meets warrior in hand-to-hand combat.   The din of battle
is deafening.   To and fro sway the fighters, many locked

Beowulf, 1546.

in a mortal grip and struggling to draw the "seax" (dagger)
from the hip; while above them and around gather the
ravens and wolves eager to feast upon the slain.   At length,
by ones and twos and threes, the vanquished begin to flee

Maldon, 189.

from the outskirts of the battle; some mount their horses,
and ride away in desperate haste.   Larger grows the crowd
of fugitives; and the victors break over and round the line
of their foes, to join again in the rear, encircling those who
cannot or will not flee.   In wave after wave they dash

Judith, 305.

furiously upon isolated groups who are fighting it out to
the death.   First one and then another group is overwhelmed;
all semblance of array is lost.   Men fight blindly hither and
thither in confused tumult, till at last the rushing to and
fro subsides, and the battered and blood-stained assailants
break asunder to reveal heaped-up rings of slain, over whom,
when night shall have set in, their women folk will sing the
mournful sorrow-song of defeat and despair.

Meanwhile the victors press their advantage home, hastening in hot pursuit of the fugitives. The remnant who have *Genesis*, 2000. escaped flee for the fastnesses and the high rocks. Some *Elene*, 132. *Judith*, 292. perish in the rivers; some are slain with spears and arrows from behind; some are cut down with the sword; and the number of those who run diminishes rapidly. The pursuit and slaughter go on till darkness mercifully interposes. Then *Genesis*, 2006. the booty is gathered in, and there is a rich harvest for the spoiler. Maids, wives and widows, cattle and arms, perhaps a slave or two, all are the conqueror's prize; what he cannot lead away with him perishes in the burning of the dismantled homestead or the ruined town. And at last, when all is over, the victorious army returns to encamp upon the battle-field, now lit up by a whole countryside in flame; and there the night is spent in excited festivity and exultant song.

Often were the bodies of the slain mutilated, and the *Beowulf*, 984, dismembered limbs raised aloft as trophies of victory, or even 1589. nailed upon the dwellings of the conquerors. Often was the *Judith*, 125. head of a famous foe struck off and carried away as a tangible proof of his defeat and death. Sometimes the captured, too, *Beowulf*, 2939. were hanged, or cruelly tortured and disfigured. When Oswald was slain by Penda (642) the heathen king ordered Ælfric, *Life of* his head and his right arm to be cut off and set up as a mark. *Oswald.* In 796 Ceolwulf, king of the Mercians, overharried Kent, *A.-S. Chron.* captured Eadberht the king, led him bound into Mercia, and caused his eyes to be put out and his hands to be cut off.

Examples of treachery were not at all uncommon among *Beowulf*, the invaders; and some of them, like Eormanric, "the wrath- *passim.* *Fight at* ful breaker of pledges," in the *Widsith*, did not scruple to *Finnsburg*, violate the oaths they had made. According to the *Gododin*, *Widsith*, 9. the Saxon herald who came to propose the truce at Cattraeth treacherously stabbed and killed the bard Owain. In 626 Cwichelm, king of the West Saxons, sent an assassin with Bede, *Hist.* a poisoned dagger to kill Eadwine of Northumbria. Eadwine *Eccl.* II. 9 and see III. 14. only escaped through the devotion of his chief thegn, Lilla, who received in his own body the blow intended for his king. Hengist's treachery was but one example of many.

Long did the bitterness of the Welshman's hate endure towards the Englishman who had won in such fierce fashion the fatherland he himself had lost. To him the conquering tribes were an abomination; and we can easily understand why Gildas applies to his country's foes the epithets "wolves," Gildas, *Hist.* "dogs," "robbers," "whelps from the lair of the barbarian pp. 310, 311.

lioness," "hateful both to God and man." We remember

Bede, *H. E.* III. 5.

that to the austere missionary of Iona they were men untamable and of hard and barbarous mind. But one of their

Beowulf, 1864.

own race says, "I know the people fast foes, firm friends, in every way blameless in the old wise." And for them it is

1005.

ordained that "by strife man shall win from man, compelled by need, the place made ready, where his body, fast upon his

1061.

bed, shall sleep after the feast;" and "many things, both dear and loathly, must he abide, who here in these days of strife lives long in the world."

But these years of warfare, of bloodthirstiness and cruelty, of sorrow and revenge, were not without their purpose. The battlefield was the first great training school of the natural man, in which he learned how to live and how to die. It made the hero a pattern to his fellows, and preached heroism as the greatest of manly virtues. It alone induced the individual to sink self in the honour and enthusiasm of a cause, and imposed upon him, at least for the time being, some sense of discipline and self-control. It forced him to appreciate the value of his friends, and to recognise the ties of friendship. It called forth strength of character, strength of will, and strength of nerve. It taught the necessity of plain, healthy living, and the stoical endurance of hardship and pain. Above all it inculcated the virtues of patriotism and obedience to the call of duty. Yet, indeed, it was the hardest and most terrible of schools, and when the unruly Englishman had passed through it he knew for the first time what it was to obey.

The typical hero of these early days will represent for us the ideal towards which the best of his race were striving, and will help us to form a conception of the better side of the Teutonic character. An accepted definition of the Teutonic hero may be found in the last lines of the *Widsith*:

Widsith, 135.

"Thus wandering on, they pass throughout the world,
Gleemen roaming through many lands of men.
They tell their needs; they speak the word of thanks,
Ever by south or north some friend they meet,
Skilled in their lays, ungrudging of rewards,
One who for glory's sake aspires for fame
And noble deeds to do.
Till all shall fade away, light and life together,
He who carves out a name has under heaven
High-wrought renown."

Thus in his wanderings the Gleeman found his hero: one whose life is spent in the quest of honour, glory and imperishable renown, a generous-hearted doer of noble deeds, a friend. So the poet's ideal is by no means ignoble, embracing, as it does, nobility, generosity, friendship. In troubled times friendship is man's greatest boon, and must be ever true. "Nothing can ever set aside friendship in him who is well-thinking." For his own safety and well-being a man must hold well his friend wherever he goes; in sorry state is he who must live alone and friendless; wretched is he who deceives his friend. It is a shameful thing, a vile, unclean thing, for an earl to speak his fellow fair before his face while behind his back he slanders him with injurious and offensive words, having deceit in his heart.

Beowulf, 2601.

Gnomic Verses (Ex.) 145, 173, 37.

Bi Manna Lease, 3.

We take three famous examples from our early poetry and find the list of heroic attributes enlarged. To Beowulf it is said: "Thy fame is upreared about the wide ways, among all peoples, Beowulf my friend. Thou holdest it all with patience, might with wisdom of heart. Thou shalt be a consolation, long granted, to thy people, a help to heroes." Offa "was the best of all men beside the two seas, the spearkeen man, for gifts and for war widely honoured; with wisdom he ruled his fatherland." Ælfwine "had of all men the readiest[1] hand to win praise, the most generous heart in the giving of rings." The hero, then, must be brave and strong, wise and patient, generous and kind. And we notice that honour is won by the *ready* hand of the warrior; it is the honour of the strong right arm and the well-fought field. We remember a parallel in this respect in the case of the historic hero Cerdic of Wessex. The record of one of his victories in which both Saxons and Britons fought with obstinate bravery, the Britons being defeated with terrible slaughter only as the day was drawing to its close, concludes: "Thus was the name of Cerdic glorified, and the fame of his wars and of his son Kenric was spread over all the land."

Beowulf, 1704.

1956.

Widsith, 70.

Hen. of Hunt. Bk. II. p. 48.

We have our typical hero almost completely drawn for us in the character of Beowulf the Geat. Born of a father mighty in deeds and wise in council, bravery and wisdom are his by inheritance. "Never heard I more wisdom in so young a man. Thou art strong of might, and wise of heart

Beowulf, 261, 459.

1842.

---

[1] "leohteste."

423. and speech," says Hrothgar to him. He is tall of stature,
247.
198. of noble appearance, and of gigantic strength; he has the
strength of thirty men in his grip. In his youth, like so many
Northern heroes, he had been despised and little accounted
2184. of; his people said that he was slack, an unwarlike atheling;
but a change came about in the man, and while yet a youth
he avenged the griefs of his people, and ground down their
379. wrathful enemies. To his foes he is a slaughter-fierce warrior,
629.
2495. a wolf of war. He is stout-hearted, resolute in thought, with
826. a quiet confidence in his own might. He says, "I will work
610.
1839. the will of your people, or fall in the attempt. I will perform
635. deeds of earl-like valour, or await my death in this mead-
hall." "I, with my sword, will gain glory for myself, or death
1443. shall take me." He cares not at all for his life. When his
1530. sword fails him in the fight still is he resolute, not sluggish
of courage, mindful of glory; he trusts in the strength of his
grip. "So must a man do when in the strife he thinks to
gain lasting praise, and cares not about his life." Ever in the
2498. host would he be in the front, and so will he fight as long as
2524. his sword endures. Not a foot will he flee, but it shall be as
860. Fate decides. Never was there a better warrior, or one more
2178. worthy of kingship. "So the son of Ecgtheow, the man
renowned in wars, showed his valour through brave deeds.
He never slew the hearth-companions who had drunk with
him; not cruel was his heart.'

His adventurous spirit leads him across the sea to take up
267. the cause of the oppressed. In kindness he lends his aid at
278. Heorot, and his sympathetic nature bids him propose a plan to
282. cool the wellings-up of care. "For our defence and for kindly
aid hast thou sought us, Beowulf, my friend," says Hrothgar,
627. the persecuted king; while the queen trusts him as a conso-
1220. lation against oppression, and desires his good-will towards
826. her boys. So the wise and stout-hearted one cleansed Heorot,
removed the pain and sorrow of heart and hard need of the
Danes, and rejoiced in his work. To Hrothgar he says as he
leaves him, "If ever I hear over the sea that thy neighbours
1827. oppress thee with dread, as thine enemies did of yore, I will
bring a thousand thegns to help thee."

915. Fair and lovable is he to all his friends. "I like thee the
948.
1480. better the longer I know thee, dear Beowulf," says Hrothgar,
1854. who, at his departure, takes him by the neck and weeps as he
1871.

kisses him ; the hero is so dear to him that he cannot restrain his emotion[1], and in his secret thought yearns for him " against his blood[2]," i.e. although he is not related to him. Beowulf cares for the thegns who follow him, and the love between them is exceedingly great. His generosity is unbounded ; 1605. and when he returns home laden with treasure he gives it gladly to his king and queen, for whom he has the most sincere affection. "For all favours come of thee," he says to 2150. his king. "No head-kinsmen have I, save only thee, O 3075. Hygelac." He was not eager after gold, rather the favour of his lord had he looked for first. When Hygelac has been slain, and the queen offers him the kingdom, fearing that 2370. Heardred, her son, is too young to hold the fatherland against its foes, he refuses to deprive the boy of his throne, but remains his protector, adviser and friend, in all kindness and honour, till Heardred is slain in feud by Eanmund, grandson of Ongentheow.

He is very jealous of his fame, and defends it with righteous indignation when it is attacked. At a banquet envy 500. leads Hunferth to impugn his prowess, alleging that he had been overcome by one Breca in a match upon the sea. The hero notices with contempt the speaker's condition. "Lo ! many things hast thou spoken about Breca, Hunferth my friend, drunken with beer," and then proceeds to give his version of the affair, adding, "Neither you nor Breca ever performed so bravely in the strife, though not of that boast I much." He concludes severely but justly and to the point, with a bitter taunt which completely silences his detractor, "But thou wast the murderer of thy brothers, for which thou shalt pay the penalty in Hell, though thy wit is so mighty. I tell thee truly, son of Ecglaf, that Grendel would never have worked so many terrors to thy lord, such shame in Heorot, if thine heart were as fierce as thou thyself showest." The hero is mighty in words as well as in deeds.

His end is worthy of his life. As he has lived, ever in the quest of honour, ever risking his life for his friends and avenging their wrongs, so he dies. His country is ravaged by a fiery dragon, and the old warrior, sad at heart, prepared 2420. for death, knowing that his fate is very near, goes out to meet it. With pagan satisfaction he looks back upon his past life

---

[1] "breost-wylm."   [2] "wið blôde."

2536. with pride. He has always "performed earlship," and will continue to do so.   The dragon is slain, but the hero lies dying,
with the treasure he has won spread out before his glazing
2733. eyes; and thus he speaks of his life: "I have ruled this
people fifty winters; no king of my neighbours, with his
war-friends[1], dared meet me in battle.   I held mine own well,
sought not treacheries, swore no false oaths, slew no kinsmen."
The moral standard may be low, but it is that of the age
over which the hero has risen superior.   His last words are of
2815. the friends and kinsmen of the days gone by.   "Fate swept
them all away, earls in their heroic strength, and I must
2889. after them."   "Death is better for every earl than life
ill-famed," said one who loved him, echoing the hero's own
3180. thought.   So the people of the Geats bewailed the fall of their
lord.   They said that he was a king, mildest to his men and
kindest, gentlest to his people, and most yearning for fame.

Thus we have in Beowulf the old ideal of manly perfection,
the hero of whom the Englishman loved to sing.   He stands
a giant figure outlined against the background of his age,
a second Prometheus, of Teutonic blood, isolated by Fate
upon the lofty peak of duty.   An atmosphere of pathos
is cast about him in life, as in death, for he is singled out
from his youth to accomplish more than mortal labours,
which demand from him complete self-sacrifice and continual
self-control.   His responsibilities are of the greatest, and his
recognition of the burden laid upon his shoulders is exceedingly vivid; but the fresh blood of healthy, strenuous life
runs in his veins, and he is perfectly human.   He has his
faults, but they are few—a tendency towards boastfulness,
one momentary outburst of passionate and violent language
under extreme provocation, a childish delight in the treasure
spread out before his dying eyes.   And who of his age had
not these faults, intensified a hundredfold?   With all his
massive frame and daring spirit, his chivalry and courtesy,
his strong sense of duty and self-respect, add to his character
an impressiveness, a thoughtfulness, an unwonted mildness
and gentleness, which raise him to the highest place above
his fellows.   Over such as he Fate herself can gain no
conquest, for though she may lead the body to destruction
yet she cannot touch the hero's fame; and even over her the

[1] "gûð-winum," with swords or allies.

immortal spirit, staunch and resolute, may claim the last great victory which counts for all.

In later days, when sorrow shall have softened the Teuton's heart and enlarged his experience, the poet's ideal will become still more thoughtful, more chastened, more introspective. " The wise man must be patient, not too hot-hearted, nor too *Wanderer*, 65. hasty of speech, nor too weak a warrior, nor too heedless, nor too fearful, nor too fain, nor too avaricious, nor ever too ready at boasting before he know well. The hero must wait when he speaks his boast until, bold of heart, he knows with certainty whither the thought of his heart will turn."

The age of Beowulf is that of a nation's childhood, with all the excesses of immaturity openly displayed. The egotism of the individual rules unchecked. Reserve and self-control are rare, emotions violent, passions strong. There is, on the one hand, a childlike delight in everything that glitters to the eye, and on the other, a childish fear of the dark, the supernatural and the unknown. But already the Teutons are beginning to discriminate, to contrast and compare. As a foil to an appreciation of Beowulf the hero we have, in the character of Heremod, a description of all that the hero should not, or rather could not, be. No consolation was *Beowulf*, 1710. he to his people ; for their pleasing he cared not, but became their slayer. Mad at heart he slew his board-fellows, his shoulder-companions, until at last he died alone and friendless. He grew in power, yet his heart was bloodthirsty ; no rings gave he. The hero should take this example to heart, for the end of such is disastrous. Similar contrasts are fairly common in the *Beowulf*. And in a later poem there is a description of the passionate frenzy of one who is deliberately portrayed as being far from heroic. When his will was *Juliana*, 594. thwarted he became rough and fierce of heart, began to tear his raiment, grinned with rage, and gnashed his teeth ; he raged in his heart like a wild beast ; he raved, wicked-minded, and cursed his gods. And his passion is translated into violent and savage deeds.

War made the hero, and after him the king. During the invasion of Britain raiding bands were continually hovering round the coast, landing in the river mouths, and pressing inland into the heart of the country. Each of these bands was under the leadership of its own chosen chieftain ; and when these scattered parties began to coalesce into larger groups of kindred tribes to give greater momentum to the attack, the leader whose prowess had been proved in some victorious engagement came to be chosen king. So, by degrees, from the marauding tribes, the nation and the monarchy were evolved. In this way Cerdic came over as an *A.-S. Chron.* "ealdorman" in 495, and in 517 became king of the West-Saxons; and thus, in 547, Ida became king in Northumbria.

As we have already seen, the kingly office had its duties, as well as its honours, clearly defined in the minds of the *Widsith,* 11. people. "Every king who would prosper upon his throne must live in accordance with custom; the earl must rule his land as others before him ruled." The king must be brave, strong and wise, liberal and free, the protector, shepherd and friend of his people. There is still much that is patriarchal in his office.

Next to the king were the military nobles, the "ealdor-men" or earls, chief among whom as a rule were his sons and kinsmen, the athelings. Cerdic's son, Cynric, was associated with his father as a sort of under-king, and afterwards succeeded him upon the throne. The monarchy was already *Beowulf,* 1180, hereditary. When the settlement had begun, each "ealdor-2470. man" usually ruled over some portion of the conquered territory allotted to him as his shire, and had a voice in the supreme council of the nation, the "Wîtena-gemôt," or assembly of the wise.

261.   In personal attendance upon lord or king were the thegns, 343. his hearth-companions or table-companions, men of noble 160. birth, usually divided into two classes, the honoured veterans and the youths[1], whose sacred duty it was to win or die with him. No service was too dangerous, no duty too arduous for the faithful thegn to perform for his lord; and the lord in return bestowed marks of his personal favour and apprecia-*Widsith,* tion upon those who served him well. A ring from his *Beowulf,* finger, a bracelet from his arm, a horse from his stable, a *passim.* valuable sword or corslet from his armoury, in addition to lands and home, were the usual rewards of faithful service. Sometimes the lord's daughter was given in marriage to a warrior especially renowned. Thus Ecgtheow, Beowulf's 262. father, had to wife the only daughter of Hrethel, king of the

---

[1] "duguð and geogoð."

Geats ; and thus Eofor, by his prowess in Ravens' Wood, won   2998.
his bride, the only daughter of Hygelac.

There was strong personal affection between the lord and
his thegns ; and the thegn was grateful, in a loyal and manly
fashion, for all the favours he received. The poet of the   2147.
Widsith, like Beowulf, was grateful to his lord at home who   *Widsith*, 93.
protected him and gave him the lands of his fathers.   One of
the most valuable rewards he had won, an armlet or collar of
beaten gold, he set aside as a special gift for his lord ; and he
leads us to infer that much real feeling accompanied it.   The
praise of his good queen he sang loyally, and prolonged her
fame wherever he went as the best of gold-adorned queens
who freely dispense their gifts.   Hrothgar feels keenly the
loss of his thegns at Heorot, and cannot control his expressions of sorrow even in public. " He sat unhappy, suffered   *Beowulf*, 130,
great pain, endured thegn-sorrow." And his grief is very   1324, 1481.
acute when Æschere is snatched away. Beowulf cares for
his thegns, and thinks of their future when he is about to
enter into the strife, commending them to the protection of
Hrothgar in the event of his own death. In turn, they seem
to think the world of him. When he attacks the mother
of Grendel beneath the sea, the conflict is long doubtful, and
time passes. The waves become tinged with blood, and to
those who sit upon the cliff, anxiously watching for his return,
there seems no longer any doubt about his fate. The Danes
depart—Beowulf is no lord of theirs—but his own faithful
followers remain. Sick at heart they gaze upon the water,   1602.
and think that they will never see their lord and friend again.
But when at last he does appear, their delight, the eager
attentions with which they receive him, their joy as they
march over the moor proudly carrying the trophies of his
victory, are quite pathetic as an eloquent revelation of the
deep love they bear him.

In the hall the thegn was his lord's trusted adviser and   1326.
councillor[1], freely offering advice ; in the battle he was his   366.
" shoulder-companion[2]," protecting his master's body with his
own. To desert his lord when in danger was for him an
everlasting disgrace ; and no other chieftain would ever give   2891.
him protection after such an inglorious deed. When Beowulf
awaits by night the attack of Grendel his thegns retire to rest   690.

---

[1] "mîn rûn-wita and mîn rǽd-bora."   [2] "eaxl-gestealla."

with sad but resolute hearts. Their thoughts are of home
and old-time friends and the scenes of childhood's days, to
which they believe that they are fated never to return. But
there is no shrinking from the ordeal, no wavering; duty to
their chief teaches them that their place is by his side whatever the end may be. Similarly, the followers of Andreas,
when the storm arises upon the sea, are fearful of the danger.

Andreas, 375, 400. None of them thinks that he will ever live to accomplish the
dangerous passage; but when it is proposed that they should
leave the ship they quickly answer that they could not leave
their master in his peril and seek safety for themselves on

405. land. "Whither should we go, lordless and sorrowful, if we
fail thee? We should be loathly in every land, despised

Beowulf, 2661. among the people." When Beowulf, in his last fight, is hard
beset by the dragon, the youthful Wiglaf says to his companions who watch the fray, "I remember the time when we
drank the mead, when in the beer-hall we promised our lord,
who gave us the rings, that we would repay him for those
war-trappings, the helmets and sharp swords, if such a need
as this befell him. He who chose us out of the host for this
adventure reminded us of honour, and gave me these treasures,
because he accounted us good spear-warriors, brave helm-
bearers....Now is the day come when our lord needs the
might of good fighting-men. Let us go and help him. I had
rather by far perish with him. It seems to me not fitting
that we should bear our shields back again home, unless we
first may fell the foe, and save the life of our king." But
their hearts fail them, and so he flies alone to his chieftain's
side, with brave words to encourage him. Beowulf's sword
breaks off short, and the dragon seizes him by the throat
with its jaws, making a ghastly wound. Then, in his lord's
dire need, Wiglaf's weapon reaches home, and between them
the monster is slain. The old hero is wounded to the death,
and his thegn tends him with faithful service, loosening his
helmet and washing his hurts, reviving him with water, and
spreading out the treasure before his eyes to please him in
his last moments. Beowulf takes the golden collar from his
neck, and gives it to the young warrior, with his gold-

2822. mounted helm, his bracelet and corslet, and then dies. "It
went hardly with the young warrior that he saw, stretched on
the earth, his best beloved at the end of life, struggling

miserably." He cannot believe that his lord is dead, but sits, wearied out, by his shoulder, trying in vain to revive him with water ; and when those who had fled return in shame, so they find him. He bitterly reproaches the cowards who had left their master to his fate. " Lo ! this can he say, who will 2865. speak the truth, that the lord who gave you those treasures, the war-trappings that ye stand in there, when on the ale-bench he oft gave to you hall-sitters helmets and corslets, the lord to his thegns,...that he altogether cast away those war-weeds. Not at all could the folk-king boast of his comrades when war befell him....Now shall all treasure-sharing and sword-giving, all home-joy, cease from your race. Every man of your family shall wander, deprived of land-right, among his own people, as soon as the athelings hear far and wide of your flight, of your inglorious deed. Better is death to every earl than life ill-famed." We may quite reasonably imagine that we are watching a closing scene upon one of the battle-fields of Britain.

Separation from his lord, either by death or exile, was always a cause of deep distress to the faithful thegn. A wanderer, who has known its bitterness, describes the sorrow of such a one. Cold with care, he sits brooding by the sea, and thinks of his home of yore :

"Remembers he the heroes and the treasure-taking,   *Wanderer*, 34.
How him in youth his gold-friend did receive
And welcome to his feast. That joy has long since passed.
Therefore knows he, who long time must forgo
The lore-speech of his dear and friendly lord,
When sorrow and strife together intermingled
Oft bind the senses of the lone, sad man.
Him thinks then in his heart that he his lord
Doth clip and kiss, and on his knee lay down
Both hands and head, as he at times before
In days of yore enjoyed his lord's dear gifts.
—Then wakens from his sleep the friendless one,
And sees before him but the fallow waves,
The sea-fowl bathing, spreading wide their plumes,
And, mingling with the hail, the falling sleet and snow.
Then all the heavier are his wounds of heart,
Sore yearned for the beloved; sorrow is renewed......."

So strong were the ties which bound the thegn to his lord.

Next in rank in the social order were the ceorls or freemen, who followed their lord of their own freewill, and by whose swords his position was won and the foundations of his power established. The Teutonic freeman might acknowledge a leader, but never a master. His duty towards his chief was rather a matter of mutual benefit than of regularly ordained service. On reaching maturity the young freeman received his war-equipment, as a mark of his manhood, and took his place among the warriors of his tribe. He then possessed a voice in the tribal council[1], and was summoned to the place of assembly[2] whenever important matters, touching the common weal, were to be discussed. He would ride in with his fellows in troops, fully armed and well mounted, and always saw to it that his opinion was not lightly disregarded. He expressed his dissent by placing his lips to the rim of his buckler and giving vent to a deep, murmuring hum of dissatisfaction ; his applause was expressed by a loud beating of spear upon shield. At home and abroad, at council or festive board, he always had his weapons near at hand, ready for feud or war. In theory his person was sacred ; his lord had no right to put him to death, or to imprison him, or to order him to be beaten. He had the right to demand from his rulers reasonable and equitable decisions. His religion was his own and not subject to the jurisdiction of any other. His blood had its price. But the criminal might be outlawed or exiled, and then all his free-rights were annulled. The outlaw, or " wolf-head," had no place in the social order, but was treated as a wild beast. He might be slain at sight, or hanged upon the gallows-tree by any who took him, without any satisfaction being required. Thus a means was provided for the elimination of those who were dangerous or unworthy.

Before we can fully understand the life and character of our ancestors we must carefully observe the great importance which they attached to liberty in all its aspects. A passionate love of liberty, born of the free and roving life of the early continental days, is the keynote to the character of the race ; and we can see the inbred craving after it working itself out as the supreme factor in the national development of constitution and religion through the Reformation to the great movements of the eighteenth and nineteenth centuries. By the Teutons a new element was introduced into European civilisation : the desire for personal independence, for free

Beowulf, 2615. *Desc. into Hell*, 70.

Andreas, 1095.

Beowulf, 2043. *Tacitus*, cc. 13, 22, 7.

Riddle, LVI. 12. *Gnomic Verses* (*Ex.*) 147.

---

[1] "folc-gemôt."   [2] "þingstede."

and adventurous experience, for the full realisation of personality; in short, the desire for all that makes one feel
oneself a man.

Liberty was denied only to the serfs and slaves, the
theows or thralls, who were lowest of degree. These were
the sad results of the darker side of conquest, men whose
lives had been spared after defeat that they might perform
the menial duties of the homestead and the farm. It is
impossible to believe that universal slaughter could have
prevailed over the whole country throughout the whole time
of the invasion; and we have seen that the Englishman was
not entirely destitute of humanity, mercy and pity. In the
first shock of race against race there was certainly much
abominable cruelty displayed; but, as the conquest progressed and the resistance became less determined, a milder
aspect. seems to have come over it. Great numbers of
captured Welsh women must have become the wives or
slaves of the conquerors, who, except in the case of the
Angles, did not usually bring their own wives with them.
And the custom of allowing the defeated the option of slavery
no doubt prevailed in the later stages of the conquest, except
where the passionate ferocity of the moment, during a revengeful fray, led to indiscriminate slaughter, and then men,
women and children alike perished. Thus we read in the *Riddles,*
literature of the thong which binds the swart Welshmen[1], of XIII. 3, XIII. 8,
the "þeow-wealh" or Welsh serf, of a swart herdsman who LIII., LXXI.
tends the cattle, of one dark-haired Welshwoman[2] who dresses *Laws of Ine,*
the hides, and of another who draws the water from the well. 74.
Then, too, though some cities, when taken by storm, were
completely destroyed, others, like London, York and Lincoln,
appear to have been spared. And here and there, in such
places, isolated communities of the Welsh no doubt remained,
quietly submitting to the conqueror's yoke, and thus escaping
massacre. It seems that some of them were even allowed,
after the wave of conquest had passed by them, to retain *Laws of Ine,*
a portion of their land with certain land-rights; and others 32.
were to be found, either as warriors or guides, in alliance with
the invaders against tribes of either nation. Thus some
intercommunication must have been established, which will

---

[1] "swearte Wealas."   [2] "wonfeax Wale."

account for the apparent influence of the Celtic imagination upon the Teutonic literature.

In addition, there were also among the slaves men of English birth who had committed some offence for which they were unable to atone, and had in consequence lost their freedom. If a freeman were taken with stolen goods upon him the king had power either to put him to death, or to sell him beyond sea, or to cause him to redeem himself by payment of his "wer-geld." Whoever seized and secured the thief had half the price that was paid for him or by him ; if anyone slew him, he received seventy shillings. If the thief's household were privy to his theft they were all sold into slavery. Tacitus says that it was a common practice among the Germans for one who had lost his all by gambling to stake himself upon one last throw of the dice, for they were always inveterate gamblers. "They two shall sit at the dice while their misery glides away from them ; they forget their heavier lot; they have their sport on the board," says an Old English poem. Inter-tribal conflicts also added to the roll of slaves. Though it was enacted, for the purpose of checking an indiscriminate slave traffic, that anyone who sold over sea his own countryman, bond or free, even though the man had committed a crime, should pay for him according to his "wer," yet in London there was a great slave market much frequented by Frisian merchants by whom English slaves were sold abroad.

The lot of the slave was by no means happy, since he possessed no rights, and therefore, if taken in a fault, might be sold or beaten at his master's pleasure. But, as opposed to wholesale butchery, enforced servitude upon the land marks a comparatively high development of morality, and long prevailed among civilised nations.

Speedily in the track of the invasion followed the settlement, as the Englishman sat down to enjoy the fruits of the victories he had won. He was soon at home in his new England, for it was for the purpose of winning a home that he had come. He found himself among the *débris* of an older civilisation, with a people already accustomed to subjection ready to serve at his call. The cities which remained undestroyed he often left to their previous inhabitants. The old remains of the Roman occupation, the stone-paved streets,

Laws of Wihtræd, 26. A.-S. Laws, Thorpe, p. 19.

Laws of Ine, 7, p. 47.

Germania, c. 14.

Gnomic Verses, III. 182.

Laws of Ine, 11, p. 48. Bede, Hist. Eccl. III. 7, IV. 6, 12, 22.

Beowulf, 2225.

Ruined Burg, 2.

the walls and pillars, the strong fortifications, greatly impressed and even overawed him, because they were new to   *Gnomic Verses*
his experience. He thought them the creations of magic   *(Cott.)* 1.
arts, the antique work of a giant race of old, far wiser and   *Andreas,* 1236,
1494.
mightier than himself[1]; and he could not accustom himself
at once to be barricaded within stone walls and battlements,
over and around which seemed to hover the spirits of the
past. Habitations of stone, which he was not sufficiently
skilful to build for himself, at first seemed to him cold and
comfortless. So he began to open up for himself fresh
ground, clearing the land, and raising in the midst of the
cleared spaces his dwelling-places of wood. The land was
held to be the common property of the tribe, and was
distributed among the freemen as "folc-land" by the king
and his council, the representatives of the people. Such land
was usually held for the term of the freeman's life, and on his
death was re-assigned to another holder, not necessarily the
dead man's heir. But there was also the "bôc-land," or
freehold, granted in perpetuity to the freeman who had
distinguished himself in the service of his king and people,
and descending after his death to his heirs.

The camp became a settlement springing up round the
hall of the chief, in much the same way as the settlement   *Beowulf,* 65,
sprang up round Heorot after the victories of Hrothgar,   665, 1237,
1300.
with bowers for the ladies, and separate habitations for the
principal men and their families. Then, after victory, was
heard "the loud joy in the hall, the sound of the harp, and   88.
the clear song of the Shaper," while the victor dispensed rich
treasures to his men. The hall itself was a long, rectangular,
high-gabled building of wood, with a door at either end, and
long, raised benches along the sides, with a hearth in the
middle of the floor, and an opening in the roof above as an
outlet for the smoke. There was often a dais for the chief,
and benches and tables for the warriors. At night men slept
on beds placed on the floor at right angles to the wall. The
interior was usually hung with banners, shields and spears,
with walrus bone, horns of stags, and other trophies of field
and flood, and was often adorned with tapestry and gilding.
Outside, the roof was sometimes crowned with wide-spreading
antlers. Near by clustered the rude huts of the poorer tribes-   *Riddle,*
LXXXV.

---

[1] "orþanc enta geweorc," "enta ærgeweorc," "eald enta geweorc."

men, together with the farmsteads and storehouses for grain. The whole was enclosed by a mound and fence, and to the enclosure was given the name "tûn."

Riddle, XXI.
Crafts of Men, 61.

In the township the art of war speedily began to give place to the manifold arts of peace, though the smith who worked upon the warriors' weapons still kept his employment and his great reputation. There the cunning craftsman

58. worked in gold, silver and precious stones, and the potter fashioned his rude vessels from the clay. There the miller plied his craft by the river side, and the brewer brewed the

Riddles, V., XXVIII., XXIX.
Crafts, 44, 75.
Riddles, XXVI., XXVII.

beer which the Englishman loved only too well, while the wise and ready-handed workman planned and built houses and halls of timber. There the women sat spinning and weaving and making rough garments, or tanned and dressed the hides, or employed themselves upon the more delicate

LI. work of embroidery, while others fed the dogs and the poultry, or saw to the bees.

In the fields and common pastures around grazed numerous herds of cattle, with herdsmen keeping close watch to prevent straying or theft. Here and there were clearly defined

XXII., LXXI. spaces marked out by the ploughman's furrow. "I trod the mark-paths; I paced the moors, bound under the beam; I had the beam on my neck; often the iron hurt me sore in

XXXV. my side," says the Ox in the *Riddles*. Upon cultivated patches the slaves worked with rude agricultural implements, raking and hoeing, sowing or reaping, as the season might be.

Fates of Men, 69, 85.
Gnomic Verses (*Ex.*) 185.
Riddle LXXVIII.
Crafts of Men, 73, 80, 81.
Beowulf, 865, 917.

At home idle warriors sat over a coloured board[1], gambling with dice; and afield their more energetic comrades rode, hunted and fished, or trained and tried their hawks. And sometimes the horsemen would choose a level stretch of ground and race against each other with great emulation and excitement. Horse-racing was already becoming a passion; and in at least one Continental tribe, the Esthonians, it had become by the days of Alfred a

Alfred's Orosius, Voyage of Wulfstan.

systematised sport. There, when a man died, his goods were divided into five or six or more unequal portions, and laid in successive heaps, of increasing value, within a mile of his "tûn," the largest portion being the farthest away, and the smallest nearest. Then all who had swift horses

---

[1] "blêobord."

assembled at a starting point, about five or six miles from
the heaps, and raced for the prizes. He who came first to
the largest portion took it as his prize; the others raced
on, and the second swiftest rider took the second portion;
and so on until all the prizes were won. Because of this
practice swift horses were there excessively dear[1].

On the outskirts of each settlement, and by the shore
if the settlement were near the sea, armed sentinels were
constantly on guard against a sudden attack or foray, ready
to challenge anyone who happened to approach. When   *Beowulf*, 230.
Beowulf and his men land near Heorot such a sentinel
rides to meet them, furiously brandishing his spear, and demanding to know whence they come. "I was the sentinel,"
he says, "I held watch by the shore, that no foes with their
fleet might ravage the land of the Danes. Now I must know
your race before ye go further hence as false spies into the
Danish land. Now, ye sailors from afar, hear my plain
determination. It is best to declare at once whence ye
come." If any stranger left the beaten path without making   *Laws of*
his presence known by shouting or blowing his horn he was   *Wihtræd*, 28,
   p. 19.
liable to be taken as a thief and either slain or held to   *Laws of Ine*,
   20, p. 50.
ransom.   Thorpe.

Round each settlement lay the mark or border land, a tract
of unexplored moorland waste or woodland, crossed only by   *Exodus*, 56.
narrow, solitary paths and secret ways. There, where all was
strange and dangerous, lurked the outlaw and the hidden   *Gnomic Verses*,
foe, the wolf and terror-demon; there, with the giant and   147, 42.
   Beowulf, 111.
the monster, lived the wood-elf and the wood-mare[2] which
lured the unwary to destruction. From the mark Grendel   711.
descends upon Heorot by night, striding across the misty
moors. "He was a fierce spirit, a notable mark-stepper, who   102.
held the moors, the fen and fastness; he guarded the abode of
the giant race." In the mark there was many an uncanny
spot where none but the bravest dared venture, sometimes "a
secret land, with wolf-haunted slopes and windy nesses, a
dangerous fen-path," with "a mere over which hang rustling   1358.
groves; a wood, fast by its roots, overwhelms the water; where

---

[1] Plan of the Course:

      6 miles   5 miles   4 miles   3 miles   2 miles   1 mile

The Start: | ⟶ | ⟶ | ⟶ | ⟶ | ⟶ | 1. 2. 3. 4. 5. 6. ☐ "tûn."
                                        Prizes in order of value.

[2] "wudu-mære," cf. nightmare.

every night strange portents may be seen, fire in the flood. No man liveth so wise as to know the bottom; even the stag when pursued by the hounds will give up his life on the shore before he will venture in to hide his head. No pleasant place is that."

The Englishman believed that he often heard from the mark the voices of many strange spirits. If he passed hastily through the woods at nightfall he could hear them moaning as if in pain, then coming up with the wind, and dashing past him over the tops of the trees, as though in pursuit of some hunted creature; and he often crouched low in the undergrowth, and feared for his own safety, as the wind and the storm passed by. Some spirits, he decided, must be suffering unspeakable agony, being banished for their crimes from the fellowship of the gods and heroes, and revenging themselves upon the human race. By day and night he could hear them echoing his call and mocking him upon the hills and wooded slopes whenever he cried afar to his companions. When tired of lying in wait for him they would often issue forth in the darkness to devastate his land. The unroofed farmstead, the levelled walls, the uprooted trees, the ruined crops, were all tokens of their malignant cruelty and ill-will. How these superstitious children feared the dark and the terror of the unseen!

Again, with the mists from the mark came strange diseases, fevers, plagues and pestilences; and the Englishman felt the evil spirits working upon his fears and oppressing his soul. He saw no connection whatever between disease and lack of sanitation, never traced his fever to the stench from the filthy fen[1]. But, in self-defence, he betook himself to witches and diviners, to magic and charms, and the many curiously fantastic concoctions of leechdom. His prescription for witlessness, devil-sickness or demoniacal possession, of the times when the medicinal methods of Dioscorides were known in the land, was to take from the body of the wort mandrake three pennies' weight and to administer the same as a drink in warm water as might be found most convenient. A sudden stitch was believed to

Elene, 1272, cf. Bede, *Hist. Ec.* (A.-S. version) and Cockayne's *Leechdoms*, III. 53.

Beowulf, 1353.

Riddle, XLI. 31. *Laws of Alf.* 30. *Laws of Edw. and Guth.* 11. Thorpe, pp. 23, 74.

Cockayne's *Leechdoms*, I. 249.

---

[1] "þis fen swearte
þat her yflê adelan stinceð"
(adela, filth).

be the work of elfin women, weird hags who rode noisily
over the land, and sent their yelling spears into skin, flesh,   III. 53.
blood and limb. The remedy was feverfew, red nettle and
dock, boiled in butter, and then, with an appropriate in-
cantation, rubbed into the parts affected, for the purpose of
melting the supposed spears. The best cure he could think
of for swollen eyes was: "take a live crab, put his eyes out,   II. 307.
and put him alive again into water, and put the eyes upon
the neck of the man who hath need; he will soon be well."
He had also an elaborate charm for bewitched land, another   I. 384, etc.
for the swarming of his bees, and many others of a like
nature, for his was an age of magic and childish credulity.
These charms and incantations were often written down   Bede,
and worn as amulets to weaken the spells of the evil   Plummer,
spirits.   II. 243.

But there were good spirits also, the Wane Deities, who
dwelt among the rustling reeds, and beside the banks of the
rippling brooks, genii of the gently flowing rivers, cool
fountains and standing waters, who soothed and comforted
and blessed him. Some there were who came with the
gentle showers of spring and the summer sunshine, who
kept their watch by day beside the growing crops and the
ripening corn. And ever there was conflict between the two,
the good and the evil.

Thus the Englishman, in his imagination, created round
about himself a world of airy spirits, personifications of his
hopes and fears, of light and darkness, emanating from the
nature worship of still earlier days.

Within the "tûn" our ancestors lived a jovial, happy life.
Even when the snow bound the earth in the fetters of winter,   *Andreas,*
and the settlement lay locked in the grip of frost, with the   1257.
ways impassable, and the streams covered with ice, when   *Wanderer,*
the terror of the dark winter nights came round about them,   103.
they whiled away the time with convivial intercourse and   *Fates of Men,*
merriment, with harp and song. They were at heart sociable   80.
and hospitable, fond of banqueting and festivity. The poet   *Widsith,* 105.
of the *Widsith* bears ample testimony to the warm welcome   4, 50, 70, 88,
which was always extended to the wandering singer and the   139.
friendly guest, and to the open-hearted hospitality which
generally prevailed. Such a welcome is given to Beowulf at   *Beowulf,* 320.
Heorot. With his troop he comes marching up the stone-

paved street to the hall; and Wulfgar, an honourable thegn
of Hrothgar's court, greets him before the door with stately
courtesy, asking his lineage and the business which brings
him thither. Beowulf replies with princely dignity: "We
342. are the table-companions of Hygelac; Beowulf is my name.
I will speak mine errand to the famous king, thy lord, if he
will be so good as to permit us to give him greeting."
Wulfgar bids them wait while he announces their presence
to his king, and they seat themselves by the door. He
hastens to Hrothgar, who is seated within, and stands re-
spectfully by his shoulder while delivering his message; for
359. he knows the usage of noble warriors, and the etiquette of
a court[1]. When Hrothgar hears who is without he says,
"I knew him when he was a boy....Hasten, and tell them
to come in....Say to them that they are welcome to the
397. Danes." But Wulfgar, observing the customary precaution,
requires the guests to lay aside their shields and spears before
they enter the hall. Under helm and corslet, at the head
of his band, Beowulf advances to Hrothgar with the usual
407. greeting, "Be thou Hrothgar hale[2]." The two talk together
for a while, and then preparations are made for refreshment.
The benches are made ready in the beer-hall, and the warriors
495. sit down. "The thegn who bore the inlaid ale-vessel did his
duty; he poured out the foaming mead. At whiles sang the
'scop,' clear in Heorot; there was joy of heroes, the noble
warriors of Danes and Weder-Geats." Then Wealhtheow,
614. Hrothgar's queen, comes in, mindful of etiquette[3], to greet
the guest in the hall. She first bears the cup to the king, as
custom ordained, bidding him be blithe at the beer-drinking,
then to the thegns, veterans and youths, going to every part
of the hall, and then to Beowulf, to whom she expresses her
1163. pleasure in his coming. It was the custom for noble women
1982. thus to show courtesy to the guests of their lords. Her duty
2021. done, she takes her seat beside the king, and the feast pro-
653. ceeds till dusk, when the warriors rise and with kindly
good-nights prepare to retire to rest.
　　While his guests remained under his roof the host was
responsible for their personal safety, and if harm befell them
1055. he was required to pay either "bôt" or "wer," as Hrothgar

---

[1] "cûðe he duguðe þeaw."
[2] "wes þu Hrôðgâr hâl"; cf. "wassail." 　　[3] "cynna gemyndig."

did for Hondscio. On the other hand if they did harm to any he was responsible for their deeds. If a man entertained a stranger, a chapman or any other who had come over the mark, for three nights in his own house, and fed him with his own food, and the stranger afterwards did harm to any man, the host had to bring him to justice, or make atonement for him.

Laws of Hlothere and Eadric, 15, Thorpe, p. 14.

At Heorot, when Beowulf had vanquished Grendel, there was a banquet on a grand scale, for which elaborate preparations were made. Treasures, to serve as decorations or to be bestowed as gifts, were taken from the hoards, which were then, with the exception of the person, the only banks. For the personal wealth of the warriors and their wives mainly consisted of ornaments of precious metal, bracelets, armlets and necklets of gold, costly flagons and drinking vessels, inlaid weapons, helmets and armour; and we hear of a valuable necklet[1], of a definitely ascertained value, which was given to Widsith: "on it were scored six hundred scots of beaten gold, counted in shillings[2]." The guest-hall was made ready by many men and women; tapestry, embroidered with gold, shone upon the walls; and there were many things beautiful to look upon. The warriors sat down upon the benches, and the mead-vessel was passed round with due observance of ceremonial. Then a golden ensign, an ornamented banner with a staff, a helm and corslet, a sword inlaid with jewels, and eight horses with gold-plated bridles, on one of them, Hrothgar's own war-steed, a saddle inlaid with precious stones, were brought in and given to the victor; and other gifts there were for his men. Song arose, and the sound of the harp, as Hrothgar's gleeman sang the Battle-Lay of Hengest, while the cup-bearers carried round the wine. When the song was ended, Wealhtheow, with her daughter Freaware, joined the company, wearing upon her head a golden circlet. She carried the cup first to the king, and then to Beowulf, with warm and gracious thanks for his help, and with still more treasures from the hoard.

Gnomic Verses (Ex.) 126, etc.

Widsith, 91.

Beowulf, 994.

1015.

1065.
1163.

At all great banquets etiquette and courteous ceremonial

---

1 "beag."
2   "on þam siexhund wäs smætes goldes
             gescyred sceatta scilling-rîme."
Cf. "paying his shot," " scot-free."

were prominent features, pointing to a fairly developed sense of order and social refinement. At least the great kings and queens of the *Beowulf* seem to have been hedged about with a certain grave stateliness and royal dignity, which were reflected by those in immediate attendance at their courts. A noble pedigree carried with it a claim to honour and respect ; and to show a ready acquaintance with the lineage and renown of all who were of noble birth was the pride of those who were themselves noble. The warriors of rank professed a courtesy of a high and long-established order ; and any intentional rudeness could usually be ascribed to over-indulgence or burning jealousy.

372.

Fates of Men, 48.
Bî manna môde, 13.
Beowulf, 480, 502.
1105, 2033.

But it often happened, when the mead gained a hold upon brain and tongue, that the warrior would boast too freely of the deeds he had done, and of those he intended still to do ; and often would envy and jealousy lead someone to belittle his fame. Then would the strife of angry words rise high ; and frequently the banquet ended in deeds of blood. The ale-vessels would be overturned in the tumult, as the warriors leapt to their feet in frenzy, with all restraint forgotten, while the women fled in terror from the hall.

770.

Andreas, 1528.

There is a word in the *Beowulf,* " ealu-scerwen " (ale-terror), which almost of itself calls up a vivid picture of such a scene ; and there is a fellow to it, " meodu-scerwen " (mead-terror), in the *Andreas.* When the settlement was completed laws were drawn up to prevent such riotous scenes, thereby furnishing a proof of their former prevalence. For one man to call another a liar, or to shamefully bespeak him with abusive words, in another's house, involved a fine ; one shilling to the man whose hospitality had been thus abused, six to the insulted person, and twelve to the king. To remove another man's drinking vessel, or to cast the contents in his face, was punished by exactly the same fine, evidently pointing to the existence of rough horse-play and drunken violence. Drawing one's weapon at a beer-drinking, and personal violence within the township, were also punishable by fine.

Laws of Hlothere and Eadric, 11.
Thorpe, p. 13.

12, p. 14.

13, p. 14.

There cannot be any doubt that the average Englishman was then addicted to frequent bouts of drunkenness, although we hear of the queens and noble women who graced his banquets, and probably, by their presence alone, imposed some measure of restraint upon him. Sometimes he even

resorted to the ale-vessel to stifle his fears of impending *Beowulf,* 480.
danger, or to screw his courage to the sticking point when
about to engage in some desperate attack. Then, half-
maddened, he must have presented a terrible spectacle. Here
is a picture of a drunken orgie very different from the
banquets in the *Beowulf.* A king summons the chiefs *Judith,* x.
of his army, and all become drunk together. "Then was
the king in wine-joy; he laughed and shouted, he roared
and dinned, so that all men might hear afar how the fierce-
hearted one stormed and yelled. Fiercely drunk, he frequently
admonished his guests to drink deeply. So the wicked one,
throughout the day, drenched his warriors with wine until
they lay swooning, made drunk all his captains as though
they had been struck down in death, drained of every good."
When at last he retires to rest, he falls across his bed so
drunken that he does not know what is happening when
he is seized by the hair and slain. The realism of the
description is altogether terrible. In the heathen days, the
Teuton's Heaven, Walhalla, was pictured as an abode to
which the warrior who died upon the battle-field passed
after death, there to sit at the banquet with the gods and
heroes, drinking mead from the skulls of vanquished enemies.
But the poet's hero was never drunken, and, indeed, could *Beowulf,* 530.
express his contempt for those who were.

No banquet was complete without the gleeman and his song.
Rich gifts were always the reward of the skilful singer, and he
was everywhere welcomed with gladness and respect. Yet it
is the conscientiousness of the man which is most striking.
The poet rejoiced in his art with a feeling akin to reverence.
Though to us it may often appear crude and unpolished, yet
to him it represented a recognised mission and a noble life's
work. He regarded himself not merely as the amuser of an
idle hour, but also as a stimulator. Hence his repeated cry
to his audience, "Hwæt!" with a sharp touch upon the
strings. He believed himself to be divinely inspired for the
purpose of setting forth noble deeds and raising the thoughts
of his fellows to higher things, as the stories of Widsith,
Cædmon and Cynewulf, the author of the *Heliand* and the
Icelander Halbjörn, go to prove. "He hath in himself the *Gnomic Verses*
gift of his glee, which God gave him." We cannot pass him *(Ex.)* I. 172.
by without giving him credit for honestly endeavouring to

fill that sphere of usefulness to which he believed he had been specially called.

The ties of home and kin possessed for the Englishman a full significance, perhaps all the more because of days of hard experience in the past. Hardship in the field must have taught him to value the rest of home when, for a brief space, he remained at ease in his hall. He was always prepared to fight to the death for his home and family. Hrothgar *Beowulf*, 656. commits Heorot to Beowulf's keeping as a precious charge which he had never before entrusted to another. When the 693. Geats retire to rest in the hall their thoughts fly back to their own home life, to the folk and the ruler's castle where they 2329. were fostered. It is a ruthful thing to the heart of Beowulf, the greatest of heart-sorrows, which makes his breast swell within him with dark thoughts, when his home among the Geats is destroyed by the ravager. The Wanderer laments *Wanderer*, 20, that he is deprived of home and far from friends, and as he 51. broods upon his woes "the memory of his kinsmen passes o'er his heart; he greets them with songs of joy, looks yearningly upon them. But his comrades float away; the spirit of the fleeting shades brings not there many of the old familiar songs. Sorrow is renewed to him who must again and yet again send forth his weary heart over the icy 75. binding of the waves....In countless numbers round this land the walls stand beaten with the wind, and coated o'er with rime, and halls are all decayed. The wine-hall crumbles; its lord lies lifeless, its warriors all fallen, the proud ones by the wall. Some war has gripped and carried hence; one a ship bore away over the tossing ocean; one the hoar wolf tore when dead; one a sad-faced earl hid in an 92. earthy grave....Where went the steed? Where the kinsman? Where the treasure-giver? Where are the seats of feasting? Where the joys of the hall? Alas, the bright beaker! Alas, the byrnied warrior! Alas, the people's pride! How that time has passed away, grown dark under the helm of night, as though it never had been!" Thus the exile's yearning for home and the life that is gone finds utterance. Very similar is the pathetic elegy of the *Beowulf*, 2245. chieftain, last of his race, who commits to the earth the ancestral treasures, a secret hoard. Death in battle has taken away all his fellow-tribesmen; all are dead who once

took part in the hall-joy. None is there now to bear the
sword, to burnish the plated flagon and the drinking-cup,
none to furbish the helmets. The mail coat rusts, which once
in battle withstood the bite of the steel; the ringed corslet is
no longer carried afar with the chieftain and his heroes. No
longer is there the joy of the harp; no good hawk sweeps
through the hall; no swift steed beats the castle-ground with
its hoofs. Death has banished far away all his comrades. 2268.
"So, sad at heart, he mourned his sorrows; last of them all,
unhappily he wept both night and day, until death's flood
touched at his heart." And yet again we have Beowulf's
description of the sorrow of his aged grandfather Hrethel
whose eldest son Herebeald had been accidentally slain by
Hæthcyn, his younger brother. "Ever, on every morning, is 2451.
he reminded of the death of his boy; he cannot bear to see
another in the place of the dead. Sore-hearted he looks
upon his son's bower, the wine-hall waste, an abode of the
winds, bereft of revelling. The riders sleep in the grave; no
sound of the harp is there, no game in the courtyards as of
yore. He departs to his bed; sings his sorrow-song, the
father for his son. All too roomy seemed to him the meadows
and the hall." Thus we see the tenderer side of the Englishman's character, and the store he set upon all the associations
of home.

In the home life the Englishwoman played a most im-
portant part. The heroines of these early days were almost 616, 1159, etc.
invariably of noble character, loving to their husbands,
affectionate to their children, tender and pure of heart, bearing
themselves with true womanly dignity and reserve, and in
every way winning the respect and chivalrous homage of the
men. Woman was no slave, but had her mission in life, and
that a noble one, making for harmony and peace. Her poetic
title, "peace-weaver" or "love-weaver[1]," is very significant, 1943.
and was derived from the custom of giving kinswomen
in marriage to settle feuds and cement alliances. In his
youth the poet of the *Widsith* had travelled in the train *Widsith*, 6, 9.
of Queen Ealdhild, "the pure peace-weaver," to the court of
Eormanric, "the wrathful breaker of pledges," evidently bent
on an embassy of conciliation. We might allow our imagi-
nations to make much of this embassy. When Wealhtheow

---

[1] "freoðu-webbe."

comes forth at Heorot after the conflict we notice at once her

Beowulf, 1172. anxiety to lay the foundations of a lasting alliance. "Speak to the Geats with mild words; be gracious to them; be mindful of gifts," she says to the king. Of Beowulf she asks friendship in the future, and adds, almost as an admonition,

1229. for she knows well the fierce hearts of the men, "Here is
1927. every earl true to his fellow, mild of heart." Hygd, the queen of Hygelac, though very young, is wise, virtuous and
1983. generous. She loves the people, and when she is left a
2370. widow, with a son too young to rule, she studies how best to further their interests and to ward off the horrors of war from the land.

Strongwilled and wicked women there were, but for them there is no praise. Such was Thrytho, the fierce queen, upon whom none dared to look; for the penalty was death. "Such is not a queen-like custom for a woman, though she

1941. be without equal, that a weaver of peace should shamefully deprive a dear man of his life." But love conquered even her at last, and as his queen Offa tamed her and changed her way of life for better things. While many

Gnomic Verses (Ex.) 102. women were "fast cautious," "firmly prudent," others were curious, prying busybodies. And there were weak and foolish women also who fell under the spells of witches, enchanters

Laws of Alf., 30. Thorpe, p. 23. and magicians to their own great harm. Alfred ordered that those who had such dealings should not be suffered to live— an evidence of the mischief which was at work, often sapping the very foundations of domestic life.

When a woman was sought in marriage the husband bought her from her kin with cattle or treasure, not so much by way of payment for her services, as once had been the

Gnomic Verses (Ex.) 11. 82. case, but as a recognition of her worth. "A king must buy his queen with cattle, with cups and bracelets. Both must first of all be good with gifts. War must wax in the earl, and the wife thrive, dear among her people. She must be light-hearted, hold counsel, be liberal with horses and treasures. At the mead-giving, before the companions, always, everywhere, she must greet the chief of the athelings first of all, must straightway give the first cup to the hand of her lord. And both of them, house-holders, must take counsel together."

Laws of Æthelbert, 77. Thorpe, p. 9. If a man bought a maiden with property the bargain was binding if it were without deceit; but if there were deceit

he could take her home again and have his property restored
to him ; such was the law. But a higher view of marriage
was already coming into vogue, and the property was often
presented to the wife herself as a dowry or marriage settlement. On the morning after marriage the husband also
presented her with the " morning-gift" which remained her
own absolute possession. Thus it was that queens, as well as
kings, had treasures to bestow as gifts.

Apollonius of Tyre.

The married life of the Englishman was usually happy
and peaceable. He was always the master[1] of the home, with
none within it to gainsay his will. He reverenced the womanhood of his wife, and she looked up to him as her lord. Nor
was deep and true affection wanting. In the *Husband's
Message*, the man who has made a home beyond the sea
sends to his wife a letter carved in runes upon a wooden
tablet, reminding her of her plighted troth, and calling upon
her to join him as soon as she hears the cuckoo in the wood,
for he is waiting and longing for her. His foes had driven
him away from her, but now, in the foreign land, he has won
much treasure and land, high rank and honour, and is the
chief of many warriors. Yet without her it brings no joy to
him. And the message ends in true lover fashion with the
binding together of the runes which represent their names,
and a renewal of his vow to keep as long as he lives the
troth which is between them[2]. The *Wife's Complaint* reveals
the sorrow, the " waking-care," of a woman, friendless and
alone, whose husband, having doubted her, had put her
from him and gone across the sea. Many of life's sorrows
had she known, but never a worse than this. They had
been so suited to each other and so loving ; often they
had vowed that nought but death should ever part them.
But his kinsmen had made mischief and plotted to put
them asunder ; and now it is all changed as though there had
never been anything between them. Her husband had hidden
his heart from her, had murder in his thought, and yet dis-

Husband's Message (Ex.).

22.

48.

Wife's Complaint, 7.

12.
21.
20.

---

[1] "hûs-hlaford," "hûs-bonda," "ætgifa."
[2] 　　　　"Gecyre ic atsomne S. R. geador
　　　　EA. V. and D. âðe benemnan,
　　　　ðat he ðâ wære and ðâ winetrêowe
　　　　be him lifgendum læstan wolde,
　　　　ðe git on ærdagum oft gespræcon."

dained to show his grief to her, bearing himself so blithely.

27. And at last she had been banished to the woods, to live alone, as though she were a shameful creature. Her heart cries out for him, and the happiness of other lovers but increases her own pain. She knows he cannot altogether have ceased to love her, and that somewhere he sits, gazing across the sea, with memories of the old home in his heart, and wearily

52. longing to have her back again. "Woe is to him who must with weary longing wait for his beloved." And there is another passage describing the home-coming of a sailor from the sea with a loving wife to greet him :

Gnomic Verses
(Ex.) 95.

> "Dear the welcomed one to the Frisian wife,
> When the ship stands by the shore.
> His keel is come, and her man is home,
> Her own food-giver. And she bids him in,
> Washes his sea-stained suit, and gives him new.
> Pleasant it is to him on land
> Whose love impels him home."

But the picture must not be too perfect. We hear another

Juliana, 166. husband addressing his wife : "My sweetest sunshine, lo ! thou hast the splendour and glory of youth, an ample gift";

187. but later, in the violence of thwarted passion, he strips her,

227. beats her, and takes her by the hair. The poet allows us to make out something of both the light and shadow of early married life, but means us plainly to understand that this particular husband was a brute.

To the Englishwoman chastity was the crown of all

Gnomic Verses virtues, and the loss of honour her greatest shame. "The
(Ex.) II. 101. wife must keep her troth to her man." To Beadohild,

Lament of drugged and wronged by Weland, her shame brought greater
Deor. sorrow than the death of her brother; and there is also a hint of the story of Hild, afflicted with a like sorrow, whose father, in the mythology, rises from the dead to fight with her ravisher night after night for many years. In the settlement so strong was the feeling against unchastity that the unchaste

Gnomic Verses woman lost her place in the tribe, and no man would take
(Cott.) 43. her for his wife. She was banished from home and kin to

Boniface to dwell in the woods with the outlaw and the wild beast; and
Ethelbald, such punishment was often meted out even to one under
Will. of Malm.
I. 4. suspicion. Among the Old Saxons, if a virgin in her father's

house or a wife living with her husband committed adultery she was either strangled and burnt, her seducer being hung over the grave where the remains were buried, or else the matrons of the tribe cut off her garments at the waist and drove her from the community, whipping her and wounding her with knives. With the marks of shame upon her she was hounded on by fresh tormentors from village to village until she perished miserably. Immorality among the English there certainly was; "oft," say the *Gnomic Verses*, which charge some women with inconstancy; that they love another when the husband departs afar. And the *Riddles* bear sufficient witness to a delight in coarse speaking, grossness and indelicacy among the men. But, with remarkably few exceptions, considering the age, Old English literature is decidedly healthy and clean; and from this we may judge that the morality of the people as a whole was, for the time, distinctly of a high order. Further evidence may be drawn from the laws, where adultery with a freeman's wife is assigned a greater penalty than the slaying of the freeman himself—the wife's honour dearer than the man's own life. The seducer must atone for his crime with his "wer-geld," and must also provide another wife with his own money, and bring her to the man he has wronged. And the penalties in other cases were also very high. If a bond-maiden were carried off by force the ravisher must pay fifty shillings to her master, and afterwards buy her of him. If she were betrothed to another man he must make "bôt" to him with twenty shillings.

But it was in the stress of war that the woman suffered most, for then fierce and lustful passions passed out of all control, and the Teutonic women were often driven to prefer suicide, or death at their husbands' hands, to the shame which awaited the captured female slave. Great was the war-terror of the women when armed men broke in upon the settlement, and the blood-stained sword beat upon the helmet's crest. And when their lords and protectors lay dead, "sadly they mourned with deep sorrow of heart, singing a woeful dirge, with hair all unbound, dreading the harm of the hard days to come, fearing the warrior, the shame and the bondage." After "the protectors of brides and bracelets had fallen, sick with wounds,...many a frightened pale-faced woman must go

Gnomic Verses (Ex.) 65, 103.

Riddles.

Laws of Æthelbert, 31, 82, 83. Thorpe, pp. 4, 10.

Beowulf, 1285.

3150.

Genesis, 1969.

trembling in a stranger's clasp." When Hildegund escapes with Walther, believing that the Huns are upon them, she *Waldhere.* cries, "Slay me, lest I belong to the Huns and not to thee"; but the strangers turn out to be Franks, and there is hope of victory, so she urges on her lover to the strife, as the Teutonic women often encouraged their lords at critical moments: "Let not thy strength fail this day; let not thy valour droop; conquer or die!"

Of their children the English were passionately fond and *Juliana,* 93. passionately proud. A father speaks to his daughter: "Thou art, daughter mine, the dearest and the sweetest in my heart, mine only one on earth, the light of mine eyes." Hrothgar *Beowulf,* 945. speaks of the pride which the mother of Beowulf must have in having brought forth so great a son, if she yet lived to hear of his mighty deeds. He himself would take him to his heart as his own son; but Wealhtheow reminds him of their own 1176. boy, who must not be deprived of his birthright. If he is left fatherless, and too young to rule, Hrothulf, their nephew, must be his guardian. Having expressed her opinion she turns 1220. to Beowulf with her gifts, and says, "Be friendly of lore to these boys. I shall not forget thy reward for it....Be kind in deeds to my son." Elsewhere we read how fathers and *Fates of Men,* 1. mothers delighted in their little ones, nourishing and feeding them with loving care, till the young limbs were full grown, 13. and the boys became men, perhaps warriors whose fate it 46. was to fall upon the battle-field. Then we hear of a bereaved mother mourning over her dead, weeping and wailing as she sees the body of her son consumed upon the bale-fire. Thus *Beowulf,* 1115. Hildeburg mourns when her son is slain at Finnsburg. She orders the last rites to be performed, but exceeding great is her sorrow. As he is placed on the pyre she lies grief-stricken upon his shoulder and sobs aloud; as the flame devours all that is dear to her she grieves and laments with mournful 2450. death-songs. And we have already seen that a father's sorrow for his son was no less grievous. In fact the English could not conceive any creature entirely destitute of parental *Riddle* xvi. affection. One of the *Riddles* describes how desperately an animal, probably the badger, works to make a way of escape for her dear ones when the hunter threatens them with death, and how fiercely she will fight in their defence if her retreat *Beowulf,* 1277. be intercepted. Even the mother of Grendel grieves over her

son's death as though she were human; and it is natural
affection which leads her forth upon a sorrowful journey to
avenge him. It will not greatly surprise us, when we come
to Christian times, to find that the Englishman also gives to
Satan a son, of whom he boasts that the creation of man   *Satan.*
is his work.

Naturally, the settlement greatly modified, or at least
restricted, many of the primitive instincts of the race. In
the heart of Britain many of the tribes became almost
completely isolated from the great Continental movements,
and their interests became more and more localised. Thus,
except when local interests clashed, life became somewhat
quieter, less fierce, less unruly, as the settler opened up the
fertile lands about his home. He was influenced greatly by
the change from the old to the new England. In part he
lost his passion for the sea as he pressed inland and became
farmer instead of sailor. By the days of Alfred it had become
necessary to re-create a navy to meet the attacks of the
Danes, for the English sailors that remained had often
changed from sea-fighters and pirates to merchant-traders,
with profit rather than conquest and adventure as their spur.
The Englishman became less and less ready to leave his   *Andreas,* 369.
comfortable hall to brave the dangers and hardships of the   *Riddle* IV.
deep, whence the grim water-terror rose in the storm
more vividly than ever before, filling his heart with fear
and the expectation of death. Thus it is that the voyage
across the sea seems so frequently to imply exile and sorrow;
and thus it is that in the *Seafarer* there seem to be two
voices, the one urging, the other dissuading. In the *Andreas*
the hero is very loath to undertake the voyage ordained for
him, and his followers are greatly distressed when the storm
comes on. Not so were those who first crossed the sea to
seek these shores.

Closely woven into the English character was a dark
strain of brooding melancholy, which again and again found
its expression in English song. In spite of all the inbred
fierceness, the pathos of sorrow lay near to every heart, being,
no doubt, the outcome of an experience of dark days of   Cf. *Wanderer,*
national stress and strain, and of personal hardship and   95 et seq.
privation. The Englishman long had felt the dread and
mysterious forces of existence pressing upon his soul, ever

bearing him irresistibly whither he would not. To find a key
to the problem of life was altogether beyond his power; and
he turned for a solution of its mystery to the dark goddess
Wyrd, or Fate, in whose hands both gods and men were
powerless, and by whose arbitrary decisions the fortunes of
men were determined. The decrees of Wyrd change all the
world beneath the heavens, and Fate goes ever as it must.
"Wyrd, cruel and fierce with hate, injures us," he says. Never
may the weary-hearted withstand his fate, nor his fierce spirit
afford him help; fate is fully ordained. Fate is all powerful,
and cannot be avoided; Wyrd is strongest; and men are
hurried blindly on upon the path she marks out for them.
Out of the past came the heroes of old; they lived in
warmth and splendour for a space; and whither went they?
"Why stand their habitations void and desolate?" asks the
Wanderer. And the answer is: "Wyrd the mighty snatched
away the earls." Of his friends of old time, Beowulf says,
"Wyrd swept them all away"; and Hrothgar uses the same
words with reference to his thegns who perished at Heorot,
"Wyrd swept them all away into the terror of Grendel." So,
too, Wyrd took away Hygelac when he raided the Frisians,
and likewise Beowulf himself when it was no longer her will
to allot him victory in the strife. She hovered over the souls
of men, sometimes warning them with the sense of impending
doom, sometimes leaving them all unconscious of the end
prepared for them. When the dragon ravaged Beowulf's
land, the hero's heart was sad, flickering, and foreboding
death; Wyrd was immeasurably near; but the thegns whom
Grendel's mother invaded at Heorot knew not their fate
when they retired to rest. Worse than useless was it to
attempt to strive against the dread power; far better to
submit at once to the inevitable; for out of such resignation
heroic courage and confidence might spring. "It shall be to
us two as Wyrd decides," says the hero, when about to go
forth against the dragon; and again, "Not yet was I fated,"
when he recounts the slaying of Grendel's mother. But best
of all was to steel the heart into callousness, and thus to bear
with equanimity whatever doom befell. None can escape
his fate, is practically the summing up of the Wanderer,
but man can harden his heart against adversity, and know
himself, by training his soul to self-restraint and absence of
excess; therefore fetter up the heart.

Beowulf, 107.
455.

Andreas, 1563.
Wanderer, 15,
5.

*Gnomic Verses
(Cott.)* 5.

Wanderer, 92.

Beowulf, 2815.

477.

1206.

2575.

2420.

1234.

2527.

2142.

*Wanderer,
passim.*

11.

And herein is revealed the philosophy of the careworn *58.*
soul in the presence of dread forces which it cannot understand.   But the man within often refused to be thus stifled;
and the hero trusted in the inherent nobility of his character
to conquer though overthrown; for the action of Wyrd was
ever to destroy[1].   And who knew but that, perhaps, after all,
Wyrd herself might, for a moment, smile kindly upon the
undaunted heart, since she could not annul the hero's fame?
"Wyrd oft saves an earl undoomed when his courage avails," *Beowulf,* 572.
says Beowulf.   And it was Wyrd herself who willed that
Grendel should take no more of Hrothgar's warriors after the *735.*
night when Beowulf grappled with him in the hall.

In the *Lament of Deor* we have fatalism blending with *Lament of*
what is almost stoicism.   Deor had been gleeman of the *Deor.*
Heodenings, and high in favour with his lord; but another
singer, one Heorrenda, had excelled him in his art, usurped
his office, and taken the lands that had been his fee.   He
is landless, homeless and destitute.   To what consolation can
he flee?   How does he strive to stifle his misery?   He knows
no resource external to himself, so summons up the resolution
which his own innate sense of manliness, his own stern
refusal to be broken by his grief, bestows.   Others overcame
their sorrows, so can he his.   He goes back to the old
Teutonic mythology for examples parallel to his own hard
lot; to the story of Weland, lamed and fettered by Nithhad,
yet bitterly revenging himself upon his captor, and finally
escaping, with mocking laughter, upon the wings he had
made; to the heart-sorrow of Beadohild, Nithhad's daughter,
whom Weland revengefully entrapped and violated before
his escape; to the sorrow of Hild, basely ravished by
Hedinn; to the love-sorrow of Geat, whose passion stole
away his sleep; to many a warrior of the cruel Eormanric,
who yearned wistfully for a milder ruler, yet forced himself
to hide his grief.   "That he overcame, so may I this[2]," repeats
Deor bravely as the refrain of his poem.   Here the darker side
of the poet's life and thought is seen; and we notice what the
Englishman felt to be the greatest sorrows which could be dealt
out to him—loss of liberty, honour, love, freedom and home.

---

[1] "wyrdan."

[2] "þäs ofereode, þisses swâ mäg!"   Cf. Shakespeare, *Rich. II.* Act v. Sc. 5,
l. 23, et seq.

The Englishman died as he had lived, stoically and
Beowulf, 26. fearlessly. At the hour chosen by Wyrd he must obey her
call; the only choice allowed him was whether he should
die like a hero or like a coward. His whole life was
but a period of preparation and training for his last great
hour. Death was ever before his eyes, ever in his thoughts.
As died the Celt Cuchulaïnn so died many a warrior of Saxon
blood, as the ethics of his time taught him. Wounded to
L'Épopée the death he gazed upon the foes who hedged him round, and,
Celtique en as his strength began to fail, he supported himself against a
Irlande, great stone, fastening his body to it with his belt. He would
p. 346. die upon his feet, neither sitting nor lying. And those who
had slain him stood and looked upon him, fearing to come
near him, for he seemed to be still alive. Brave and resolute
Beowulf, 2721. also is the death of Beowulf, with full confidence and satisfaction that he has done his duty, as long after him Nelson,
the great hero of the sea, was to die. Grievously wounded
he sits by the wall, while his faithful thegn washes his hurts,
recalling his past life spent in the service of his people; no
need is there for him to be ashamed. He desires to look
upon the treasure, the fruit of his victory; then he can die
2748. easily. He bids his thegns build a bale-fire on the ness. and
raise a barrow to his memory; and so he dies a warrior's
death, without the least regret, except that he has no son to
succeed him. His thegns raise high upon the cliff a funeral
3140. pyre, greatest of bale-fires, hung round with helms and
shields and shining corslets, and with bitterest lamentation
lay their dead lord upon it, and set fire to the pile. The
wood-reek rises, dark above the quivering, roaring flame,
until the body falls asunder in the midst of the bale-fire.
1119. So, too, is the pyre raised for Hnæf and the athelings
who have fallen at Finnsburg; blood-stained corslets and
crested helms surmounted with the boar of gold or iron
are heaped upon it; the bodies dissolve in flame; the
warrior ascends to the skies. Beowulf's thegns obey his
last command, and raise a mighty barrow which can be seen
afar across the sea; and there they bury the treasure. It
3086. was not fitting that they should enjoy that which had
cost them the life of their lord; the fate was too harsh
which had drawn their king thither. Around the heaped
3157. up mound, before they depart, twelve athelings ride, mourning

their king, and recounting his mighty deeds of valour and self-sacrifice.

Such was the end of the hero who died in battle; to die otherwise was the warrior's greatest shame. When, in later times, the brave Earl Siward of Northumbria was stricken with dysentery, and near to death, he cried out, "Shame on *Hen. of Hunt.* me that I did not die in one of the many battles I have *Bk.* VI. p. 205. fought, but am reserved to die with disgrace the death of a *Ant. Lib.* sick cow! At least put on my armour of proof, gird the sword by my side, place the helmet on my head, let me have my shield in my left hand, and my gold-inlaid battle-axe in my right hand, that the bravest of soldiers may die in a soldier's garb." Those who died a natural death were usually buried in graves, or caves cut in the rock, and with them also were often buried arms and treasure. Loeghair the Celt *Book of* directed that he should be buried like his ancestors, on the *Armagh,* folio 10. rampart of his fort, girt in his armour, with his weapons by his side ready for combat, and with his face turned towards the home of his hereditary foes, where their chief likewise lay similarly buried, ready and willing at a future day to arise and renew the combat, because of the endurance of their hate. Such thoughts and such burials were not confined to Celts alone, but were common to many related peoples of the Aryan stock, though the English chieftain long attached to burial something of disgrace. Sad and tear-stained is the face of the earl who must thus hide away in an earthy grave *Wanderer*, 83. the body of an old-time friend.

Sometimes the sea-king was buried with his ship; sometimes, like Balder, he was laid on a pyre in its bosom, and thus sent blazing out to sea. Haki, in the Ynglinga Saga, being grievously wounded, loaded his ship with weapons and the bodies of the slain, with a pyre in the midst. Then, when the land breeze blew, he hoisted sail, and so put out to sea, with his ship enwrapped in flame. Scyld, the mythic Danish hero of the *Beowulf*, was carried by his best loved friends to *Beowulf*, 26. the shore, as he himself had given command, and there laid in the bosom of a ship, with many treasures, weapons and 35. armour, thus to depart afar into the possession of the sea. With a golden ensign set on high above his head, he was 47. given back to the ocean; they let the sea bear him, even as when a child he had come at the beginning, alone over the

waves, to be the consolation of the Danes. And sorrowful
were their hearts at his passing. None could truly say
who took up that burthen. Some had it that it was to Odin,
chief of the gods, that the souls of heroes thus passed out
across the unknown sea. When Sigmund bore the body of
Sinfiötli to the shore it was Odin himself, clad in a garb of
grey, who came with his skiff to receive it.

Thus far and no further had the attempts of the thoughtful to solve the mysteries of life and death progressed. The
old tradition ran that the gods had once found upon the
shore two trees, Ash and Elm, drifted in from the sea, and
out of them they fashioned the first human pair. So, too,
Scyld floated in from the sea to become the ancestor of the
English and the Danes ; and thus, in a figure, was set forth
the mystery of the living soul. Man came as a child from
the great and boundless ocean, Eternity, to sport awhile,
perchance to weep awhile, upon the shores of life, and then
put out again to the deep, bound whither no one knew[1].

There is another figure like to this, but inland and not of the
sea, which points to the universality of the fundamental idea.
At the Council of Godmundingaham (627) one of Eadwine's
thegns spoke thus to his king : " The present life of man
upon earth, in comparison with the time which is unknown
to us, appears to me, O king, as if, when thou art sitting at
the banquet with thine ealdormen and thy thegns in the
winter time, when the fire is kindled and thine hall warmed,
while the rain and the snow and the storm beat without,
a sparrow should come and fly swiftly through the hall. It
enters through one door and departs through the other. Lo !
in the time that it is in the hall it is not beaten by the
winter's storm ; but that is but the twinkling of an eye and
the least moment of time. It soon passes from the winter
out into the winter again. So, then, the secrets of life are
revealed for a short space. What has gone before, what shall
follow after, we cannot tell."

Bede, *Hist. Eccl.* II. 13.

That these men believed in the immortality of the soul
is clear, though of the nature of that immortality they
could not definitely speak. Eternity for them partook of the

[1] Cf. *Coming and Passing of Arthur*:
    "And therewithal came on him the weird rhyme
    'From the great deep to the great deep he goes.'"

nature of the endless sea, and of the dark and the cold of
the long winter's night. Life alone was sure, representing, in
comparison with the unknown, all that there was of warmth
and joy, and that but for a brief space, for the twinkling of
an eye. The warrior's soul passed finally either to Walhalla,
the abode of the gods and heroes who died in battle, of which
the Englishman says little but implies much, or to the dim
world of mist and cold and wind, of fiery dragons and *Satan,*
serpents, where the grim death-goddess Hel, daughter of *Eddas,*
Loki the Evil One, with dreadful countenance and body of *passim.*
horrid hue, had rule throughout an endless night.

It was difficult to believe that the mighty personalities of
the heroes had entirely ceased to be. Somewhere or other, the
ancestral hero must surely be still exerting the majestic powers
which had raised him upon a pinnacle above the heads of
his fellows while he yet lived upon the earth. As his might
had won for him in life sovereignty and fame, so after death
it must have won for him a place in the gathering of the gods
themselves; and the lapse of centuries, while memories faded *Cf. A.-S.*
away into traditions, but added a more god-like lustre to his *Chron.*
name, until his apotheosis was complete. And it was just as *A.D. 855.*
difficult to escape from the deep impressions made by Nature
in her variable moods; so that the Old English heathenism
remains an evident growth from a blending of ancestor and
nature worship.

In the earlier days, various deities seem to have been
worshipped as personifications of Heaven and Earth, and
Summer their son, against whom were arrayed the forces of
the evil powers of darkness, of Winter and Night. Later, as
the mythology became more concrete and more complicated,
the beneficent deities came to be represented by the ancestral
Woden, from whom came Hengist and Horsa and the royal
line of Wessex, with Friga his wife, and Thor; though it
would seem that Sceaf, the father of Scyld, was once the
father of the gods. But, sooner or later, the chief of the gods
was Woden, or Odin, the god of the storms and winds, the
furious deity who inspired men with the passionate frenzy
of war. Tyw, Woden's son, was the great god of the sword;
Thunor, or Thor, the god of thunder and the ruler of the
stars, was the protector of the husbandman, and the giver of
fertility; Friga was the goddess of generation. Then there

were Eostra, the goddess of the radiant dawn, whose cult was widespread among the English, and Hreda, the goddess of brightness; while Niörd, or Nerthus, seems to have been the friendly deity of the sea. These beings, though mighty, were not all-powerful. Even they could not oppose the dark decrees of Wyrd, or interfere with the jurisdiction of Hel; even they were compelled to engage in long and dubious conflict with the powers of evil. Their home, according to the Teutonic mythology, was Asgard, where Odin, as All-Father, reigned over the mighty Æsir[1], where the fairest and brightest hall was Gimli, an eternal abode which should remain when heaven and earth had passed away, and to which the souls of the good should be translated. Niflheimer, a nine-fold world, shrouded in mist, and girt with horror, in which was situated the hall of Hel, was the abode of the evil and malignant spirits. Between the two was Midgard, the Earth, the abode of men, round which lay coiled the great serpent which was born to Loki, the spirit of evil; and here was the battle-ground on which the fight for supremacy continually raged.

To propitiate the gods, and to ward off the enmity of the evil spirits, the English made prayers and incantations, and offered sacrifices, sometimes of beasts, sometimes of human beings. That their religion had not yet become much more than a service of terror these last seem certainly to prove. At Heorot Hrothgar's thegns vowed sacrifices at *Beowulf*, 175. the temples of the gods, and prayed that the spirit-slayer would afford them help in the general distress. "Such was their practice, the hope of the heathen; they remembered Hell in the thoughts of their hearts; they knew not the Lord God." There is an after-reflection of human sacrifices in the Cædmonic Genesis, where the Teutonic imagination transforms the offering of Isaac into a heathen rite: Abraham *Genesis*, 2901. "then began to upraise a pyre, to kindle a fire, and fettered the feet and hands of his son; then hove him on the bale-fire, and quickly grasped his sword by the hilts. He purposed, with his own hands, to slay his son, to quench the fire with his kinsman's blood."

The Teutonic religion is best revealed in the Icelandic Eddas, where, though an overlay of Christianity is evident, the

---

[1] The gods of the Northmen of Iceland and Scandinavia.

essential foundation of the myths seems distinctly heathen, dating, according to Professor Warsoë, perhaps as early as the sixth or seventh century, possibly being even earlier. And certain coincidences with the heathen elements of Old English literature seem to suggest that the germs of the Eddaic myths were once well known in England. The eternal conflict between good and evil is the most prominent feature of the Icelandic poems and sagas. Again and again does evil prevail, but good must conquer in the end. Then will come a Judgment, and the world will be destroyed by fire ; the just will be translated to Gimli, in Asgard the Holy City, where, in its temple, shrines will be set up for Odin and his twelve attendant deities ; while the wicked will be cast into an abode of everlasting woe.

The most beautiful part of this mythology is the story of Balder, son of Odin and Friga, fairest and best and purest of all beings. He dreams that he is soon to die, and makes known his doom to the gods, who, by consulting the oracles, find that his dream has shown him the truth. Whereupon they take measures to ward off his impending fate, for Balder is beloved by all the good ; and Friga is sent to exact an oath from every created thing that it will not harm her son. She obtains the oath from all but one, for, though she had pleaded successfully with the oak, she had overlooked the mistletoe which climbed about it, because she thought it too young to take the oath. Then, secure in Balder's supposed invulnerability, the gods mock at fate, and in sport set him up as a mark for their missiles. But Loki, taking the appearance of an old woman, goes to Friga, and learns from her that the mistletoe is exempt from the oath. He tears up a root of the fatal tree, forms it into an arrow, and gives it to Hoder, Balder's blind brother, offering to direct his aim. To the consternation of all, the shaft pierces home ; the god they love is stricken down ; and there is awful silence in Heaven at his fall. As he dies, the whole creation breaks forth into universal weeping and mourning. Efforts are made to redeem him from Hel's abode, and all nature weeps and pleads for him, until Hel promises that if unanimous petition is made she will release him. But Loki renders the petition futile, taking again the guise of an old woman, and refusing to join in the tears and prayers. "I, Loki, will weep with

Cf. Keary,
*The Mythology
of the Eddas—
How far of
true Teutonic
Origin.*
*Dr. of the
Rood*, 55.
Christ, 1128,
1175.
Satan, passim.
*Genesis,
passim.*

Volospá.

dry eyes the death of Balder. Let all things, living or
dead, weep if they will, but let Hel keep her booty." Then
Loki fled and hid himself, but Odin found him out, and Thor
caught him, and the gods bound him in strong chains, with
the serpent Skada hanging over his head ; and ever above his
face its venom fell drop by drop into a bowl held by his
wife Siguna, who sat continually beside him, emptying the
vessel as often as it was full. So he is doomed to endure
until the Twilight of the Gods draws near, and the end of
all things is at hand. Then Loki will break his chains ; and
the earth will dissolve into the sea ; the sun and the stars
will be blotted from the heavens ; the sky will be consumed
in fire ; and gods and men alike will perish. Then, when
the woe is done, there will be a new Heaven and a new
Earth ; all evil will have passed away ; and Balder will again
appear in his beauty as conqueror over all.

CHAPTER II.

THE ADVENT AND INFLUENCE OF CHRISTIANITY.

UNLIKE many of their kinsmen on the Continent, the Teutonic tribes who invaded and conquered Britain had not as yet come in contact with Christianity. In England, for many years, they held to the old heathenism and nature worship, to the old mythology, to the old sacrificial and ceremonial rites. The Welsh, who had been either absorbed or driven into the fastnesses of the western mountains, had been Christians from about the second century, but it seems that they had little to do with the conversion of the English. While the warfaring was at its height it was scarcely possible that either nation could have had much opportunity for converting the other, or indeed would have cared to avail themselves of it if opportunity had offered; and when the fighting was over, the Welsh were far too weak to effect much. The religion of a conquered and disorganised people rarely has immediate influence upon the conquerors, who establish the potency of their own deities by the plain fact of the victorious issue. It is to the influence already at work among the southern Continental tribes that we must ascribe the conversion of the English; for their earliest Christian literature reveals a blending of the deeply rooted myths of Teutonic heathendom with the theology of Latin Christianity; and Welsh influence, in this particular direction, is scarcely, if at all, apparent. The results of the contact of Teuton and Celt seem to have been literary, intellectual and imaginative rather than religious.

At this period the Englishman's admiration was always given to that which was strong. Weakness he utterly despised; and the weakness of the Welsh system in religious as well as in secular matters was but too plainly seen. Before the invasion the religion of the Celts represented a strange admixture of Christianity with polytheism, mysticism and magic. The Brython who embraced Christianity was, it is true, called upon to renounce his heathenism; but the Goidel superimposed the Faith upon a foundation of old beliefs of Aryan origin[1]. To him Christianity was simply the mightiest magic; he regarded his Christian priest as a magician, and judged him by the same standard as that by which he judged the heathen magicians and wizards. Gildas, professing to give a faithful account as an eye-witness of the state of affairs which prevailed in Britain, describes his fellow-countrymen as "an indolent and slothful race," by whom "huge and heinous sins" are committed, in whom "an innate, indelible and irremediable load of folly and inconstancy" is found, among whom "every kind of luxury and licentiousness" flourishes. "They are addicted to fornication and adultery," he says, "are ever ready to take oaths, and as often perjure themselves." The shepherds of the flock, who should have set an example, "slumbered away their time in drunkenness," in envy and strife, in ravening and immorality. While making all due allowance for the constant tendency of Gildas to paint with the darkest colours, we cannot but perceive that the Englishman's development could not be carried on through the influence of the Church of the Welsh. Again, among them the old tribal life remained almost unchanged, practically precluding the making of proselytes. Outwardly a quasi-monastic system was in vogue, in which families lived together as "Tribes of the Saint"; the continuance of the holy rites was provided for by regular ordinations within the tribe; and each tribe preserved its own individuality as an isolated sphere of life and discipline. Converts were not sought; a stranger could claim no sympathy, since he was not of the blood of the tribe. It was practically impossible for an Englishman to embrace Welsh Christianity without first enrolling himself as a member of a Celtic tribe, which was for him an even greater impossibility. In fact, at first, all friendly communication with the English seems to have been forbidden, and, of deliberate intent, no efforts were made to go out of the way to convert them. When

Gildas, Pref.
Sect. 1.
Epist. Sect.
65.
Six O. E.
Chron.

Hist. Sect. 21.

Epist. Sect.
27, 66.

Bishop Collins,
Beginnings of
Engl.
Christianity,
pp. 44–94.

Bede, *Hist.*
Eccl. II. 4, 20.

---

[1] The Celts were divided into two branches, the Brythons and the Goidels, the former including the Welsh and the Celts of Cornwall and Brittany, the latter the Celts of Ireland, the Scottish Gaels, and the Manx.

St Beino was travelling by the banks of the Severn he heard
upon the opposite side of the stream the loud voice of an
Englishman crying to his hounds, whereupon he returned
to his companions, and bade them put on their clothes and
shoes and leave the place at once, " for the nation of this
man has a strange language and is abominable." Even the
later political alliances did not remove this aloofness in
religious matters. The Welshman who broke away from
his tribe could never return, but was absorbed by the
English, and, having no influence himself because of his
position, soon lapsed into religious indifference, or became
a convert to Teutonic heathenism.

On the other hand, the barbarians of the Continent had
recognised the greatness of the institutions of glorious though
fallen Rome, and craved for a development and civilisation
for themselves equal in all respects to that upon which they
had descended from the north. They admired the grandeur
of the Empire, and perceived the eminently practical nature
of its system, face to face with which a sense of their own
deficiency seems to have come upon them. Therefore, instead
of completely destroying all marks of the civilisation of the
past, they frequently assumed for themselves the insignia of
Roman authority, and attempted to carry on the administration as before. Barbarian kings, seated securely upon the
Imperial throne, strove to develope themselves so as to
understand and fulfil the functions of an office which held out
to them an ideal of civilisation, sovereignty and power.

Under the ægis of Roman greatness, stamped with the
seal of Imperial authority, a recognised institution of the
Empire, Christianity was introduced to the Teutonic tribes
as an important factor in Roman civilisation. Their leaders
intuitively perceived its immense value as a political and
social institution much more highly developed than anything they themselves possessed ; and on that account they
first began to embrace its precepts. The past glory of the
Empire was reflected upon the Christian Church, upon its
bishops, even upon its simplest priests, while its power gave
a real sense of system and solidity which served it well in
the presence of the Teutons. The day came when the word
of a Roman bishop was as good as that of a Teutonic king ;
when the Christian altar took the place of a Teutonic law-

Cf. Bede,
Hist. Eccl.
II. 16.

Laws of Wihtræd, 16, 18, 20.
Thorpe, p. 18.

court. Thus in the English laws we find it written that the word of a bishop and of the king shall be without an oath, incontrovertible; that a priest shall clear himself by his own sooth, standing in his holy garment before the altar, and saying, "I speak the truth in Christ; I do not lie"; that a deacon shall clear himself in like manner; that a stranger shall clear himself with his own oath at the altar; and likewise a king's thegn. We may estimate the magnitude of the benefits of Latin Christianity by contrasting the stagnation and decay of the Welsh Church, after the withdrawal of the Roman legions, with the systematic growth and active spirit of the Church of the English, as it developed with the help and guidance of Roman churchmen; for the conquerors of Britain, like the rest of their race, were always strongly attracted by the prestige of Rome.

The English found in Britain Roman cities, Roman roads, and many other marks of the Roman civilisation which had passed away; and from the Continent they must have learned much more of Roman glory. Rome came to them, therefore, as an ideal, almost beyond comprehension, to be regarded with reverence and awe, to be ardently sought after. The landing of Augustine appeared to Æthelbert of Kent to be an event of as great political as religious importance. Here at last he saw himself in actual touch with the great Empire, receiving an embassy which betokened the right of himself and his people to a place among the nations. Connection with Rome meant connection with the centre of existing life and thought, and introduced into England not only a new religion, but also new learning, new literature, new thought, new laws, new arts and manufactures. It determined the direction of the national development, and tended to bring about a rapid modification of political and social life. Under this influence London became a busy mart and flourishing port, keeping up continual intercourse with the merchants of Roman Gaul, and adding an increased impetus to the civilising movement which had already begun.

Bede, *Hist. Eccl.* I. 25.
A.D. 597.

We turn to the *Historia Ecclesiastica* of Bede for a full account of the conversion of the English to Christianity. Æthelbert, king of Kent, had raised his kingdom to the first place among the English nations, and had asserted his supremacy northwards as far as the Humber. Through his queen, Bertha, a Frankish princess, he had come to hear of the new faith, and was brought in contact with the thought of Western Christendom, at first without there being aroused in him anything more than vague curiosity. But it seems that where the Frankish priests of Bertha's household had been unable to make any deep impression upon him, the rumour of an approaching mission from Rome itself at once excited his attention. After his great political success in England, it would, no doubt, appear to him that the Empire was greeting him as an ally and an equal. When, however, more of the purport of Augustine's mission was made known, when he heard that it was of an everlasting kingdom that the Roman taught, he began to show signs of uneasiness, and bade the monks remain in the island where they had landed, while he considered what he should do with them. When at last he received the missionaries, his uneasiness became still more manifest. As we have already seen, the English believed in ancestral and nature deities who inhabited the air and sky ; and they thought that under a roof any magic arts and spells which the strangers possessed would be most potent, since they themselves would be cut off by it from the protection of their gods. This superstition led the king to receive the missionaries in the open air. The procession of strangely robed priests, with a silver cross borne before them, and with a picture of the crucified Christ upraised in their midst, as they advanced singing a solemn litany, must have greatly impressed the wondering onlookers, and added to their superstitious fears. But here, at last, within his borders, Æthelbert looked upon the symbol of civilisation, though it struck him as weird and partaking of the nature of witchcraft. His reception was kingly and courteous; and he heard Augustine patiently as he told "how the merciful Jesus, by His own suffering, redeemed this sinful world, and opened the gate of heaven to all believers." When he had made an end of speaking, the king answered him: "The words and promises which you bring are indeed pleasant to me, but, because they are new to us, and of uncertain meaning, I cannot so far yield to them as to abandon all that I and the whole English people have for so long observed. But, since you are strangers, and

Ælfric,
Homilies.

Hist. Eccl.
I. 25.

have come hither from a distant land, and desire, as I see, to communicate to us what you believe to be true and good, we will not molest you, but will receive you with kindly hospitality, and will furnish you with necessary food, and not forbid you to win over by preaching as many as possible of my people to your belief." No reception could have been fairer, more tolerant, more generous, and at the same time more cautious.

I. 26.   The missionaries took up their abode in Canterbury; and there they began to imitate the apostolic life of the primitive Church, with continual prayers, vigils and fasts, preaching the Word of Life, as though despising all things of this world. And of the English some believed and were baptised, wondering at the simplicity of their innocent life and the sweetness of their celestial doctrine. Many began to come together daily to hear the Word, and, putting aside the heathen rites, believed, and joined themselves in the unity of the Holy Church of Christ. Soon, Æthelbert too, believing, was baptised, being pleased with their life, and with their most sweet promises. But he compelled none to Christianity; he only treated believers with a closer affection as fellow citizens with himself in the Kingdom of Heaven. Such was the success of Augustine's mission for the conversion of the English; and when he died, worn out with unceasing labours, a great work had been accomplished. The poetical record of his death is this:—

Menologium, 96.

"......that the Lord took
    To another light Augustinus,
    Blithe in his breast, because that he in Britain here
    Disposed the earls with humble hearts to Him,
    To God's will, as the wise Gregorius
    Bade him. Never heard I of men of old
    Any before ever bring
    Over the salt sea a better lore,
    A more famous bishop. Now he rests in Britain,
    In Canterbury, near the royal seat,
    In the noble minster."

Hist. Eccl. II. 13.

Very similar in many respects was the conversion of Eadwine of Northumbria and his people some thirty years later. For two years the king hesitated, and then decided to put the matter before his council. At Godmundingaham the great question was debated, and Cefi, the chief priest of the heathen temple, answered the king in a very matter-of-fact speech, of which it is hard to say whether cynicism or dissatisfaction with the outworn tenets of heathenism is the predominant element. He said that he had learned for certain that the old religion had nothing at all of virtue, nothing of utility, for no one had been more devoted to the heathen gods than he, and yet others had received greater benefits. If their gods had been true gods they would have aided him most. Therefore, if the king thought that the new religion was better than the old, it seemed reasonable to him that they should embrace it. Evidently the priest had perceived the desire of his king, and framed his words accordingly. "Verba prudentia" is the term applied to them by Bede. "Gross materialism!" some may say, for his reasoning seems simply "Shall I lose or gain materially by becoming a Christian?" That he cannot lose much he is sure, but rather stands to gain, since the sympathies of his king are already enlisted on the side of the new faith. The speech is illuminating when regarded as the outcome of the first contact of a heathen Englishman with Christianity.

Afterwards another councillor rose and made the deeply thoughtful speech already quoted; after which Cefi spoke again in a somewhat better spirit. "For a long time past I have understood that what we worship is nothing, because, forsooth, the more zealously I sought truth in that religion, the less I found it. But now, openly, I confess that in this teaching that truth shines clear which is able to give us the gifts of life, salvation and eternal happiness. Wherefore I suggest, O king, that the temples and altars which we have sanctified, without any practical benefit, we should speedily hand over to anathema and to fire." When it was asked who first should profane the altars and temples of the idols, he answered, "I; for who, more fittingly than myself, for the example of all, may destroy, through the wisdom given me by the true God, those things which I have served through foolishness?" The council broke up resolved upon embracing Christianity; and Cefi, to the wonder of the common folk, who thought him insane, armed himself, and rode like a warrior upon a war-horse, as no English priest had ever been known to ride before, to hurl the first spear against the temple of the heathen gods.

Supra p. 56.

Thus the Englishman took to himself Christianity, following, as a faithful thegn, the evident desire of his king, and, like all barbarians, advancing through that which was material to that which was spiritual. The illustrious Eadwine founded ample churches in his domains, and drew up laws for the just government of his people, leading them on to keep the faith by rewarding the good and threatening the wrongdoers. And so the reign of Christianity in the North began, to culminate in the grandest church of mediæval times. "O pietas, O celsa fides!" exclaims Alcuin, looking back upon the glorious past.

As to how far the influence of the Empire had a place in the workings of the royal mind we may judge from Eadwine's adoption of the dignity and symbols of Imperial authority. The royal ensigns constantly made known his presence; and wherever he travelled upon the roads the standard which the Romans called "Tufa," and the English "Tuff," was borne before him.

It is conceivable, and indeed very probable, that the English, great with barbarian ideas of Roman citizenship, may have readily enrolled themselves as citizens of the kingdom of Heaven long before they could in the least appreciate the difference between the spiritual state and the earthly Empire of Rome. Politics and religion had always blended as closely in Teutonic conceptions as in Roman institutions; and Christianity in the West had become so thoroughly Roman, so impregnated with the idea of the "Civitas Dei," that the substitution in the English mind of the concrete example for the abstract idea is not to be wondered at. The fact that the glory of Rome was then but a reflection from the past, and not a living actuality, had not as yet been fully realised by the barbarian mind. The idea of "the kingdom" was always put forth prominently by the missionaries, and sank deeply into the minds of their converts, to be again and again repeated in speeches and writings. Thus Gregory writes to Æthelbert that in former times the pious Emperor Constantine had recovered the commonwealth from the perverse worship of idols, and had subjected it, together with himself, to Almighty God and the Lord Jesus Christ, and bids him follow the admonitions of Augustine, and further his endeavours, that he may be

Alcuin, De Pont. et Sanct. Ebor. 216.

284.

Bede, Hist. Eccl. II. 16. *Hen. of Hunt.* Bk. II. p. 57. *Ant. Lib.*

Hist. Eccl. I. 29, 32, II. 5, 9.

Epist. Greg. Hen. of Hunt. Bk. III. p. 74.

made a partaker of the kingdom whose faith he has caused
to be received and maintained in his own.   And Daniel of
Winchester writes to Winfrid, advising him as to his methods   *Epist. Bonif.*
of converting the heathen, that he must tell them of the
greatness of Christendom, in comparison with which they are
themselves so insignificant.   It is very improbable that the
Teutonic warrior could at first understand clearly what the
Latin theologian was trying to teach him, for there was so
little in common between them.   And, just as so many trans-
formations took place in the passage of Christianity from
the Latin to the Teutonic mind, so it would be with "the
kingdom."   But, with time, there came an increasing comprehension of the true meaning, as the germ developed, and as
the Englishman made the Latin thought his own ; and then,
at length, "regnum caeleste conscendit" became a common   *Hist. Eccl.*
formula when speaking of a death.   From this time onwards   II. 7, etc.
thoughts of eternity and immortality begin to have a clearer
definition and more complete expression ; and the English-   *Wanderer,*
man will soon be able to contrast for himself the transitori-   110, 114.
ness and vanity of an earthly kingdom with the eternal
security of those who seek mercy and consolation of the
Father who is in Heaven.

Yet there were many who, caring little or nothing for
Rome, refused to be converted, and met the missionaries with
fierce defiance and contempt.   Such were the three sons of
Sæberht of Essex, who, "being puffed up with barbarian   *Hist. Eccl.*
ignorance," broke in upon Mellitus, the bishop, while he was   II. 5.
celebrating a solemn mass, demanding "Wherefore do you
not give us the white bread which you gave our father Saba ? "
When the bishop explained to them that they must first be
baptised, they answered, "We do not desire to enter that
font because we know that we have no need of it, but,
nevertheless, we wish to be fed with that bread."   He refused
to give way, and, stirred up with anger, they said, " If you do
not please to give us what we ask in so simple a matter you
shall stay no longer in our province."   Evidently the Englishman knew his strength, and felt himself master of the
situation.   This outbreak led to a council of the missionaries,
in which it was decided to return home, since it seemed vain
to expect to win over men of such headstrong character.
Mellitus and Justus, another bishop, fled to Gaul, and the

others were about to follow, when a better aspect came over
the situation, and the fugitives were encouraged to return.
II. 6, 14. Such fluctuations were common. Again and again were
wholesale baptisms followed by wholesale apostasies; for
untoward events were interpreted as disasters brought about
through the wrath of the gods who had been deserted. In
the year 664 there was an eclipse and also a plague, and
III. 30. the king of Kent, the Archbishop of Canterbury, and other
bishops and religious men died; the consequence was the
apostasy of the East Saxons.

Penda of Mercia was a typical example of one who
was a stout opponent of the new faith. With true sceptic
instinct he discovered for himself the weak place in its
armour—the professing Christian whose practice was not in
accordance with precept. In his latter days he ceased to
III. 21. persecute, and did not prohibit the preaching of the Word,
but he hated and despised those who, having embraced the
faith of Christ, did not strive to have the works of faith,
saying that they who refused to obey the God in whom they
believed were contemptible. Nor was it always possible, at
the beginning, to lead the Teuton to appreciate the Christian
III. 22. virtues. When the thegns who murdered Sigbert were asked
why they had done so, they could answer nothing but that
they were angry and enemies of the king because he was
wont to spare his enemies too much and, when they besought
him, soon forgave, with placid mind, the injuries done by
them.

At Tynemouth, when five ships, which had sailed up the
Vita Cudb. Tyne from the monastery to gather firewood, were carried
out to sea by an unexpected gale, the slumbering hostility
of the peasantry suddenly blazed out. The monks gathered
upon the rocky shore to pray for the safety of their brethren,
but the fury of the storm remained unabated, and the
country people assembled in crowds, mocking and jeering at
their ineffectual prayers. Cuthbert remonstrated with them.
Ought they not rather to pray for the safety of the monks
than to rejoice over their misfortunes? But they replied
obstinately, " No one shall pray for them. May God spare
none of them. They have taken away the ancient worship, and no one knows how this new worship is to be
performed."

With such a spirit among the people we can understand why it was that for centuries Christianity and heathenism in England existed side by side, in the same centres, in the same homes, even in the same hearts, and why the old religion did not pass away without leaving so many vestiges of its influence upon the new. Thus it is that the Old English Christian literature contains so much that is heathen percolating through and lying beneath the teaching of Latin Christianity. The presence of two such elements is but the outward sign of an intermediate stage in the course of a natural development, and will be fully accounted for when we remember the prevailing tendency of all polytheism to find a place for an ever increasing number of deities. To lead the barbarian to embrace Christianity was usually a comparatively easy task; the difficulty arose when the first attempts were made to get him to renounce the old ideas and the old practices.

The wise Gregory, with a deep knowledge of human nature, and foreseeing this opposition, sent a message to Augustine by Mellitus advising that the heathen temples among the English should not be destroyed, but only the idols which were in them. Holy water should be sprinkled in those fanes, altars constructed, and relics placed therein. Because, if the temples themselves were well constructed, it was necessary that they should be converted from the cult of demons to the service of the true God; that while the people saw not their fanes themselves destroyed, they might lay aside error from their hearts, and, knowing and adoring the true God, might assemble in familiar fashion in the places where they had been wont so to do. And since they were accustomed to kill many oxen in sacrifice to demons, any religious solemnity ought to be changed among them concerning this. They must not sacrifice animals to the devil, but to the praise of God; so that while any rejoicings not involving the root of the matter might be reserved to them, they might be won the more easily to consent to the rejoicings within the Church. Bede also gives very similar advice, citing the example of St Paul; and Bishop Daniel of Winchester counsels Winfrid, the English missionary to the Germans, not to attack their false divinities, but to appeal to reason without provocation or

Hist. Eccl.
I. 30.

Com. on the Acts.
Epist. Bonif.

insult. To teach from and through the known to the unknown has always proved the soundest method; to modify
is often more profitable than to attempt to destroy. We
cannot but think of the eagerness with which Gregory would
have seized upon such myths as that of Balder had he heard
of them ; and certainly some less famous Christian teachers
must have done so in later days, since there are so many
traces remaining of contact between them and the divine
story of the Christ. There is the closest connection between
parts of the story of Balder and passages in the works of
Gregory, Cædmon and Cynewulf; but to discuss it here
would be to launch out upon one of the most intricate
literary problems connected with the myths. It is sufficient
to mark the fact that not only is there a conversion of the
Englishman in process, but also a corresponding conversion
of his mythology; and that for some time the tendency
will be not to eradicate but to blend and to assimilate from
either side.

So it came about that, at first, the Englishman, though
a professing Christian, often retained his belief in his
ancestral and nature deities, and his fears of the demons and
evil spirits. The case of Redwald of East Anglia was far
from being an exception : " After the manner of the ancient
Samaritans he was seen to serve both Christ and the gods
which he had before been wont to serve, and in the same
temple had both an altar for the mysteries of Christ, and
also an altar for the victims offered to demons." All the
Latin monk could do was to direct the classification of the
heathen theogony so that it might better conform to Christian
theology. Thus the Englishman came to believe that Woden
and Scyld derived their origin from a certain Hreathra who
was born in the Ark; and that the descent of the demons was
to be traced from Satan and from Cain. And, in his new
cosmography, the heathen goddess Hel gave more than her
name to the Christian hell. So, side by side with Christian
teaching and Christian practice, there long remained idola-
trous rites, sacrifices, incantations and divinations, with
belief in magic arts, witchcraft, charms and auguries, in
senders of tempests and foretellers of future events by the
inspection of runes. In the *Anglo-Saxon Laws* it is seen
that the offering of heathen sacrifices had to be punished

*Cf. Greg.
Hom.* x.
Christ, 807,
1128, 1175.
*Dr. of the
Rood,* 46, 55,
62.
Genesis, 107,
etc.
Voluspá.

Hist. Eccl.
II. 15.

A.-S. Chron.
A.D. 855.
Beowulf, 111.

Hist. Eccl.
I. 30. 25,
II. 10,
IV. 22, 27.

*Laws of
Wihtræd,* 12,
Thorpe, p. 18.

by heavy penalties of fine and confiscation; while Alfred
thought it his duty to visit such practices with the extreme
rigour of the law, so long did the old ways survive.   In the
Charm for Barren Land may be found a *naïf* example of   Charm for
the way in which Christian and heathen elements were   *Barren Land.*
intermingled.   Four pieces of turf were to be taken up from
the field, and oil, honey, balm and milk poured into the holes
where they had been, while holy water was sprinkled around.
The turfs were then taken to the church and placed with
their green sides turned towards the altar while four masses
were sung.   Next, four crosses, upon which the names of the
four Evangelists were carved, were placed in the holes, and
the turfs relaid thereon.   Then the Paternoster was sung
nine times, with a Christian litany, hymns and prayers, the
ceremony being concluded with a prayer, supposed to be of
great antiquity, to "Mother Earth."   The annual festivals
also came to possess the same twofold character; for in
social life the tenacity of the customs of heathenism was
even greater than in religious life.   For instance, Christmas
blended with Yule, the heathen festival of the New Year:
within the church, the priest directed the thoughts of his
congregation to the mystery of the Incarnation and the
circumstances attendant upon the Saviour's birth; without
it, the good cheer and festivity, the jollity and buffoonery,
the gathering of the mistletoe (a touch of the Balder myth),
the bringing in of the boar's head and the burning of the
Yule-log, remained just as popular as before.   In a similar
way, the lighting of fires at Epiphany, the Whitsun ales, the
May games, beating the bounds, whipping the fruit trees in
spring, the harvest rejoicings on Thor's day, remain as traditional observances which once possessed a certain heathen
significance.

    Christianity itself was, to a certain extent, modified by
the impact of the two systems.   The barbarian, a worshipper
of ancestral deities, and an idolater, was at first utterly
incapable of conceiving a God not of like body, parts and
passions with himself, or of appreciating a religion which was
entirely spiritual: and when his tribe, at the desire of its
chief, became converted to Christianity *en masse*, and not
through definite individual conviction, it was but to be
expected that his Christianity would take a form very

different from that held by the monk who had called him to conversion. In fact, the Englishman seems to have read himself, his own motives, his own instincts, his own life, thought and character, into his new religion; and the more sincerely religious he became, the greater was often the change from the apostolic ideal. That which was in spirit Hebrew or Roman soon became Teutonic, and took a more martial guise. God and the Christ became more like mighty Teutonic chieftains; just as Chaucer's God sometimes appears with the qualities of a French gallant. The apostles and patriarchs became English thegns; and the dread majesty of Satan and his followers required that they should be "heroes stern of mood." Even the word for *creed* in the Anglo-Saxon version of Bede's *Ecclesiastical History*, rendering the post-classical Latin "symbolum," is "here-bêacen," the war-standard.

Parl. of F.
197.
Dethe of B.
675.
Leg. of G. W.
1035.
Genesis, 285.

Hist. Eccl.
IV. 17.

Thus the Englishman made Christianity his own, and gave it a form which especially appealed to him; and thus the final victory of the faith was assured. As time went by, the impression made went very deep; and the influence of the conversion upon both character and social life became exceedingly great. A deeper charity towards the unfortunate, and even the criminal, was inculcated, to be increased still more by the gentle teaching of the pious Aidan and the monks of Iona; and an organised attack was made upon all that was harsh and brutal in the national temperament. Through the influence of the Church laws were drawn up for the protection of serfs and slaves; and the "thêow" at last ceased to be treated as a wild animal deprived of all social rights and recognition. He was at least human, and therefore was to be treated with humanity. He must not be deprived of the scanty savings he had so hardly won, and must not be slain or beaten to death without judgment. The chastity of the female slave must not be ruthlessly violated to satisfy the wanton lusts of a vicious master; she must not be brutally beaten by a passionate mistress. For the slave, too, had an immortal soul, and therefore, as the Church steadfastly maintained, an appointed place in the ranks of her disciples. Failure to recognise this claim was visited with a heavy penance. In Sussex, through the influence of Wilfrid, King Ecgfrid freed the slaves who were

A.-S. Laws,
Thorpe,
pp. 20, 31,
35, etc.
Laws of Alf.
11, 25.
Laws of Ine,
etc.

baptised. " All of whom," says Bede, " since by baptism they were saved from the servitude of demons, moreover he freed from the yoke of human servitude by giving them their liberty." And the *Laws of Alfred* ordained that the Christian " thêow " should go free in the seventh year. *Hist. Eccl. IV. 13.*

In every way morality benefited by the advent of Christianity. Among the chiefs it seems to have been customary for the eldest sons of the deceased to marry their stepmothers; and this the Church stigmatised as a grave sin. " But in truth there are many among the English people who, while as yet they were heathen, are said to have been joined in this wicked marriage; these, coming to the faith, are to be admonished that they abstain, and recognise it to be a grave sin. Let them fear the heavy judgment of God, and not for carnal pleasure incur the torments of eternal punishment,...but, having sinned in ignorance, they are not to be deprived of the Communion of the Holy Body and Blood of the Lord." Yet a thegn who persisted in keeping an unlawful wife was excommunicated by his bishop, who commanded the faithful neither to enter his house nor to partake of his food. The Church set itself inflexibly against immorality in any form; and its teaching evidently went home. In the *Wise Words of a Father to his Son* we find the sin set down as a social disgrace, a source of strife and loathly shame, a long hostility and unbounded presumption against God. *I. 27.* *III. 22.* *Fäder Lârcwidas, 37.*

Of marriage itself a more austere view was taken by the monks; and, as the English became enthusiastic about the new faith, this view became widespread. Gregory, Bede and Ealdhelm, in agreement with the usual teaching of the Church, taught that, though marriage in itself was good, virginity was better; and on this subject Ealdhelm wrote in Latin prose his *De Laudibus Virginitatis sive de Virginitate Sanctorum*, and in Latin hexameters his *De Laude Virginum*. Others, following the *De Exhortatione Castitatis* of Tertullian, and Jerome's *Hieronymus contra Jovinianum*, alleged that not only were second marriages adulterous, but that every marriage partook of the nature of sin, only to be atoned for by penance. In England this view seems to have been due to the teaching and practice of Theodore. This austerity led many noble and devoted women to give themselves up entirely to the

Will. of Malm.
I. 2, 3, 4.

Hist. Eccl.
IV. 23.

Eddius,
ch. 60.

Cf. Boniface
to Æthelbald,
Will. of Malm.
I. 4.

Daniel, 15.

Exodus, 2634.
Daniel, 116,
703, 750.

Judith, x.

Juliana, 483.

service of the Church, and communities of nuns were scattered throughout the land.   Among such Hilda, Werburga, Etheldreda, Ermenilda, Hereswitha and Elfleda were especially famous.   Of Hilda of Whitby it is said that all who knew her were accustomed, on account of her distinguished piety and grace, to call her "Mother," and that kings were wont to seek counsel of her wisdom.   Elfleda was a most wise virgin, always the comforter and the best peace-maker of the whole province.   So far did this influence go that we hear of several queens who left their lords after conversion. Among others, Hereswitha, sister of Hilda, left her husband, the king of East Anglia, for the celibate life, and he seems to have quietly married again.   But in this unnatural segregation of the holiest and best men and women there lurked a dangerous germ which, in the times when enthusiasm waned and ideals became less sacred, would tend to deterioration in both Church and State.   For while, on the one hand, the elimination of the best did not make for the continuance of the purest home life, on the other, the linking together of marriage and immorality as cognate sins naturally lowered the standard of the one, and blunted the national conscience with regard to the other.

Against the national drunkenness the Church arrayed all her forces.   The Old English Christian literature is very definite upon the subject, teaching that the vice is the root of all evil, the work of the devil, the destroyer of the soul. In the *Daniel* the moral is pointed that the Hebrews were the chosen people of God, Who gave them victory over many nations, until drunken thoughts possessed them and they turned aside from Him.   Drunkenness is usually attributed to the enemies of the godly as a besetting sin and the cause of their downfall.   Abimelech, Nebuchadnezzar and Belshazzar are all drunken.   Holophernes, "the wicked one," is held up to scorn in the *Judith* entirely by a description of his besotted condition, and is seen lying "drained of every good."   The poet's abhorrence of the vice is distinctly shown ; and he takes great care that the sympathy of his audience shall not be on the side of the drunkard.   In the *Juliana* the Fiend is forced to confess that he draws men on when they are drunken with beer, and the outcome is strife and slaughter : "Some, drunken with beer, I drew on with my teachings, made them ready for strife, so that they suddenly renewed old enmities. I gave them to drink strife from the ale-vessel, so that they should lose their souls through the sword-grip in the wine-hall." The drunkard must answer at the Judgment for his sin; though little he thinks of that when he sits at the banquet with wine at his will. He does not trouble himself about what shall happen to him after this world. And again we hear the bitter reproach of a *Lost Soul to its Body*: "Thou wast rich in food and sated with wine; in lordly fashion thou didst hasten on through life, and I was thirsty for God's Body, for the drink of the Spirit." But great shall the shame of that body be on the Judgment Day.

Bi Dômes Däg, 77.

Soul to Body, 39.

That thoughts of beer are still, in spite of all this teaching, continually present in the minds of even the best of the English is very evident. In the *Andreas* there is an altogether unpleasing and uncalled-for comparison of a miraculous flood breaking over the land of the heathen to mead spilled after a feast. "This was a bitter beer-feast; the cupbearers, the attendant thegns, delayed not; there was to each, from break of day, enough drink soon ready." It possibly marks an upward development in this respect when we find Ælfric, in the tenth century, omitting this simile from his Life of St Andrew; though we find the same author, in his Homily on the Assumption of St John, representing Christ Himself as saying to the beloved apostle, "John, come to me; the time is come for thee to banquet with thy brethren in my 'gebêorscipe.'" Here is an evident modification of the Christian Heaven towards the heathen Walhalla, to which the incongruous note is due.

Andreas, 1528, 1535.

Ælfric, *Homilies*.

Even upon the battlefield the influence of Christianity was often manifest. What a chastened picture of resolute faith is Ælfric's description of the victory of Heavenfield! "Oswald had with him but a little company, yet faith upheld him, and Christ aided him to overthrow his enemy. Before the battle he raised the Cross, and cried to his men, 'Let us fall before the Cross, and pray to the Almighty to save us from the proud enemy who is about to fall upon us. God knows well that we fight in a just cause against this cruel king to save our land.' They all fell to prayers, and, on the morning after, advanced to the fight, and won the victory." Wholesale slaughter becomes much less frequent, and the

Ælfric, *Life of St Oswald*.

lot of the captive less severe.   The Church deliberately
sets itself to curb the violent and savage passions by which
blood is shed.   Thus the Christian poet adds to and emphasises the words of God to Noah in Genesis ix. 5.   " Every one
Genesis, 1518. who with point of spear takes the life of another destroys
himself with the strength of his spirit first of all.   He need
not rejoice in his heart at the requital, but I will require much
more heavily the life of man at the hands of the slayer and the
murderer of a brother, at the hands of him who accomplishes
bloodshed and slaughter of man with weapons, murder with
his hands."   Within the settlement, the Church laboured for
quietness and peace, imposing, in the laws which she inspired,
Cf. *Laws of* frequent penalties for killing, wounding, bruising, breaking
Æthelbert,
Thorpe.   and stealing, until, in the days of Eadwine, so great was the
peace throughout his dominions that a woman with her little
Hist. Eccl. child at her breast might travel from sea to sea without fear
II. 16.   of molestation.

   With the decrease of violence, charity and care for the
needs of others became more widespread.   In his thoughtfulness for his people Eadwine caused posts to be fixed upon
the highways beside the clear springs, and hung upon each
post a brazen cup for the comfort and refreshment of travellers.
Ælfric, *Life of* Oswald was as pre-eminently distinguished for charity as for
St Oswald.   humility, ministering continually to the wants of the sick and
poor ; and, in imitation of a Roman tradition, a story arose
that the right hand with which he dispensed his charities
Hist. Eccl.   remained after death undecayed.   At Whitby, Hilda taught
IV. 23.   of justice, piety, chastity, and other virtues, but especially the
keeping of peace and charity.   No one there was rich, no one
poor, but all things were common to all, when nothing that
belonged to anyone was held to be his own.   Thus the first
principles of the Christian socialism of the apostolic times
came to be practised in England.   So far had the Englishman
already assimilated the primary Christian virtues.

   In the year 664 an important conference was held at
III. 25. Whitby, then called Streoneshalh, at which the Northern
English were asked to decide between the systems of the
two rival churches, Rome and Iona.   The bent of their minds
towards Rome was there clearly seen.   In reply to Colman,
Bishop of Lindisfarne, Wilfrid, the young enthusiast, pointed
with fiery eloquence to the universal nature and authority

of the Church Catholic, which was of the whole civilised
world, and with which the Church of two remote and semi-
civilised nations ought not to be compared. He questioned
the authority of St Columba of Iona as opposed to that
of St Peter; and the king, Oswiu, took up his argument.
"Did Christ really say, 'Thou art Peter, and upon this rock
I will build My Church'?" "Did He ever say anything
of the like to St Columba?" "Did He give to St Peter the
keys of heaven?" were the questions he propounded to
Colman, who was forced to concede each point. "Then,"
said the king, with a smile at his own rude wit, "for my part,
I shall obey the authority of the doorkeeper, lest, when I come
to the gates of the kingdom of heaven, I may, perhaps,
find no one to unlock them for me." Of course the people
followed the decision of the king; and thus the character
of the Englishman's Christianity was determined. In this
connection we may note Wilfrid's cleverness in controversy.
Already an Englishman of pre-eminent intellectual ability,
who is a match for both Celtic and Roman bishops upon
their own ground, has been found. The same argument was
used again in the south when Ealdhelm wrote to Geruntius, the
Celtic king of Cornwall, "If, therefore, the keys of the kingdom of heaven were given by Christ to Peter, who, despising
the ordinances of his Church, may enter through the gate of
the heavenly Paradise?"

Plummer,
Bede, II. 192.

The outcome was decisive; and the Roman organisation
became paramount. By degrees the Church introduced law
and order in place of the chaos which had existed. Civil
and ecclesiastical codes of law were drafted under its influence;
and the country was parcelled out under the jurisdiction of
bishops who were pastors of the people and counsellors
of the kings. For this, Theodore of Tarsus, who landed in
669, was mainly responsible. He united the scattered
bishoprics into one corporate body; and a national synod
of the clergy of the whole country was instituted. Oswiu
greatly appreciated what he did; and the two leaders appear
to have worked well together for the country's good. A great
advance towards just and righteous government was made;
and the kings were taught that their kingdoms were sacred
trusts specially committed to them by God. In the *Widsith*,
as we now have it, a Christian has written: "In his youth he

Widsith, 131. had always found that the king, to whom, while he lives here on earth, God has given the rule over men, is dearest to the dwellers in a land." In later history we shall find that certain English kings made much of this divine right of their kingship.

Henceforth the great ambition of the saintly Englishman is to see Rome at least once before his death, and, if possible, *Hist. Eccl.* v. 7. to die there, believing that thus he ensured for himself the benefits of "the kingdom." In those days many of the English people, nobles, commoners, clergy, laity, men and women, were wont to vie with each other in this ambition. In 688, Cadwalla, king of the West Saxons, left his realm for the sake of Christ and the eternal kingdom, and went to Rome, desiring for himself the singular glory of being washed in the font of baptism in the holy city, by which the gate of celestial life was opened, and hoping that, as soon as he was baptised, being freed from the flesh, the world might at once be changed for the joys eternal. Thirty-seven years afterwards, Ine, his successor, followed his example. Coinred of Mercia also went to Rome, received the tonsure, v. 19. and became a monk, remaining there in prayers, fasts and almsgivings to the day of his death. Offa, likewise, left wife, lands, kindred and country on account of Christ, and went to Rome, and, becoming a monk, lived there for the remainder of his life.

There is, however, another side to the picture. Visits to Rome, ostensibly as religious pilgrimages, grew to be a mere fashion; and, as time went on, many pilgrims, unsupported by any great depth of faith, succumbed to the many temptations and licentious pleasures of the south. Where so much was expected, disillusionment on account of worldly failings speedily usurped the place of zeal, and from many a pilgrim's heart the Christ departed at the entering in of the seductive gaieties of the new world. Winfrid (Boniface) goes so far as *Epist. Bonif.* to say, in one of his letters, that of those who travelled to Rome few remained sound, and that there were but few cities of Lombardy where there was not an adulteress of English birth. And this was but the beginning of the cycle of the influence of Italy upon the travelled Englishman, which, in many different phases, long endured.

Though, at home, Rome was the pattern upon which the

English churches and kingdoms sought to model themselves, the papal authority was not permitted to usurp the office of the king; the Englishman was too strong for that.   When Wilfrid, taking a high view of his ecclesiastical position as Bishop of York, began to interfere in secular and domestic matters, he was deposed from his bishopric and banished from the kingdom.   He laid his cause before the Pope, who received him with great honour, and delivered to him a papal bull drawn up in his favour.   But when he returned home and appeared before the king and the Witan, confident that his bull had gained the day, he was quickly undeceived. The papal jurisdiction was promptly and warmly repudiated; he was thrown into prison, and his sentence of banishment was renewed.   Some time passed before a reconciliation was effected, with which the Pope was not concerned, and then Wilfrid was permitted to return and resume his office. A second appeal to Rome in later days, on the matter of the division of his diocese, resulted in a letter of advice, not of command, from the Pope, but even to that the king refused to listen.

By now, the English had begun to benefit greatly by the new teaching; and we have the spectacle of a strong and virile, though for the most part an untrained and unpractised people, set to work within the domains of learning by an impulse from without.   For the first time in their history they found themselves aiding in an organisation in which intellectual rather than physical force held sway; in which the subtle power of the teacher and the priest transcended the warrior's strength of body and skill in arms.   Monasteries sprang into being throughout the land; and to these the best youth of England flocked to partake of the new learning. At Canterbury Augustine had founded a Latin school round which grew up the schools of Kent, and probably of East Anglia also, in imitation of the schools of Gaul.   Perhaps one of the most striking products of this movement was the compilation of the "Dooms" of Æthelbert, the first codification of English law.   This education of the south was altogether Roman.   The Roman curriculum and Roman art were introduced, and under Theodore great progress was made.   Latin, Greek and Hebrew were taught by him and his assistants, Hadrian the African, and Benedict Biscop the Englishman. Students came from all parts, even from Ireland, to learn from the lips of Theodore. Later, many other famous schools arose, chief among which were Malmesbury and York, until, in the eighth century, the glory of York quite eclipsed that of Canterbury. So set upon learning were the English that the monastic schools were not sufficient for them, and they crossed to Gaul and Rome or to Ireland, to return bringing with them new arts and new thought. We are told by Ealdhelm that whole fleets were filled by the students who flocked to Ireland.

The usual subjects of instruction in the monastic schools comprised the Trivium—grammar, rhetoric, logic—and the Quadrivium—arithmetic, geometry, astronomy, music—with theology. Though the theologian was often disposed to forbid the study of the classics, Virgil and Ovid were read and quoted by the monks; and even the nuns could read and write letters in the Latin language, could quote Virgil, and had some acquaintance with Greek. Cicero was a great favourite; Plato and Aristotle seem to have been known; and a Greek source is to be found for at least one of the Old English poems, the *Andreas*, and perhaps also for the *Elene*. Music, especially sacred music, received great attention. James the Deacon first taught it at York, and until the time of the Danish invasion the northern monasteries never lacked a famous teacher of singing. To the sound of the horn and trumpet and the melody of the harp is now

Phœnix, 136. added the harmonious note of the organ[1].

De Pont. et Sanct. Ebor. The picture of the daily routine at York, as given by Alcuin, is beautiful in its simplicity. Ecgberht, the bishop of the province and head of the school, devoted the morning to the training and education of the young students; at noon he celebrated mass; at the mid-day dinner and afterwards literary questions were discussed; after evensong each student came and knelt before him to receive his blessing

1435. before retiring. Æthelbert, his successor, gathered about him whatever youths gave promise of exceptional natural ability, and taught, fostered and loved them. To some he imparted assiduously the art of grammar, to others the art of rhetoric. Some he carefully trained in the refinements of the law, some in the beauties of classic verse. To others

---

[1] "organon swêg."

he made known the harmony of the heavens, the toilsome courses of the sun and moon, the five zones of the world, the wanderings of the seven stars, the laws which rule the movements of the stars, their rising and setting, the lofty uprisings of the sea, the tremors of the earth, the natures of men, of cattle, birds and wild beasts, with the diverse kinds and properties of numbers. He taught, too, the appointed times of the Paschal feast, especially opening the mysteries of Holy Scripture.

With such teaching and such enthusiasm England became the home of Latin learning at the time when, upon the Continent, it had reached its lowest ebb. In the Continent's darkest age, when all interest in learning seemed to have ceased, when even the Roman priests were unable to read or to understand the Latin tongue, and therefore took no pains to preserve the treasures of the past committed to their keeping, the English churchmen in their pilgrimages were indefatigable in rescuing, collecting and copying manuscripts, in founding and augmenting the monastic libraries. In England, books multiplied with the greatest rapidity. Those who returned from abroad brought with them as many as they could obtain, and, where purchase was impossible, made skilful and elaborate copies with which they returned joyfully home. Merchants and pilgrims vied with each other in presenting to their favourite monastery rare and valuable manuscripts, to obtain copies of which other houses, less favoured, sent their most skilful penmen from far and wide. Even kings engaged in the fascinating pursuit of book collecting. Aldfrith of Northumbria was content to give to Ceolfrid land sufficient to support eight families for a splendidly adorned Cosmographorum Codex from the library of Jarrow. By the end of the eighth century the library at York was second only to that at Rome, and its contents, as given in the *De Pont. et* contemporary Latin verse of Alcuin, mark the industry and *Sanct. Ebor.* zeal of the men by whom it had been collected. This is the *1535.* library of which Alcuin laments his loss while engaged at Tours in educational work for the Emperor Charlemagne. "Give me," he says, "the more polished volumes of scholastic *Alc. Op.* I. learning, such as I used to have in my own country, through *p. 52.* *Will. of Malm.* the laudable and ardent industry of my master, Archbishop *I. 3.* Ecgberht. And, if it so please your wisdom, I will send some of our youths, who may obtain thence whatever is necessary, and bring back into France the flowers of Britain; that the garden of Paradise may not be confined to York, but that some of its scions may be transplanted to Tours." In the list of authors whose writings it contained may be found the names of many whose work and thought formed the basis of the literature of the Middle Ages, upon which young English students were for centuries nourished and brought up, Jerome, Ambrose, Augustine, Athanasius, Orosius, Gregory, Chrysostom, Bede, Boethius, Pliny, Aristotle, Cicero, Alcuin, Clement, Lactantius, Virgil and Statius being the most important.

Theology was the end of all the learning of the age, and many came to believe that all learning which was not theological was sinful. Alcuin, the most famous scholar of York, afterwards forbade the reading of Virgil in his monastery in Gaul, telling his young monks that the sacred poets were sufficient for them, and sharply admonishing those who persisted in secret. "Gentile poems are but the husks which the swine do eat," says Bede, though he himself seems well read in the classics. He retells the story of an Irish monk who devoted himself to literature and neglected the study of the sacred books. When smitten with the plague he began to quake lest hell should be the well-merited punishment of his wickedness. To one who stood near he said: "Thou seest how I am brought to the moment of death; and after the death of my body I shall be brought to the perpetual death of the soul, and the torments of hell, because often in the studies of the divine readings I was wont to serve rather the enticements of vicious things than the divine mandates."

But the schools did not lack what was then practically a technical side. The arts of sculpture, painting and embroidery were carefully cultivated; and the adornment of the churches testified to the progress that had been made. Books were bound in the most precious materials, often with settings of gold or precious stones, as though the contents were worthy of no less costly a covering. The *Lindisfarne Gospels*, of entirely English design and workmanship, shows the care which was often thus bestowed. Architecture, too, found many votaries. One of the results of the conversion was that whereas the heathen Englishman had built his halls and temples of timber, now his Christian kinsman, under the

Bede,
Plummer,
I. liii.

Hist. Eccl.
III. 13.

teaching and supervision of the Roman, began to build more permanently with stone. Fine churches of stone in the Roman style were built at Wearmouth, Hexham, Ripon, Canterbury, Crowland and Bradford-on-Avon, the latter remaining as an almost unique specimen of its kind.

So we see the Englishman at work in a new direction. An end has been pointed out to him which he believes can only be achieved by profound scholarship, and therefore his desire to develope himself, coupled with his strong sense of duty, leads him to spare no pains to acquire such scholarship as speedily as possible. All this points to the strength and earnestness of his character. No other conversion was ever so real, or had such immediate and practical results, as his. Within a century from its beginning the English could train *Hist. Eccl.* their own bishops and archbishops, and were in possession v. 23. of a thoroughly organised church. While Bede, the quiet recluse of the North to whom all the West yielded the palm for faith and authority, illuminated the whole civilised world *Will. of Malm.* with the brilliancy of his learning, Ealdhelm of Sherborne, I. 2, 3. of immortal genius, was wonderful and almost unrivalled in all the liberal arts, and Daniel of Winchester had more than a national reputation as one of the most learned bishops of his time. Nor must we forget the fiery eloquence and zeal of Wilfrid, and the fervent spirit of Benedict Biscop, with, a little later, the brilliance of the teachers and scholars of the school of York, Ecgberht, Æthelbert and Alcuin. Of all the English, Alcuin was, as author and scholar, inferior only to Bede and Ealdhelm. By these men, and such as they, were the foundations laid upon which rose the noblest church and the grandest literature of the age.

But the greatest glory of the English Church was the noble band of men and women, missionaries and teachers, saints and martyrs, who passed across the sea to the Continent in its darkest hour, carrying with them the light of learning and the hope of the Gospel. The English were already strong enough to give of their best that missions and schools might be planted among the Germans, Franks and Saxons. By missions, as well as by pilgrimages, an outlet was afforded for their roving and adventurous spirits, no longer bent on foray but on the preaching of the Gospel of enlightenment and peace; and the stream of enthusiasts was ever increasing.

The names of Willibrord, trained at Ripon, and consecrated Archbishop of Utrecht in 696, Winfrid, or Boniface, trained at Exeter, and afterwards Archbishop of Mayence, Lullus, trained at Malmesbury, and the successor to Winfrid in his archbishopric, Willibald, a West Saxon, Bishop of Eichstadt, and Willihad, a Northumbrian, Bishop of Bremen, are but the most famous among many. When the progress of the national development was stayed by the descent of the Danes in the ninth century, it was in the schools of Charlemagne alone that learning was preserved to Western Europe, and those schools owed their excellence solely to the efforts of such teachers and organisers as Alcuin of York and the band of young disciples whom he gathered round him.

Bede, *Vita Abb.*
Will. of Malm.
I. 3.

Chief among the young men of noble birth who gave up the court for the monastery was Benedict Biscop, a thegn of Northumbria. On several occasions he journeyed to Gaul and Rome collecting books, pictures and relics, and, as his store grew, he received a grant of land at Wearmouth on which to build a monastery. This work entailed a visit to Gaul to procure masons and glassworkers, as there were then none to be found in England. He was the first to introduce into the country from abroad constructors of stone edifices and makers of glass windows ; for rarely before his time were buildings with regular courses of stone seen in England, and windows fitted with transparent glass were practically unknown. His love for his country and his devotion to art led him to spare no pains to fulfil his earnest desire to benefit his fellow-countrymen, and to raise their life to a higher plane.

V. Abbat.
p. 30.

At Wearmouth he furnished the interior of his church with pictures, from which even the unlettered might learn. Across the nave, from wall to wall, he hung pictures of the Virgin and the twelve Apostles ; the south wall he adorned with pictures of scenes from the Gospel history, and the north with pictures of the visions in the Revelation of St John ; so that all who entered the church, whether they could read or not, wherever they turned, might gaze upon the loveliness of Christ and His saints, or meditate with more vigilant mind upon the blessing of the divine Incarnation, or examine themselves more closely, having the peril of the Last Judgment before their eyes. Later, at Jarrow, he pursued a similar

p. 36. plan. One representation of Christ bearing His Cross he

hung beside a picture of Isaac carrying the wood for his
sacrifice, and another of the crucified Son of Man beside
the Lifting up of the Serpent in the Wilderness. All were
meant to direct and to render more definite the thoughts
of worshippers and visitors alike.

These pictures, and the like in other churches, stamped
an indelible impression upon the English religious mind.
Again and again does it seem that this influence is working
itself out in certain portions of our literature down to the
time of the Miracle and Mystery Plays. The *Dream of* Cf. *Christ*,
the Rood, the Cross upon the Hill of Zion in the *Christ*, 71, 265, 500,
with the description of Mary, the Descent into Hell, the 558, 807, 866,
Ascension and the Last Judgment in the same poem, the 1081, 1250.
appearance of Satan and his angels and the sacrifice of
Isaac in the *Genesis*, the many portrayals of the terrors
of hell in various poems, certainly seem to owe the vividness
of detail which they possess as much to the pictures within
the churches as to the poet's imagination. In the Homilies
delivered in the churches in later days, and in the beginnings
of the drama, which had its birth within the church itself,
it is more than probable that what was continually before
the eye had a much greater influence than can now be
completely ascertained. Thus Ælfric's description of Satan, Ælfric, *Ser-*
all black, with pointed visage and flowing beard, with locks *mones Cath.*
hanging down to his ankles, with hair like feathers upon his
body, with eyes scattering sparks of fire, and mouth sending
forth sulphurous flames, seems undoubtedly to have come
from an English picture, to pass through the Homilies into
the Miracle Plays. And we know that there were painted on
the walls in many churches, as there were once at Stratford
in the Chapel of the Holy Cross, representations of Paradise
and the mouth of Hell, with gilded angels and black devils,
similar to those of the Miracle Plays. When Chaucer gives
to his Summoner "a fire-red cherub's face" it is plain that *Cant. Tales*,
he is making use of a common feature of such pictures, well *Pro.* 624.
known to his readers, in which the Cherubim were invariably
painted red and the Seraphim blue. And yet again, the step
from the pictures to the drama, which often represented, in
the Middle Ages, the sum total of the uncultured Englishman's theological knowledge, may be seen in a Wicliffite
sermon denouncing the plays, where the common argument

in favour of the drama is set forth in order to be demolished:

Eng. Mir. Plays, Pollard, p. xxiii, note.

" Also, since it is lawful to have the miracles of God painted, why is it not just as lawful to have the miracles of God played, since men may better read the will of God and His marvellous works in the playing of them than in the painting, and they are better kept in men's minds and more often rehearsed by the playing of them than by the painting, for this is a dead book, the other a quick?" Certainly the use of the picture of the Crucifixion by the mission of Augustine reveals one of the methods, and that the most striking and impressive, of the Roman teacher. In Cynewulf's *Christ*, when the Saviour displays His wounds before the host of the lost, we almost see the Christian priest with hand outstretched towards a picture of the Crucified, and catch an

Christ, 1455.

echo of an old-time sermon: " See now the deadly wounds which once they made in My hands and likewise in My feet, by which I hung, fastened cruelly. Here, besides, now may'st thou also see, manifest in My side, the bloody wound"; and the words of the preacher, fired with his theme, must have gone home to the newly converted. At least the poet had never forgotten that picture and that sermon. And here

Davis, *Antient Rites of Durham*, Pollard, *Eng. Mir. Plays*, p. xv.

again is the same method: " Within the church of Durham, upon Good Friday, there was a marvellous solemn service, in which service time, after the Passion was sung, two of the ancient monks took a goodly large crucifix all of gold of the picture of our Saviour Christ, nailed upon the Cross."

The depth of the impression made upon the Englishman by pictures, in the early days of the Church, may be gauged by the story of Drihtelm, who saw in the night a vision of death and hell, no doubt arising from the suggestion of such

Hist. Eccl. v. 12.

pictures as those at Wearmouth. He saw the restless, awful agony of the lost souls who leapt incessantly from the hottest flame to the bitterest cold, and then back again to the flame, never finding ease. He saw the damned hurled up from the pit of hell by dense masses of flame, and then carried back again as the fiery tumult subsided. He heard the laughter of the demons mingling with the shrieks of the tortured ones, as the fiends dragged down their souls and plunged them deeper and deeper into torment. The vision seems to have turned his brain, for ever afterwards he was wont to perform his devotions while standing in the river, though, in winter, ice

formed upon the surface of the water. When his friends
wondered at his strange conduct, and remonstrated with
him, he would say, " I have seen much more cold, I have
seen much worse austerity than this."

The influence of Benedict Biscop and his work was great
and lasting, and cannot possibly be overvalued. Through
him and the monasteries he founded, civilisation, learning
and Christianity came to the North and flourished. At
Wearmouth and Jarrow Bede acquired his great store of
learning which descended after his death to the more famous
school of York, and thence, through Alcuin, to the schools
of Charlemagne upon the Continent, from which schools
the whole culture of Western Europe in the Middle Ages
took its source.

Bede, the greatest scholar of the age, the lover of books,
the untiring and faithful worker who, it is said, refused to
become abbot of his monastery that he might not be
separated from his beloved manuscripts, whose eyes, in old
age, became dim through toil, is the outstanding figure of the
English monasteries. How far removed is he in character
from his own heathen grandsires! And yet the older English
traits are not altogether absent, though with him the sword
has yielded place to the pen. No life of warfare and strife
is his; but his story forms a simple narrative of quiet, steadfast work within his monastery, which he never left except
to make short visits to such places as Lindisfarne and York.
Ever delighting in learning, teaching and writing, for more *Hist. Eccl.*
than thirty years he occupied himself with the study of the V. 24.
Scriptures, the observance of the monastic rule, and the daily
offices of the Church. Numerous, and on all the known subjects of knowledge, were the treatises which came from his pen.
Thus writes the Christian scholar : " And Thou, great Father *Com. on*
of Lights, from Whom cometh down every good and perfect *Nehemiah.*
gift, Who hast given to me, the humblest of Thy servants,
the desire and means to see the wondrous things of Thy
law, and the grace to bring forth, out of the treasure of the
prophetic volume, things new and old for the use of my
fellow-servants, remember me, O my God, for good." Again,
at the conclusion of his great work, the *Historia Ecclesiastica
Gentis Anglorum*, he says : " And I pray Thee, good Jesu, *Hist. Eccl.*
that, as Thou hast mercifully granted to me sweetly to drink concl.

in the words of Thy knowledge, so Thou mayest grant me of Thy goodness some day to come to Thee, the Fountain of all wisdom, and to appear continually before Thy face." Each is a scholar's prayer, breathing out the spirit of simple piety and true religion. The truest Christian charity, humility and unselfishness are almost everywhere present in this great man's work.   Only against the adversaries of his Church, the heathen and the Celtic monks, does he ever show any signs of bitterness. But the Englishman was always a strong partisan.   When the faithful worker grew feeble with age and sickness, the brethren tried in vain to persuade him to be less regular in his attendance at the daily devotions, and Alcuin ascribes to him the beautiful thought : " I know that the angels visit the canonical hours and the congregations of the brethren. What if they do not find me among them ? Will they not say ' Where is Bede ? Why comes he not to the prescribed devotions with the brethren ?' "

Bede, Plummer, I. xii.

Epist. of Cuthbert to Cuthwin.

An eye-witness gives an account of his death. From about two weeks before Easter until Ascension Day he lingered, without any great pain, but weighed down by weakness, and especially by a difficulty in breathing.   He continued daily his readings to his disciples, and spent the rest of his time, except when he fell into a light sleep, in singing psalms, in prayers and thanksgivings. He bore his affliction cheerfully, but sometimes he would repeat, " It is a fearful thing to fall into the hands of the living God," and would admonish the brethren to arise from the sleep of the soul by meditating upon their last hour.   Also he composed the following verses in English, for in addition to his other attainments he was learned in the native songs :

> "'Fore the need-journey no one becometh
> Wiser of thought than his need may be,
> Prone to consider, ere his hence-going,
> What to his spirit of good or of evil,
> After his death-day, doomed shall be."

He also sang the antiphon for Ascension Day, " O King of Glory...leave us not comfortless," and at these words he burst into tears and wept much.   Often he would repeat the words of St Ambrose, " I have not so lived as to be ashamed to live among you, but neither do I fear to die, since our God is good."   His last hours were spent in dictating the last chapter of his translation of the Gospel according to St John. " I would not that my disciples should read a lie and labour in it without fruit after my departing," he said. Also he distributed among the brethren the little treasures in his chest—pepper, napkins and spices. No earthly rewards, other than the esteem and love of all Englishmen, came to him from his long life of arduous toil. He spoke to them as they mourned and wept over him: " I have lived long, and the merciful Judge has well ordered my life. The time of my departure is at hand, and, moreover, my soul yearns to see Christ my King in His beauty." The closing scene is very characteristic. The boy Wilbert, who acted as his scribe, said to him, " Beloved master, yet one sentence remains un-written"; and he replied, " Well, write it." A little after the boy said, " Now it is finished." And the old man answered: " Good ! it is finished ; thou hast said the truth. Take my head in thy hands, for it pleases me much to sit opposite my holy place where I was wont to pray, that so sitting I may call upon my Father." So upon the floor of his cell, chanting " Glory be to the Father and to the Son and to the Holy Ghost," he passed away.

So an Englishman can die now, and in spite of his Latin culture I fancy that in many of the details of the close we may see some parallels with the death of Beowulf which show that the Christian scholar is the true descendant of the heathen warrior. It seems quite clear that the former is the Christian development from the latter. There is an added atmosphere of piety and faith, of a deeper tenderness, to mark the change. This latter characteristic may be as clearly seen in the touching description of the death of Benedict Biscop. As he lay, worn out with toil and para- *Vita Abbat.* lysed, his great friend, Sigfrid, who was also paralysed and Sect. 13, p. 41. dying, was carried into his cell and laid beside him so that their heads lay upon the same pillow, and thus, without speech, they took farewell of each other.

Under this influence all the ideals of the race are changing. In the monastery the hero, " the best of all men beside the two seas," is no longer merely " the spear-keen man, for gifts and for war widely honoured," like Offa, but is also the Christian warrior, fighting his battle alone in seclusion against *Guthlac*, 107. the powers of darkness, and winning his victory over the

temptations of Satan and all his host. Such is Guthlac of
Crowland, who is called by the messenger who announces
his death to his sister, "My lord and thy brother, the prince
of heroes, the best beside the two seas."

1331.

315.

> So must a hero ever in his heart
> Fight for God, and bear his spirit
> Oft in zeal 'gainst him who will persecute
> Every soul, where he may light upon him."

Bede,
Plummer,
ii. 68.

Vita Cudb.
Bede and
Anon.

Already to many of the English the contemplative life
had usurped the place of the active strenuous life of old.
Bede distinctly states that the former is preferable to the
latter, though the two ought not to be entirely dissevered.
Cuthbert, the hermit saint of Farne, led a life very similar
to that of Bede, though he was pastor rather than scholar.
"He was as an angel in his look, graceful in his language,
holy in all he did, pure in body, brilliant in genius, great
in counsel, catholic in faith, most patient in hope, and unbounded in charity." A Northumbrian thegn of high spirit,
blessed with strength of body and skill in leaping, running
and wrestling, a champion in all youthful sports, he nevertheless possessed a strong imaginative and poetic temperament. From his youth he was a seer of visions and a dreamer
of dreams, and the deep thought and meditation which came
upon him amidst the northern moors and mountains led him
to the monastery of Melrose and a monkish life of strictest
austerity. Patiently he toiled among his fellow countrymen
in continual meditation and prayer, but his trials made their
mark upon him. The vanity of the world and of humanity,
even the vanity of work itself, appalled him ; and he who once
had said that to counsel and console the weak was equivalent
to an act of prayer, at last sought to withdraw himself from
the world and to take refuge in complete seclusion, "where
I have fought my little wrestling (such as it was) for the
Lord." The desire for seclusion, with the corresponding
practice of asceticism, rapidly increased in many of the
monasteries until self-denial became nothing less than fanaticism. The ties of kin and the claims of society were alike
disregarded in that form of selfishness which secluded its
possessor, despairing of a general victory in the conflict of
good and evil, so that he might at least save his own soul.

There had been nothing akin to it in the Englishman's previous experience; but excess of zeal for the new faith led him on upon the mistaken path. To what lengths this fanaticism could go we see in Cuthbert's practice of washing his feet at Easter only, and in his refusal to keep a cow to supply his wants on Farne, alleging as his reason that where there is a cow there must be a woman, and where there is a woman there must be mischief.

Again, these dwellers in narrow cells and cloisters had been nourished from early youth upon narratives bristling with recitals of supernatural events. Their fathers before them, while yet heathen, had given all credence to tales of magic and mystery, and the minds of the children were impregnated with the prevailing tendency. In the early days of history, men appear to have come into the world with eyes opened wide in credulous wonder at all they saw and heard. Accumulated experience was, after all, so very limited, and the world of nature so mighty in comparison. Given a feebly stirring and often almost irrational brain, who can foresee the angle at which an idea may strike, or say to what depth it may penetrate, or calculate the tangent at which it will glance away? False readings of nature, false assumptions, false theories, built up a stock of erratic judg-ments which even an age of science and criticism has not been able altogether either to meet or to remove. Through his imagination the Aryan had peopled heaven, earth and sea with a host of spirits to whom he ascribed supernatural powers, and to whom he had recourse for a theory whenever some unwonted phenomenon passed before his eyes. The minds of the heathen English were saturated with wonderful stories of elves and demons, of wizards and witches, whose existence the cloistered monk felt himself unable to deny, and whose creation he could only ascribe to the Evil One. And, as though these were not sufficient, before reason had time to develope, fresh additions were made to the store from Latin mythology and Christian legend. The theology over which the Englishman pored, the classics he read in secret, were authorities for strange and wondrous hap-penings. And when one works continually in a narrow cell, or lives entirely in a world of books, neglecting to walk abroad in the sunshine and to refresh the brain with the health-giving vigour of the free winds of heaven, authority is everything. That miracles occurred in every age and in every part of the earth could easily be proved by authority. The Roman monk boasted to his English brother of the wonders which the merits of the saints of his blood had brought to pass, and from what we know of the Englishman he was not at all inclined to admit the inferiority of his Church even in the matter of miracles. The Roman told of a monk whose tomb was opened twenty years after his death, when it was found that, though the body had turned to dust, the hand which had held the pen still remained sound and undecayed; and the Englishman soon found a fellow to it in the undecayed right hand of Oswald. Such stories of pre-

Hist. Eccl.
III. 9, 10,
V. 2.

eminent sanctity increased till at least five other English saints were said to have been found incorrupt long after burial.

Will. of Malm.
II. 13.

"I believe you can nowhere find the bodies of so many saints entire after death, typifying the state of final incorruption," says William of Malmesbury. And since the

Guthlac, 1256.

miraculous light of heaven had shone upon the last resting places of many foreign saints to mark their distinguished

Will. of Malm.
I. 3.
Hen. of Hunt.
Bk. III.

virtue and devotion, it was necessary that that light should likewise shine about the shrines of England.

The brain of the ascetic monk, bent only upon subduing the flesh in solitude, was frequently the wicket through which many such records entered into the world; and the ascetic himself came to be regarded as the holiest of men when holiness was measured by the frequency of visions and miraculous experiences. Such hallucinations were never set down to their true causes. It was never seen that the self-tortures and macerations, in extreme cases often resulting in chronic weakness and incipient insanity, naturally tended towards a distorted imagination, an unbalanced intellect and a fevered brain, upon which a little brooding in an hour of weakness was quite sufficient to stamp the most vivid pictures. It was not perceived that in such an estimate of holiness there lurked a strong temptation for the monk who was at all unscrupulous. And, in isolated communities of simple-minded men, the ordinary occurrences of the outside world, often brought in and heightened in colour by an ignorant peasantry, would receive their miraculous settings, gradually to increase in definition and in marvel as they were

passed by word of mouth or by letter from one monastery
to another. Often such occurrences became adorned with
appropriate miracles modelled upon those of the Bible; often
plain statements of fact became entangled in old myths and
tales culled from the classics or the folk-lore of the countryside. Sometimes an example of medical skill, more highly
developed or more sensible than usual, became an accepted
instance of miracle working. It took very little then, we
may suppose, to translate "nothing less than a miracle" into
an authentic example of the miracle itself. We know that
at least one poultice, properly applied, brought its com-
pounder a great and widespread reputation. Cuthbert, in Bede, *V.*
his youth, was suffering from a grievous swelling on the knee, *Cudb.* and
                                                              Anon, I. 7.
and one who was riding by advised the application of a hot
poultice, which broke the swelling and gave immediate relief.
And afterwards Cuthbert knew by revelation that the man
was an angel sent by our Lord to heal him of his great sickness and disease[1]. So a general acceptance of the miraculous
in everyday life came about, and the manifestations of the
divine power of the Christ were feebly imitated by tales of
fanciful marvels said to have been brought about by the
many virtues of human agents. Even the wise Bede, having
no precedent for refusing to accept such accounts, and being
faithfully devoted to authority, did not scruple to insert
miraculous episodes into the text of his history, all of which
he himself firmly believed. But we must not forget that
men are always as their time is, and condemn too harshly
the credulity and simple-mindedness of the Englishman in
affairs which, as yet, he could but partially understand.

There is, however, a darker side to the monastic life which
cannot be so easily passed over. As time went on some of the
monasteries became notoriously dissolute and corrupt; and of
these Bede speaks in his *Epistle to Ecgberht of York.* There *Epist. ad*
are monks without any religion whatever, who are wanting *Ecgb.*
in self-restraint, and, so, easily succumb to the temptations
of the flesh in many ways. They give themselves up to
ribald jokes and tales, to feasting and drunkenness and other
unseemly vices, rather than to the ministrations or the studies

---

[1] "Agnovitque sacer medicum venisse superni
Judicis a solio summo, qui munere clauso
Restituit visus piscis de felle Tobiæ."

to which they have pledged themselves.   Others there are who preach the Gospel in order to heap up riches for themselves, giving no heed to Christ's commands.   And, to add to the evil, there are many fraudulent monasteries founded and inhabited by communities of laymen for their own profit and advantage.   Such are useful neither to God nor to man, for they do not carry on the work of the Church and yet escape the levies and tolls which they ought to pay to the State.   Bede's *Epistle* is throughout a loud cry for reform. His statements are corroborated by the *Guthlac*, where we

Guthlac, 459.

hear again of the loose discipline and violent habits of "the young men in God's temples."   They delight in vain riches

388.

and pride and presumptuous array, "as is the practice of youth where fear of the elder restrains not."   They pamper the body with the delights of feasting and foolish revelling.

433.

"Many things ye hide before men which ye ponder in your hearts, yet your deeds are not hidden, though ye perform them in secret."   Alcuin, too, advises that the young monks

Will. of Malm.
I. 3, 4.

of Wearmouth should attend less to hunting foxes and hares, and more to the study of the Scriptures and the praise of God.   He also reflects upon the love of some of the English clergy for parti-coloured and gaudy garments which do not befit their office.   In an age when a certain element of coarseness in manners and thought and speech was present in all but the very best of men, it is scarcely to be wondered at that the greatest possible difficulty was experienced in eliminating the corresponding coarseness of fibre from the nature of the average monk.   Even some of the bishops, we are told, were not altogether spotless in this respect. Thus we have the first appearance in England of the taint which, in later times, will become one of the causes of the Reformation; but so far it seems to have reached no very great magnitude and to have been confined to a very small

Guthlac, 383,
et seq.

section of the Church.   Still there was just sufficient of the evil to cause uneasiness and distress in the minds of the leaders, who saw in it the presence of Satan amongst them, actively working to compass the destruction of the faith.

The account of the poet Cædmon throws into strong relief not only the spirit which generally possessed the workers in the monasteries, but also the social life which was centred

Hist. Eccl.
IV. 24.

in them.   He had been a servitor or lay brother at Whitby

for many years before the divine inspiration came to him. It was customary for his companions to meet together in the evenings, after the English fashion, to while away the time with harp and song. What were the songs they sang we can only guess, but most probably they were of the olden time, of warfare and feasting, heathen or semi-heathen songs like the *Beowulf*; for Cædmon must have heard many such, as the setting of his own poems goes to show. When the harp came near him he would rise and leave the gathering; and it may well have been that, though he could not altogether deny himself the warmth and light and festivity of the hall, he could not bring himself to frame in his turn heathen songs. "He could never make any frivolous or empty poem," says Bede. On one such night, when the duty of attending to the cattle had been assigned to him, he left the company and betook himself to the out-buildings; and there he saw in a vision, as he slept, an angel visitant who set free the thoughts long locked within his heart. The voices of his native hills and of the sea, the whispers of the moorland, the lowing of the cattle in the steads, the sympathy of a full-hearted creature for all created things, coupled with devout and grateful appreciation of the goodness of the All-Creator, welled up in his heart to express themselves in his song. For it was of the wonders of creation and of the Creator that he sang:

"Now must we praise the Warden of heaven,
 The Creator's might and His heart's deep thought,
 The work of the Father of glory, as He, the eternal Lord,
 Of every wonder ordained the beginning.
 He first shaped for the sons of men
 Heaven as a roof, the holy Creator;
 Then the mid-world[1], the Warden of mankind,
 The eternal Lord, after created,
 The ground for men, the almighty Ruler."

On the morning after his vision Cædmon was brought before the abbess and many learned men to tell his dream and to repeat his song; and it was seen by all that the heavenly grace had been given to him by the Lord. Then they expounded to him some portion of sacred history and doctrine, and bade him turn it into song. Next morning he

---

[1] "middangeard," Midgard.

returned with it expressed in most excellent verse. Where-upon the abbess at once perceived the grace of God in the man, and received him into the monastery as a monk, com-manding that he should be taught the whole series of sacred stories. And he, by meditating and ruminating like a clean animal, converted into sweetest song all things whatsoever he could learn by hearing; and by the very sweetness of his song he made learners of his teachers. He sang of the creation of the world, and the origin of the human race, and the whole story of Genesis; of the exodus of Israel from Egypt, and their entrance into the Promised Land; and many other stories from Holy Scripture of the Incarnation, Passion, Resurrection, and Ascension into heaven of the Lord, of the coming of the Holy Ghost, and the doctrine of the apostles. He made songs of the terror of the Judgment to come, the horror of the punishment of Gehenna, and the sweetness of the kingdom of heaven, and very many others of the divine benefits and judgments, in which he strove to draw men from the love of sin, and to stir them to choose and practise good deeds. For he was a very religious man, and subjected himself in all humility to regular discipline; but he was kindled with fervent zeal against those who were minded to do otherwise; wherefore he concluded his life with a beautiful end. " Many others indeed after him, among the English," says Bede, " made religious poems, but none could equal him, for he learned the art of song not from man nor taught through man, but, aided by divine inspiration, he received freely the gift of singing."

So, in Cædmon's verse, we have a new departure which reflects the change now being gradually brought about in the English character. The elements of the ancient poetry become a medium for the transmission of the religious thought and teaching of the Church which the English have already to a great extent made their own. The Catholic Scriptures and Catholic dogma find their expression in the vernacular in " sweetest song," which has a peculiar and national interest, and which all can understand. There is something exceedingly practical underlying Cædmon's out-pouring of song. As our forefathers have been taught by the Scriptures, by the traditions of the Roman priests, by the works of Latin bishops and the Fathers of the Church, so they sing. But they add an original element of character and feeling, and a Teutonic atmosphere which is distinctly their own, and which marks the blending of the old and the new. They feel deeply; they speak earnestly and sincerely; and, at least among the singers, hypocrisy is nowhere evident. Let us examine and analyse what they have made of the Bible story.

First of all, as the primary foundation of the fabric, there is the plain Bible history of the Latin Vulgate, the medium through which the Hebrew theology of the Old Testament and the Christian theology of the New Testament were introduced to the English by the Catholic Church.

Next, there is the secondary influence of the traditional teaching of the Church, which incorporated itself into pure Christianity, forming an exceedingly complex system of theological thought, with sources manifold and various. In the early Græco-Jewish school of Alexandria, about the year 20 B.C., Hebrew theology seems to have blended with the Platonic philosophy, in which many Magian elements may be discovered, to find an expression in the figurative language and allegorical interpretation of the nations of the East. As a later development from this school, Origen began, about the year 185 A.D., to combine Neo-Platonism with Christian dogma; and thenceforth the influence of this combination was exceedingly strong in the teaching of the Church. It appears very plainly about the last decade of the fifth century when Avitus of Vienne wrote his *De Spiritalis Historiæ Gestis, Libri V*, with the suggestive sub-titles, De Origine Mundi, De Originali Peccato, De Sententia Dei, De Diluvio Mundi, De Transitu Maris Rubri. About the same period were put forth three works, ascribed to Dionysius the Areopagite, *The Celestial Hierarchy*, *The Interpretation of Celestial Names*, and *The Mystical Theology*; and, that the cosmography might be complete, there also appeared the *Pseudo-Gospel of Nicodemus* containing a description of Christ's descent into hell. The influence of this Neo-Platonic Christian school culminated in the Commentaries and Homilies of Gregory the Great, by whom the mission for the conversion of the English was planned and the designs for the development of the new Church first formulated. Naturally, this school of thought took root and flourished exceedingly in the monasteries; and Old English Christian literature, of monastic origin, reveals an almost complete assimilation of the system. The works of Avitus seem to have had a direct influence upon Cædmon and the poets of his age; Benedict Biscop, we know, had visited Vienne, and had thence brought books to the monasteries of the north of England; but it was the teaching of Gregory which first and foremost directed the English theological mind.

The third feature of Old English poetry, the Teutonic element, is easily seen as the Englishman begins to make the Bible story his own. God, the Almighty, is represented as a *Genesis*, 79. Teutonic chieftain surrounded by his host, a "lord and protector dear to all His thegns"; and Satan and his followers are held up to scorn as traitors and oath-breakers. Satan, too, is a lord who has bound his thegns to him by gifts : "If 409. I to any thegn princely treasures gave of yore, when we in the good land sat happily and held our seats, then never in a dearer time could he to me with service repay my gift," says he when planning the seduction of Adam. On the strength and number of those who follow him he prides himself in Teutonic fierceness of spirit, and refuses longer to serve his 278. Lord. "Lo! shall *I* toil?" he cries; "there is to me no need at all to have a lord. I can with my hands as many wonders work as He. I have enough of might to make a goodlier throne than His, and higher in the heavens. Why should I after His bidding serve, bow down with such vassalage? I can be God as well as He. Strong thegns stand by me, who will not fail me in the strife, heroes stout-hearted. Me have they chosen for their lord, these noble warriors. With such as these may one think out a plan, and win it with such helpers. My devoted friends they are, faithful in their heart's best thoughts. I can be their lord and govern in this kingdom. So to me it seems not right that I should need to cringe at all to God for any good. No longer will I be His servitor." We can easily imagine some fierce Old English rebel having such thoughts in his heart, and thus expressing himself in 65. proud and angry words. But Satan and his host are crushed and beaten; their pride is humbled, their arrogance brought to nought, their threatening rendered futile. Crestfallen and woeful they are banished on the long journey, on the dark path of exile, and cast into hell.

Even there the archangel retains his fierceness, and speaks with jealous fury: "Satan spake, spake mournfully. Within him welled fierce pride about his heart; and hot without him was the angry flame: 'How different is this narrow place 356. from that other which once we knew, high in the heavens, given me by my Lord, though it, through the Almighty's power, we may not hold and roam our realms. He hath not justly felled us to the depths of fire, to this hot hell, deprived of heaven. He hath planned to people it with human kind. That is my greatest sorrow, that Adam, who was formed of earth, should hold my mighty seat and live in bliss while we this flame endure, harm in this hell. Oh! if I could but free my hands, and might a space get out, escape one single hour, then I with this host'"—but words cannot express all he would do. How thoroughly human this Satan is, transformed from the traditional to the Teutonic mould.

The hell in which he lies is a dreary, hopeless abode, shrouded in unending night, filled with torment, with broad, 41. fierce-burning flame, with bitter reek and smoke and darkness, 324. swept through and through by fire and sudden cold. "There have they at even, excessively long, all of the fiends, fire 313. renewed. Then comes at the dawn the wind from the east, frost and piercing cold; ever the fire or the smart of the cold." The Gehenna of the Bible, and of tradition, is a place of fire only, but the Teutonic poet's conception of it is here blended with the heathen Niflheimer, the place of mist and cold. Among southern races the greatest hardships and sufferings have always been caused by exposure to the burning heat of a tropical sun in a parched and waterless region, where the awful agonies of thirst rack the body and craze the brain; the barbarian of the north knew more of the privations of the wintry steppe, ice-bound and lapped in snow, whither came at intervals the thick mists from the warmer sea.

Another picture of hell is given in one of the shorter *Satan.* poems. It is there an abyss of mingled heat and cold in the 30. nether world of the north, so deep that it seems a hundred 721. thousand miles from the bottom to Hell-gate. It is a dire, loathly, woeful, dim abode, a windy, accursed hall, a bitter ground, containing a tumultuous sea of poisonous fire sur- 133. rounded by lofty nesses, beneath which the devils lament and

mourn without hope; a place of serpents, adders, dragons,
and demons howling in their misery; whither the light of
heaven never comes to disperse the shades; and where often
in the gloomy horror terrible scenes are enacted: "at whiles
naked men struggle against the worms." The gnashing of
the teeth of those in torment may be heard for twelve miles
without the gate, beside which dragons, hot in heart and
breathing out flame, eternally dwell. The whole pit rages
with fire and venom; and when Satan speaks the words fly
from his lips in venomous sparks. The hall, the serpents and
the venom are other Teutonic additions to mediæval tradition.

    The poet's art rises in vividness and power whenever he
treats of warfare, a subject dear to the heart even of the
cloistered monk, and reminiscences of scenes from such
poems as the *Beowulf* frequently appear. When Satan
rebels, the wrath of God comes upon him, and he and his
followers are handled much in the same way as Grendel was
by Beowulf. "Stern the mood He had, bitterly angered;
in His wrath He gripped His foes with hostile hands, and
broke them in His grasp; angry at heart He cut them off
from home," and hurled them into hell. Even the Hebrew
in his bitterest moments could not have devised a fiercer
ending for the enemies of Jehovah. Before the Flood God
determines to avenge the evil upon the generations of men,
"to grip mankind grimly and sorely with hard might." And
in the *Exodus*, after the destruction of the Egyptian host in
the Red Sea, we find a similar passage: "There the more
mighty Warden of the sea-flood, angry and terrible, with his
battle-grip would decide the conflict." When the first-born
of Egypt are smitten, we are reminded of the bale at Heorot.
The land is full of mourning, and joyful song is no longer
heard in the hall. God Himself fells the persecutors of His
people, and the Destroying Angel strides far and wide.
When the Exodus commences, the march is over the moorland by narrow, solitary pathways, an unknown road; all
around lies the habitation of undefinable terror, evidently an
English mark.

    In the *Genesis* the Flood is God's war-feud. Elsewhere,
Christ's work on earth is His feud against the Evil One;
those who crucified Him recked not of the feud to follow;
He opens His war-feud when He enters hell. The *Pseudo-*

(marginal references)
111.
135.
338.
98.
39.
78.
162.
Genesis, 60.
1273.
Exodus, 500.
33.
58.
Genesis, 1351.
Christ, 1441.
Satan, 405.

Gospel of Nicodemus tells how a glorious light heralded the approach of the Saviour; how the summons to open was heard at the gate; and how the Saviour entered and released the spirits in prison. But in the Cædmonic rendering the descent into hell becomes a Teutonic surprise attack. " Then came the shout of the angels, din in the dawning; the Lord Himself had overthrown the Fiend. Then yet was his war-feud open at morn, when the terror came." Satan's seduction of Adam is also of the nature of a feud, revenge the motive. When Adam eats the forbidden fruit, the fiend who had been sent to tempt him cries aloud, " All our harms are avenged, *Genesis*, 759. the injuries which we long endured." So it is quite in keeping when, in a later poem, we find the apostles represented as armed warriors, heroes of English likeness, glorious upon the field of battle; to be less would have robbed them of their dignity in the Englishman's eyes.

> "Lo! we have heard in days of yore   *Andreas*, 1.
> Of glorious heroes twelve beneath the stars,
> Thegns of the Lord. Their glory failed not
> In the fight, when banners crashed together,
> After they dispersed, as the Lord Himself,
> High King of heaven, assigned their lot,
> That o'er the earth they should be famous men,
> Folk-leaders stout, keen on the path of war,
> Illustrious warriors, when the shield and hand
> Upon the field of strife warded the helm."

John the Baptist is said to have received from the Christ, *Desc. into* his protecting Lord, at the outset of his mission, helmet, *Hell*, 70. corslet and sharp sword, as though he were a young warrior receiving his arms from his chief. " I kept that always even until now," he says of the sword. Abraham and his men are *Genesis*, 2033. represented as typical English warriors, with English customs, weapons, fierceness, and methods of attack, as are also the *Exodus*, 155. hosts of Pharaoh in the *Exodus*. When the four kings from *Genesis*, 1965. the north raid the five kings of the south it is as though a Teutonic raid were in progress. The whole face of the country is covered with foes, " wolves of war, exulting in victory and spoil," and for the women the great horror is near. The levy is called out to meet the invaders, and fierce is the conflict. The defenders are smitten; their gold is shared among their foes; and maidens, wives and widows flee away from their devastated homes, since their lords and kinsmen are no more. " Many a frightened, pale-faced woman must go trembling in a stranger's clasp; the protectors of brides and bracelets have fallen, sick with wounds."

Adam becomes a typical Englishman, slow and cautious in his thought and speech, faithful to his Lord, and distrustful of the beguiling counsels of the stranger spirit, whom he rebuffs with a few gruff words, direct and to the point:

533. " I cannot at all recognise thee, neither thy words nor ways, but I know what He Himself, our Protector, bade me when last I saw Him. Thou art like no angel of His that I have yet seen; neither showest thou me any token from Him as a pledge. Therefore, I cannot listen to thee, but thou canst get thee gone. I have firm faith in the almighty God who made me with His hands." Thus foiled, the Tempter turns to Eve, hinting at the wrath of God which will follow this

580. rejection of his message. " Adam spoke sharp words, accused me of deceit," he says. He tells her of the superhuman power which the acceptance of his gift will bestow; and, knowing that Eve is in truth a very woman, he says that by its power she will be able to turn Adam after her will. The poet deals very tenderly with the fall of the woman, chivalrously inventing an unselfish reason for her weakness, emphasising her devotion to her husband, and depicting her as a model English wife, though a thoughtless, beauteous woman[1], unskilled to meet the Tempter's subtlety. She takes the fruit and eats; and by the deceiver's art a glorious vision of heaven rises before her eyes. Then, all unsuspicious of harm and from the best of motives, that Adam may share the gift with her, she tells him what she sees, and prevails upon him to follow her

684. example. It takes a whole day before he is persuaded, and at last he yields, partly because of the love he bears her, partly wearied out by her importunity. " The most beautiful of women spoke then to Adam full closely, until in the thegn his thought began to change, so that he believed in the promise which the woman made him. Yet she did it through devoted heart, knew not that therefrom so many harms, so many ills, should follow to mankind, because within her heart she listened to the counsels of the loathly messenger. But she thought that she had won with her

---

[1] "unræde idese scîene."

words the favour of the King of heaven." Was it thus, we think, that English wives in the olden days so often swayed the minds of their husbands? At the mocking laughter of the fiend disillusionment comes to them, and stricken with 777. horror at their sin they fall to prayer and ask forgiveness. Hell now they see before their eyes instead of heaven ; and in his misery and foreboding Adam speaks bitter words of reproach, and rues the day when first he asked the good God to give him the woman for his wife. " See'st thou now the 792. swart hell, greedy and devouring ? " he cries. " Now may I repent me that I prayed the God of heaven, the good Ruler, 816. that He here should work thee for me from my members, now thou hast seduced me into the hate of my Lord ; so now may I rue me for ever and ever that ever I saw thee with mine eyes." Eve answers with pathetic tenderness that her grief is as deep as his ; and apparently she feels more for him than for herself. " Thou canst make me know it in thy words, my 825. dear Adam, yet it cannot repent thee in thy thought worse than it grieves me in my heart." Adam breaks into a passionate cry of penitence and regret, a cry to know the Almighty's will, what punishment they must endure. In the sea, the flood, the ocean, the abyss itself, no terror shall make him quail if only he may work the will of God. Oh ! that God may remember and direct them ! " But they fell to 850. prayer both together every morning, prayed the Almighty not to forget them, but to teach them how they thenceforth in life should live." Immediate repentance has followed upon their fault ; a passion of penitence sweeps in upon their souls, and they cry to the Almighty with an exceeding bitter cry. In their distress they now cling to each other in all tenderness and love; and Adam's brief words of anger fade away altogether before the loving words of sorrow-smitten Eve.

These two sorrowful ones are more than mere Biblical figures. They are of the north, Teutonic and English seekers after God, faithful and devoted though fallen. Their penitence is that which comes from the monastery and the hermit's cell. Here we have the veil lifted for one short moment that we may catch a glimpse of the passionate workings of the grief-stricken heart crushed under the sudden recognition of its sin. We may well believe that Adam's cry was but an echo of many such, which, in the England of the early Christian days, when faith was strong though the flesh was weak, passed upwards from earth to heaven. This deep consciousness of sin was one of the most marked consequences of the conversion, and seems to have made its impress upon much of the literature of the period.

For Adam and Eve the punishment is exile; and the heart of the poet goes out in pity to the unhappy pair. This pity for the unfortunate and fallen is now an ever-present element in the English character; the pathos of sorrow has rarely failed to have an influence upon the English heart. *Satan*, 324. Even Satan's hard lot, as he lies fast bound with fire and flame, excites pity, just as his fierce majesty seems to have won reluctant admiration. The poet can hardly bring himself to leave the fallen archangel in hell, deprived of all hope, and so in the concluding portion of his work he puts into his mouth words in which there is a note of penitence and regret for the past. " Now am I stained with deeds, wounded with 156. sins; now must I bear this bond of torment burning in my back, hot in hell, deprived of hope." Abject, despairing, he raises a passionate cry to God, to earth and heaven. Never again can he be able to attain to heaven with his hands, to look upward with his eyes, to hear with his ears the resounding song of the trumpets of God. For his strife against the Lord of Hosts he must suffer exile, torment and sorrow, must 202. wander wretched and full of care. Oh ! let men take warning, cries the poet, lest like him they lose the joys of heaven.

Many other Teutonic modifications there are. Pagan *Genesis*, 103, 116. ideas, of hoary age, blend with the Bible story of creation. From the hollow abyss of shadow, clothed in the darkness of eternal night, the earth rises, and the darkness and shadow give place to light. Dark is the world, wrapped in the wan waters of the ocean, until the grass grows green at God's 197, 511. command. When Adam is created he steps forth upon the hallowed greensward of the Teutonic peoples. The offering of Isaac changes, as it passes through the English mind, into 2855. a heathen sacrifice. God's command to Abraham is: "There thou must prepare a funeral pile, a bale-fire, and thyself kill for a sacrifice thy son with the sword's edge, and burn up the body of thy dear one in the swart flame."

Thus, with all their growing enthusiasm for Christianity, it was a difficult matter to root out the old ideas from the

national mind. The race has always been one of the most
conservative. In spite of all the Latin learning, a great
love for the old songs remained among the dwellers in   Cf. *Hist. Eccl.*
the monasteries as well as among the laity ; and similar   IV. 24.
blendings, proceeding directly or indirectly from the active
spirit of the monks, may be found in many poems whose
authors and dates are matters of conjecture. It was but
natural that the earnest-minded monks, while satisfying their
own tastes, should blend the old with the new in their
additions to the national literature. The convert could not
have become Christian all at once, perhaps for years never
proceeded further than a very simple faith, perhaps indeed
was never so much at home with Christian thought as with
the ways of heathenism, though anxious to seize every
possible opportunity of obtaining a wider hearing for the
religion he had embraced. Besides, the national life itself,
as we have seen, possessed the same two-fold aspect. Thus it
is that, when the Englishman comes to write, memories, and
sometimes more than memories, of the songs he has heard his
heathen father sing mix with what he himself has learned
from Christian lips, so that to us the same poem may appear
in some parts to be the work of a heathen, and in others the
work of a Christian. I think we may take it that whenever
warfare, adventurous exploits and old-time customs are the
theme the poet is apt to forget for the moment that he himself
has embraced Christianity, and when he does recall himself
from the past it does not always add to the literary excellence
of his work.

That all the Old English poems we possess were, in their
final form, the work of the same class of men as those who
worked upon the songs of Cædmon is, I think, evident from
their parallelism of thought, sentiment and phraseology. All
these poets are the offspring of heathen ancestors and have
been brought under the influence of the same Latin training.
In the *Beowulf*, best of its class, the burden of the song when
Heorot was completed was of the creation, and was just such
a song as those which Cædmon and his followers sang. " He
said, who could recount the first shaping of the men of old,   *Beowulf*, 90,
that the Almighty made the earth, the brightly gleaming   and cf. *Æneid*,
plain which the water engirdles. He, the Victorious,   I. 740.
appointed the shining of sun and moon for a light to the

earth-dwellers, and adorned the fields of the earth with
branches and leaves. He also gave life to every creature
that lives and moves." Carved in runes upon the hilt of the

1689. sword found by Beowulf in the sea-cave "was written the
beginning of the strife of old, when the Flood, the poured-out
ocean, destroyed the race of the giants, who fared perilously.
They were a people hostile to the eternal Lord; to them the
Disposer gave this requital through the water's up-welling."

104. Again, the origin of Grendel is linked on to the story of Cain.
"He, hapless creature, had kept ward of the land of the giant
race since the time when the Creator had condemned him.
Upon the race of Cain the eternal Lord avenged the slaying
of Abel. He rejoiced not in that feud, for the Creator
banished him from mankind on account of the crime. Thence
awoke all the evil race, monsters, elves and ogres, and likewise

1262. the giants who strove against God for a long time; but He
repaid them for it." This is emphasised by repetition later.
It would seem that the poet knew something of the Titans

1683. of classical mythology. Grendel becomes "God's adversary,"

853, 1275, 712. "a heathen soul," "a spirit of hell." He "bore the anger of

812, 789. God," was "hostile to God," was "fettered by hell," and

853. "when he laid down his life hell there received him." It is
difficult to say whether it is not the heathen goddess Hel who
is here referred to, so close is the blending. He met his

1272. death at the hands of one who "trusted in the strength of the
might which God had given him, a bounteous gift, who placed
his confidence in the grace of the All-Disposer for help and
consolation."

Hrothgar, though a heathen king, is made, with great
inconsistency, to speak as a Christian, and becomes the
mouthpiece through which the poet expresses his own

1717. thought. Concerning the wicked Heremod he says: "Though
the mighty God exalted him in the joy of might and strength,
advanced him above all men, yet in his heart sprang up
bloodthirsty thought....By such do thou take warning....
Wonderful is the story how the almighty God, through His
omniscience, bestows wisdom, land and fame upon mankind.
He is omnipotent. Sometimes He causes the thoughts of the
heart of man, high-born, to turn unto love; gives him in his
land earthly joy, to possess the lordship of men; and so puts
into his power great portions of the earth, a wide dominion,

that the man himself, through his folly, may not think upon his end. He lives in pleasure; nothing afflicts him, neither desire nor old age. Remorse never casts a shadow upon his heart. Neither strife nor enmity anywhere shows itself. But for him all the world goes according to his will, and the worse he knows not, until within him a deal of pride waxes and flourishes, when the warder, the guardian of the soul, sleepeth. His sleep is too sound, bound up with troubles. The slayer is very near who shoots maliciously with his bow. Then, under his guard, he is smitten in his heart with a bitter arrow. He cannot protect himself from the strange, sinful biddings of the accursed Fiend....He forgets and slights what God before gave him....It happens in the end that the mortal body passes away; doomed it falls." Then follows an admonition which was intended to be taken to heart by every English warrior: "Guard thyself from the deadly enmity, dear Beowulf, best of 1758. men, and choose for thyself that more excellent part, the everlasting life. Eschew arrogance, O famous hero. Now is the fulness of thy might but for a time. Soon shall it be that sickness, or edge of sword, or fire's embrace, or surge of flood, or gripe of sword, or flight of spear, or dire old age, shall rob thee of thy strength, or brightness of eye shall fail and sight grow dim, so that death shall conquer even thee, O noble warrior."

A great change is now beginning to come over the old fatalistic conception of life. No longer is Fate the blind *Gnomic* force before which even the gods must bow; "God is to us *Verses*, I. 8. eternal; the decrees of Wyrd change not Him," says the Christian. Soon we shall hear of the heathen coming to learn of him, and asking him to dispel his doubt. "Full often I heard wise men long ago debating which of the two without *Sal. and Sat.* doubt was the stronger;...there was none upon earth who 424. could dispel the doubt." But the Christian replies that Wyrd goes hard, surges very near, awakens weeping, heaps up woe, destroys the soul, bears the spear, yet nevertheless the wise-thoughted may moderate every fate if he be prudent of heart, reliant upon his friends, filled with the Holy Spirit. "But why is it that Wyrd afflicts us so?" asks the heathen. "That," replies the Christian, "is the work of the devils cast into hell; they are those who fight against us; therefore is there increase of weeping to each of the wise." Again we

Andreas, 613. hear that it was Wyrd who deceived and seduced the Jews
Guthlac, 1030. so that they crucified the Christ. But Wyrd cannot set
aside the ordinances of God, and, indeed, must further His
work. Of one convert who was baptised we read that "Wyrd
Elene, 1044. determined that in the kingdom of this world he should
become so faithful and so dear to God, acceptable to the
Christ." So now Wyrd has become almost synonymous
with Providence, the power through which God works, even
Beowulf, 478. God Himself, almost the grace of God. "He whom death
shall take shall believe it to be the judgment of God": "It
2527. shall happen to us two at the wall as Wyrd, the Creator of
2815. every man, ordains": "Wyrd swept away all my kinsmen to
the doom of the Creator," are all from the lips of Beowulf.
God, not Wyrd, now rules the affairs of men. When Beowulf
671. waited for Grendel to appear he "surely trusted in the grace
479. of the Creator," knowing that He "may easily restrain the
fierce foe from his deeds." Before he lay down to rest he
expressed his intention to decide the conflict by handgrips,
686. "since the wise God, the holy Lord, may award the glory on
whatsoever hand seems to Him best." His company were
698. sorrowful, but "the Lord gave them the woof of war-speed,"
701. and "the truth is made known that the mighty God has
always wielded the affairs of mankind." Then it was made
707. known to men that when the Creator willed otherwise the
Harmful One could not drag them off into the shades.
1056. Grendel would have killed more of them had not the wise
968. God warded off such fate from them; "the Creator had
charge of all men as He has even now." He wills that
Grendel shall escape from Beowulf's grip. The struggle in
the demon's cave would have gone ill with the hero had not
1554. "the holy God, the wise Lord, decided the war-victory; the
Ruler of the heavens easily decided it aright." "Almost was
2294. an end put to my war-faring, only God protected me," he
says. "The undoomed one, whom the grace of the All-
Ruler upholds, may easily survive the woe and the exile."
2858. God's will alone is unalterable. Wiglaf was unable to recall
his dead lord to life, or change at all the will of the All-
Ruler: "The doom of God would govern the deeds of every
man, as it does even now." It was God who sent Beowulf to
1315. Hrothgar and his people as a respite to their woe, and placed
13. wise words in his heart. It was He, too, who sent Scyld as

a consolation to the Danes. So we are not surprised that
when the sentinel upon the Danish shore bids farewell to
Beowulf's band he says, "Now I must go; may the almighty   316.
Father hold you by His grace safe in your journey."

The Almighty is now to the Englishman God of all gods
and Overlord of all lords. As a faithful thegn he renders
Him all thanks, esteem and praise, in gratitude for his goodness. Again and again are thanks offered to God in the   1627, 929,
Beowulf for blessings vouchsafed. As soon as Beowulf and   1398, 1779,
his men landed near Heorot they returned thanks to God   2795.
that the voyage had been easy for them ; and on the hero's   227.
return home Hygelac says, " I give thanks to God that I may   1998.
see thee safe and sound."

On the other hand misfortune was thought to be a mark
of God's anger on account of sin committed ; an idea firmly
rooted in the English mind, which frequently appears in the
literature and with increasing intensity. When the dragon
burns Beowulf's hall, and lays waste his land, it is a cause of
great grief to him, greatest of heart-sorrows. " The wise   2328.
one thought that he had bitterly angered the All-Ruler, the
eternal Lord, that he had sinned against the old laws [the
Ten Commandments]; and his heart boiled within him with
dark thoughts, as was not his wont." This darker shade is
often apparent, in the poetry of the north of the later eighth
and ninth centuries, as the shadow cast by the hard days of
the fading glory of the Northumbrian kingdom, when the land
was wasted by dissensions within, and by foes from without,
when disaster and defeat brought home to the heart of the
chastened monk a deeper conviction of his sin. With it
appears an increased complexity of thought and character as
the age closes in despondency and gloom, brightened only by
the light which shines from the Cross.

The great poet of the period is Cynewulf, who, like
his predecessor Cædmon, was the product of the northern
monastic schools, and also like him seems to have had a host
of followers and imitators. In the work of the Cynewulfian
school minute details of the life and character of the Englishman are given.

In the days of his youth he is gay and thoughtless, given
to sport and song and the joys of the hall. He is a lover   *Riddles, Gifts*
of animals, of nature, of humanity; one whose life is bound   *of Men*, etc.

up with the lives of many friends. As yet life is to him more than religion; his morality is by no means spotless; his speech often tends to coarseness and indecency. He plays upon the harp, or reads the stars, or builds his houses and ships; he runs, and shoots with the bow, and trains his hawk; he rides, hunts and fights. He steers his warship across the sea; he engages in forays and invasions. He makes and mends his weapons of war, or plies the gold-smith's craft. He sits in the hall, now drinking, now gambling, now joining in the tribal councils, now distributing or receiving gifts. He makes love to the maidens of his settlement with passionate fervour. So he lives until the Christian preacher crosses his path. Perhaps he has met with disaster; perhaps his tribe has been overwhelmed upon the field of battle. His world has become empty, his life darkened, his thought more serious. He listens, is attracted, hopes, hesitates. He listens again and is won, and soon presents himself for baptism; conversion has now become a matter of individual conviction. Most probably he enters one of the monastic schools to be educated and grounded in the faith. Perhaps in the end he becomes a monk, perhaps, as time goes on, even an abbot or a bishop.

He now reads far more widely and more deeply than did his predecessors in the early days of English Christianity. He increases his knowledge of the Bible and the traditions and legends of the Latin Church, which he makes more completely his own. The great monastic schools have already borne much fruit. Now he loves to read and ponder over many tales of spiritual conflict and temptation in which the Evil One is dismayed and overcome, and these stories have a great influence upon him, as we see in the *Juliana*, *Guthlac* and *Andreas*. He orders his religious life after their example, and believes their minutest details. His brain is nourished upon Homilies, Lives of the Saints and Martyrs, Christian Latin poems and hymns of variable quality, with Physiologi, fanciful descriptions of birds, beasts and fishes, with alle-gorical explanations of religious import. Especial favourites are the *Carmen de Phœnice* of Lactantius—expanded from the Phœnix story of Ovid into an allegory of the Resurrec-tion, as in the *Epistle* of Clement and the *De Resurrectione Carnis* of Tertullian—the *Panther*, another allegory of Christ and the Resurrection, and the *Whale*, an allegory of the wiles of Satan and the danger of sin. The last two are from a Latin translation of a Greek original. There are also collections of Latin riddles, Enigmata, which he copies and improves, the books of Avitus, the Commentaries and Homilies of Gregory, and the Commentaries of Augustine, with, perhaps now, certainly a little later, Gregory's *Dialogues* and *Pastoral Care*, the *De Civitate Dei*, Augustine's great philosophical and historical apology for Christianity, with its companion handbook the *Universal History* of Orosius, the *De Consolatione Philosophiae* of Boethius, and translations of Aristotle, whose philosophy thus gains acceptance in England. And he now begins to have some slight acquaintance with the medical prescriptions of the Greeks and Romans. For centuries these manuals remain as the great monuments of English reading, mines of information worked and re-worked in season and out of season, till by their influence the English learned mind becomes fixed in the one stereotyped and invariable form of the Latin scholastic system.

But the natural instincts of race, the moulded products of centuries, could not be altogether eradicated by learning. Even as monk and scholar the Englishman could not always cut himself off from the influence of the world without the monastery to live his life alone in the world of books. In his walks abroad the life of the countryside spoke to him, and memories of the worldly days of youth arose in his heart. Sometimes the stress of circumstances, an invasion, a foray, a council, recalled him to active participation in mundane affairs. Sometimes, like the Bishops Ealhstan and Heahmund, he buckled his armour on again when the tide of war passed near him ; and his courage and old-time fierceness came back once more as he fought against the heathen adversaries of God. Sometimes, when forced to flee from his retreat by marauding bands, he took refuge wherever he might find it in the homesteads of the people. When next he began to write, all such experiences found their natural expression, blended with his reading ; and thus the spirit of his race was kept alive in his poems.

Thus it is that in the early years of the eighth century, when the glory of the Northumbrian kingdom was already

A.-S. Chron.
A.D. 823, 845, 871.

D.   8

departing, the literature of the age preserves for us a reflection of the despondency which settled upon the inhabitants, clergy and laity alike. The outcome of this period of disaster is that the character of the religious Englishman is softened by his chastening of sorrow; his thought becomes deeper and more tender; and there is found in him a new element of introspectiveness born of the age of adversity in which he finds himself. He searches his heart; conscience awakens; and he stands before the Cross convicted of his sin. The terrors of death and the Judgment loom large before his eyes and nearer to him than ever before; and he takes to his heart with morbid satisfaction the various apocryphal writings which profess to delineate the dreaded future with minutest detail. He sees visions and dreams dreams; he accepts voraciously, as prodigies and omens, comets and eclipses and other phenomena of the heavens. Surely the end of the world is near, and these strange, unexplainable happenings are but signs of the approaching doom. His prayer goes up to heaven: " O beloved Lord, O righteous Judge, eternal Ruler, prepare me. I know my soul wounded with sins; heal Thou it, Lord of heaven, and search it, Prince of life, for Thou canst most easily of all leeches, far and wide, who ever have been."

A.D. 793, 806.

Prayers, Cott. MS. 1.

Cynewulf tells us much about his own conversion, his hopes and fears and final peace in Christ. When he puts into English verse the *Life of St Juliana, Virgin and Martyr*, he says, " There is to me great need that the holy Maid should help me when my soul must depart from my body on the journey I know not whither." Sad at heart he wanders, stained with sins, waiting in fear what the great Judge will doom for him after his deeds. He trembles, oppressed with care, remembers all the sore, the wounds of sins of former days, weeping he mourns them with tears. And he signs this lamentation with his name in runes[1]. Too late was the

Juliana, 695.

704.

704.

---

[1]   "Geomor hweorfeð
C. Y. and N. cyning bið rêþe
sigora syllend þonne synnum fâh
E. W. and U. acle bîdað
hwæt him æfter dædum dêman wille
lîfes to leane L. F. beofað
seomað sorgcearig sâr eal genom
synna wunde þe ic sîð oððe ær
geworhte in worulde."

time when he became ashamed of his evil deeds in the days of health. There is need for the holy Maid to intercede for him. Will every man who reads his poem pray that God may help him at the great Day.

He makes a similar request in the *Fates of the Apostles*; that the reader will pray for the help of the apostles for him when he must seek alone the long home, the dwelling unknown. Elsewhere, in the *Christ*, he tells us that he expects for himself and dreads the sterner doom[1], when the Lord of angels shall come again, because he kept not well what his Saviour bade him in the books; and again he appends his signature as before. All joy has departed from his life because of his fears; and he turns to the Christ with penitence and prayer: "We humbly pray Thee, Christ our Healer, to hear the voice of the captives Thy servants, O God and Saviour, how we are afflicted through our self-will. The avengers, the accursed beings, the hateful fiends of hell, have cruelly constrained us, bound with baleful bonds. Thou alone, eternal Lord, canst help us, penitent and sorrowing, that Thine advent may comfort our misery, though we have made feud with Thee through lust of sin. Pardon now Thy servants, and remember our wretchedness, how we stumble in our frailty, wander in weakness. Come now, King of heroes; delay not too long; we have need of comfort; that Thou mayst save us, and give us Thy true salvation, that we henceforth may do Thy will continually." "Come now, Warden of victory, and give Thy gracious mercy here." "Come now Thyself, high King of heaven, bring us salvation, to weary ones oppressed, worn out with weeping, with bitter burning tears. Thou alone canst help us in our great necessity."

And the Christ does come to him, and gives him faith, hope and peace. His gloom vanishes; his terrors disappear. Henceforth the Cross has the chief place in his life and in his song. "Now is to me the hope of life, that I may seek to honour well, oftener than all others, the Victory-Tree alone. That desire is great within my heart; and my refuge is made ready near the Cross." So deeply does the divine Atonement for human sin appeal to him that glorious visions come

Fates of the Apostles.

Christ, 789.

357.

243.

149.

Dream of the Rood, 126.

---

[1] "dôm þý rêðran."

in the night to inspire his soul. In the *Dream of the Rood* there is a description of the Crucifixion, imaginative and eloquent with feeling. At midnight, as the poet sleeps, it seems to him that a wondrous tree, brightest of all trees, radiant with light, adorned with gems and gold, is led out into the sky; and upon it gaze the angels of God and the spirits of the holy ones, men who dwell upon the earth, and all created things. And at the sight his heart is filled with

13. awe and the sense of guilt. "Wondrous was the Victory-Tree; and I was stained with sins, wounded sore with defilements." With wondering eyes he sees, through the gems and gold, marks of the Passion of by-gone days. From its right side the Rood begins to sweat with blood; and he is troubled and afraid. He sees it change in covering and in hue; now it is clouded over with moisture, soiled with streaming blood; now it is decked with treasures. The Cross begins to tell its own story: how it was cut from the end of a wood, and set up on Calvary; how all the earth shook when the Lord stepped up to it, and it dared neither break nor bend because of His word; how it trembled when He clipped it round, fastened with dark nails; how it would have fallen upon those who hung Him there, but dared not injure any; how the blood poured out from the wounded side and covered them both together; how, when His Spirit passed, the dark came down and wrapped the Body with clouds, the shadow overcoming the bright light of day. "All

55. creation wept, bewailed the fall of the King; Christ was on the Cross. But there hastening came from far to the lonely One a noble band. I beheld it all. Sore I was with griefs afflicted, bowed myself humbly to the hands of the men with jealous care. There they took the God almighty, raised Him from the heavy pain; and the warriors left me standing, streaming with the bloody sweat; I was all with arrows wounded. There they laid Him down, limb-weary; stood beside Him at His head; gazed upon the Lord of heaven; and He rested there for a while, weary after the great strife. Then began the men a grave to make for Him on the mountain side, cut it from the native rock, and set therein the Lord of victory. A sorrow-song the mourners sang in the even-tide."

In the *Christ* there is, I think, a reflection of the sermon, or
at least of the teaching, which, after Cynewulf's conversion, first
opened up that deeper feeling which led him to tell the story of
the Cross.   He pictures to himself the Tree on Calvary, red
with the blood of the Christ crucified upon it, rising to shed its   *Christ,* 1081.
radiance throughout the world.   He sees the Saviour point-
ing to His wounds, openly displayed; and hears Him speaking to the host of the lost assembled before Him, making
His appeal, direct and personal, to each individual soul.
" See now the deadly wounds which once they made in My   1455.
hands and likewise in My feet, by which I hung fastened
most cruelly.   Here besides now mayst thou also see, manifest in My side, the bloody wound.   How uneven there the
reckoning between us two!   I received thy sore that thou,
happy and blessed, mightst enjoy My kingdom in heaven,
and dearly bought for thee, with My death, the everlasting
life....Why didst thou forsake that glorious life I bought for
thee through love?   Wast thou so witless that thou knewest
not how to thank thy Lord for thy redemption?   I ask not
now about My bitter death which I endured for thee; but
give me back thy life, the price of which I long ago paid
for thee with My suffering.   I claim the life which thou hast
sinfully slain with sins to thine own shame....Oh! why hast   1488.
thou crucified Me heavier upon the cross of thy hands than
ever I hung before?   Lo! this seems to Me the harder; now
is heavier with Me the cross of thy sins."

The poet grows old and feeble, and feels that the day of
his death is near, but it causes him now no sorrow, for he   *Elene,* 1257.
knows that his salvation is assured.   He falls in prayer before   *Dr. of the*
the Cross, eager, with passionate longing, for death to release   *Rd,* 122.
him from the flesh, and to open for him the joys of heaven.
Life is but the crossing of a dangerous ocean to the rest with
Christ.   " Now is it most like," he says,

......" as if on ocean's flood   *Christ,* 851.
O'er the cold water in our keels we passed,
O'er the vast sea on our ocean steeds,
Guiding our barks.   It is a dangerous stream
Of waves high-tossed which here we sport upon
Through this vain world of stormy ocean-steeps,
Over the deep sea-road.   Then was our peril strong
Before we to the land had safely sailed

Over the sea's rough back, and help to us appeared;
Till us to safety in salvation's haven led
God's ghostly Son, and gave His gift of grace
That we might rightly know, o'er bulwarks see,
Where we should bind our stallions of the deep,
Our old wave-horses, with the anchors fast.
So let us in that haven place our hope
Which for us there th' All-Ruler has prepared,
The Holy in the Highest, when He uprose to heaven[1]."

Dr. of the Rd, 131, cf. Augustine, *Com. St John*, XIV. 15.

To die will be but going home to the joyful welcome of old, long-lost friends in the light and warmth of heaven, where the evening meal is spread, with a place prepared for the faithful one. In contemplation of the Christ he sees heaven

Phœnix, 595.

open with shining fields and sunny groves dancing in light, while the song of the angels and the joy of the saints are borne to his ear. "There is the song of angels, bliss of the

Christ, 1650.

blessed, there the Lord's beloved countenance, to all the happy ones brighter than the sun. There is love of loved ones, life without the end of death, glad the host of men, youth without age, glory of the hosts of heaven, health without pain for the righteous, rest without strife, glory of the blessed, day without darkness, bright and glorious, bliss without sorrows, peace between friends henceforth without variance among the blessed ones in heaven, love without hatred among the saints. There is neither hunger nor thirst, sleep nor heavy sickness, neither the burning of the sun, nor cold nor care. But there the company of happy ones, brightest of hosts, enjoys for ever the grace of the King, glory with the Lord."

The personal note in Cynewulf's work cannot possibly be mistaken ; we know that he is always speaking from his heart, and expressing his true feelings. We feel that he is a zealous enthusiast, by nature introspective, sensitive and imaginative, one in whom the religious conscience is fully awakened. Throughout his work we see that passionate yearning for the religious life which is so marked among the English of this age. His poem, the *Christ*, has been called

---

[1] This is the English expansion from Gregory's Latin: "Quamvis adhuc rerum perturbationibus animus fluctuet: iam tamen spei vestrae anchoram in æternam patriam figite, intentionem mentis in vera luce solidate." Greg. *Hom.* II. 29, par. 11.

"the epic of salvation," and he himself may be fitly styled
"the poet of the Cross."

That he is a product of the schools is clear, for the
foundations of all his works are drawn from the monastic
learning and experience. Some portions of the *Christ* are
based upon Gregory's Homilies on the Epiphany and the
Ascension, with the Latin Hymn on the Day of Judgment,
but the spirit of the poem is more than these could ever give.
The source of the Life simile has been already noticed; and
from Gregory he also expands the simile likening the sun and
moon to gems shining in the highest heaven, and figuring
thereby God and His Church:

Greg. *Hom.*
I. 10, II. 29.

II. 29, par. 11.

par. 10.

> "What are those gems so bright
>   But God Himself?
> He is the soothfast gleaming of the sun,
> To angels and to men a noble light.
> As o'er the earth the moon, a ghostly star,
> Gives shine, so God's own Church
> Through congregations of the truth and right
> Gleams bright[1]."

Christ, 694.

Again, where Gregory describes the effect of the Crucifixion upon the inanimate world[2], Cynewulf inserts additions,
both in the *Christ* and the *Dream of the Rood*, so entirely
Teutonic in sentiment and imagery that we are led to believe that he is making use of the Balder myth. All
creation, heaven and hell, earth and sea, the sun and
the stars, are moved by what is taking place. Nature
herself, "the earth all-green," is fearful at the Saviour's
pangs, and suffers in sympathy with Him. The trees run
with tears of blood, red and thick; their sap is turned to
blood. When the Cross tells of its wounds Cynewulf seems

Greg. *Hom.*
I. 10, par. 2.

Christ, 1128.

1175.

---

[1] Cf. Gregory: "Quis enim solis nomine nisi Dominus, et quae lunae nomine
nisi ecclesia designatur?"

[2] "Omnia quippe elementa auctorem suum venisse testata sunt. Ut enim de
eis quiddam usu humano loquar: Deum hunc coeli esse cognoverunt, quia sub
plantis ejus se calcabile praebuit. Terra cognovit, quia eo moriente contremuit.
Sol cognovit, quia lucis suae radios abscondit. Saxa et parietes cognoverunt,
quia tempore mortis ejus scissa sunt. Infernus agnovit, quia hos quos tenebat
mortuos reddidit. Et tamen hunc, quem Dominum omnia insensibilia elementa
senserunt, adhuc infidelium Judaeorum corda Deum esse minime cognoscunt, et,
duriora saxis, scindi ad poenitendum nolunt; eumque confiteri abnegant, quem
elementa, ut diximus, aut signis aut scissionibus clamabant."

Dr. of the Rd, 46, 62.

to be moving still further away from Christian teaching into details of the heathen myth: "On me the dagger-wounds are seen, open wounds of malice,....I was all with arrows wounded." We also find this tendency in another poet's

Satan, 509.

work, where the Saviour says, "I pleaded for you when the warriors pierced Me with darts on the gallows-tree." And

Guthlac, 1261.

Guthlac, like his Master, is pierced to the heart by the arrow-shower, by the death-darts of the fiends.

Again, in Cynewulf's work there are many signs which point to the use and amplification of Latin hymns and quasi-dramatic portions of Roman ritual. For example, the

Christ, 70.

dialogue between Mary and the people of Jerusalem, with the chorus in praise of the Christ which follows, may perhaps have been drawn from an antiphonal setting for one of the great festivals, or may even have come from part of some simple dramatic representation within the church, one of the germs from which the Miracle and Mystery Plays developed later. But when the Immaculate Conception is made known to Joseph we have a dialogue more essentially English in spirit, of a nature closely akin to the later plays, which proves that the poet has not ceased to be influenced by the social life he sees about him. His Joseph and Mary possess all the characteristic traits of an English husband and wife: "Wilt

166.

thou lose my love?" asks Mary; and Joseph answers: "Now am I deeply troubled, robbed of honour, for on account of thee have I heard a multitude of words, vast sorrows, bitter speeches, slander; and shame they speak of me, many grieving words. I must pour out my tears, sad-hearted. God may easily heal the sorrow in my heart, console my misery. Alas! young maid, maid Mary!" Mary altogether ignores the implied reproach, and answers as though it were some fault in himself which has caused his grief; a truly feminine method of defence. Joseph's tears change to sternness: "Too many woes have I received from this child-bearing. How can I stay the loathly tale, or find an answer against the wrathful ones? It is widely known that I, from God's bright temple, freely received a maiden, pure and guiltless, now changed by some deceitful art. Impossible it is for me either to speak or keep silence. If I shall speak the truth, then must David's daughter die, slain with stones; yet harder far that I should hide the crime, to live henceforth a perjurer, loathsome to all, despised among the people."

There are in Cynewulf's work two elements, very unlike each other, and yet seemingly not incompatible, which are also to be found in Cædmon and in Bede, and which must have been very common in their day. One is a stern, uncompromising opposition, a fierce, unmeasured hostility, to all adversaries of the Catholic Church and to those who differ from the orthodox religious opinions. The beautiful Juliana *Juliana*, 149, is aggressively hostile to her persecutors as well as to the Evil 176, 210, 509. One; neither torments nor loving words can for one moment shake her firmness. In the *Christ* this feeling is carried to its utmost when the righteous find great joy in regarding the sufferings of the lost. The third cause of their happiness is that "in the bale of darkness the happy host see the *Christ*, 1248. damned suffering pain as a punishment for their sins, the surging flame, and biting of the serpents with bitter jaws, a school of burning creatures. From that sight waxes for them a winsome joy, when they see the others enduring the evil that they escaped through mercy of the Lord." The Teutonic temperament was well fitted to receive this teaching Cf. Psalm from the Hebrews of old. On the other hand, from the lviii. 9. monastic training comes that emotional excitability which often leads to weeping. Cynewulf sheds passionate tears when he thinks of his past sins; Cuthbert cannot refrain from tears when celebrating mass; Bede on his death-bed bursts into tears and weeps much; and often we read of weeping monks, and even kings.

Though he has his moments of sadness and despair the Englishman is far too healthy to remain long in the depths. For him the brighter hope arises, and it is a consolation to his soul to know that after death he shall possess the light of *Bi Manna* heaven, up among the angels; that he shall behold with his *Lease*, 43. eyes the King Himself, Who shall be an eternal consolation to *Creation*, 93. the blessed. Though from the dead none return to tell of the heavenly mansions, and God alone knows whither the *Gnomic Verses* soul passes to await the Judgment, yet it is sufficient to know (*Cott.*), 57. that, whatever the place may be, it is "the bosom of the protecting Father," and that all are safe with Him. Here and there in portions of the *Beowulf* there is the same Christian teaching. Scyld departed at the appointed hour to commit *Beowulf*, 27.

2470. himself to the keeping of his Lord.   The chief of the Weders
3109. gave up man's joys, and chose the light of God.   Wiglaf bids
the people carry Beowulf where he shall long in the safe
keeping of the Almighty patiently wait.

So now the Englishman, after conversion, looks forward,
like Cynewulf, to his end, and is eager for death, no longer
death upon the battle-field, but a glorious close to his spiritual
wrestling for the Lord.   When the time comes, like Bede,
Cædmon, Cynewulf and Guthlac, he is quite prepared to
depart, for he is full of faith and assured of salvation.   But
no longer does he trust entirely in himself and in the merit
of his own great deeds; it is upon the Christ that his confidence is placed, and He is a Healer and Saviour, a Protector
against all terrors.   Guthlac says that his spirit "is now
Guthlac, 1017, ready, eager for the journey thither....It is to me no hardship
1038. to submit to the will of my Lord.   I have not in this sick
time sorrow in my heart."   When he died, "angels bore him
1280, 1288. to the long joy,...troops of angels sang the victory-song";
and, to mark his holiness, a heavenly light, reaching down
from heaven to earth, shone about the place where he lay.

Many excesses may be discovered in the work and
thought of this period, but they are usually excesses of
youthful ardour, of inexperience, of passionate impulse.   We
shall not be very far wrong if we style this age "the age of
zealous enthusiasm."   From the state of chaos the Englishman has advanced far and learned much; and the motive
force which has impelled him onwards has been the quickening, civilising spirit of Christianity.   He and his fellows are
now much more than the fortuitous concurrence of atoms
of the old tribal days.   They have found that which will tend
to bind them into one compact and organised whole, with
common sympathies, common ideals and a common faith.
Such is the result, under the grace of God, of Augustine's
mission and the Roman teaching.   Now the poet can sing
from his heart his Anglo-Latin song of redemption, so typical
of his own twofold character :

Phœnix, 667.

"Hafað us âlŷfed lucis auctor
ðæt we môtun her mereri,
gôddædum begietan, gaudia in celo,
ðær we môtun maxima regna
sêcan and gesittan sedibus altis,

lifgan in lisse lucis et pacis,
âgan eardinga almæ letitiæ,
brûcan blæddaga, blandem et mitem
geseon sigora frean sine fine,
and him lof singan laude perenne,
eadge mid englum, Alleluia[1]!"

[1] "He hath redeemed us, the Author of light,
That we may here merit,
Gain with good deeds, rejoicings in heaven,
Where we may seek the greatest of kingdoms,
And sit in the high seats,
Live in enjoyment of light and of peace,
Possess habitations, happy and joyful,
Enjoy glorious days; gentle and mild
See victory's Lord for ever and ever,
And sing to Him praise, praise without ceasing,
Happy with angels, Alleluia."

CHAPTER III.

THE DISCONCERTING FACTORS.

IN the preceding phases of development an attempt has been made to show the advance of the Englishman from barbarism to civilisation, from heathenism to Christianity, from chaos to comparative order. That advance was seen to have been accompanied by, if not actually carried out upon, a great wave of zealous enthusiasm, which arose from an almost spontaneous leaping into life of the vital principles of an exceedingly complex development. And, as is usually the case when enthusiasm lacks the aid of experience, a tendency towards excess was discovered, which on closer examination always seems to hint at hidden dangers and pitfalls by which the risk of ultimate failure is greatly increased. Some weak spots have already been pointed out among much that gave promise of high excellence in the future; and in the course of the next two hundred years the number of these will be seen to increase rapidly, until in a time of stress and trial a blight seems to set in. Then the Englishman's high ideals collapse; the fabric of his civilisation begins to crumble away; and all is uncertainty and suspense. How does his character stand the test? How will he emerge from his trial?

Sometimes we see him rousing himself for a space to the most strenuous efforts, struggling to cast off the incubus from his shoulders, fighting desperately to free himself from the toils which check every attempt at expansion or improvement. Sometimes we see him galled by failure, reckless, careless of honour, and almost entirely destitute of self-respect, a very barbarian, cunning and treacherous, with no thought but for the passing moment. Sometimes we see him chastened and subdued, morbidly accusing himself of manifold crimes, looking continually upon the darker side of all things. That which strikes us most, no doubt, is the abject despair, the awful vacancy, which settles over him when his best endeavours lead but to failure. With a sigh he seems to resign himself to the inevitable. That consciousness of sin, coupled with the belief that misfortune is always the immediate consequence of wrong-doing, which appears in the *Beowulf* and so frequently in the poetry of Cynewulf, takes hold upon him. Against God he has sinned, and therefore has this evil come upon him. " Who can stand against the wrath of the Almighty?" is the burden of his thought.

But it is ever the darkest hour before the dawn. Birth always implies pain ; and from this travailing of sorrow a new man will be born, brighter, stronger, more joyous than of old, an Englishman with an expanded destiny, a leader of men and of nations, one who has gained his experience in the hard school of adversity, and is all the better for it. In these two hundred years comes the crisis of the Englishman's development, in which again and again, despite his frantic battlings, he seems to be almost overwhelmed and doomed to extinction. The old tribal spirit is still strong within him ; he is always more ready to divide than to unite ; and this makes for internal dissension and consequent weakness when face to face with his foes. If his people are to take a place among the nations they must free themselves from many instincts of the older mode of life, to become a united nation with one determined policy and one chosen leader. It would seem that only by crushing and bruising could this result be brought about. Whenever a leader arises, strong enough to bind all men to him, and experienced enough to plan a skilful policy, then the tide of fortune turns repeatedly in favour of the English; when such a one is lacking, their best efforts become spasmodic and without effect. O for born leaders of multitudes of men ! But these, like everything else, have to be developed from the lower to the higher order ; and their development takes time and training. The Englishman must learn from the great leaders of his conquerors what it is to lead. Yet, though he is conquered for a while, the natural virility of the individual does not completely fail, refuses to be stamped out entirely, flickers, it may be, but never dies, till the time comes when the leader is found to lay the foundations of the national prosperity and freedom.   After these centuries we shall have a united and compact England, able to offer a firm and unbroken front to all who dare assail her, mighty and vigorous enough to continue, on the grander scale which her fortunes impose, the career of expansion, conquest and settlement to which she has been impelled from her earliest days.

A.-S. Chron.
Hen. of Hunt.
Bk IV.
Will. of Malm.
I. 3.

The eighth century had been mainly occupied with the struggle for supremacy among the three great kingdoms, Northumbria, Mercia and Wessex; and a tumultuous sea of troubles had resulted from the clashing of the three great tribal waves.   By the year 756 the hopes of Northumbria had been completely destroyed; and we have a sad record of insurrection, usurpation, bloodshed and murder.   For more than a century no Northumbrian king died in peaceful possession of the throne.   Some were murdered; some were banished; some in despair abdicated and took the monastic vows.   An insane spirit of insubordination seems to have possessed the people; the nobles were continually in rebellion, and the country was wasted by unceasing strife, while pestilence and famine intensified the horror which prevailed.   In the year 823 the power of Mercia was broken by Ecgberht of Wessex on the bloody field of Ellandune,

Hen. of Hunt.
Bk IV.

and "Ellandune's stream ran red with blood, was choked with the slain, became foul with the carnage."   Shortly afterwards all the tribes of the centre and south submitted to his sway.   In 827 he advanced against the Northumbrians, who met him with offers of submission and allegiance.   By 828 he had made himself overlord both of the English and the Welsh.   Are we now to have a united people, owning the same king, pursuing a common destiny?   Such was Ecgberht's aim.

In his youth he had been forced to take refuge at the court of Charlemagne, and there, in the great Empire of the West, he had seen and learned much of the art of the con-

Will. of Malm.
II. I.

queror and administrator.   To Charlemagne's example he was indebted for the formation of his ideal of a united England, as well as for the methods by which he achieved his great political success.

But scarcely had England attained so far towards unity when the blight set in, first in the north, and then working southwards through the whole country. For a time all progress was stayed, and even the ground which had been gained was lost. The Danes had begun to appear upon the English coast as early as the year 787; and the manner of their reception was in some respects not unlike that of Beowulf and his men upon the shore near Heorot, though with a very different ending. The Englishman was suspicious of the strangers, and not without just cause. "Three ships came first in the days of King Beorhtric, and the reeve rode to them, and wanted to make them go with him to the king's 'tûn,' because he knew not what they were; and they slew him."

A.-S. Chron. 787.

A superstitious sense of impending doom, which shook the Englishman's courage and unnerved his arm, began to settle over the land. In 793 "many dire prodigies came upon the land of the Northumbrians and miserably terrified the people; there were great flashes of lightning, and fiery dragons were seen flying in the air. A great famine soon followed these tokens; and a little afterwards in the same year, on the 8th of January, the ravaging of heathen men wretchedly devastated the Church of God on Lindisfarne with plundering and slaughter." Such forebodings were by no means confined to the ignorant and foolish. Alcuin, the most learned scholar of the time, lately come from the court of Charlemagne, believed that he saw, in the time of Lent, a rain of blood falling from the summit of the roof of the northern side of St Peter's Church at York, though the day was fair. "Is it not a sign that blood must come upon the land from the north?" he asks. The carnage came, and the North was overwhelmed. "Behold, every holy place is laid waste by the heathen; the earth is stained with the blood of princes." "Behold, the Church of St Cuthbert is sprinkled with the blood of God's priests, stripped of all its ornaments, given up to the spoiling of the heathen."

793, E.

Alc. Epist. Will. of Malm. I. 3.

The Danish attacks soon became regularly organised and much more formidable; and the English were called upon to face just such an invasion as they themselves had inflicted upon the earlier inhabitants of Britain. The Danes disembarked in the river mouths in unexpected quarters, pushed rapidly into the heart of the country, and seized various strategical points as centres for further raids. Often they found horses for themselves, and so pushed on with double speed, while the people fled in panic before them. Their attacks were usually unexpected and bewildering. Devastation marked their path; everywhere they ravaged the

Hen. of Hunt.
Bk v. Pref.
Ant. Lib.

towns and villages, carrying fire and sword throughout the land, sparing neither age nor sex; and unspeakable horror prevailed. To meet them the English levied their fighting strength, and prepared to follow up their foes and force them to give battle. Usually they tried to cut off the raiding bands, or else to make a sudden attack upon the Danish camp. But the invaders seemed to be everywhere. If the English heard of them towards the east, and hastened to meet them there, the next report would be of ravages in the south; if they turned towards the south, the Danes would appear in the west; and soon would follow like tidings from the north. "Whither are ye marching, O noble chieftains? The Danes have descended upon the north. Already have they burnt your halls; even now are they carrying off your wealth; they are tossing your young children aloft on the points of their spears; of your wives, some have they forcibly dishonoured, others have they carried away with them into slavery." And the warrior bowed his head in despair that his sin had brought this requital upon him. "Both kings and people, in bewilderment, lost their vigour both of mind and body, and were utterly prostrated." When at last they encountered the enemy, stubborn and bloody was the warfare; each side fought with determination to the last, and victory was now to the one, and now to the other. Often the invaders lost heavily, even more heavily than their adversaries, and yet it frequently happened that the English attack died away, and the Danes were left in possession of the battlefield. Then they would afterwards depart to the coast and put to sea with immense booty. If the English won, the victory could rarely be pressed home, for the Danes would hasten to escape under cover of night to commence fresh raids elsewhere.

Naturally, a warfare of invasion and plunder is always the most ruthless and ferocious; ferocity upon the one side begets its like upon the other. A measure of the cruel character of the Danes may be seen in the fact that one Keary, *Vikings in West. Christm.* p. 145. of their leaders, who once protested against the inhuman practice of tossing little children upon the points of spears, received the derisive nickname of " Börn" (the Child). And the Englishman was no less severe in his methods of re- taliation. In 794 " the heathen ravaged among the Northum- *A.-S. Chron.* 794, E. brians, and plundered Ecgferth's monastery at the mouth [of the Wear]; and there one of their leaders was slain, and also some of their ships were wrecked by a storm, and many of them there were drowned, and some got to the shore alive, and those were soon 'slain-off' at the mouth [of the river]." Thus the merciless struggle began. To the Englishman, embittered by the ravaging of his land, the Dane was a heathen, an accomplice of Satan, and as such received less consideration when taken than was accorded to the wild beast on the wold. It was not till later, in the brighter days when the Dane after defeat became a Christian, that he was regarded as a man and a brother.

In the year 832 the Danes harried Sheppey; and in the 832. next year Ecgberht was defeated by them at Charmouth in Dorset, where there was a great slaughter. Two years later they formed an alliance with the Welsh of Cornwall, but Ecgberht defeated the combined forces at Hingston Down. Shortly afterwards, however, the king died; and all hope of the realisation of his dream of sovereignty was soon dispelled.

In the year 851 the purpose of the struggle under- 851. went a partial change. Then, for the first time, the Danes wintered in England, and the raids developed into a war of occupation. Three hundred and fifty of their ships lay at the mouth of the Thames, and devastated all the country near. The English were fully aware of the danger which threatened them, and made a brave attempt to rid themselves of the intruders. Though the king of Mercia was defeated, three victories were gained at " Wicganbeorge[1]," Sandwich and Ockley, and in the last of the three " there was the greatest slaughter in the heathen army that we heard tell of until this present day." Yet the hold of the Danes upon the country, though severely shaken, was not lost. In 867 they 867. dashed across the Humber from East Anglia, and occupied York, which lay open to surprise owing to internal dissen-

[1] Identification doubtful.

sions in Northumbria. A belated attempt to retake the city failed, and a great number of the Northumbrians were slain, together with their two rival kings who, when it was too late, had joined forces against the common foe.

In such dissensions and general disunion in face of the enemy the weak spot appears among the English of the north. The lessons which the Church had tried to teach, and the unity for which Ecgberht had striven, were alike forgotten in the crisis. For two centuries the Danes will be predominant in the north and east; and York has already become the centre from which they make their raiding expeditions. The glory of the famous school passes away, though it may be that some small remnant of its learning still lingers in quiet and secluded places. But most of its scholars have already fled southwards, bearing with them the manuscripts they value most. The blight has set in; monasteries, abbeys, churches, schools, all perish in the general decay. In East Anglia the Danes destroyed all the monasteries they came to, among others that at Peterborough, 870, E. which they burned. "They slew the abbot and the monks; and all that they found there, that before was very rich, they made so that it became nothing." In Wessex, in 871, "there 871. were nine pitched battles fought with the Danish army in the kingdom south of the Thames, besides which Alfred, the king's brother, and single 'ealdormen' and king's thegns often rode on raids which were not counted; and this year nine earls and one king were slain." What scant opportunity was there remaining for the preacher and the scholar! Surely

Alcuin's *Ep.* this is the work of the Great Adversary, thinks the pious
Wulfstan's Englishman bitterly. Surely he is in league with the foe
Sermo ad Angl. to overthrow the Church of God, and to afflict His people;
Asser's *Life of* and the Almighty has given them over to destruction be-
Alfred. cause of their sins. This is but the beginning of the end; these are but the signs of the great Day of the Lord, when the thousand years shall be accomplished.

So the English were tried, and in their trial were bent and strained, almost to the breaking point, by their own blood brothers, in whom were to be found just those characteristics they themselves had possessed some three centuries before. Again the warrior rushes to seize his weapons with thoughts of revenge and slaughter uppermost in his mind, and without any preconceived and regularly concerted plan. The barbarian is once more supreme in England; the scholar and priest take refuge in flight; and the hand of progress is set back upon the dial-plate of time. The line of development is, as it were, bent over and turned backwards upon itself. But from this warfare the Englishman will learn three great lessons of vital importance: that he must unite with his fellows, with one to lead; that one definite and national policy must provide for the defence of the whole country; that again he must turn his attention to the sea, whence his enemies had descended upon his shores where and when they willed. Otherwise it had proved quite impossible to cope with the elusive Danes. Thus it is that the world is ever directed onwards by means of its very failures.

During the time of this terrible visitation there were some men of noble character who rose above their miseries to the most heroic patriotism and self-sacrifice, whose adversity but brought out all that was best in them to oppose the widespread degeneration which had set in. One such was Edmund, king of East Anglia. Rather more than a hundred years after his death Ælfric told his story in his *Lives of the Saints*, alleging that the ultimate authority for it was the king's own swordbearer, who, when very old, told it to King Athelstan in the days of Dunstan's youth. Dunstan, in turn, told the story, three years before his death, to a certain monk, who wrote it in a book; and this book Ælfric says he has translated into English. The Christian idealisation of the monk is, of course, clearly apparent, the story being closely modelled upon the popular Christian legends, but it will serve to illustrate, not only the time, but also the monkish mind at a period when the Danes were again threatening to overwhelm the country. It certainly reveals the Englishman's ideal of the Christian patriot and saint. *Ælfric, Life of King Edmund.*

Edmund the Blessed was a wise and worthy king who always honoured the Almighty. He was virtuous and humble-minded, ever remembering the precept, "If thou art set up as a ruler, exalt not thyself, but be among men as one of them." He was charitable to the poor and widows as a father; with benevolence he guided his people always to righteousness, and restrained the cruel, and lived blessedly in the true faith. In his reign the Danes came with a fleet, *Ibid.*

harrying and slaying throughout the land, "just as their custom is." Under the leadership of the chieftains Hinguar and Hubba, "united through the devil," they landed first, with their ashen war-ships, in Northumbria, laid waste the land, and slew the people. Then, in the year 870, they divided their forces, and Hinguar stole suddenly, like a wolf, upon East Anglia, and slew the inhabitants, men, women and innocent children, and shamefully treated the guiltless Christians. A messenger was sent to Edmund demanding his submission: "Hinguar our king, brave and victorious by sea and land, has command of many peoples, and now has landed here with his army in haste to find winter quarters for himself and his host. Now he bids thee quickly to divide with him thy secret gold-hoards and the treasures of thine ancestors, and to become his under-king, if thou wilt live, because thou hast not the might to withstand him." Edmund sought the advice of a certain bishop who was nearest at hand, but the bishop, being afraid, counselled him to do as Hinguar bade. The king remained silent, and looked upon the ground; then at last replied in kingly fashion, "Lo! Bishop, too shamefully are these poor people ill-treated; it were dearer to me now to fall in fight, if only my people might keep their land." The bishop replied, "Lo! dear King, thy people lie slain, and thou hast not the force to fight, and these pirates will come and bind thee alive, unless thou save thy life either by flight or ransom." Then said King Edmund, so very brave was he: "I neither purpose nor desire in my heart that I alone should remain after my dear thegns, who, in their beds, with children and wives, were suddenly slain by these pirates. It is not my wont to flee, and I would rather die, if need be, for mine own land. God Almighty knows that I will never depart from His worship nor from His true love, live I or die." He then turned to the messenger and said: "Surely thou art worthy of death; but I will not defile my clean hands in thy foul blood, because I follow Christ, Who so taught us. Go now quickly and say to thy cruel lord, 'Never will Edmund bend to Hinguar, the heathen chieftain, in life, except he first bend in this land with faith to Christ the Saviour.'" This answer was conveyed to the Dane who was already advancing. When he came to Edmund, the king stood within his hall unarmed, having cast away his weapons, mindful of the example of Christ when He forbade Peter to use the sword against His captors. The Danes took him, bound him, and treated him ignominiously, beating him with rods. Then they led him to a tree, tied him thereto with strong bands, and again beat him for a long time with many strokes. And he cried continually between the strokes with true faith to Christ the Saviour. Then the heathen became mad with rage because of his faith, and because he called upon Christ to help him. They shot at him as though in sport, until he was all beset with their arrows like the bristles of a hedgehog, "just as Sebastian was." At last Hinguar, despairing of breaking down his faith, ordered him to be beheaded, and so the heathen drew the holy one to slaughter, even then still calling upon Christ. With one stroke they struck off his head, and his soul departed, blessed, to be with the Saviour. "There was a man near by, hidden by God from the heathen, who heard all this, and told it afterwards as we here say it." Whatever strokes have been added to the picture by the monkish pen, the details of the Danish raid seem to be correct, and the character of Edmund is true to the Anglo-Christian ideal.

Of like devotion to his people, and of like piety, but far stronger, far more practical, far more patient, was Alfred, rightly called "the Great," and long remembered as "the shepherd and darling of the English." By the year 874 the Danish occupation had reached southwards to Mercia, which became a vassal state, the king, a nominee of the Danes, swearing oaths of fealty, and giving hostages that he would come to the aid of the Danes with all his followers whenever they were in need. Nothing could lay greater emphasis than this upon the lack of unity among the English, though the Danes were so nearly akin to them that alliance first and absorption afterwards were no difficult matters. Apparently the Mercians, tired of the incessant strife in which they have suffered most severely, see both reason and advantage in exchanging the alliance of straitened Wessex for that of the conquering Danes; and loyalty to the national cause is not strong enough to forbid. The state of the country is deplorable; life in its every aspect is altogether precarious. The age is an age of deterioration. In the midst of it a strong man

Proverbs of Alfred, 10.

A.-S. Chron. 874.

arises, Alfred of Wessex, and for a time, by the strength
of his own personality, delays the catastrophe, nay, even
gains ground against the forces of decadence; and round
him he gathers a meagre band of helpers, all too few to stem
the tide completely. He is a genius of manifold parts, with
all the characteristics of the Teutonic blood united to the
experience and balance of mind which proceed from the Latin
culture. He is dogged and wonderfully cautious, thoughtful
and pious, with an unbounded confidence in the destiny of
his nation, refusing to despair at the critical state of its
fortunes. He is no fanciful dreamer, no self-centred ascetic,
but a plain, practical man of affairs, and yet one who can
transmit something of his own enthusiasm, something of his
own energy, into those who move around him. In the
Proverbs of Alfred, written some time after the Norman
Conquest, we see what the Englishman has always thought
of him:

Proverbs of
Alfred, 17.

"Alfred he was in England
And king exceeding strong.
He was king, and he was clerk,
Well he lovëd Godës work.
He was wise in his word,
And ware in his work;
He was the wisest man
That was in England."

A.-S. Chron.
878.
Asser's *Life of*
Alfred.

    In 878 Alfred and Wessex alone remained as the last
hope of England, and they also were in a perilous state.
That year the Danes overran Wessex, and many of the
folk were driven over sea. Of the others the greater part
were ridden down and compelled to surrender, but the
king himself escaped. With a little troop, after much hardship, he got away through the woods and moorland fastnesses
till he came to Athelney, a hidden retreat in the midst of
treacherous marsh and bog. There he made a fortified camp,
and sat close, waiting his opportunity. All England was
now practically in the hands of the Danes; but Alfred was
resolute, and far from giving up all as lost. There is a secret
gathering of his forces, a sally, a sudden attack, a rout of
the Danish host, a fortnight's siege of their camp, a surrender, and the south is saved. The Danes give hostages,
and swear great oaths that they will leave the kingdom, and
also promise that Guthrum their king shall be baptised.

Three weeks afterwards Guthrum comes to fulfil his pledge with twenty-nine of his most honourable men, and remains twelve days with the king, who honours him and his men greatly with gifts. At the same time a treaty is made by which all the south is won back from the Danes, and other laws are drawn up "which all have decreed and with oaths confirmed...who reck of God's mercy or of ours." In spite of all his anxieties and trials his religion stands first with the king; and he seems to value his victory all the more because he has tamed and made Christian the king of his foes. This desire of the English to baptise a defeated enemy is remarkable, and seems to have been fairly common. In or about the year 943 King Edmund in the same way received two kings, Anlaf and Regnald, in baptism.

Alf. and Guth. Peace.
A.-S. Laws,
Thorpe, p. 66.

A.-S. Chron.
943, D.

The dark cloud has broken in the south, and the horizon begins to clear; but the fighting still continues in many places, for the Danes have several leaders. Alfred is extremely practical in all that he does, and takes advantage of his victory to set his forces on a sound footing. He organises patrols where the country is defenceless; he divides his levy into two parts, so that half are at home and half afield in turn, and thus a constant force is provided, with a fixed term of service and a fixed period for rest and refreshment; and he organises a defence for the towns. Henceforth the danger of unexpected attack is greatly decreased. But he also sees the great advantage which the Danes derive from their superior fleet. The eyes of the land-dweller cannot follow their path upon the deep, and from the sea they descend rapidly, and work their mischief before the levy can gather in sufficient strength to meet them in the field. When outnumbered they can easily depart to their ships, and then pursuit of them is impossible. If defeated with heavy loss they speedily reinforce their depleted forces with fresh bands from beyond the sea. As long as they hold command of the sea their numbers increase continually, "so that though thirty thousand were slain in one battle, others would fill their places to double the number." Means must therefore be devised to meet them upon the water with a fleet equal, or if possible superior, to their own; and Alfred at once proceeds to build one. The design of the ships is his own, and after neither the Danish nor the Frisian model. They are nearly twice as

894.

cf. 885.

Asser, *Life of Alfred.*

A.-S. Chron.
897, A.

long as the Danish ships, and swifter, steadier and higher, with sixty oars or more. He appoints regular crews for these vessels, and gives them the duty of watching the coasts, and preventing the enemy from obtaining supplies from abroad. The wisdom of the plan is soon evident, for the Danish ships are compelled to put out in all weathers; many of them are wrecked, and the remainder rendered less capable of offering a stout resistance when attacked.

Asser, Life of Alfred.

In the year 897[1] there was a sharp engagement on the southern coast, noteworthy as the first exploit of the new navy. Six Danish war-ships, after doing much mischief, were lying in a harbour on the south coast, and Alfred ordered nine of his new ships to cut them off from the open sea. When the English arrived at the harbour mouth three of the Danes were aground, but the remaining three, perceiving their danger, came out in a brave attempt to escape. Six of the English intercepted them, and a running fight seems to have taken place, in which two of the Danish ships were captured, and their crews slain; one escaped with the loss of all its crew save five. The other three English ships rowed close in to attack the Danes who were aground, but ran aground themselves; and when their consorts came up later they also did the same, but on the opposite beach. When the tide ebbed, the Danes left their ships to attack the three English near them, and a fierce fight took place upon the shore, the English losing sixty-two of their number, and the Danes a hundred and twenty. Meanwhile, according to one chronicler, the English across the channel could be seen beating their breasts and tearing their hair while they looked on, unable to cross over to assist in the fray. The English seem to have been hard pressed, when at last the tide turned, and floated off the Danish vessels before they could push off theirs of deeper draught. The Danes seized the opportunity to escape, and rowed out of the harbour, pursued, when too late, by the attacking fleet. But they were in such a sorry state that two of the three ships were cast upon the coast of Sussex, and there captured. Their crews were led to Winchester, and hanged by order of the king. The remaining ship escaped to East Anglia, then in the hands of the Danes, its crew

A.-S. Chron. 897, A. Hen. of Hunt. Bk v.

Hen. of Hunt. Bk v.

[1] The dates from 893 onwards have all been increased by one by the scribe; probably the original dates were correct.

being sorely wounded. In that same summer no less than twenty Danish ships, men and all, perished by the south coast. Alfred's severe treatment of the captured crews shows that he regarded them as pirates and oathbreakers, and this makes it clear that he had now the upper hand. He did not always make such stern reprisals, for when the wife and sons of Hæsten were captured in 894 he gave them back again, because one of them was his godson.

A.-S. Chron. 894.

After his treaty with Guthrum, Alfred's main policy was to consolidate that portion of the country which his victories had preserved, and to make his own kingdom strong against attack, rather than to extend his frontiers. Not only was his plan successful, but by degrees the Danish power was rendered weaker and weaker, until in the days of Edward his son, and Athelstan his grandson, expansion became possible, and the north as well as the south again came, at least nominally, under English rule. Then it seemed as though the English might after all weather the storm.

Throughout this trying time the English had maintained their close relationship with Rome, to whom they looked for comfort and sympathy in their affliction. The faith of many was indeed sorely tried, since the Church could lend no great material aid. When the first onslaught came, and Lindisfarne was destroyed, even Alcuin had cried out that St Cuthbert could not save his own, but yet his belief that the outcome was in the hands of the Almighty never wavered. Many fell away, and relapsed into heathenism or religious indifference; but the faith of those who still remained true shone all the brighter. They saw the hand of God in all things, and when at length a time of rest came to the weary land, it was "through the mercy of God" that their prayers were answered. Nor did they forget their thank-offerings to the Church. After his great victory at Ockley King Athelwulf granted by deed the tenth part of his land throughout all his kingdom to the praise of God and for his own eternal salvation, and in the same year went to Rome with great splendour. Alfred is especially noteworthy in this respect after his victories, as he frequently sends alms to Rome by a messenger of high rank, so frequently indeed that an omission receives comment in the *Chronicle* in 889: "In this year there was no journey to Rome, except that King Alfred

A.-S. Chron. 883, E, 897, A.

855.

889.

sent two couriers with letters." Against one of the records
of these alms-bearing missions some later scribe has written

887, E. in the margin, "Elemosinā nō Debitū!" thus showing that
the Englishman did not regard himself as being a tributary
to Rome. In return, the Roman, perhaps being himself
deceived rather than wilfully deceiving, seems to have imposed
upon the Englishman, whose credulity made deception easily

883. possible. In 883 Pope Marinus sent to King Alfred what
was professed to be a piece of the wood of the true Cross.
We can easily understand with what veneration such a gift
would be received by those among whom the poetry of
Cynewulf had been preserved.

When victory in the field has given respite for a season
from the anxieties of war, Alfred turns to educate the people
over whom he rules. Though he loves, and is well acquainted

Asser, *Life of Alfred*. with, the old songs of his fatherland, he has no time to spare
to add to their number, for he is too busily employed upon
more urgent matters. Little leisure has he also for the learned
vanities and conceits of the pedant, but true learning has for
him a certain substantial value of its own, and this he has
determined to acquire both for himself and his people. There
are laws to be made, and much lawlessness to be checked.
Therefore he draws up a national code of law which includes

A.-S. Laws, Thorpe, p. 26. Laws of Alfred, 49. the chief tenets of the Old and New Testaments, and is
supplementary to the laws of Ine, one of his predecessors.
There is one law which in his opinion includes every other
law: "And that which ye will that other men do not unto
you, do ye not that to other men. From this one doom
a man may remember to judge every one righteously;
he need heed no other doom-book." How modest is the
king! He dare not set down many laws of his own making;
for who can say how posterity will regard them? So he is
careful to follow the established laws of the land to which his
Witan give assent. "I, then, Alfred, king, gathered these
together,...for I durst not venture to set down in writing
much of my own, for it was unknown to me what of it would
please those who should come after us." The Englishman
can already give his laws their just value.

Again, he prepares to raise the intelligence of his people
by translating those books which seem to him most famous
and most useful; and so once more the English come in

touch with Latin learning. His own desire for knowledge is insatiable; and he confesses with sorrow that one of the greatest difficulties and impediments in his life has been the lack of teachers when he was young. He tells us that he often thought of the days that were past, how prosperous they were, how distinguished for wisdom, piety, peace and morality. Then the nation extended its borders, and had good success both in war and in learning. Then ecclesiastics were zealous about teaching and learning and the services of God. Then men came from abroad seeking wisdom and learning in England, but now the English themselves must go abroad for them if they desire them. So completely has all learning passed away that there are very few south of the Humber who can understand their mass-book, or even translate a letter from Latin into English; and he imagines that there are not many beyond the Humber who can do so. "So few of them there were, when I succeeded to the kingdom," says the king, "that I cannot call to mind even a single one south of the Thames....Think what punishments then came upon us before this world, when we neither loved wisdom ourselves nor allowed other men to do so. We loved the name alone that we were Christian, and very few of us loved the Christian virtues." He remembers how, before the harrying, the churches were full of books and treasures, and there were many servants of the Lord all over England; but now, through wilful neglect, wisdom has passed away. He purposes, with the co-operation of the bishops, to remedy the evil. "Therefore it seems to me better, if it seem so to you, that we also should translate some books, which it is most necessary that all men should know, into the language which we all can understand; and that we should bring it about, as we very easily may with God's help, if we have peace, that all young freemen now in England, who are rich enough to devote themselves to it, may be set to learning while they can find no other occupation, until such time as they can read English well. Let one then teach further in Latin those whom it is desired to teach further, and to advance to a higher order." And so the king himself sets the example, planning and working that his people may recover the ground which has been lost. The books upon which he works, with the help of the band of teachers whom he has

Asser, *Life of Alfred.*

Pref. Trans. Greg. Past. Care.

invited into the country, and which he considers to be most beneficial to his people, are the Histories of Bede and Orosius, the *Pastoral Care* of Gregory, and the *Consolation of Philosophy* of Boethius. No light or frivolous books are these, nor are they creations of the poet's art; all are representative of the learning of the age. "When I then remembered how the Latin lore before this was fallen away among the English, and that, nevertheless, many could read English writing, then began I among other various and manifold cares of this kingdom to turn into English the book which is called in Latin 'Pastoralis,' and in English 'Hierdebôc,' sometimes word for word, sometimes sense for sense, as I learned it from Plegmund mine archbishop, and from Asser my bishop, and from Grimbald my mass-priest, and from John my mass-priest. When I then had learned it, so that I understood it and could translate it most intelligibly, I turned it into English; and to each bishopric in my kingdom I will send one; and in each shall be a book-mark worth fifty 'mancessa.' And I command in God's name that no man remove the mark from the book, nor the book from the minster; it is unknown how long there may be bishops as learned as now, thanks to God, there are nearly everywhere. Therefore I would that they should be always at the place, unless the bishop desires to have his book with him, or it be somewhere for a loan, or someone be making a copy of it."

Alfred's own children are carefully educated, either privately at court, or in the schools with the children of the nobility and of many who are not noble. In the schools both

Asser, *Life of Alfred.* Latin and English books are read, writing is taught, and the Psalms and English poems committed to memory, so that before the boys are old enough to engage in the manly arts, such as hunting and the pursuits befitting their birth, they may become studious and practised in the liberal arts. The sons of the nobility who are brought up in the royal household Alfred causes to be carefully instructed "in all kinds of good morals," and provides, among other things, that they shall receive regular instruction in literature.

It is a time of work to make up for that which has been lost. The Englishman seems to have laid aside for a space his power of original composition, but still retains his love for the songs of the past. He has lost, too, something of his dreaminess, something of his passionate inspiration. Time must be given him before he can recover his elasticity, and become completely himself again. For the present he is humble, practical, useful and prosaic. His weakness has been revealed to him, and his sole aim is to overcome it by closest application to the task which his king has set before him. But he will sing again before many more years have elapsed, when the danger will seem to have been for the time surmounted.

Alfred was succeeded by his son Edward who, by a series of brilliant victories, made himself overlord of the English, Welsh, Danes and Scots, thus completing the design which his father had left unfinished. His success greatly inspirited his people. Their fear of the Danes began to disappear, and indeed they came to regard their enemies with contempt and derision. No small share of the credit for this success was due to his sister Ethelfled, Lady of the Mercians, a worthy daughter of Alfred, " as she was a powerful accession to his party, the delight of his subjects, the dread of his enemies, a woman of an enlarged soul." It was commonly reported of her that she thought it unbecoming to the daughter of a king to take delight in conjugal ties and family cares, since her country demanded of her duties of a wider range. Following the example of his own training, Edward carefully provided for the education of his children. His daughters devoted themselves to literature, and to the use of the distaff and the needle ; his sons were educated so that first of all they might have the fullest benefit of learning, in order that when the duty of governing the state should devolve upon them they might rule " not like rustics but philosophers."

The afterglow of Alfred's success, and the fruits of his thoughtful care, remain for many years after his death. Again for a time the Englishman is master in his own land, and prides himself upon his birthright, while he makes strenuous, though perhaps erratic, efforts to attain to his former excellence. Now he begins to cast off his depression, and to recover his buoyancy of temperament; and again his heart swells proudly as he dwells upon the glorious deeds of his countrymen. Once again the voice of the gleeman is heard in the land, exulting over the great day at Brunan-

A.-S. Chron. 921, 924.

Will. of Malm. II. 5.

burg in 937, when the Danes and their allies, the Scots, were
driven in flight to their ships, leaving behind them five
under-kings, seven earls, and many warriors, dead upon the
battle-field.

> "937. Here Athelstan the king, lord of earls,
> Ring-giver of heroes, and his brother also,
> Edmund the Atheling, life-long glory
> Won in the strife with edges of swords
> Around Brunanburg. They clove the shield-wall,
> Hewed down the linden shields with the forged swords,
> The offspring of Edward, as was natural to them
> From their lineage, so that they oft in the field
> Against every foe defended their land,
> Their hoard and their homes. The enemy bowed low,
> People of the Scots and the sea-rovers,
> Doomed they fell. Warriors brave
> Covered the field, since the rising sun
> In the morning tide, the glorious star,
> Glided over the grounds, bright candle of God,
> The eternal Lord, until the noble creature
> Sank to its rest. There lay many a warrior
> Of the northern men laid low with spears,
> Shot over the shield, and the Scottish too,
> Weary, sated with war. The West Saxons forth,
> All day long in pursuing troops,
> Followed on the track of the loathly people,
> Hewed down the fugitives severely from behind
> With swords mill-sharpened. The Mercians refused not
> Hard hand-play to any of the heroes
> Who with Anlaf o'er the waves' blending,
> In the ship's bosom, sought the land,
> Doomed in the fight. Five young kings
> Lay dead on the battle-field,
> Put to sleep with swords; seven also
> Of Anlaf's earls; a countless host
> Of sailors and Scots. There was put to flight
> The lord of the Northmen, compelled by need
> To the prow of his ship with a little troop.
> The galley hurried to sea; the king escaped;
> Out on the fallow flood he saved his life.
> Likewise also the old one came in flight
> Into his north country, Constantinus
> The hoary warrior. He needed not exult
> In the meeting of swords; he was shorn of his kinsmen,
> Deprived of his friends, on the battle-ground,
> Bereft in the strife. And he left his son,
> Young in war, mangled with wounds,

On the slaughter-field. He needed not boast,
The grey-haired hero, of the slashing of the bills,
The old malignant, nor Anlaf the more.
With their host's remnant they needed not laugh
That they were better at the war-work,
On the battle-field, at the clashing of banners,
At the meeting of spears, the contest of men,
At the exchange of weapons, after they on the slaughter-field
Had played with the offspring of Edward.
    Departed then the Northmen in their nailed galleys,
Bloody spear-remnant, on the dashing sea,
Over the deep water, to seek Dublin,
Their own land again, disgraced in mood.
    Likewise then the brothers, both together,
King and Atheling, sought their own people,
The West Saxon land, exulting in war.
Behind them they left to divide the corpses
The dusky-coated one, the swart raven,
With horny beak, and the grey-feathered
Eagle, white of tail, to enjoy the carrion,
The greedy war-hawk, and that grey beast
The wolf on the wold. Never was there greater slaughter
In this island ever yet,
Of folk cut down, before this,
With edges of swords, of which the books tell us,
And the old sages, since hither from the east
Came Angles and Saxons, earls eager for glory,
O'er the broad wave, and Britain sought,
Proud smiths of war, and conquered the Welshmen,
And won this land."

And five years later there is a poetical record of Edmund's 942, A.
re-conquest of the five Danish burghs, Leicester, Lincoln,
Nottingham, Stamford and Derby.

Light shines once more upon the dark places. After all,
it is good to be strong and brave and successful in war.
After all, the delights of victory are very sweet; and the
Englishman feels that he is back again in the heroic age as
the impassioned phrases of the war-songs of old leap once
more to his lips.

Other monkish chroniclers, less poetically gifted than their
predecessors, break into song when recording the coronation 973, A,
of Edgar and the glory of his reign, with his death in 975. 975, E.
" Kings honoured him far and wide, and submitted to him,
as was fitting. The Danish fleet was not so proud, nor the
Danish army so strong, that in England they gained for

themselves booty while the noble king held the throne."
Of Edgar's reign the Saxon chronicler is always enthusiastic.
In his days the kingdom prospered greatly, and God granted
him peace to the end of his life; and he did that which was
right and merited his prosperity. He upreared the praise
of God, and loved His law, and increased the security of the
people more than any of the kings who were before him in
the memory of man. God aided him, and kings and earls
eagerly inclined to him, and subjected themselves to his will,
so that without fighting he soon won over what he would.
He was greatly honoured throughout the land, because he
zealously revered the name of God, and obeyed His law,
and governed his people wisely in the sight of God and the
world. Nevertheless one fault was thought to attach to him
because he seemed to love foreign customs, and introduced
into the land heathen practices, inviting hither outlandish
men and people who harmed the land. "But may God grant
him that his good deeds be mightier than his misdeeds for
the protection of his soul on the long journey." These
so-called misdeeds sprang from his desire to deal out even-
handed justice to all who came beneath his sway, making no
distinction between Englishman and Dane, while attempting
to weld the two peoples into one nation. Defeated Danes
had submitted to him; many of them he had advanced to
high office; and this had not met with the approval of the
native-born, who could never free themselves from racial
prejudices. But already a strong Danish element had been
absorbed into the English stock, to bring about a general
hardening of character, and to make the national type more
like what it had been in the days of heathenism. It must be
added that some chroniclers make serious charges against
Edgar's private character, alleging gross immorality and
wanton lust; but usually these charges are overshadowed by
accounts of his personal bravery and capability as a ruler.
There is a story told concerning him, that Kinad, king of the
Scots, was overheard to say at a banquet that it was remarkable that so many kingdoms were subject to such a sorry
little fellow; and this remark was repeated to the king.
Soon afterwards Edgar invited the Scot to meet him privately
in a wood, ostensibly for the purpose of discussing matters
of great political importance. When they met, however, the

959, E.

Cf. *Will. of Malm.* II. 8.

Ibid.

Ibid.

king produced two swords, and offered to prove which of them was the more worthy to command. Kinad at once fell on his knees, and begged for pardon, which the king magnanimously granted him.

But another aspect of manners and character, beneath this recrudescence of the heroic spirit, remains to be unfolded. The violence of the age had its influence among men, even among the kings. It is said that Edgar took stern measures to check criminal violence and lawlessness, meeting wrong-doing with punishments of outrageous cruelty, putting the robber to death, often after terrible mutilation. With eyes put out, nostrils slit, and ears torn off, with hands and feet cut off, and scalps torn away, miserable wretches were exposed to the ravenings of birds and beasts of prey, and left to die. King Edmund, brother of Athelstan, banished a robber named Leofa, but at a royal banquet the latter was seen seated among the guests. This audacious act so enraged the king that, losing all sense of kingly dignity, he leaped upon the outlaw, seized him by the hair, and dragged him to the floor, whereupon Leofa drew a hidden dagger and mortally wounded him. The king's thegns then closed with the slayer, and tore him limb from limb, though not before he had wounded several of them.

Vita Swythuni, Will. of Malm., Ant. Lib. p. 158, note.

Will. of Malm. II. 7.

On the other hand, after their victories, many suffered their muscles to relax, and their hearts to grow cold, while they indulged in pursuits which added to their own pleasures but sapped their country's strength. In those days the Englishman never saw very far ahead, and Alfred's influence was already on the wane. The clergy, upon whom so much depended, to whom the country should have looked for light and leading, had soon begun to forget their high calling, and to busy themselves with worldly affairs. Frequently, contrary to the ecclesiastical vows, the priests took to themselves wives, and among them cases of divorce and bigamy were not unknown. The pleasures of the chase, of eating and drinking, occupied the minds of many of them more than the oversight of their cures. There was again a great need for reform ; and, naturally, when the reaction set in, the reforming party went to the other extreme of strictest asceticism, being influenced to a great extent by a similar movement then in progress across the channel, originating from the monastery of Cluny.

The heart and soul of the new movement was Dunstan, who, amid much opposition, gradually won his way to the achievement of his stern ideal. He was a keen, intellectual and strong-willed man, whose personality dominated all with whom he came in contact, whose zeal for the Church and monasticism took precedence of every thought and care. He was the greatest patron of the liberal arts throughout the kingdom, and a most munificent restorer of monasteries. He never shrank from denouncing in words of righteous indignation the wickedness of kings, nobles and clergy, but to the poor he was ever fatherly and kind. Though Hallam and Milman formed no high opinion of him, Bishop Stubbs regarded him as a good and faithful servant, with nothing grotesque, nothing of the tyrannical ascetic in his character, as "a constructor not a destroyer, a consolidator not a pedantic theorist, a reformer not an innovator, a politician not a bigot, a statesman not a zealot," though filled with zeal for the purity of marriage. Yet it seems that in his iron-bound plan there was insufficient place for that free, intellectual and individual energy which speaks of vigorous life and growth. He seems to have held that man was not made to think and reason for himself, but only to obey, and that in temporal matters, as in spiritual, the sole ordaining and governing power upon earth was the outward and visible Church of the West, represented, in his eyes, by the monastic party, and exercising authority by means of the representatives of the monastic brethren. For the secular clergy he seems to have had neither respect nor regard. Striving to eliminate all that was weak and evil, he came to uphold that which had become in those days nothing but the narrowest and most domineering monasticism.

But the time for such a system to pass unchallenged and unopposed was well nigh past. The monks were no longer what they had been ; and, through the efforts of Alfred, the English layman had emerged from his former state of darkest ignorance. He had begun to know his own mind, and to exercise the faculty of reason with which he was endowed ; and the after-glow of this enlightenment had not altogether died away when Dunstan became strong enough to enforce his views. In consequence, for a time, he was the most hated man in England, but the strength of his personality gained him a party, and ultimately victory.

II. 8.

Stubbs, *Memorials of St Dunstan,* civ, cviii.

The despotic tendency of the monks and their jealousy of the secular clergy were at this period almost incredible. Though in a time of pestilence and plague Ethelwold, "the benevolent bishop," could break up the sacred vessels of the Church to feed the destitute, and much true-hearted charity was undoubtedly displayed, yet, when face to face with opposition, desire for the mastery appears to have carried many beyond themselves, and excesses of cruel austerity became quite barbaric in character. The story of the young king Edwy and his queen Elgyfa presents a tangled skein of mingled truth and fiction, but reveals the methods of Dunstan's party, and also the strength of the opposition which was aroused. It is said that Dunstan dragged Edwy with violence, on his coronation day, from Elgyfa's chamber, and that they were afterwards divorced by Archbishop Odo because they were related within the forbidden degrees, while some say that the unhappy woman was seared and hamstrung by order of the monastic party. Edwy may have been a wanton boy of fifteen ; Elgyfa may have been an abandoned woman ; Dunstan may have been actuated purely by righteous indignation ; but whatever the truth may be, and whatever happened, public opinion seems to have been on the side of the king. "This king wore the diadem not unworthily," says Henry of Huntingdon; "but after a prosperous and becoming commencement of his reign, its happy promise was cut short by a premature death." However, a storm of indignation arose which drove Dunstan and the monks into exile, leaving their places for the secular clergy. "At that time the face of monachism was sad and pitiable. Even the monastery of Malmesbury, which had been inhabited by monks for more than two hundred and seventy years, he [Edwy] made a sty for secular canons."

Shortly afterwards Edwy died ; Edgar came to the throne, and Dunstan was recalled in triumph, to become within three years bishop of the sees of Worcester and London, and archbishop of Canterbury. Thenceforth until his death the monastic influence was supreme. At once a great cleansing and restoration of the monasteries was begun at the instigation of Dunstan and Ethelwold. The secular clergy had the option of taking the monastic vows or resigning their offices, and when they refused to do either, they were driven out, and

A.-S. Chron. 984, A.

Will. of Malm. II. 7. *A.-S. Chron.* 958, D, etc.

Hen. of Hunt. Bk V.

Will. of Malm. II. 7.

A.-S. Chron. 963, E.

their places were filled by monks. Edgar tells us how he found
the monasteries in a ruinous condition, decaying, worm-eaten
and neglected, almost destitute of God's service, and how
"ejecting those illiterate clerks, subject to the discipline of
no regular order," he appointed in their stead "pastors of
a holier race, that is, of the monastic order," and found
them ample means out of the royal revenues to repair
their churches. The number of the monasteries was greatly
increased, and many bequests were made to provide
endowments for them, the privileges of the monks being
safe-guarded by the pope under a threat of a perpetual curse
and excommunication against any who should violate them.
Edgar supported Dunstan in all his projects; and from his
confirmation of the charter to Malmesbury he appears to
have been a strong partisan of Rome and the monks.
The papal mandate ran: "We ordain, moreover, that no
person shall have liberty to enter this island [Malmesbury],
either to hold courts, to make inquiry, or to correct"; and
Edgar writes[1]: "The decrees of pontiffs and the decisions
of priests are fixed by irrevocable bonds, like the foundations
of the mountains"; and again: "Let the same liberty and
power also as I have in my own court, as well in forgiving as
in punishing, and in every other matter, be possessed by the
abbot and monks of the aforesaid monastery within their
court. And should the abbot or any monk of that place,
upon his journey, meet a thief going to the gallows, or to
any other punishment of death, they shall have power of
rescuing him from the impending danger throughout my
kingdom. Moreover I confirm and establish...that the bishop
of Wells and his ministers shall have no power whatever over
this monastery, or its parish churches." William of Malmesbury comments thus upon the decrees: "If then the ordinance
of St Peter the apostle be binding, consequently that of
John the pope must be so likewise; but not even a madman
would deny the ordinance of Peter the apostle to be binding,
consequently no one in his sober senses can say that the
ordinance of John the pope is invalid. Either, therefore,
acknowledging the power conferred by Christ on St Peter
and his successors, they will abstain from transgressing

---

[1] Or is represented as writing. The acceptance of the record, even if forged,
is sufficient for our purpose.

against the authority of so dreadful an interdict, or else
contemning it, they will, with the devil and his angels,
bring upon themselves the eternal duration of the curse
aforewritten.... Wherefore let no man reading this despise it,
nor make himself conspicuous by being angry at it.... The
monastic order, for a long time depressed, now joyfully reared
its head."

But a change again took place in the fortunes of the
monastic party after Edgar's death. His son, Edward, was
but a "child unwaxen," and the feud broke out anew between
the monks and the secular canons, who desired, now that
Edgar's influence was no longer against them, to recover the
ecclesiastical possessions which had been theirs in Edwy's
days. Of course the monastic chroniclers make out a strong
case against their rivals. "In his days, on account of his *A.-S. Chron.*
youth, God's adversaries, Ælfere the 'ealdorman' and many *975, D.*
others, broke God's law and marred the monastic rule, dispersed the monasteries which King Edgar before commanded
the holy Bishop Ethelwold to establish, drove away the
monks, and put to flight God's servants. They despoiled
widows often and repeatedly, and many wrongs and evil
customs arose up afterwards, and ever things became rapidly
worse and worse." In Mercia, especially, we hear that the
monks had happened upon evil times. Many of the servants *975, A.*
of God and men of learning were driven out and scattered
abroad; everywhere the worship and praise of the Almighty
were overthrown and destroyed. "That was great mourning
to him who bore in his breast burning love for the Creator;
then was the Author of glories too greatly despised." But
here lie disclosed the seeds of that long-enduring contention
which ended only at the dissolution of the monasteries in the
reign of Henry VIII. There is already a strong popular
party to espouse the cause of the secular clergy against the
monks: "the principal people, as is the custom of the laity, *Will. of*
exclaiming more especially that the injury, which the [secular] *Malm.* II. 9.
canons had wrongfully suffered, ought to be redressed by
gentler measures." To settle the controversy, a synod was
held at Winchester, where the monks declared that the
crucifix spoke miraculously in their favour; and also again
a council at Calne, where the matter was debated with much
vehemence, Dunstan himself being especially singled out for

attack, and men of every degree fiercely upholding their several sides of the question. While the tumult was at its height the floor suddenly gave way, and all present, save Dunstan who stood upon a beam which retained its position, were either killed or severely injured. This event was regarded as a miracle approving Dunstan's cause, and henceforth the party of the secular canons made little headway against his authority.

It is but to be expected that at such a period there should have been a general recrudescence of a theological literature, such as the Homilies of Ælfric and the Blickling Manuscript. Again the Christian Englishman begins to think upon his end; and the near approach of the year 1000 A.D. fills him with dread. He has quite made up his mind that then the end of the world shall be.

A.-S. Chron.
973.

> "......And then were passed and gone
> Ten hundred winters of the tale of years
> From the birth-tide of the glorious King,
> Guardian of lights, save that there yet remained
> Of the count of winters, of which the writings speak,
> Twenty and seven. So nearly was the thousand
> Of the Lord of victories spent when this occurred."

Ælfric, Hom.
Blickling
Hom.

The sermons of the day harp upon this theme: Though none but God Himself can tell exactly when the day will fall, yet all the signs which Christ foretold have come to pass, save that Antichrist has not yet appeared; therefore the time must be at hand. Nation rises against nation; shameful and wicked wars are prevalent; deaths of men of high estate are frequent; diseases and famines are increasing; many evils are common, and no good remains. Every earthly thing is sinful; man's love for Christ has grown cold, and good works are neglected. Everywhere is lamentation and weeping, mourning and breach of peace, everywhere evil and slaughter, and the end is bitterness. The terrors of death and the Judgment, of hell and its torments, are again painted with vivid detail; and when the preacher has by this means sufficiently impressed his hearers, he turns to exhort them to repentance and faith, and to a pure and pious life. Ælfric, the disciple of Dunstan and Ethelwold, and the greatest prose writer of his day, firmly believes that the Judgment is at hand, and writes his homilies in order that by reading and learning men may be brought to resist the temptations of Antichrist when he shall appear. "Everyone may the more easily withstand the future temptation through God's support, if he is strengthened by book-learning." Preface, Ælfric, *Hom.* Thorpe, p. 4.

Yet at this time the Englishman was perhaps not so credulous as he once had been. The education of the generations past is now beginning to bear fruit, and his faculty of reason is already developing and beginning to work upon the heterogeneous mass of unsifted material which has been imposed upon him. In many matters of tradition and common report he has already a tendency towards scepticism, for he has come upon so much that will not stand testing. It is now possible for him to appraise authority at something approaching its just value, to weigh evidences, to choose and reject. "I have seen and heard," writes Ælfric, "of much error in many English books which unlearned men, through their simplicity, have esteemed as great wisdom." To realise that it is possible for even a book to lie is always the first great step towards purer truth. Ælfric questions the authenticity of the apocryphal narrations of the *Vision of Paul*, and notes that the apostle himself said that when he was caught up into Paradise he heard unspeakable words which it is not lawful for a man to utter. His criticism extends even to portions of the Bible itself, for, when asked to translate Genesis, he thinks that there are many things in the lives of the patriarchs, especially their polygamy, which are not suitable to be set before English Christians. He does not believe that miracles ever happen in his day, though he relates many concerning English saints: One who plants herbs or trees only waters them until they begin to grow, and then ceases; so God at the first worked miracles among the heathen, but when their faith was established then He ceased. The Englishman has already begun to discriminate between good and evil so far as to judge a dignitary according to his deeds rather than his office. He could oppose Dunstan when he thought that the reformer had gone too far. King Edred imprisoned an archbishop who had been strongly accused of treachery; and yet in the same year when the people of Thetford slew an abbot he punished them by putting many to death. So it seems that the crisis appertained not only to the national fortunes but also to the Pref. p. 2. *A.-S. Chron.* 952, D.

intellectual side of the national development. Just at this time no one could have ventured to prophesy what direction the line of the Englishman's development would take ; the Englishman himself saw nothing but the end of all things with the close of the century.

Will. of Maim. 11. 9.
A.-S. Chron. 979, E.

Greater troubles, however, were in store, amid which the ecclesiastical strife was forgotten. In 979 King Edward, tired and thirsty after hunting, came at eventide to the gate of Corfe Castle, and, while drinking, was stabbed by order of his step-mother, who had plotted to gain the throne for her own son Ethelred. Though severely wounded, the young king put spurs to his horse to escape, but one foot slipped from the stirrup, he fell, and was dragged along by the other and killed. " Never was a worse deed done to the English than this was, since they first sought Britain," says the Saxon chronicler. Ethelred succeeded to the throne, only to prove weak and absolutely incapable at a time of sorest need, when England required the strong hand of a soldier and statesman to meet the onset of her foes.

Battle of Maldon, 7.

Once again, in the year 991, the Danes descend upon Folkestone, Sandwich, Ipswich and Maldon, demanding as alternatives tribute or war. And the English warrior lays aside the chase ("he let then from his hand the dear hawk fly to the woods") and prepares his weapons, vowing that he will perform his boast that he would fight before his lord as long as he could hold shield and broad sword in his hands. Byrhtnoth, the "ealdorman," gathers the levy, and the two armies come face to face at Maldon. The English are drawn up in array by the bank of the Blackwater, and a messenger 29. from the Danes shouts his errand across the stream : " Bold seamen sent me to thee, bade me say to thee that thou must quickly send rings for your protection ; and better it is for you that ye buy off this spear-rush with tribute than that we should deal out strife so hard. We need not slay each other, if ye are rich enough ; we will, in return for the gold, confirm a peace. If thou, who art highest here, agreest that thou wilt ransom thy people, and give to the seamen, at their own choice, money for friendship, and wilt take peace from us, we will with the 'scot[1]' depart to our ships, sail away on the sea, and hold you in peace." And scornfully Byrhtnoth

---

[1] "sceattum."

answers, uplifting his shield, and brandishing his slender ashen spear: "Hearest thou, sea-rover, what this folk sayeth? 45. Spears will they give you for tribute, the venomous point and the old sword, war-weapons which shall not be good for you in the strife. Messenger of the seamen, return again and say to thy people a spell much more loathly to their ears, that here stands an undaunted earl with his host, who will defend this home-land, the country of Ethelred my prince, the people and their ground; the heathen shall fall in battle. Too shameful it seems to me that ye should go unfought to your ships with our tribute, now ye thus far have come hither into our land. Not so easily shall ye gain treasure; point and edge shall reconcile us, grim war-play, ere we pay tribute." But neither host can cross the river, now high with the flood tide, though some fall beneath the arrow-shower. When the ebb comes, Byrhtnoth bids three brave warriors, Wulfstan, Ceola's son, Ælfere and Maccus, hold the causeway across the ford by which alone a crossing can now be made. With his spear Wulfstan pierces the first bold Dane who sets his foot upon it, and the three fearlessly resist all attempts to force a way. Then the Danes ask free passage to lead their troops across the ford, and, in his pride, the Englishman grants their request and withdraws his men from the bank. It is a chivalrous, but foolish, piece of conceit and over-confidence when the fate of a nation is at stake. "Now that room is made for you, come quickly to us for the fight; God 93. alone knows who shall have the victory," Byrhtnoth cries. He trusts in his strong right arm, and the prestige of past victories, and scorns to take advantage of his position. They are in the hands of God. Then the slaughter-wolves wade over; they care not for the water; the viking host carry their linden shields westwards over the stream, over the shining water, to the bank. And Byrhtnoth is ready for them with his men in close array, hedged round with shields.

A cry goes up; spears fly, and the bows are busy; the shields receive the sharp-pointed darts; many fall on either hand. The English stand fast; Byrhtnoth incites them to the fray, to win glory from the Danes. Beneath his shield the chieftain steps out to meet a Danish warrior, and the viking's spear goes through the wood and enters the hero's body. He thrusts forward the shield, and the spear springs and breaks. With his own spear he pierces his enemy's throat, reaches his life. A second foe he hits, breaking through the ringed corslet till the spear-point stands at the 146. dead man's heart. "The earl was the happier; laughed then the proud man; said thanks to God for the day's work which the Lord had given him." But a third Dane casts a spear which pierces him through. The young Wulfmær, Wulfstan's son, an ungrown boy, draws the spear, all bloody, from his leader's side, and with it slays the Dane. Another foe rushes upon the wounded hero to take his bracelets and rings, his armour and inlaid sword. Byrhtnoth snatches his broad, brown-edged bill from its sheath, and smites him on the corslet; but yet another Dane, with a quick blow, cripples his arm, and the fallow-hilted sword falls from his grasp. Defiantly he cheers on his warriors, but he staggers and can no longer stand firm on his feet. He knows that death is near, and looking up to heaven thanks God for the joy he has had in life, and prays that He will receive his soul. Then the Danes cut him down; Ælfnoth and Wulfmær bestride his body, and they too are slain. Some of his men lose heart, forget their pledges, and flee. Godric, Odda's son, first of all, leaps upon Byrhtnoth's own horse, and rides for the fastness of the wood with his two brothers and many more than is fitting, if they but remember all their lord has done for them. Cowards are they, and scorn their portion.

The others draw closer together; they all will do one of two things, either lose their lives or avenge their dear one. Ælfwine, a warrior young in years, encourages his fellows to 216. remember their boasts. "I will make known my noble birth to all....None shall twit me at home that I fled when my lord lay dead. That is greatest of harms to me." Brave words of encouragement are upon their lips, and indomitable courage in their hearts; in defeat, the doggedness of the race makes itself known: Godric has betrayed them, for many thought from the horse he rode that it was their lord who fled, therefore was the shield-burg broken up. But not a foot will they flee; they care not for their lives; they will avenge their lord with heaps of the slain; they will not return home lordless men. They rush among the Danes and break their array, cleaving the shields, smiting, slaying and dying. One of the last of them, Byrhtwold, an old comrade of Byrhtnoth, raises aloft his

shield, brandishes his spear, full boldly exhorts his comrades
to brave deeds: "Thought must be the harder, heart the
keener, courage the greater, as our might lessens[1]. Here lies
our lord, all hewn in pieces, the good one on the ground.
May he who now thinks of turning from this war-play ever
have sorrow. I am old of years, but hence I will not. I mean
to lie beside my lord so dear." And thus the fight to the
death draws to its close.

3[1]2.

So passes the spirit of the heroic age, overwhelmed by
its foes, but chivalrous and loyal to the last; and with it
also fades the age of the old Anglo-Saxon song. Sad is the
tale of the years to come. The brave are dead; the cowards
live; and the coward's heart is always base and treacherous.
The Englishman will now be seen in his very worst aspect.

Later in the year, after the battle, he pays the tribute
which has been demanded, "an infamous precedent," and it
amounts to ten thousand pounds. In the next year there is
a scheme afoot for entrapping the Danish army, which fails
through the treachery of the "ealdorman" Ælfric, who had
previously been harshly banished by King Ethelred and
afterwards restored to favour. Though now one whom the
king trusts most, he sends to warn the Danes. On the night
when they are to be surprised their army breaks away, and
with them escapes the "ealdorman," while the king wreaks
his vengeance upon Ælfgar, Ælfric's son, causing him to be
blinded. Others also of those about the king were wont to
divulge his designs to the Danes and bring his efforts to
confusion. In 994 the attack is again bought off with a
ransom of sixteen thousand pounds; and the payment of
tribute becomes a regular practice. The English are now
very weak indeed.

A.-S. Chron.
991.
Will. of
Malm. ii. 9.

A.-S. Chron.
992.

It is the age of Ethelred "the Unready," the foolish leader
without a plan for the defence of his country in its need, the
base, effeminate and indolent man who can devise nought
but what is treacherous and cruel, the vicious coward who
can make the brutal mutilation of innocent hostages his
boast. When Thurkill the Dane sends to invite the assistance
of Sweyn, king of Denmark, he tells him that the English
king is a driveller, given up entirely to women and wine, that

Will. of
Malm. ii. 10.

---

[1] "Hige sceal þê heardra, heorte þê cênre,
    Môd sceal þê mâre, þê ûre mægen lŷtlað."

war is the last thing in his thought, that his own people hate him and foreigners despise him, that the leaders of the English are jealous of each other, and the people weak and ready for flight the moment the onset is sounded. It is a pitiable picture of the leaderless Englishman, hesitating and unnerved.

At rare intervals Ethelred rouses himself to propose plans of defence, which all end in empty words: "And it will be prudent that every year, immediately after Easter, ships of war be made ready"; but nothing is ever carried through. In the year 999 it is decided that a fleet shall co-operate with an army on land against the enemy, but when the ships are ready the leaders delay from day to day, and so cause much suffering and wretchedness among the men who man them. The more need of haste there is, so much the greater is always the delay; ever the troop of the enemy increases, while the English retire before them; and in the end the naval force effects nothing but unavailing toil, waste of money, and encouragement of the enemy. Evidently the Englishman, in some dim, hazy fashion, still grasps the idea that without a fleet he is all but defenceless, but how to make skilful use of it is beyond him. In 1001 the Danes come to Exmouth and attack the town, and for once meet with a desperate resistance. Then they turn aside through all that district, and do as they are accustomed, slaying and burning. An immense levy of the men of Devonshire and Somerset is gathered, and battle is joined at Penho, but as soon as the attack begins the English give way, and there is a great slaughter. The Danes ride over the country, and ever their latter expedition is worse than the former; and they bring with them to the ships enormous booty, and afterwards depart to Wight. They fare about just as they please, and nothing withstands them. Neither the fleet on the sea nor the levy on land dares follow them up. "It was then in every wise a heavy time because they never ceased from their evil," says the Saxon chronicler. The efforts of the English are always vain, "for the army, destitute of a leader and ignorant of military discipline, either retreated before it came into action, or else was easily overcome."

Many of the Danes are now settled among the English; some of them even fight upon the English side against the

Laws of Ethelred, 33. *A.-S. Laws,* Thorpe, p. 138. *A.-S. Chron.* 999, E.

1001, E.

Will. of Malm. II. 10.

later raiding bands.   Then opportunity arises for the general
massacre of the year 1002, in which many Danes throughout the country, at the instigation of the king, are seized
unawares and ruthlessly butchered.   Among them Gun-
hilda, sister of Sweyn, is beheaded, after her husband and
son have been put to death before her eyes.   The Danes
take a terrible revenge, and for four years the land *Will. of*
is ravaged with fire and sword.   So completely is the *Malm.* II. 10, and *Hen. of*
national spirit broken that the victorious army passes *Hunt.* Bk VI.
"boldly and insolently" and unattacked before the gates
of Winchester, carrying with it the booty and supplies
it has gathered fifty miles inland.   Now we begin to hear
of the "Den-geld" as the name of the regularly levied
tribute.

Again, in 1015, there is another resort to treacherous
slaughter at a great council of the leaders of both peoples
held at Oxford ; and again the crime is expiated in a deluge
of blood.   At this period there seems to be treachery heaped
upon treachery.   How soon does the thin veneer of their
civilisation, learning and Christianity, wear away from these
men!   How sadly they have deteriorated!   The only ex-
planation of their conduct that can be offered is that the
best of the race have fallen, and that the remnant are panic-
stricken under the burden of their sad affliction.   The
Englishman himself can only say weakly: "All these mis- *A.-S. Chron.*
fortunes happened to us through folly[1], because one would 1011.
not in time offer tribute to them, or fight with them, but
when they had done most evil then one made peace and
league with them."

It is a relief to turn for a moment to the account of the 1012.
brave Archbishop Ælfeah in 1012, for true courage such as
his seems to have been rare in Ethelred's reign.   He was
captured when Canterbury fell through the treachery of the
Abbot Ælfmær, whose life he had previously saved.   The
Danes took him away with them in their ships ; and when
he refused to promise them money, and forbade that any
should ransom him, they led him to their "husting," and
there, in a fit of drunken frenzy, shamefully killed him.   They
pelted him with bones and the heads of cattle, perhaps in
derision because he was a bishop and not a warrior, until at

[1] "þurh unrǽdas."

last, to end his misery, one of them struck him on the head with the back of an axe. In strong contrast to his resolute refusal to pay ransom is the subsequent conduct of the king, who paid the tribute asked for, and then subsidised five and forty ships of the Danish fleet to protect his realm.

Sermo Lupi ad Anglos, Wulfstan's Homilies, Napier XXXIII. (5), p. 156.

The *Sermon to the English* of Wulfstan, archbishop of York 1002—1023, contains some plain speaking which gives a vivid impression of the terrible demoralisation and depression which prevailed: Though the thousand years are past, the doom is at hand; and in the world it grows ever worse and worse, because the sins of the people increase greatly from day to day before the coming of Antichrist. And then shall it indeed become terrible and fearful widely in the world. It is clear that it is the devil who is responsible for all the mischief; for he has too greatly led astray this people for many years past; and though men speak well, yet there has been little truth among them, and too many wrongs have prevailed in the land. Evil has been heaped upon evil, and in consequence many losses and indignities have been experienced. The only remedy is to turn again to God, for the wretchedness has been well merited. Everywhere God's dues have been withheld; His house has been despoiled within and without; His servants have been everywhere deprived of reverence and protection, and have been treated as men never dared treat the ministers of the heathen gods. Widows are frequently forced wrongfully into marriage, reduced to poverty, and brought low. Poor men are sorely deceived, and cruelly deprived, by treachery, of benefit, of food, of property and life; and, though innocent, are sold out of the land into the power of foreigners; and little children are enslaved for petty thefts, through cruel laws. "Free-right" is annulled, and "thrall-right" preserved; and "alms-right" is curtailed. Freemen may not control their own actions, nor go where they will, nor do with their own property as they choose. Thralls may not possess what they have gained in their own time and won with hardship, nor what good men have given them, by the grace of God, as alms. God has been rejected; therefore has this insult and injury come upon the land. It is clear to all that there has been more breaking than making good; therefore many things are impending to this people. There

has been no worth now for a long time, within or without;
but instead there has been harrying and hunger, burning
and bloodshedding, repeatedly on every side. Stealing and
killing, sedition and pestilence, cattle-plague and dire disease,
slander and hate, and the ravaging of spoilers, with excessive
taxes, and storms which often cause barrenness, have severely
injured the people. The result is that much wrong and unreliability are everywhere among men. For often kinsman
protects kinsman no more than the stranger, nor the father
his child, nor at times the child his own father, nor
one brother another. No one has ordered his life as he
should; neither the monk according to his rule, nor the
layman according to the law; but all have done as they
pleased. Treachery and injury by word and deed have been
common; men slander their fellows with scandalous attacks
and calumnies; they would do more if they could. Treachery
towards one's lord has been rampant in the land; and many
lords have been slain or driven from the country by most
heinous treason. Too many Christians have been slain, or
sold out of the country; and too many holy places have
perished through unworthy men being placed in them. The
father has sold his child for a price, and the child his mother,
and one brother another, into the power of strangers out of
the land. Many are forsworn and greatly perjured; pledges
are given only to be broken; and it is evident that the anger of
God sits severely upon the people. Serfs escape from their
masters and join the Danes; and encounters between thegn
and thrall are common. There is no worth in the land;
all is harrying and hate; and the English have long been
without victory and greatly disheartened through the anger
of God. The Danes have become so strong, by God's permission, that often in fight one puts to flight ten, and two,
twenty, sometimes less, sometimes more, all for their sins.
Often the thrall binds fast his lord, and makes him a thrall,
through the anger of God. Often two or three Danish seamen drive in bonds a drove of Christians through the country
from sea to sea, to the shame of all, if indeed they can know
any shame. And all the insult they endure they repay with
honour to those who shame them. They pay tribute continually, and the Danes humble them daily. They harry and
burn, rob and plunder, and lead captives and spoil to their

ships. In all these sad happenings the anger of God is
plainly visible. It is no wonder that such things happen; for
men have, for a long time past, cared not what they did in
word or deed. The nation has become very sinful. Murder
and crime, avarice and greediness, robbery and rapine, be-
trayals and heathen vices, treacheries, breakings of law and
seditions, attacks upon kinsmen and manslaughters, incests
and various fornications abound. There are in the land
adversaries of God, degenerate apostates, hostile church-
haters, and fierce haters of the people, despisers of the divine
laws and Christian customs, and there is derisive foolishness
towards the most sacred things. Men are more ashamed of
good deeds than of evil deeds. They cover good deeds with
derision, and revile the pious, and insult and blame all who
love right and the law of God. And among the women
there are harlots and child-slayers, and many foul prostitutes,
and witches and sorceresses. Gildas had said that the Welsh
were destroyed by God for their wickedness; but, truly, they
know some worse deeds done among the English than they
anywhere heard of among the Welsh. Let them therefore
take warning by such an example. Let them repent and
turn away from their sin, and creep to Christ with trembling
hearts. Let them call upon Him without ceasing, and merit
His mercy. Let them think frequently upon the great
Doom, to which they all must come, and so save themselves
from the fiery upwelling of the torment of hell, and win for
themselves the glories and the joys which God has prepared
for those who work His will in the world.

What a sad picture of decadence is this! It is only
relieved by the patriotism of the two archbishops, who see
how and why the nation is driving on to destruction, and
strive to keep it from the rocks, the one by the example
of his deeds, the other by his words.

Even when a strong man arose later, in the person of
Edmund, son of Ethelred, a worthy son of an unworthy
father, his country was quite unprepared to support him.
A.-S. Chron. "And then after his [Ethelred's] end, all the Witan who
1016. were in London, and the citizens, chose Edmund king; and
he bravely defended his kingdom while his time was." His
great strength of body and resolution in war won for him
the title "Ironside"; and in seven great battles, waged with

varying fortune, and always robbed of results through treachery, he disputed the possession of the kingdom with Cnut, the son of Sweyn. At Assandune, the greatest fight of all, Eadric, the arch-traitor of his time, betrayed his lord, and set the example of flight. Cnut won the victory and gained for himself the kingdom, the flower of the English army being totally destroyed. Edmund fled to Gloucester, and yet again gathered the shattered remnant of his forces; but it is said that before engaging he challenged his rival to decide by single combat which of them should hold the realm, an action quite in keeping with what is told of his character. Henry of Huntingdon, in fact, gives a brief but vivid description of the *Hen. of Hunt.* combat, which it is just possible may have actually taken Bk VI. place, and says that Cnut, when his strength was failing, offered a fair division of the country. William of Malmes- *Will. of* bury asserts that the challenge was sent and refused. The *Malm.* II. 10. *Anglo-Saxon Chronicle* is silent on the point, but says that the nobles brought about a peaceful division. However it came about, Edmund still ruled in Wessex when he was shortly afterwards assassinated by Eadric; and then Cnut became king of both the English and the Danes.

After some two hundred years of discord, invasion and adversity the nation at last finds some measure of repose in its humiliation. The Englishman seems too overwearied to care how or by whom the cessation of his misery is brought about; and thus becomes accustomed to the rule of a foreign king. By the strength, wisdom and just dealing of Cnut the disunited members are for a space drawn into one body. No *A.-S. Chron.* longer will there be so much meaning attached to the names *Hen. of Hunt.* Angle, Saxon, Mercian, and Dane; Englishman and Dane are *Malm.* II. 11. now allied in blood, in sympathies, in language, in policy, in character, with a general hardening in all directions. Through adversity the nation begins to know itself, and submits to the welding process. And it soon becomes possible for Cnut to make himself not only a popular king, but also a national hero, in rendering obedience to whom the Englishman can feel no shame. He brings peace to the distressed country; he recognises English customs and English law, and makes no distinction between the natives and the new-comers; he punishes the traitors as they have deserved. He becomes a Christian, and the friend of the pilgrim and monk.

Will. of
Malm. II. II.
Ant. Lib.

As "king of all England, Denmark, Norway, and part of
the Swedes," he sends greeting "to the whole nation of the
English, high and low," and sets forth his policy. "I have
lately been to Rome, to pray for the forgiveness of my sins,
for the safety of my dominions and of the people under my
government....I have been the more diligent in the performance
of this, because I have learned from the wise that St Peter, the
apostle, has received from God great power in binding and in
loosing: that he carries the key of the kingdom of heaven....
Again I complained before the pope, and expressed my high
displeasure, that my archbishops were oppressed by the immense sum of money which is demanded from them when
seeking, according to custom, the apostolic residence to receive
the pall: and it was determined that it should be so no longer....
I have vowed to God Himself henceforward to reform my life
in all things, and justly and piously to govern the kingdoms
and the people subject to me, and to maintain equal justice in
all things; and have determined, through God's assistance, to
rectify anything hitherto unjustly done, either through the in-
temperance of my youth, or through negligence....I command
all sheriffs and governors throughout my whole kingdom...to
allow all, noble and ignoble alike, to enjoy impartial law....I
have no need to accumulate money by unjust exaction....I am
now going to Denmark...to make peace and firm treaty....
When I have established peace with the surrounding nations,
and put all our sovereignty here in the east in tranquil order,
so that there shall be no fear of war or enmity on any side, I
intend coming to England, as early in the summer as I shall
be able to get my fleet prepared. I have sent this epistle
before me, in order that my people may rejoice at my prosperity; because, as yourselves know, I have never spared, nor
will I spare, either myself or my pains for the needful service
of my whole people." What nation would not be won over
by such words? What king speaking thus, and backing his
words by deeds, could fail to be popular, especially so when
he had proved himself a hero of the antique type? There is
a certain likeness in this respect between Cnut and Alfred,
which the English, with their hero worship no longer dormant,
could not fail to recognise. The popular songs of the next
century seem to have retained many memories of Cnut, which
show how completely the people accepted him for their own;

and there is in them a joyous note which has been but too long absent. The monk of Ely records how gladly the monks showed their pleasure in him as he passed by:

> "Merrily sang the monks in Ely
> When King Cnut rowed thereby.
> Row, knights, nearer the land,
> And hear we the song of these monks."

How thoroughly the Danish influence permeated English taste and character may be seen in the stories of *Horn* and *Havelok* of a subsequent period.

After Cnut's death the throne passed to Harold his son, who was chosen king by a national Witan assembled at Oxford. Though many of the English thegns, under the leadership of Earl Godwin, dissented, his election was carried by the Danes and the Londoners, "who, from long intercourse with these barbarians, had almost entirely adopted their customs." And when he died, both English and Danes unanimously elected Hardicnut, his half-brother. The weakness of these two kings stands out in great contrast to the strength of Cnut. Violence and cruelty again were prevalent ; and Godwin became a power in the land, gathering a party in opposition to the Danish faction. When Alfred, brother of Edmund Ironside, landed in England in 1036 he was taken and blinded, and then left miserably to die. Every tenth man among his followers was put to death, some were tortured and mutilated, others were sold as slaves. "Never was a bloodier deed done in this land since the Danes came," is the indignant comment of the Saxon chronicler. Somehow, perhaps by the intrigues of his enemies, Godwin was said to be implicated in this deed, and in the next reign was obliged to clear himself by oath, and to make satisfaction to the king. Living, bishop of Crediton, also implicated, was expelled from his see, but regained it within the year by bribery. How far the churchmen had deteriorated may also be seen in the significant admission that Ulf, bishop of Dorchester, at a synod held at Vercelli, narrowly escaped being removed from the episcopate: "And afterwards the pope held a synod at Vercelli ; and Bishop Ulf came thereto, and they were very near breaking his staff, if he had not given the greater treasures, because he could not do his offices as well as he should."

A.-S. Chron. 1036.

Hen. of Hunt. VI.

Will. of Malm. II. 12.

A.-S. Chron. 1047.

In 1042 Edward the Confessor, son of Ethelred, succeeded to the throne, a succession fraught with lasting consequences.

1065. "Then came forth, lordly in his trappings, a king pre-eminently good, pure and mild. Edward the Noble protected his native land and his people, until, forthwith, death the bitter came and took the noble one so dear from the earth. Angels bore his soothfast soul into the light of heaven," is the eulogistic record of the Saxon monk. But Edward, the saint, seems strangely placed upon the English throne at such a juncture. Gentle, unassuming, easy-going, his very self-depreciation, coupled with natural indolence, rendered him quite incapable of resisting the influence of strong-willed and energetic men. "From the simplicity of his manners he was a man little calculated to govern," says William of Malmesbury. His deficiencies were more than covered by his great nobles, who became all the stronger because their king was weak ; and in consequence faction and feud again were rife. Three great men there were about the throne upon whom the fortunes of the country depended ; and each of the three presents a different type of character. Godwin, strong, masterful, unscrupulous, "trusting in the consciousness of his own merits," had little respect for the king, and often bore himself insolently among his fellow-countrymen ; while Leofric, loyal, generous, and liberal of heart, strove to protect his sovereign from Godwin's ambition. Siward, the brave earl of the Northumbrians, a giant in stature, and vigorous both in mind and body, was the mightiest hero of the three. When his son was slain in war with the Scots he asked of the messenger who brought the news, "Was his death-wound before or behind?" "Before," was the reply. "Then," said the old warrior, "I greatly rejoice ; no other death was fitting either for him or me[1]."

Supra, p. 55   Siward's disappointment at his own peaceful end has been already told.

Little more do we hear of the Danes ; they are absorbed, and are themselves henceforth English. But now another influence begins to bear upon the people, which becomes

Will. of Maim. ii. 13.

[1] Cf. *Macbeth*, Act v. Sc. 8, l. 46:
   Siward.   "Had he his hurts before?"
   Ross.   "Ay, on the front."
   Siward.   "Why then, God's soldier be he."

irksome and galling.   Edward had been nourished among the
Normans, and was himself Norman on the mother's side.   He
had Norman friends and Norman tastes ; and so through him
the Englishman was first brought into contact with the
strongest and most practical race which the world had yet
seen ; a race of conquerors born and bred.   It is in its first
direct contact with the Normans that the English nation
again becomes truly conscious of its own individuality, and
that the instinct of self-preservation again grows strong.
Norman friends passed to the king's court, and many received
high positions in the land.   Robert, a monk of Jumièges,
eventually became archbishop of Canterbury ; and this man,
the English say, was the cause of the discord which arose.
The Englishman finds the haughtiness and overbearing
temper of the foreigners more than he can endure.   He has
regained something of his former sturdy confidence in himself,
and refuses to permit his rights to be impaired.   On one oc-   *A.-S. Chron.*
casion Eustace the Norman returns from visiting the king,   1048.
and, before entering Dover, arms himself and his men, with
the intention of forcing the townsmen to provide food and
lodging wherever they chose to stay.   A people among whom
hospitality is always due to the friendly guest naturally resent
such an ill-mannered intrusion.   One of the Norman men-at-
arms chooses to lodge at the house of a certain tribesman ; the
two come to blows, and the Norman is slain, after wounding
the Englishman.   Eustace and his men avenge the death of
their comrade by slaying the householder, and then proceed
to attack the town-guard.   In the conflict twenty English
and nineteen Normans are slain, the latter also losing many
wounded.   In the end Eustace escapes with a few men, and
flies back to the king with a biased account of what has
occurred.   Edward's anger is aroused against the townsmen,
and he bids Godwin punish them.   Godwin sympathises with
his countrymen, and refuses to harm his own province for the
sake of a foreigner.   So the matter seems to end, but later in
the year a false accusation is brought against the earl and
his sons by the Welsh, and the king seizes the opportunity
to banish them from the country.   In the following year,
however, Godwin returns with a powerful force, and the king
is compelled to annul his sentence of banishment, and to expel
the Normans in disgrace from his realm.   A little longer and

this sturdy independence and growing national spirit would have made the country strong against every attack, but the strength of the Englishman is now muscular rather than mental. He lacks the power to will and to plan great things for himself, and it is ordained that that intellectual quality shall be given him by a second conqueror, by one who is strongest where he himself is weakest, by one who can deal effectively with the most subtle combinations of strategy and statecraft.

In 1066 Edward died childless; and, since Edgar the Atheling, his nephew, was but a boy, too weak to rule in turbulent times, there arose three strong claimants to the throne: Harold, son of Godwin ; William, duke of Normandy ; and Harald Hardrada, king of Norway. To two of these, Edward, with his customary weakness and submissiveness to the dominant will of the moment, and without consulting the nation, seems to have made some promise of the crown. *A.-S. Chron.* *1065.* " And the wise one committed the kingdom to the illustrious man, to Harold himself, to the noble earl, who always faith-fully served his lord in words and deeds," says the *Chronicle*, *Will. of* *Malm.* II. 13. thus asserting the English view of the matter. The Norman chroniclers allege a similar bequest to William, and say that Harold coerced the nobles and seized the crown. It certainly seems as though Edward, upon his death-bed, had more than a suspicion of the mischief his weakness would cause. But apart from the bequests, Harold was undoubtedly the popular favourite, as the support he received in the subsequent struggle goes to prove. If Hardrada relied upon anything but the right of the sword, it was a supposed compact between his predecessor, Magnus, and Hardicnut, son of Cnut.

Ibid. *Hen. of Hunt.* Bk VI. *Wace, Rom.* *de Rou.* The story goes that Harold had once been cast by a sudden storm upon the coast of Ponthieu, and was there surrounded and captured by the peasantry, who handed him over to Guy, their count. William heard of the capture, claimed the prisoner, and received him at his court with all out-ward courtesy and hospitality. But when Harold's confidence was won, the duke began to broach the subject of the English succession, and required the Englishman's allegiance to his cause. Harold felt himself compelled to assent in order to regain his liberty ; and a further agreement was made that he should marry Adela, William's daughter, and espouse his own sister to one of the Norman barons. Then William craftily proposed a solemn ratification of the promise by oath. Before a public assembly of the Normans, Harold knelt before William, and, placing his hands between those of the duke, swore to become his man, and to do him loyal and faithful service. And upon a missal, laid on a chest covered with cloth of gold, he placed his hand by William's command, and confirmed the oath which he had made. But those who looked on saw that his hand trembled and his body shook as he did so, foreseeing the death-blow to his own ambitions, though not knowing that to make the oath still more sacred the Norman had placed within the chest all the holy relics of the saints which he could gather from the Norman churches. But the oath was taken, and Harold had promised to surrender England to the duke, while many cried, " May God grant it ! " And then the cloth was removed, and the relics lay revealed. Harold departed for England sorely troubled and fearful for what he had done. But of this visit to William's court, and of what took place there, the *Anglo-Saxon Chronicle* makes no mention. The Saxon Englishman never acknowledged the oath ; and when the king died shortly afterwards, Harold was elected by the nation to succeed him.

So it came about that, no sooner was the son of Godwin seated upon the throne, than he was called upon to face two mighty foes, one from the north, the other from the south. Messengers arrived from William, asserting his claim, and reminding Harold of the oath he had sworn. Whereupon Harold repudiated his pledge as having been obtained under compulsion, as being invalid because it had not received the consent of the English nation : he had promised what did not belong to him. Then William published the perjury through-out Christendom, and declared his intention to win his right by force. He laid his cause before the pope, who declared that England was the lawful possession of the Norman, and forwarded a consecrated banner with his blessing upon the Norman arms. Upraising this mark of papal favour, William began forthwith to levy the mightiest arma-ment Christendom had ever yet seen. From all quarters the chivalry of western Europe, French, Normans, Bretons, Aquitains, and many others, gathered round him, a conti-nental league against the islander, attracted by the splendid

promises the duke held out. From the outset nothing but
the conquest and spoliation of England was determined upon.
For several months the cosmopolitan army was mustering in
array upon the northern shores of France ; and in every port
the carpenters and shipbuilders were at work throughout the
spring and summer, preparing the hulls, setting up the masts,
and bending the sails, with the greatest industry and activity.
And strenuous preparations for defence by sea and land were
also in progress on this side of the Channel.   The Englishman
was fully aware of his peril, and knew quite well that he was
to fight for life, home and country.   In the face of danger
he wins our highest admiration as he nerves himself for one
supreme effort.   Had there been but a single enemy to meet,
one might venture to assert that the outcome would have
been very different.

But there was the one great and ever-present weakness to
throw all plans awry. Tostig, Harold's elder brother and
rival, who had been banished in the previous reign, joined
Hardrada, and with him descended in force upon Northumbria, defeated the northern English, and occupied York. This
attack in the rear rendered Harold's position precarious, and
multiplied his difficulties. Instead of devoting all his attention
to making a resolute defence in the south he was called upon
to solve a most intricate strategical problem. He decided
upon a bold stroke, left his fleet to watch the coast, and in
four days made a forced march with his army into Northumbria. At Stamford Bridge he took the Northmen by surprise,
threw their ranks into disorder by stratagem, drove them

Hen. of Hunt.
Bk VI.

across the river, "the living trampling on the corpses of the
slain," and won a great and decisive victory after nine hours'
fighting. Tostig and Hardrada were slain with the flower
of their army, and the power of Norway was completely
shattered. Harold, decisive, energetic, and, above all, so far
successful, had proved himself a leader of consummate
ability.

But the English, too, had lost heavily ; and their army
had spent its best efforts when news came that William had
taken advantage of a temporary dispersal of the fleet for
refitting and re-provisioning to land along the southern coast,
and that the work of laying waste had already begun.   In the
absence of its directing brain, the fleet had failed to achieve

the object for which it had been prepared. Nothing remained
but for Harold to make a second forced march with the remnant of his force, and to levy fresh warriors from the midlands
and south as he went. His second call to arms met with a
ready response, for his people saw in him alone all the qualities
which a crisis demanded. But it was impossible for him as
he marched to make full use of the resources of the country.
He reached London, and after a short halt pushed on again,
hoping once more to strike a decisive blow upon an unprepared
foe. But surprise was soon found to be impossible, and being
numerically inferior to the invaders Harold took up a strong
defensive position, skilfully chosen, upon the hill of Senlac, near
Hastings, in the direct line of their advance. Had he been less
impetuous, or less anxious for the people whose houses and
lands the Normans were destroying, he might have retired
slowly, drawing the invaders after him further and further
from the sea, until with augmented numbers he could have
taken them in front, flank and rear. Delay would have
favoured the Englishman, for his fleet had now regained
possession of the sea; immediate action was William's great
hope. No safety could be found in flight if they were defeated,
William told his men; escape by sea was impossible, for he
had given instructions to his sailors to render the ships un-
seaworthy by breaking them up and piercing holes in them.
But when fighting was afoot the Englishman thought it
shameful even to appear to hang back from the fray. One
doubt alone possessed him now, and that was concerning the
oath upon the sacred relics which it was alleged his king had
sworn. That oath hung heavily upon the hearts of simple-
minded men, and filled them with foreboding. In spite of all
their reckless violence, religion was a very real thing to them,
and they believed, as they had been taught and as their
fathers before them had believed, that the consequences of
such sin were immediate and inevitable. Was not the might
of Rome, the holy Mother, behind the invaders? This uneasiness led to dissensions in the camp. Gurth, Harold's
brother, even proposed that the king should withdraw and
leave the battle to those who had sworn no oaths and were
fighting in a just cause in defence of their country. To that
suggestion Harold at once refused to listen: it would be
cowardly to let others fight for him when he dared not fight

himself. Again Gurth proposed that the host should retire, laying waste the country as they went, that the Normans might be forced to capitulate through lack of supplies; but Harold refused to adopt this course, and much wrangling ensued. It is even said that Gurth so far forgot himself as to strike his royal brother. Their forebodings were intensified when a Norman monk, Maigrot of Fescamp, came with a message from William offering Harold choice of three things: to deliver up the crown, to submit to the arbitration of the pope, or to decide the matter by single combat. Harold would have struck the monk to the earth, but Gurth restrained him; and the messenger was sent back with Harold's refusal to accept any of William's conditions: his crown and his life belonged to his people. But when the monk returned again to say that William denounced the king as a liar and a perjurer, and that a papal bull, excommunicating him and all who fought for him, was already in William's hands, the faces of the English chiefs showed the deep impression his words had made. I fancy that the Saxon Englishman never forgot or forgave the part played by the pope and the see of Rome in the downfall of his fortunes. Still it would never do to yield; their lands were already parcelled out; their homes, their goods, their wives and daughters were at stake; if they laid down their arms the nation would be ruined for ever. And they swore an oath that they would make neither truce nor treaty with the spoiler, but would conquer him or die.

Harold planted his standard at Senlac upon a steep slope facing a break in the Sussex hills, and fenced in his position with a palisade of stakes intertwined with osiers. The night before the battle was spent after the English fashion, for, now that the fighting was near, the spirits of the warriors rose in anticipation of yet another victory. In the early morning Harold gathered his men about him in compact array upon the hillside on which gleamed the Golden Dragon of Wessex.

Rom. de Rou,
13109, *etc.*

They were clad in short garments to the knee, with shirts of mail covering their bodies, and with great helmets upon their heads. They were armed with large two-handed axes and bills, with swords, spears and shields. Even the neighbour-

12839.

ing peasantry had come in with such arms as they could procure, clubs and long staves, forks and implements shod with iron. Bows and arrows seem to have been little used by the English, perhaps because at this period they relied upon hand-to-hand fighting, perhaps because they were outnumbered and outshot by the Norman archers. "Hold together; smite with your spears and bills; cleave with your battle-axes; strike with all your might, and spare not," was the substance of their leader's charge. It seemed almost impossible that their defences could be penetrated; and up the slope the charge of the heavy-armed chivalry of France must surely falter and die away to invite a terrible onslaught from above.

12911.

On the other side, it is said that the invaders spent the night confessing their sins, and receiving absolution, knowing that many of them must die before the battle was done. At dawn masses were sung, and the army was marshalled in array. Three divisions there were, with archers in the van to prepare for the attack, and with cavalry in support and on the wings to drive it home. The duke's instructions were to strike hard and to give no quarter: "Show no weakness towards them, for they will have no mercy on you."

Will. of Malm. Bk III. *Rom. de Rou.*

12605.

From the English position first one division, then a second, and then a third, could be seen advancing along the crest of the opposite ridge and then descending the slope, till the valley seemed to be alive with men. In the last division, near the duke and surrounded by his choicest vassals, was the standard which had come from Rome. And a company of priests and clerks ascended a hill near by to offer up prayers to God for the success of the Norman arms. On both sides, horns, trumpets and bugles sounded. Loud, deep cries, like the baying of hounds, rose from the English ranks; while their adversaries broke into the stirring *Battle-Song of Roland* as they marched. And from the later form of this song, the work of a Norman who had sojourned in England between 1066 and 1096, who, perhaps, had even been with William's army in the battle, we may obtain additions to our picture of the invading host, and catch a further reflection of the spirit which animated it.

13066.

And cf. *Ch. de Rol.* 3527.

Léon Gautier, *Ch. de Rol.* Introd. xx—xxvi, and xlix.

Down the hill they come in glittering array; first the archers, light-armed and active, quick to advance or to fall back upon their supports, clean shaven, with steel caps upon their heads, and quilted leathern coats upon their bodies, each carrying sword and bow; and following them the knights

Rom. de Rou, 11628, 12805, 11638, 12816. *Ch. de Rol.* 2999, 3001, 1808, 1799.

and barons, distinguished by their cognisances, in complete armour of steel mail, mounted upon their destriers. The inlaid helms and hauberks of the chevaliers gleam like points of fire; great lances, from which the pennons, red, white and blue, hang down about their heads, are held aloft; round their necks are hung their shields, painted with flowers. One Taillefer, the minstrel, leads the army and the song. To him is given the honour of being the first to slay and the first to be slain. A cloud of arrows carries death among the fighters;

3349, 3541, 3165.

and then the onset is made. The reins fall upon the charger's neck; the cruel spur goes deep into the flank; the blood flows clear in trickling streams. The French break into a

1183, 1116.

gallop, into a charge. How they ride! With what fire, with what furious speed they throw themselves upon the enemy[1]! Not a coward amongst them[2]!

They mount the hill; the palisades are gained; now

Rom. de Rou, 13183.

comes the shock of the onset. Lances are shivered; mace and sword and battle-axe rise and fall and crash together, and

Ch. de Rol. 3482, 1945.

break in twain helmet, hauberk and shield. Pieces of mail are shorn away, or driven into the body. Girths are broken; saddles overturn; brave men are thrown to the earth and die.

1883, 1056, 2060.

"Ferez, ne's espargniez!" "Strike! Spare not!" And the swords are red even to the gold upon the hilts. How they smite! What terrible men[3]! Red with blood are the hands

1979, 1343, 3389, 1995.

and arms of the fighters; their faces too are discoloured, ensanguined, livid; all their proud array bears traces of the strife; even the necks and shoulders of their steeds are red;

Rom. de Rou, 13193.

and the grass is no longer green. "Dex aïe!" "God aid us," cry the French; "Out! Out!" the English; and the great axes, held in mighty hands, cleave and crush and kill. Back, down the hill, roll the French, horse and man, one over the other, all struggling together in indescribable confusion, into the deep trench which lies below; often friend strikes friend,

13227.

fighting blindly. The English follow, smiting and slaying; and many of them too are drawn into that terrible pit. Many are trampled underfoot and never rise again. Javelins and rocks are hurled from the heights above; and the carcases

Ch. de Rol. 1183.

[1] "Pois, si chevalchent, Deus! par si grant fiertet! Brochent ad ait pur le plus tost aler; Si vunt ferir,—que fereient-il el?"—

1116.

[2] "Nen i out un cuard."

2060.

[3] "Feluns humes ad ci."

heap up till the trench is levelled with the plain. Already
the varlets who guard the harness in the rear are in flight.
But the Frenchman rallies. Better death than dishonour!
Death before flight! Fight for the honour of France[1]! "The
Normans die, but they retreat not; no race under heaven is
hardier in fight," is his boast. "No race under heaven is
better than the French; they are brave as lions; before
they die they will sell their lives dearly; they fail not their
leader for death or distress."

So from nine o'clock till three the fight goes on, up and
down, to and fro; and none can say who will gain the day.
Then the Norman archers are again advanced, and a thick
arrow-flight falls upon the English, who cover themselves with
their shields. So the word is passed to shoot not with direct
aim but upwards, so that the points may descend over the
shields and upon the faces of the fighters. The plan is immediately successful, and many are blinded. An arrow from
above pierces Harold's right eye to the brain. In agony he
draws out the shaft, and breaks it in his hands; and the pain
of his wound is so great that he bows himself and leans upon
his shield. But still his men maintain about him their dogged
defence of the position; and no assault can break them.

Late in the day, when every other device has failed, by the
stratagem of pretended flight the French draw the defenders
from their impregnable hold upon the hill to the level plain
below. With their leader unable to forbid, the English break
their ranks, and throw themselves fiercely upon the retreating
foe, jeering and mocking with insulting words as they pursue.
"Cowards who came in an evil hour to seize our lands! Fools
were you for coming! Never will you see Normandy again.
You cannot escape by running, unless you can take the sea
at a leap. Your sons and your daughters have you lost for
ever, unless you drink the whole sea dry before you." But
now above the din again the cry is heard, "Dex aïe!" fierce
and exultant. It is the signal to stay the flight and turn.
The snare is sprung; and back upon the pursuers come the
French in impetuous career. The English are broken; their

Ch. de Rol.
1091, 1701,
2127, 1926,
3048,
1441, 1888,
1690, 3417.

Rom. de Rou,
Will. of Malm.
Hen. of Hunt.

Rom. de Rou,
13353.

13373.
Ch. de Rol.
1091.
1701.
1926.

---

[1] "Mielz voeill murir qu' à huntage remaigne."
"Einz murreit il que il voeillet fuïr."
"Si calengiez e voz morz e voz vies,
     Que dulce France par nus ne seit hunie!"

foes press in among them and on every side; the battle becomes a *mêlée*, with indiscriminate fighting, hand to hand. With their huge axes, some of them a foot long in the blade, the English strive to retrieve the day, hewing down horse and man, beating through the defence of the shield, crushing in helmets and coats of mail. One of them, swift of foot, rushes into the thick of the fight, and aims a blow at a mounted Norman knight; but the sweep of the axe falls short, glances from the saddle-bow, and cuts completely through the charger's neck. The French are afraid of him, and begin to draw away, but one, bolder than the rest, pierces him through with his lance. Two Englishmen, comrades in arms who fight together, work havoc with long-handled bills upon both horse and man, until a French knight, attacking warily, slays one with his lance and the other with his mace. Another Englishman, a helmet of wood covering both head and neck, does great execution before a foe strikes him upon the head and, as he puts up his left hand to re-adjust his headpiece, severs his right hand with a blow, so that his axe falls to the ground. A Frenchman who stoops to grasp it is hit in the back by another Englishman with a great double-handed axe; his bones are broken, and his bowels and lungs gush out. But the defenders are driven back up the hill with sadly diminished numbers, to make their last stand about the royal ensign.

13689.   Again for a while, despite the odds, they hold their own against the onset, the Frenchmen striving to break their ring. One of the knights penetrates alone, and is afterwards found dead by the standard's foot. William rides at the head of his men, urging them on, seeking in vain for Harold, to end the strife with his death. He spurs on fiercely, knowing that his men will follow wherever he leads[1]. An Englishman, a mighty wrestler, holds the foe at bay and, when the duke rides at him, smites him upon the helmet, and runs back among his fellows. But several knights pursue him in the press, and pierce him through and through. Still, the English cannot endure for ever; the defence weakens, and now gives way. The French are through; the standard is overthrown. Harold, bowed down with his grievous hurt, is struck upon

Cf. *Ch. de Rol.* 3344.

Rom. de Rou, 13930.
Ch. de Rol. 3344.

[1] "Dient Franceis 'Icist Reis est vassals.
    Chevalchiez, ber, nuls de nus falt.'"

the helmet, and beaten to the ground; he tries to recover his feet; half rises, receives another wound deep in his thigh, and falls again. At last the end has come. Beside the body of the king fall his brothers, Gurth and Leofric, and his most devoted thegns. The height is taken, and the victory is won. Manfully some of the survivors rally in the wood behind the hill, and cut off many of the pursuers; but night falls with England in the Norman's hand. The price it has cost him is not less than one fourth part of his host of sixty thousand men.

Thus at Hastings the English were vanquished, "ingenio circumventi, ingenio victi," and their fate was decided. Yet even the Norman chronicler is forced to record his appreciation of the prowess of those who defended the hill that day. "They were few in number and brave in the extreme; sacrificing every regard for their bodies, they poured forth their spirits for their country." *Will. of Malm.* II. 13 and III.

The struggle proceeds no further. No longer have the English a king to lead them; there is no one sufficiently able to oppose William in the field; it is vain to offer further resistance. They are in the hands of Providence, they say, and He has decided against them because of their sins and the oath which Harold swore. There is no singer on the English side to tell of the fight they made, though surely there was no need to hang the head over the deeds done that day; and this silence shows how completely the heart of the nation is broken. Edgar the Atheling might have been chosen king had the chiefs and bishops been able to agree; "but as it ever should be the forwarder, so was it ever from day to day slower and worse, as at the end it all went." *A.-S. Chron.* 1066. "Thus the English, who, had they been united in one opinion, might have repaired the ruin of their country, introduced a stranger, while they were unwilling to choose a native, to govern them," says William of Malmesbury. The *Chronicle* but reflects the general gloom when it describes the reception which William received: "And there came to meet him Archbishop Ealdred and Child Eadgar, and Earl Eadwine and Earl Morkere, and all the best men of London, and then from necessity submitted when the greatest harm had been done, and it was very imprudent that it was not done earlier, as God would not better it for our sins. And they gave hostages and swore oaths to him; and he promised them that *Will. of Malm.* III.

he would be a kind lord to them, and yet, during this, they harried all that they passed over....And Bishop Odo and Earl William[1] remained here behind, and wrought castles widely throughout the nation, and oppressed the poor people; and ever after that it greatly grew in evil. May the end be good when God will."

In later days, when Englishman and Norman were at one, the general feeling with regard to the Conquest may be seen in Mannyng's *Chronicle*:

Mannyng's
Chronicle.

"Alas! for Sir Harold, for him was mickle ruth,
Full well his own should hold, if he had kept his truth.
But that he was forsworn, mishapping therefore he found;
Should he never else have lost for William no land,
Nor been in that bondage, that brought was over the sea;
Now are they in servage full many that ere were free.
Our freedom that day for ever took the leave,
For Harold it went away, his falsehood did us grieve."

[1] Fitz-Osberne.

CHAPTER IV.

[To about 1272 A.D.]

THE BLENDING OF THE RACES.

BEFORE the battle of Hastings the Normans had already appeared in Europe as a conquering nation. In the early years of the tenth century they had descended from Norway upon the northern shores of France in much the same fashion as their blood-brothers, the Danes, had descended upon England. There they had made for themselves a dukedom and a name; they had settled upon French lands; they had taken to themselves French wives; they had become fathers of French children. In a very short space of time many of the outward characteristics of the northern race had been lost or greatly modified. The old speech had been forgotten; the old manners, tastes and customs had been laid aside. French mothers had taught their sons to call themselves Frenchmen, and to be as French as the French themselves, to become Christian, to become sharers in the Latin civilisation and culture of the south, until at last the memories of the land whence their fathers had come appeared to them but as dark and shadowy myths. They themselves had entered into a warmer and brighter world. Yet still within their breasts the fierce spirit of the Norseman ruled; still all the vitality and freshness of a youthful race remained. They scarcely seemed to know what it meant to be tired or to be afraid. With clear eye they perceived where their best advancement lay; with ready brain their course was laid; with strong hand their project was carried through. Dauntless, enthusiastic, but above all things eminently practical, what they willed they did, and always more successfully than any other nation. When their own lands became too small to hold them, again the roving spirit urged them;

and their neighbours knew and feared them as the great conquering nation of the age. As Frenchmen quick-witted, as Northmen ready-handed, whoever else failed they were the men who were bound to succeed.

The chroniclers are very careful to give a complete description of the Norman-French. They are a "fierce and crafty race," "more fierce than any other people"; "their fierce temper never abates," says one[1]. Another speaks of them as being "proudly appareled, delicate in their food, but not excessive. They are a race inured to war, and can hardly live without it; fierce in rushing against the enemy; and, where strength fails of success, ready to use stratagem, or to corrupt by bribery....They live in large edifices with economy; envy their equals; wish to excel their superiors; and plunder their subjects, though they defend them from others; they are faithful to their lords, though a slight offence renders them perfidious. They weigh treachery by its chance of success, and change their sentiments with money." Yet they are hospitable and devoted to the observances of religion.

Hen. of Hunt.
VI.

Will. of
Malm.
Ant. Lib. III.
p. 280.

In the French *chansons* we have undoubtedly a reflection of the spirit which possessed the conquerors of England, a reflection of their character and their life. Here we find ourselves still in the heroic age; here are still the hero's deeds of single-handed valour, his fall after a desperate resistance against fearful odds, and his final apotheosis. The Norman-Frenchman seems to have entered the heroic age almost where the Anglo-Saxon left it, as a comparison of some parts of the *Song of Roland* and the *Battle of Maldon* will show. And this literature proves, what history advances, that the political instinct of the Anglo-Saxon was more highly developed than that of the Norman-Frenchman. The former had already caught a Pisgah view of a national and patriotic commonwealth, with the social orders closely knit together in allegiance to an elected king; the politics of the latter were still mainly tribal and local, weaker bands linking the king to the greater vassals of his realm. So much then could the conquered give the conqueror in the blending of

---

[1] And cf. *Rom. de Rou*, 13005,
"Tuit cil ki vienent d'outremer
Sont mult à craindre è à doter."

the races. The *chansons* reveal an age beset with tragic situations, with feuds and forays, with anarchy. Ignoble jealousy as well as honourable rivalry, treachery as well as loyalty, are in turn pronounced features of the characters which move across the stage. Violent passions and barbarous excess are everywhere, and, if seen to be evils, are taken at least as necessary evils inseparable from the time. Two wrongs always make a right; revenge is the prime principle of life. Raoul de Cambrai is unjustly deprived of his heritage, *Raoul de* and advances to claim his own with fire and sword. It is a *Cambrai.* mere incident when he attacks and burns a nunnery in which is the mother of his best friend; even the friend himself seems to take it all very much as a matter of course. But friendship is evidently a secondary matter when running counter to revenge, although there is the standing example of Roland and Oliver. Ganelon, the traitor, who brought upon his country the dolorous defeat of Roncesvalles, defends *Ch. de Rol.* himself with the plea that he has but claimed his right of 3778. vengeance upon Roland; he has done no treason[1]. Charlemagne calls upon his barons to avenge the dead; they know 3405. that the right is upon his side. His words when the Saracens flee form a striking parallel to Beowulf's "Better it is for every 3627. one to avenge his friend than to mourn much": Let them avenge their griefs and so console their hearts and cease from their tears. And another parallel to the *Beowulf* is his prediction that old enmities will break out again when it is made 2920. known abroad that the mighty Roland has been slain.

An adventurous spirit was ever one of the chief characteristics of the Norman, and when we examine the literature he brought with him we find this spirit everywhere prominent. The earlier portion is, in many respects, much more nearly related to that of the Anglo-Saxon than we might have expected. Again we catch the chant of the harper and the martial strains of the war-song. It is always of battle that he sings, for his heart rejoices in daring and bloody deeds. The love of woman is almost forgotten in the stirring story of the well-fought field, though surely he cannot have been altogether destitute of the tender passion. When Roland lies dying he remembers many things: his many conquests, 2377. sweet France and the men of his line, Charlemagne his lord

---

[1] "Vengiez m'en sui, mais n'i ad traïson."

who nourished him, and the French who were so devoted to him; and he cannot but weep and sigh.   But there is neither sigh nor tear for "Alde la bele," his lady love; not even a word.   Is it that the hand which wields the sword so effectively hesitates as yet, with a feeling of unaccustomed awkwardness, to touch upon the tender theme of love?   These men are no carpet knights, lounging in ladies' bowers, but rough, strong men of iron nerve and frame, who appear to love their swords more than their mistresses.   Thus Roland cries to his sword: "Oh! my Durendal! how bright and white thou art! how beautiful and holy!   It is not right that the paynims should possess thee."   Patriotism is ever present, almost to the exclusion of all other sentiment; and France is everything, a veritable passion.   It is always France the sweet, the beautiful, the free.   The dying pray to God to bless her; her misfortunes give rise to the most extravagant expressions of frenzied grief; the warrior swoons when he thinks of her widowed and bereaved of her good vassals.   And in this connection we have that deep feeling which finds a voice when one of her sons laments over some fallen comrade in arms, whose life has been bound up with his life by like aspirations, like perils, like deeds of valour in her service. Yet mothers, wives and families are not always forgotten. When, from the heights of the Pyrenees, the French behold once more their native land, there is a softer and more homely touch; their feelings are deeply stirred, even to tears, by remembrances of the maids and wives at home.   And French fathers boast of their little sons, the warriors of the time to come.   "I have a son, named Baldwin; there never was a finer child; if he live he will be a valiant man," says Ganelon.

At Hastings the Normans had advanced into battle chanting this true soldier's song of the paladin *sans peur et sans reproche*, of the hero who fought and died for his country and his God, whose soul the angels bore to Paradise when he fell upon the field of Roncesvalles, stricken down by infidels, traitors and felons, and disdaining till too late to sound his horn to recall the emperor to his side.   And those who found him there remembered his boast that if ever he died in a strange land his body would be found ahead of his fellows with his face turned towards the country of the foe, that he would die conquering.

2316, 2344, 2349.

1695, 2311, 1861, 2017, 2930, 1985.

1402, 1425, 361.

295.

2067.

2863.

Such is the Frenchman's ideal; and in many respects the Norman has read himself into the song, which a Norman pen has preserved for us. It is the creation, severe and unadorned, of a plain and practical people, a soldier's song of soldiers' deeds simply set forth ; and yet how great is its forcefulness, how intense its fire, how masterful and purposeful, how symmetrical and complete it is, pervaded throughout by the one grand, all-dominant ideal. The Norman himself always had an all-dominant ideal, invariably of his own personality, springing from his stern determination to make his mark upon the world, to make all men and all things bow before the majesty of his will. What a master, what a teacher, what a partner he will make for the erratic Anglo-Saxon, now disheartened by the pressure of his heavy fate !

William, the bastard son of Robert of Normandy by a tanner's daughter, who had fought his way first to a dukedom and then to a crown, was a typical Norman. See how cleverly he had laid his plans that the unfortunate Harold might seem to be always in the wrong ! See how he made the Church his friend, professing himself her zealous son, that his expedition might appear more like a Crusade than like a raid ! He had spared no pains to equip his army as perfectly as possible, and yet, knowing the moral advantage it would give him when pitted against a foe who was called forsworn, had not forgotten to obtain a blessing from the pope, and to carry into battle a consecrated standard, with certain holy relics of wonderful efficacy. Thus had an invasion of aggrandisement, whereby the younger sons of Normandy, France, Brittany and Aquitaine hoped to raise themselves to wealth and power when the throne was won, become converted into a holy war. The Anglo-Saxon had been out-manœuvred at all points, even in the battle itself. Well might the story of Renard the Fox afterwards become popular among these men.

In the field William had set a ready example to his knights. He had stumbled and fallen as he landed, and that was an evil omen ; " mal signe est ci." Had not their fathers *Rom. de Rou.* a story that the elves beset the path of one whose fall they desire to see ? Have not they themselves a tale which tells *Huon of* *Bordeaux.* how once Earl Amaury stepped forth sore afraid and swore that his challenger's oath was false ? And when he had so sworn he stumbled and almost fell as he turned to re-mount his steed. And those who saw him stumble took it for an evil sign, and thought within themselves that the matter would go ill with the earl, as indeed it did that day. But William was up on his feet with an oath and a laugh, gripping some of the sand and holding out his hands: "By the splendour of God, I have taken hold of the land with my two hands"; recalling Cæsar's famous "Teneo te, Africa," in similar circumstances. Through the haste of his squires before the battle, his hauberk had been put on the wrong way round, and that again was bad. But he was ready for every emergency. It was but a sign of the coming change in his fortunes: "King shall I be who duke have been." Nor had he forgotten to challenge his rival to single combat for the crown, well knowing the moral confidence Harold's almost certain refusal would give; and the message had been delivered by a monk. He had two horses slain under him; and at the very crisis of the conflict a shout had gone up that the duke was slain, and the host was on the verge of panic, so much did his leadership mean for them. But at once his helmet had been doffed that all might see his face: "Behold me, I live, and, God helping me, shall conquer yet."

He did conquer, and so came into a kingdom by the strength of his own personality which impressed both friends and foes alike. The English had always admired the strong man and the hero, and never had they met a greater than he. After a few vain struggles they all submitted to his rule, and hailed him as their king. This is the estimate formed of him by an Englishman who had sojourned at his court. "That King William of whom we speak was a very wise man and very powerful, more dignified and stronger than any of his predecessors were. He was mild to the good men who loved God, and over all measure severe to the men who gainsaid his will....So also was he a very rigid and cruel man, so that no one dared to oppose him. He had in his bonds earls who had acted against his will. Bishops he cast from their bishoprics, and abbots from their abbacies, and thegns he cast into prison; and at last he spared not his own brother Odo....Among other things is not to be forgotten the good peace that he made in this land, so that a man who had any confidence in himself might go over his realm unhurt with his bosom full of gold; and no man dared slay another,

Rom. de Rou, 11716.

7751.

Ordericus Vitalis, *H. E.* xiii.

A.-S. Chron. 1087, Thorpe.

though he had done never so much evil against him." But, for one thing which was never forgotten, the peasant bore him a grudge. " He had fallen into covetousness and altogether loved greediness. He planted a great preserve for deer, and he laid down laws withal that whosoever should slay hart or hind should be blinded. He forbade the harts and also the boars to be killed. As greatly did he love the tall deer as though he were their father. He also ordained concerning the hares that they should go free. His great men bewailed it, and the poor men murmured thereat, but he was so obdurate that he recked not of the hatred of them all." In consequence the peasant replenished his larder at the risk of his life. Moreover, to make the New Forest, he turned out of house *Rob. of Glou.* and home a great multitude of men, and took their land for thirty miles or more thereabout, to make it all forest and meadow for wild beasts; he took little thought for the poor who had lost their all. William never did things by halves. If he gave a reward, his gift was magnificent; but if he punished, his punishment was cruelly severe. Others emphasise other points in his character; it almost seems as though the Englishman had made a special study of it. He was "a young man of superior mind, who had raised *Will. of* himself to the highest eminence by his unwearied exertion." *Malm.* II. 13. " He was wise but crafty; rich but covetous; glorious, but his *Hen. of Hunt.* ambition was never satisfied." VI.

England is won ; and the practical man at once sits down with pen in hand to sum the profits of his venture. The result is the *Doomsday Book*, a minute inventory of every detail of land, house and man, a unique achievement. Saxon kings indeed, in former days, had attempted some such account, but their efforts were of little value, and fade into insignificance beside that of William.

Such is the leader; such in lesser degree are his followers; self-willed and headstrong men, who have a sublime confidence in themselves, conquerors born and bred, to whom the joy of battle is the very breath of life, to whom slaying and taking possession is the supreme end of existence. Their restless, all-pervading energy dominates all the world they know. Before the century closes, England, Wales, Portugal, Sicily, Naples, Venice and Antioch are in their hands ; and they style themselves "the conquerors of realms[1]." Pope and emperor,

---

[1] *Ch. de Rol.* 3032 : "cels de France ki les regnes cunquièrent."

Turk and Christian alike, know what it is to experience their variable moods. Hard-headed and good at a bargain, they see to it that all their efforts receive a fitting recompense. So they deal with the pope; so they deal with their patron saints; so they would attempt to deal with God Himself. A French knight is engaged in a quarrel. To him says his uncle, an abbot of the Church, "Fair nephew, offer thy gage, for the right is with thee. If thou be vanquished in this quarrel, if ever I return to my abbey, there is no saint in my church but I shall with a staff beat and break to pieces; for if God will suffer such a wrong, I shall give such strokes upon the shrine of St Peter that I shall leave neither gold nor precious stone whole upon it."

Huon of Bord.
Steele, pp. 39,
40.

Wherever his fancy or his advantage leads him, the Norman follows whole-heartedly. Sometimes he is a knight incomparable; then again he is a statesman of highest excellence; and yet again he is a scholar, a theologian, a preacher, an architect, a musician, an orator. The very face of the country he has won is changed to meet his desires. He builds monasteries and abbeys, churches and cathedrals, of Norman architecture, after a style before unknown. He upraises massive towers and castles, that his home may be undisturbed and his possessions secure. The whole country becomes the absolute possession of the king, to be parcelled out in fiefs in accordance with feudal rights. "Folc-land" and "bôc-land" are heard of no more; the Witan is practically a thing of the past. Absolutism and feudalism sweep away the free-rights and liberty of the native, and the Saxon thegn is quite insignificant beside the Norman's greatness. Any attempt to kick against the goads is rudely put down. Saxon lands are devastated, and more and more Norman-French are planted upon them, with more and more castles, which defy assault, for their protection. So it happened in the north after the insurrection in 1068. York was almost annihilated, and the towns and fields of the whole province were laid waste; the produce of the country was destroyed; and the people perished by famine and sword. For sixty years the effects of this devastation were to be seen in the district about York; and for many years, in Northumbria, families of Norman blood outnumbered the original possessors of the soil. A similar insurrection in East Anglia, in 1075, was stamped out at its commencement with like severity;

Will. of
Malm. III.

Will. of
Malm. III.

the leaders were imprisoned and beheaded, and of the rest Hen. of Hunt. VI.
many were exiled and many deprived of sight."

"Lo! thus," says Robert of Gloucester, "the English folk Rob. of Glou. Chron.
came to the ground for a false king, who had no right to the
kingdom, and came to a new lord who had more right. But
neither of them, as men may see, was purely in the right.
And thus, certainly, the land was brought into the Norman's
hand, and it is doubtful if ever it may be recovered. Of the
Normans are the high men of England, and the low men
of the Saxons....And men of religion, of Normandy also, he
endowed here with lands and rents, so that there are few
districts in England that the monks of Normandy have not
somewhat in their hand." It was brought about by God's
will because the people "turned to sloth and pride and lechery
and gluttony,...because of robbery of high men and whore-
dom of clerks."

So it came to pass that it was deemed a disgrace even to
bear the name of Englishman. Instead of freeman and thrall,
it is now Frenchman and Englishman who are not equal in
the eyes of the law. For slaying a Frenchman there is a
penalty; the Englishman may be slain with impunity. The
rightful owners of the land are bowed down by extortions
and burdensome taxes, that the avaricious Norman lords
may heap up the riches for which they have fought. "Whence Hen. of Hunt. VI.
it was got no one asked, but get it they must; the more they
talked of right, the more wrong they did."

The age after the Conquest was, naturally, a period of
unrest and tumult. The infusion of fresh blood added to the
robustness of the nation, but, for a time, the various discordant
elements jostled each other in utter confusion. The feudal
lords became mighty barons, each envious of his neighbour,
his castle a centre of turbulence and strife. Again and again
the smouldering fires of racial hatred blazed out afresh to
be quenched in rivers of blood. Scenes of wanton cruelty
were rife; and it was no uncommon thing for captives to be
brutally mutilated and deprived of sight.

This turbulence seems to reach its height in the reign of
Stephen, when the historians give us an exceedingly vivid
picture of the times. At the outset, calamity is presaged
by the appearance of brilliant meteors in the north, "fiery Acts of Stephen, Ant. Lib.
sparks like a furnace, and balls of fire of wonderful bright-

ness, like the sparks of live coals," shooting through the air, accompanied by a vivid aurora, "luminous flashes floating densely in the blazing sky." Stephen's right to the crown is disputed by the Empress Maud, daughter of the late king; two factions are formed, and the whole country becomes embroiled. In 1136 the Welsh seize the opportunity to rise; and in 1138 the Scots invade the north on behalf of the empress. In both cases extreme barbarity is displayed; and old men, women and children suffer unspeakable atrocities. The Welsh, only partially subdued, are left to themselves to work out their own destruction by internal quarrels until they "perish by famine or cut one another's throats." The Scots, after throwing themselves upon an impenetrable wall of mail-clad knights, are shot down by the archers, and routed with heavy loss at the Battle of the Standard. At home, the barons fortify strong castles, from which they issue, in the name of the empress or king, to harry their neighbours for their own advantage. At Bristol, the stronghold of Robert, earl of Gloucester, half-brother of the empress, the whole country round is terrorised by men "having licence for every sort of villany." Men of substance are taken by force, blind-folded, gagged, and led away into the city, so that their wealth may be extorted from them. Other ruffians, of more subtle cunning, betake themselves further afield into the quieter districts, and frequent the highways in the guise of humble travellers of gentle bearing and courteous address ("nor did they swear and use violent language, as robbers generally do"), until someone appears for whom it is worth while to throw off the mask. So it comes about that when a traveller espies any stranger upon the road, he fears for his life, hurries away down by-roads, or seeks refuge in the woods. Stratagems, ambuscades and surprise assaults are matters of almost daily occurrence, and Stephen's best efforts do little to mitigate the evil. When he advances with an army, the marauders retire to their strongholds, and greet him with defiance. Rival armies take the field; and at Lincoln, in 1140, the king is captured, to his own great humiliation and grief, and imprisoned at Bristol. It is reported that while being disarmed he frequently exclaimed that this shameful disaster had befallen him as a punishment for his sins.

By both sides castles and cities are invested, and earth-
works raised around them to prevent a sudden sally. Engines
are set up which hurl huge stones against the walls and crush
those upon whom they fall. Battering rams are brought up
to make a breach; miners are set to work to sap the fortifications; and firebrands are thrown upon the houses. The
engines are supported by archers and slingers who grievously
distress the defenders. Sometimes there is a stealthy night
attack, when scaling ladders of thongs bound together are
thrown over the battlements. Sometimes there are daily
assaults by the bravest knights and men-at-arms who rush
up to the ramparts under cover of a shower of arrows. If
these methods fail, it only remains to reduce the garrison by
starvation. On one occasion, when the castle at Hereford is
attacked, the citizens are horrified to see armed men quartered
within their cathedral, and its tower converted into a station
for engines of war; and greater still is their horror when the
grave-yard is dug up to make a rampart, the bodies of the
dead being rudely disinterred.

The Norman bishops are like the barons. They carry
arms and ride in shining armour, they build strong castles,
and possess numerous retainers; they ravage, torture and
kill. William of Canterbury, a man "broken down and completely enervated by luxury" and impurity, is notorious for
his avarice. His nephew, the bishop of Ely, becomes strong
enough to oppose the king on the marshes surrounding his
cathedral city; his son, by Maud of Ramsbury, narrowly
escapes being hanged upon a lofty gallows before the castle
gate at Devizes. The bishop of Winchester, brother of the
king, holds his castle against a host of besiegers who are
themselves surrounded by a royal army without the city.
"All England was there in arms," with a great gathering
of foreign mercenaries. The rebels are routed and dispersed with heavy loss; the royalists spread over the whole
district in pursuit, and take enormous booty. Riderless
horses gallop hither and thither, or, over-ridden and foun-
dered, lie dying; armour, weapons, shields, robes, vessels
and ornaments strew the ground in profusion. Defeated
knights and barons doff their cognisances and flee away on
foot, "disguising even their names in shame and fear." Some
are slain by the peasantry; others take refuge in caves, and

well-nigh perish through hunger. The archbishop and other bishops and eminent men, "separated from their attendants, their horses and clothes carried off, or barbarously torn from them, were scarce able to creep to some safe hiding-place after the fearful rout."

The Empress Maud comes to London at the invitation of the citizens; but her haughtiness and hard dealing soon bring about a change of feeling. She is sitting at dinner, all unconscious of danger, when the bells ring out a summons calling the whole city to arms. She hears the tumult; that she herself is the object of attack; and there is just time to mount and gallop away before the angry citizens break in, and pillage the quarters she has quitted. She flees to Oxford; but Stephen has now been exchanged for the earl of Gloucester, and she is there besieged. Then follows her romantic escape, accompanied by three of her knights, through the outposts of the royal army, when the country lies deep in snow and the rivers are frozen hard, "while the silence of night was broken all around by the clang of trumpets and the cries of the guard."

But, at Wilton, Gloucester defeats the royal forces, and reduces the country far and near to subjection, utterly destroying the royal castles, and strengthening his own, till half the kingdom is in his hands. The people suffer from both parties. "What with the tyranny of the one and the turbulence of the other, there was universal turmoil and desolation." Many flee from the country; others take sanctuary in the churches. Famine appears; the wretched peasantry are forced to eat the flesh of horses and dogs, and uncooked herbs and roots, and they die in heaps. However, with the fall of Farringdon Castle, the tide of fortune turns once more in favour of the king; and finally in 1153 an amicable agreement with regard to the succession is arrived at by the Treaty of Winchester.

For the Norman it is all a stirring tale of the romance of war, of strenuous life, of daring deeds and thrilling escapades. Perils and combats are dear to his adventurous heart; and the more thrilling they are, the greater is the zest with which he enjoys his life. But the romance of the Anglo-Saxon has died out long ago; and he is now too much overcast by his troubles to return to the romantic mood.

See what the Saxon says who has contemporaneous know- *A.-S. Chron.*
ledge of all these things: "When King Stephen came to
England he made his gathering at Oxford; and there he took 1137.
the Bishop Roger of Salisbury, and Alexander, bishop of
Lincoln, and the Chancellor Roger, his nephews, and put
them all in prison till they gave up their castles. When the
traitors perceived that he was a mild man and soft and good,
and never did justice, then did they all mischief. They had
done homage to him and sworn oaths, but they held no faith.
They were all forsworn, and broke their troth; for every
powerful man made his castles, and held them against the
king, and filled the land full of castles. They cruelly afflicted
the wretched men of the land with castle-works. When the
castles were made, they filled them with devils and evil men.
Then they took, both by night and day, those men whom
they thought to possess any goods, peasant men and women,
and put them in prison to get their gold and silver, and
tortured them with indescribable torture, for there were never
martyrs so tortured as they were. Men hanged them up by
the feet, and smoked them with foul smoke; they hanged
them by the thumbs or by the head, and hung corslets on
their feet; they put knotted strings about their heads, and
twisted them until they cut to the brain. They put them in
prison where there were adders and snakes and toads, and so
slew them. Some they put in a 'crucet-hus,' that is, in a
chest that was short and narrow and not deep, and put sharp
stones therein, and pressed the man in it, so that they
broke all his limbs. In many of the castles were bolts and
shackles, neck fetters, such that two or three men found it
hard to bear one. Each was so made that it was fastened to
a beam; and they put a sharp iron about the man's throat
and neck, so that he might nowhere sit or lie or sleep, but
bore all the iron. Many thousands they killed with hunger.
I neither can nor may tell all the awful wickedness or all
the tortures, that they did to wretched men in this land; and
it lasted the nineteen winters that Stephen was king, and
ever it was worse and worse. They laid tribute on the towns
continually, and called it 'censerie[1].' When the wretched
men had no more to give, then they ravaged and burned all
the towns, so that you might easily go a full day's journey

[1] taxation.

and never find a man sitting in a town, or the land tilled. Then was corn dear, and flesh and cheese and butter, for there was none in the land. Wretched men died of hunger. Some went begging who were at one time rich men; some fled out of the land. There was never more wretchedness in the land. Never did the heathen worse than they did, for everywhere at times they spared neither church nor church-yard, but took all the property that was therein, and then burned the church and all together. They spared neither bishops' land, nor abbots', nor priests', but robbed monks and clerks; and every man robbed his fellow wherever he could. If two men or three came riding to a town, all the township fled because of them, judging that they were robbers. The bishops and clergy cursed them ever, but that was nothing to them, for they were all accursed and forsworn and utterly abandoned. Wheresoever a man tilled, the earth bore no corn, for the land was all destroyed with such deeds ; and they said openly that Christ and His saints slept. Such, and more than we can say, we endured for nineteen winters, because of our sins." Truly a pitiful, heart-breaking tale !

In the next reign the state of affairs does not seem to have been much better ; and the historian again points with an accusing finger to the plague-spots of his time. Now the churchmen are the objects of his denunciation. They follow Satan rather than God, and their evils are many and various. A hundred murders have been committed by clerks alone since the commencement of the reign. The Church is care-less in her choice of servants, and her discipline is lax to the very extreme of disorder. That she may swell her numbers and add to her power, she opens her doors to those who would more fittingly grace the gallows than the altar. Her leaders are joyous-hearted, worldly-minded Normans, warrior-prelates, who serve for ambition's sake and not for love, for self rather than God rules in their hearts, and sways their every action[1]. There are the fighting bishops, Hugh de Puset, William de Longchamp and Geoffrey Plantagenet, whose

---

[1] Is not Turpin the prototype from which they have degenerated? Cf. *Ch. de Rol.* 2242 :

> "Morz est Turpins el servise Carlun.
> Par granz batailles e par mult bels sermuns
> Cuntre paiens fut tuz tens campiun."

lives and morals will not bear close inspection, to undo all
that such men as Lanfranc and Anselm could do.   Hence
the chaos within the Church; a chaos from which, when
the Englishman can analyse its causes, a mighty Reformation
will spring.   But for the present there can be no strong opposition to the evil, when even the court itself is said to be   Map, *De*
like the infernal regions, and no place for the quiet, con-   *Nug. Cur.*
centrated mind.   Wright,
                                                                 pp. 14, 141-2.

By the Conquest an all-powerful foreign element was
introduced into England.   The king and his nobles were
foreigners, and so, too, were most of the bishops and leading
clergy, the judges and court officials.   "England is become
the residence of foreigners and the property of strangers,"   *Will. of*
says William of Malmesbury; "at the present time there is   *Malm.* II. 13.
no Englishman either earl, bishop, or abbot; strangers all,
they prey upon the riches and vitals of England; nor is there
any hope of a termination to this misery."   Everywhere in
court and castle one heard the French language spoken; and
the literature also became for a time Norman-French.   Even
the place of the Witan was usurped by a Norman assembly.
Scholars pursued their studies in Latin and French; and it
became the fashion for a youth to finish his course at the
University of Paris.   Thus England was closely linked with the
Continent; and by this connection its thought, its character,
its life, were cast in the continental mould; the national
insularity being thus for a time broken down.   Ignorant was
he held to be who could only speak the native English
tongue; uncouth and rude, a very boor, he who persisted
in the manners and customs of his fathers.   Language long
formed the line of demarcation between the aristocracy and
the people.   "Lo! thus came England into Normandy's   *Rob. of Glou.*
hand," says Robert of Gloucester, "and the Normans could   *Chron.*
speak then but their own speech, and spoke French as they
did at home, and did teach it also to their children, so that
the high men of this land that came of their blood all hold
that speech which they had from them.   For unless a man
know French one accounts of him little.   But low men hold
to English and their own speech yet."

So, for many years, the national thought is French, the
politics French, the interests French; the education, manners
and morals are French.   Kings of England are buried in

Normandy, the fatherland, whither they have constantly turned their eyes and aspirations in life; for France, "la belle France," is still the ideal. Long afterwards the young king Edward III. will tell his queen that, in his mind, there is no realm to be compared with the realm of France. In England they have their knighthood and their chivalry just as they had in France; they hold jousts and tournaments, such as the home-staying Englishman had never seen before; they fight their battles in the French fashion with the shock of the cavalry charge to complete the devastation which the bows have made. Their dress is after the French mode; French dishes are upon their tables; French songs are heard in their halls, French sermons in their pulpits. The social organisation and administration are likewise French. When they commence their University of Oxford it is modelled upon that of Paris. French scholars are brought in to become English teachers, French priests to become English bishops; so that the native-born Englishman who has ambition becomes himself a pseudo-Frenchman.

Froissart,
Chron. Globe
ed. p. 32.

Usually the Saxon stands without the pale of Norman life. Norman chivalry has little attraction for him; rarely does he join in a Crusade; rarely does he read the Norman books, or learn to chant the Norman songs, for he knows but little French, and such things are beyond the circle of his desires. There are now two national literatures in the country, the courtly French and the popular English, with two great classes of the people to correspond. And in addition there is another literature between the two, the learned Latin, in which the educated of both races may meet on common ground. Here, to a certain extent, opportunity is offered to the few for an interchange of opinions and ideas.

Little by little, however, the points of contact increase; the two great classes are gradually drawn together; and the leaven of the French influence begins to work in the whole people. The Norman nobles had at first usually married only Norman or French wives; and in their families the pure Norman strain continued. But many of lower rank married Englishwomen, and, as such marriages increased in frequency, the result can easily be foreseen. Just as the older Norseman had been absorbed by the French, so now the

Norman-French began to be absorbed by the English, to
result in a blended nation possessing the traits of both races.
By the reign of Henry II. intermarriage had already so far *Dial. de Scac.*
brought about a blending that it had become difficult to say I. 10.
who was of the Norman-French and who of the Anglo-Saxon
strain. Only in the case of the villeins and serfs was the
difference plain. Among these latter the older English
characteristics were still preserved, and thus of necessity,
from their numerical preponderance, and from the nature of
their life, the condition was imposed that the direction of the
blending should always incline rather towards the Anglo-
Saxon than the Norman type.

Again, the clergy in religion and learning, the harpers
and minstrels in romance and song, were the especial
means of communication between the extreme parties,
gathering from either side to form a literature which
afterwards became national in language, custom, habit and
thought. The roving clergy were everywhere, and knew
every side of life, forming a body of men predominantly
cosmopolitan in training and experience. The wandering
minstrels were no less so, and perhaps through them the
literary fusion first began.

In warfare, too, Englishman and Norman often fought
side by side. They fought together at the Battle of the
Standard for England against the Scots; they fought
together in France for the king of England against the
duke of Normandy; and, in politics, there came to be a vast
difference between Anglo-Norman and Norman-Frenchman,
especially so when the barons who held fiefs in England were
not allowed to hold others across the Channel.

And among those who suffered through royal oppression
were men of both races who made common cause against
the tyrant. Besides men of the poorer classes, upon whom
the severity of the game laws pressed most cruelly, there
were famous leaders of the type of Hereward the Saxon and
Fulk Fitz-Warin the Norman. Many of the English who
had risen against the Conqueror and his sons took refuge in
the fastnesses of the woods and fens, and there lived as outlaws; and to them were added men of Norman or mixed
blood who had incurred the displeasure of the king or the
powerful nobles. These were the outcasts of feudalism, who

supported themselves by the game they slew, or by chance plundering of their oppressors. In the greenwood they seem to have lived a merry, independent life, owning allegiance to none but their own elected leaders. Many a rich noble or prosperous ecclesiastic, when entrapped by them, was compelled to pay a heavy ransom before he was permitted to depart; but the old songs have it that women and the poor always met with generous treatment at their hands. Everyone on the countryside seems to have known and loved the memory of Robin Hood, around whose name was built up a tale of daring deeds, which was, no doubt, of mythical origin, but yet portrays the character and life of many a forest outlaw. Here again the sympathies of the two races meet on common ground.

By the reign of Henry III. the blending was practically completed. Normandy and Anjou were no longer domains of the English kings; and so little did the new Englishman care about their loss that the barons refused to fight to get them back again. With the loss of these provinces the ties which bound the Norman to the Continent were broken. Instead he had the ties of home and the society in which he moved. And when we turn to the political songs of the reign we see that these new ties were sufficiently strong to bind together the barons and the people against the king and his favourites. Already the new nation has begun to know its strength, as the Constitutions of Clarendon (1164) and Magna Carta (1215) will show. In 1265 popular representation in Parliament begins with the first assemblage of the representatives of the cities and boroughs at Westminster.

By degrees it is almost forgotten that any real distinction of race has ever existed, and history is strained that the historian and the poet may invent a common origin for all. Britons, Angles, Saxons, Danes, Normans and French alike become the reputed offspring of the sons of Troy. How closely their belief in this fictitious common origin knits together both sections of the people may be seen in the roll of heroes of whom the poets sing, including Brutus, Hengist and Horsa, Alfred, Arthur, Cnut, Edward the Confessor and William the Conqueror. By their hero-worship the races are united; and there is much in common between the heroic

Hen. of Hunt.
VII.
Geof. of Mon.
I. 16.

ideals of both which leads them to a wider appreciation of each other. The motive which leads Beowulf to die for his people is not a little akin to that which leads Roland to his death at Roncesvalles. Either hero might have been accepted as a true son of fallen yet glorious Troy. In the heroic ideals of both peoples the highest place, even above that of the victor, is given to him who displays undaunted valour and unconquerable spirit in the face of certain defeat and death.

Naturally it takes time before the Saxon has thoroughly assimilated the French influence. In the *Story of Horn* and the *Lay of Havelok* it may be seen how he is striving to imitate his model, though it must be confessed that he does so in a very rough and ready fashion. Evidently he is not as yet distinguished for courtliness, and in his manners there is a great lack of social refinement; but still it is just as clear that the effort is being made. Even when the two nations have progressed far towards unity their differing characteristics may be seen existing side by side. There is still the recurrent strain of melancholy which is a prominent feature of Old English poetry, to form a decided contrast to the youthful happiness and gaiety of the Norman, who has not yet sounded the depths of life's experience of sorrow, but advances gaily over the heights where the breeze is fresh and the air exhilarating. Neither strain will ever be completely lost. The *Fliting of the Owl and the Night-* *Owl and* *ingale* shows both strains very clearly; the owl being, *Nightingale.* apparently, the embodiment of the Saxon temperament, the nightingale of the Norman. The one is sober and severe, more ready to weep than to sing, with the ever-present consciousness of sin and the necessity of winning salvation by self-denials and mortifications; while the other makes of life a merry song, a time of rejoicing, a season of gallantry. It is almost the contrast of grey old age with joyous youth. The Norman lives in the present, or looks forward with hopefulness to the prime which is yet to be; the Saxon looks back upon the years that are past with melancholy and regret. Such is the effect of the moulding of character by circumstances. It may be that the poem is a reflection of the contest within the Church, between the more ascetic and reforming party and their brethren of more lax discipline and morals; or it may shadow forth the opposing parties of the troubled years of Henry III., 1264–5; but its ultimate dissection reveals the contrast of two temperaments, the Anglo-Saxon and the Norman-French.

When the races have blended, the Englishman will not spend so much time brooding over his sins and his sorrows. He will again take a pride in himself, his country, and all that is in it. "England is a very good land, best of all lands," he will say. "It is an island, and so they need fear no foes except through treachery within. Men may see in England plenty of all goods...for it is full enough of fruit and trees, of woods and parks, of birds and beasts and fish, of rivers and wells, of meadows and pastures, of minerals, of corn, of trade....Its people are the fairest and the cleanliest in the world. So clean is the land, and so pure the blood of the people, that the great evil comes not there as it does in France." Another stage further and we shall hear of "the English people of Merrie England," with a land "full of mirth and of game, and men ofttimes able to mirth and game, free men of heart and with tongue." This will be when the Norman's romance and song and tale have had their full effect.

Rob. of Glouc. Chron.

Cursor Mundi. Trevisa, De Prop. Rerum, XV. 14.

The French *chansons* had been sung by the minstrels just as the Saxon gleemen had sung their national songs; but when we find the written romances ousting them from their former popularity the natural deduction is that, at least in the castles and halls, a reading public has developed, which can not only read, but is, moreover, sufficiently proficient to derive pleasure from its reading. At first there must have been many listeners and few readers, but the number of the latter grows till even the *chansons* are written down for the reader's pleasure, and not left altogether to the minstrel's art. Then the minstrel's profession begins to decline, till at last he is banished to the streets and marketplaces with the unlettered for an audience. With the growth of the reading public, which argues a corresponding intellectual development in social life, the romance takes to itself an increased complexity in art, in motive, and in characterisation, just as the more primitive *chanson* had begun to change under the influence of the manners and ideas of early feudalism. In French romance the life of the later feudal

age is perfectly reproduced. And this upward development and change of fashion has very far-reaching consequences, in that it prepares the way for that intellectual
quickening which is known to us as the Renaissance. Even
in themselves the romances show not only a confluence of
influences from afar, but also a certain amount of originality
and experiment. In them the western mind is seen bent
upon the pursuit of new things and new ideas, to be expressed with all the elegance, fluency and sentiment which
are characteristic of the latter half of this period. A most
striking change will be seen in the representation of love
as an all-consuming passion, and not merely as an art but
also as a science, with a well-defined psychology of its own.
The world in which the heroes move becomes a world of
ideals; the heroes themselves are ideal; their chivalry is
ideal. It is as though the men of the age have felt the
need of ideals to raise them out of themselves. Perhaps the
Anglo-Saxon of the preceding age had felt the need of some
such new stimulus from without when he had strayed upon
the *Epistle to Alexander* and *Apollonius of Tyre.* It is in the
transition from the *chanson* to the romance that the future
imaginative and intellectual life of England and of Europe
is foreshadowed; for all modern imagination seems to have
its roots in the literature of this period. The transition itself
is gradual and, at first, merely a matter of social class and
of intellectual appreciation. The older and more primitive
literature still remains among the poorer and simpler classes
after the later has won its way into the aristocratic and more
cultured circles, who have come more speedily, and with
greater receptivity, under the influence of the many complex
movements of the age. For the old is simple, individual;
the new, complex, semi-political. It may even be said that
the period is an age of the awakening of political science.
Men are more generally swayed by the motives of a wider
patriotism and religion, of empire and Christendom, than by
purely selfish considerations. There is to be seen a general
knitting together of men with common political interests to
make new nations; and character receives an enhanced importance, inasmuch as it influences, no less than it is influenced by, the state of society in communities of wider
growth and with greater responsibilities than before.

As the mind of the uncultured barbarian had been most susceptible to that aspect of the mysterious which he called magic, and as the mind of the monk had been most deeply impressed by stories of miracles, so now the mind of the adventurous soldier is turned to the romantic tales of chivalry. As magic had previously opened the way for miracle, so now both these prepare the way for romance. If there had not been a romantic element even in everyday life the tanner's bastard grandson would never have been seated upon the throne of England as William the First. The very quintessence of romance is in the air these men breathe; all that remains is to commit it to the written page. Even their better knowledge cannot resist the spell. Does not one of them travel into Brittany to the far-famed forest of Broceliande, led by the expectation of seeing with his own eyes some of the marvels of which all men speak, but only to make an unsuccessful quest? "Fool I went; fool I returned." It is no wonder that the *Brut* and the *Roman de Rou* of Wace appear to mark the age, and with them the *Roman de Troie*, the *Roman de Thebes*, and numerous other kindred romances, whose heroes are of the Norman type, with Norman manners and Norman dress, with Norman barons and tonsured monks, with a Venus as a princess of chivalry, and a Queen Penthesilea who rides astride with great red spurs upon her heels.

Wace, *Rom. de Rou*, 11534.

In the *Brut* for the first time there appear signs that not only is the Norman impressing himself upon the nations, but that he himself is also undergoing a subtle change. In Brittany and in Wales he has been brought into contact with the imaginative Celt, to whom he is drawn by a sympathy intellectual and artistic; and he now begins to acquire that which he has hitherto lacked. It has been said that the Cymry were the most intellectual people of the mediæval age; and in them it seems that the spirit of individualism and independence, which the feudal system of the Normans tended to strangle, was kept alive upon their impregnable mountains and rock-bound coasts. In them, more highly strung, more fanciful, than any other people, there was a strong belief in the supernatural, with the corresponding tendency towards mysticism; while dim traditions from ages long since past had been preserved among them

Thierry, *Norm. Conq.*

with tenderest veneration. Upon all these the Normans seized greedily. They were strange; they were new; they were fascinating. So we have soon the Arthurian cycle of romance, with its mystery, its elves and wizards, its magic and supernaturalism, its enchanted horns and mystic Graal, all expressed with a delicacy of touch which the heavy-handed Norman had to set himself to school to acquire. Then, everywhere in the wonderful tales of Troy and Thebes and Rome, of Britain and the East, of Arthur and Alexander and Charlemagne, all endued with the imaginative fantasy of the Celt, there is heard the weird and plaintive spell, the enchantment of romance. And, blended with all this, there is the softness and tenderness of love, at first merely as a secondary adjunct to the action, but later its primary motive force, as the character of the age changes from barbaric heroism to knightly chivalry. The influence spreads till it enters the lays of Marie de France, and even colours much of the religious thought of the day. Women, as well as men, both read and write these romantic tales. So popular are the new elements that the Breton has the place of honour among the minstrels; and we also find a high dignitary of *Geof. of Mon.* the Church going out of his way to set forth the professedly ¹·¹· true history of Arthur and his knights, that all may know whence come the fabulous stories in which men find delight. But the leopard cannot change his spots, and there are to be found, side by side with idyllic passages of extreme beauty, episodes of fierce passion and unlawful love, even of incest, which befoul the arms of the most gallant knight, and rob him of perfection.

With the spirit of romance is blended that of the Pro-vencal lyric poetry, which thrives upon the works of Ovid and other classical amatory poets. Hence the warmth of the south is transfused into, and kept alive in, the northern character, with all the idealism, formalism, pedantry and manifold conceits which are the chief features of Provençal song. Those who are thus influenced make love the main motive of existence, and all other questions pale before the many psychological problems which the subject presents. The Norman, in his own hardy character representing the masculine side of chivalry, its " prowesse," which delights in the brave deeds of warlike heroes, now takes to himself its feminine side, its "courtoisie," which embraces all the love, the tenderness, the courtliness which prevail among the Provencals of the south.

Still another great change in life, thought and morals comes at this time from the East. The adventurous knight is always ready to embark upon a holy war, especially so since there are new lands to be seen, and new territories to be conquered. He had made of his invasion of England a quasi-Crusade even before the Crusades; and, when the Conquest is complete, the roving spirit within him leads to a ready acceptance of the call of the Church to free the Holy Sepulchre from the infidel. The consequences of the Crusades can never be completely told. First of all, there is the mixing together, in the same cause, of men of almost every European nation, leading to an interchange of ideas and the sharpening of the faculties of those thus brought into contact with each other. There is a widening of the social horizon; and the circumscribed fatherland opens out into a Christendom where all are animated with the same desires. And this horizon again extends itself when the East, the land of all marvel and strange mystery, is reached; so that even the religious and chivalrous spirit which has prompted each enterprise is almost obscured by the manifold influences which are brought to bear upon every individual, who becomes the more susceptible the further he travels from his home. Round eastern camp-fires the Crusader catches the Oriental passion for tale-telling; and soon stores of Indian, Persian and Arabian tales are brought to Europe, full of every exaggeration and wonder, for the East has never been entirely comprehensible to the West. He has seen and plundered the costly treasures of cities and palaces, and is dazzled and spell-bound by the glamour of their magnificence. When he returns home he brings with him a confused impression of magnificent buildings of costly stone, of rich furniture and splendid ornamentation, of priceless jewels and wonderful raiment, of every luxury and every delicacy. Henceforth he will talk of the silks of Constantinople, of the cloth of Tars and Alexandrian purple, of embroidered satins and superb palls fringed with gold, of golden candlesticks and silver censers, of basins of enamelled gold and golden boxes studded with gems, of rich girdles and mantles of ermine, of beds of gold and ivory, curiously carved and inlaid with precious stones, dazzling in the splendour of their ornaments and worth more than the price of a castle, of embroidered pillows, rich coverlets edged with sable, and finest linen. And all this magnificence he will strive to imitate until the climax is reached some centuries later on a certain " Field of the Cloth of Gold."

Henceforth the writer of a romance must possess a certain amount of taste in such matters. He must be able to group together the choicest examples to add to the richness of his tale. He must read books of all descriptions to supply the garnishment of his story ; and where his reading falls short he must be ready with a fecund imagination to furnish any amount of improvised detail. A strict regard for plain truth is not at all desirable, for with an uncritical audience it pays better and wins more fame to excel in the art of heaping astonishment upon astonishment, wonder upon wonder.

At Constantinople the Crusader seems to have made the acquaintance of the Greek romances, dealing subtly with the subject of love and the adventures and sufferings of lovers. He studies the intricacies of the Greek plots, and, in consequence, his own thought becomes deeper and more subtle. He makes the Greek methods his own, but substitutes heroes of a more sturdy and valorous type, men of his own blood, whose hearts he knows, for the effete and unknightly characters whose motives he can but darkly understand. His own idea of love, which has been to him in the past, except so far as Christianity has chastened it, a mere animal passion, now becomes more sensitive, more subtle, more analytical. And thus from the Greek *Habrocomas and Anthia*, through the French *Roman de Cliget*, the way is prepared for future enjoyment of the story of *Romeo and Juliet*.

One great development, which springs from within rather than from without, directly fostered by the religious spirit which led to the Crusades, remains to be noted ; and that is the advance of the knightly ideal, in which the sense of honour appears in a threefold form, involving the inviolable sanctity of an oath, the regular performance of religious duties, and an almost sacred regard and reverence for womanhood.

Thus innumerable influences are brought to bear upon the minds of men at this period when the Anglo-Saxon and Norman-French races are blending, and when, in consequence, the men themselves are more susceptible than ever before to new impressions from without. To both races the old life seems far behind; the new, so pregnant with manifold possibilities, lies so near, as they step together upon the threshold of modern civilisation. The receptive and appreciative Anglo-Norman is especially well equipped with a large endowment of varied experience at the outset of his national career.

The home life of the period presents to us, on the whole, a not altogether unpleasing picture. In the intervals of war, the baron dwells at ease in his castle in the midst of wide *Gawain and Green Kn.* domains. His home is a massive pile, uprising from a lofty eminence, with turrets and towers, with windows, chalk-white chimneys and painted pinnacles "powdered everywhere,"

802.　　　　　　"That pared out of paper purely it seemed."

A moat, deep and broad, sometimes a double ditch, crossed by a drawbridge defended by barbican and portcullis, winds round the walls of squared stone, strong and thick, fortified *Morte D'Arth.* with curiously carved battlements, and flanked by heavy *Mallory,* *VII. 10.* buttresses. The lofty parapets, mounted with warlike engines, *R. de la Rose,* are pierced through with embrasures for the archers, and with *Chaucer, 4148.* holes through which stones or molten lead may be poured upon the heads of those who attempt to scale them. Within, there is an ample courtyard; and without, before the great gate, there is a level space or lawn where the knights and men-at-arms may practise their martial exercises. Usually at the foot of the hill nestles the village where the poorer retainers dwell. For two miles or more about may lie the *Gaw. and Gr.* park or meadow-land, dotted with trees, and enclosed by *Kn.* a spiked palisade. Still further away stretches the woodland, or the rugged slope of valley and hill, with here and there a hamlet or homestead surrounded by cultivated fields.

Garin le Within the castle we find its owner, and his lady is by his *Loherain.* side. He kisses her upon the mouth, and we know that in his own way he has a very tender affection for her. Other lords we know are not always so affectionate, and are apt to think that one love is as good as another. "Much more

I am sorrier for my good knights' loss, than for the loss of my fair queen," says King Arthur ; "for queens I might have enow, but such a fellowship of good knights shall never be together in no company." Our baron looks with pride upon his sons as they come through the hall accompanied by a band of youths of gentle birth. They run and leap with one another, playing, laughing and sporting in all youthful merriment.

M. D'Arth. xx. 9, and cf. *Ch. de R.* 3714.

Perhaps the morning mass or matins has just been sung, and they are about to break their fast before entering upon the pleasures or duties of the day. The knights are wont to take a hasty sop after matins before hunting. To begin the day with religious observances is the universal custom. Gawain, while on his adventures, is troubled lest he should miss matins, though the indolent and luxurious sometimes make a mere pretence of worship. "The nobility, given up to luxury and wantonness, went not to church in the morning after the manner of Christians, but merely in a careless manner heard matins and masses from a hurrying priest in their chambers," says William of Malmesbury.

M. D'Arth. vII. 9, 10, etc.

Gaw. and Gr. K'n. 1135.

750.

Will. of Malm. III.

A little later in the day, and we may see the hunters ride away with coupled hounds in leash and hawks on wrist, with a merry clatter and noise and the sounding of horns, while the ladies stand in the bay windows to watch them as they go by. We notice how carefully here and there someone handles a favourite hound or well-trained falcon, as though its value were above price. Perhaps it has been won as the prize of a tournament at the risk of life and limb. Those who once found a knight lying slain in the forest, and his three hounds raging and howling with grief over his body, said : "This was a true man ; his dogs loved him." There was once a knight who loved a lady, but she ran away from him, and took with her two of his hounds ; and when he came home and missed them, "then was he more wroth for his brachets than for the lady." On rides the cavalcade in quest of the hart, the hare, the fox and the boar, the latter being especially esteemed a noble quarry ; and now that there is no more to see the ladies descend from the windows.

M. D'Arth. xIX. 4.

Gar. le Loh. *M. D'Arth.* Ix. 40.

Perhaps, if it is the month of May, some of them will choose to go a-maying in the woods and fields, and call upon their swains, who have forgone the pleasures of the chase for

xIX. 1.

their society, to accompany them. So they make themselves ready, each cavalier decked out gaily in green silk or cloth, each with a lady behind him, to ride singing into the woods, and there to make from the groves garlands of woodbine or of hawthorn leaves, to cover themselves with herbs, moss and flowers, after the true fashion of the merry month.

Chaucer,
Knight's Tale.

Court of Love,
1436.

> "Eke each at other threw the flowers bright,
>   The primërose, the violet, the gold."

Neckam, De
Nat. Rer. I. 23,
II. 165, 166.

Those who remain disperse about the castle and grounds ; some see to the rare beasts and birds which were then kept in all great mansions ; some visit the poultry-yard ; some wander arm in arm into a pleasant garden of flowers of many hues, but with the national colours, red, white and blue, predominating. The garden is well kept, with shady alleys of blossoming trees and sanded paths. Somewhere is heard the babbling of a brook ; and in the midst there may be a fountain with a pipe of silver throwing aloft a sparkling jet which descends in spray into a marble basin. In a secluded corner a goodly old gentleman is reclining upon cloth of silk, leaning upon his elbow, and listening to a fair and gentle maid who is reading aloud from a romance, while an older lady has drawn fondly near to catch the tale, for the maiden is their only child.

Troilus and
Cress. II. 51,
820,
Pearl.
M. D'Arth.
IV. 8.

Chev. au Lion.

Troilus and
Cress. II. 83.

Within doors, in a paved parlour, other ladies are likewise engaged in reading and listening to romances. Another, love-sad and alone, sits in her chamber with her harp, and sings "a piteous lay of love." She "sings sweetly ; the voice accords to the instrument ; the hands are beautiful ; the lay is fine ; sweet the voice and low the tone." And this lonesome lady, we learn, is as clever as she is beautiful. She can not only read and write, but she knows many lays and can compose her own songs. She is the far-famed Iseult. And yet another lady appears to be reading hard under the tuition of learned masters :

Tristan and
Iseult.

Guy of War.
Ellis, *Met.*
Romances,
p. 190.

> "Gentil she was, and as demure
>   As ger-fauk, or falcon to lure,
>   That out of mewë were y-drawe,
>   So fair was none, in soothë sawe !
>   She was thereto courteous, and free, and wise
>   And in the seven arts learnëd withouten miss.
>   Her masters werë thither come

> Out of Thoulousë, all and some,
> White and hoar all they were;
> Busy they were that maiden to lere.
> And her lerëd of astronomy,
> Of ars-metrick, and of geometry;
> Of sophistry she was also witty,
> Of rhetorick, and of other clergy.
> Learned she was in musick:
> Of clergy was her none like."

The higher education of women is evidently no modern invention.

Thus the day is spent till nightfall; and with the dusk the merry-makers return; and shortly afterwards the hunters, too, appear. Horns wind without the walls; there are lusty calls for the porter to open speedily; the drawbridge descends; the portcullis, with its great sharp teeth, is raised; the gate is thrown wide open; and into the courtyard rides the clamorous company. Squires and serving-men rush out to take the horses, and to assist their masters to bring in the quarry. The whole courtyard is full of bustling life and merriment. And, perhaps, while the confusion is at its height, some stranger knight rides in to seek hospitality for the night. He is courteously welcomed by the lord of the castle; his horse is led to the stables; knights and squires come forward to relieve him of his weapons; and pages show him to his chamber. *Gaw. and Gr. Kn.*

All now prepare for the evening meal. Pages carry water *Guy of War.* for their masters and mistresses, and sometimes prepare baths with herbs for their refreshment after the exertions of the day. Splendid robes and embroidered mantles are donned; and *Eliduc.* all begin to descend into the great tapestried hall. The stranger is seated by the hearth, but, as the ladies enter, rises to greet them courteously with a kiss, after the fashion *Guy of War.* of the day. The tables are spread, and the knights and *Gaw. and Gr. Kn. 974.* ladies are seated. Hawks sit on perches about the hall, and *Knight's Tale, 2203.* dogs lie on the floor near their masters. A blessing is asked; *Havelok,* 1723. the squires carve, and wait upon their masters, or act as cupbearers. One of them "gives the says[1]," and the meal *Froiss. Chron.* commences. There is profusion everywhere, fancy bread, *III. 26. Globe ed.* fish, venison, pasties, boar's heads, game, wines, and fruits *P. 332.*

---

[1] Performs the office of taster: "Faisoit essay de toutes ses viands."

M. D'Arth.
XVIII. 3.
of many kinds. Some of the knights are especially fond of apples and pears, as well as—

Cœur de Lion,
Ellis.
"......of bread and wine,
  Piment, clarry, good and fine,
  Of cranes, and swans, and venison,
  Partridges, plovers, and heron,
  Of larks and small volatile."

M. D'Arth.
VII. 31.
They eat their food "knightly" and "eagerly," using knives and fingers, with the eyes of the ladies upon them, for the manner of a knight's eating proclaims his birth and breeding. One or two of them, perhaps, forget themselves, *Stans puer ad mensam.*
Petit Jehan de Saintré, p. 71,
Vance.
Gaw. and Gr. Kn. 116, 1652.
Havelok, 1717. and use a knife as a toothpick; one lady uses a pin for a like purpose. While the dinner proceeds there is much mirth and minstrelsy, sometimes the music of trumpets and pipes from a gallery in the hall, with the laughter of ladies to cheer the guests. Sometimes partners are exchanged between the courses.

After dinner usually follows evensong in the chapel; and then the evening is spent in merry conversation and social intercourse. Perhaps there is dancing; perhaps the company proceeds—

Ipomydon,
Ellis.
"Some to chamber and some to bower,
  And some to the high tower;
  And some in the hall stood,
  And spake what hem thought good;
  Men that were of that citee
  Enquired of men of other countree
  Of Calabre land who was king."

Guy of War.
Isumbras.
The traveller is always assailed on every side for the latest news of the lands through which he has passed, and is always sure of an interested and attentive audience.

When his tale is told, one of the knights brings out his harp, and accompanies himself as he sings his lay; for the *Trist. and Is.* perfect knight is always musical. We notice the rapt attention of his audience, since he is a famous harper, and his exquisite music is ever a potent spell. This same knight is also renowned for his knowledge of all that appertains to venery; and from him come all the terms of hunting, hawking and blowing the horn, so "that all manner of gentle-*M. D'Arth.*
X. 52.men have cause to the world's end to praise Sir Tristram

and to pray for his soul." Skill in hunting is likewise one of the first of knightly accomplishments; so much so that if a man were seen to be expert in the chase it was assumed that he must of necessity be well-born. There was once a princess who fell in love with a mysterious youth, and, to test his birth, devised a hunting party. When she saw how skilfully he began to "undo" the deer, and how fairly he "dight" the venison, she was sure that he knew enough of hunting, and thought in her heart that he was come of gentle blood. *[Ipomydon, and cf. Gaw. and Gr. Kn. 1319.]*

At the close of the song some of the knights sit down to play chess with the ladies; the game is always a favourite. One of them had once gone on board a Norwegian ship to buy falcons, and had stayed to play chess with the merchants; *[Trist. and Is.]* so engrossed had he been in the game that he had not noticed when the ship put out to sea, and so he had been carried to a distant shore. One incident mars the pleasure of the evening. From a corner of the hall we hear hot and passionate words; a lady rises angrily and accuses her opponent of not playing fair, calls him a cuckold and an ass, and knocks the board over. Such exhibitions of temper are not at all uncommon. *[Bk of the Kn. of the Tour Landry, ch. xv.]* Occasionally, when the knights play against each other, hot disputes arise, and after a checkmate the board or the larger pieces become weapons of offence. So Prince John of England once struck Fulk Fitz-Warin with the chess-board. And there are several instances recorded in the romances where the victor receives such a blow as to cause death. *[Fulk Fitz-Warin, Wright, p. 63. Guy of War. Quatre Fils Aymon, Ogier de Dan.]*

Others of the company engage in conversation, and, as their talk is often about themselves, let us pass among them and hear what they have to say; then we shall begin to know them better. *[Neckam, De Nat. Rer. ii. 184.]* Here is one, a smart, handsome, well-built young fellow, who is giving out the roll of his infinite accomplishments: "I can mew a sparrow-hawk, and I can *[Huon of Bord. Steele, p. 200.]* chase the hart and the wild boar, and blow the prise, and serve the hounds their rights, and I can serve at table before a great prince, and I can play at chess and tables as well as any other can do, nor did I ever meet man who could win off me unless I chose." We wonder, by the way, why he ever did choose; but he goes on: "I can write well, arm me, and set the helm on my head, and bear a shield and spear, and ride and gallop a horse, and when it cometh to the point where strokes should be given you may well send forth a worse than I. Also, sir, I can right well enter into ladies' chambers to embrace and kiss them and to do them any service." Incidentally we hear that many of the ladies are in love with this accomplished young man ; and there is a tale told of him that in the East a Saracen princess risked her life for his, and offered to become a Christian if he would marry her.

Some of the knights are talking among themselves of the qualities with which a peerless knight must be endued ("This talking was in the houses of kings"), and we are interested to know what they are. "Sufferance, largesse, bounty, and courtesy," says one. "Noble knighthood, courtesy, prowess, gentleness," says another ; and others, "clear knighthood, pure strength, bounty and courtesy." Someone turns to a noble lady, and asks for her opinion ; she says that a knight must not be envious, "for, and it happeth an envious man once to win worship, he shall be dishonoured twice therefore. He that is courteous, kind, and gentle, hath favour in every place." And yet another of the knights holds that his own brother, whose death they remember, had been in his own person the goodliest knight of all ; and everyone seems to agree with him. "Ah ! Lancelot," he says, "thou were head of all Christian knights ; and now I dare say...that thou were never matched of earthly knight's hand ; and thou were the courtiest knight that ever bare shield ; and thou were the truest friend to thy lover that ever bestrode horse ; and thou were the truest lover... that ever loved woman ; and thou were the kindest man that ever strake with sword ; and thou were the goodliest person ever came among press of knights ; and thou was the meekest man and the gentlest that ever ate in hall among ladies ; and thou were the sternest knight to thy mortal foe that ever put spear in the rest." Evidently the way is already preparing for the ideals of Castiglione (*Il Cortegiano*), Spenser and Sidney.

We, too, recall to memory two knights we know ; one, Gawain, "fine father of nurture," who bore upon shield and coat a new pentangle, to signify that he was faultless in his five senses, that his five fingers never failed him, that he placed

M. D'Arth.
x. 72.

x. 82.

XXI. 13.

Gaw. and Gr. Kn. 929, 638.

all his trust upon earth in the five wounds of Christ, that in battle he deemed he drew his strength from the five joys of the Virgin; and the other an old favourite—

> "That from the timë that he first began   *Cant. Tales,*
> To riden out, he lovëd chivalry   Pro. 44.
> Truth and honoúr, freedom and courtesy.
>
> .   .   .   .
>
> At mortal battles had he been fifteen,   61.
> And foughten for our faith at Tramissene
> In listës thriës, and aye slain his foe.
>
> .   .   .   .
>
> And though that he were worthy, he was wise,   68.
> And of his port as meek as is a maid,
> He never yet no villainy ne said,
> In all his life, unto no manner wight.
> He was a very perfect, gentle knight."

Then they begin to talk of the qualities of the peerless lady, and we learn that she whom we have seen in her chamber playing upon the harp is their ideal. "She is peerless of all ladies," they say; "for to speak of her beauty, *M. D'Arth.* bounty and mirth, and of her goodness, we saw never her *x. 81.* match as far as we have ridden and gone."

While they are conversing, "knights and squires of honour *Froiss. Chron.* going up and down and talking of arms and of amours," we *III. 26, p. 330.* observe them closely. We notice that in all of them there is a certain readiness of thought and speech[1], combined with an *Ch. de Rol.* extravagance of manner and gesture which extends even to the *2930, 426.* garments they wear. Some of the younger and more dandified knights rival the women in the delicacy of their persons *Will. of* and in their mincing gait. They pride themselves upon their *Malm.* IV. 1. *Petit Jehan de* beautiful, white hands[2]; their embroidered garments are cut *Saintré.* short and tight-fitting; their shoes are of the newest fashion, *Ch. de Rol.* with long, curved points; their flowing locks hang down about *2250.* their shoulders. It is even whispered that the glorious tresses, *Will. of* in which the daintiest of them take such evident pride, are *Malm.* not always entirely their own hair. Here is a portrait of a *Bk I.* typical youthful gallant: "Aucassin was the name of the damoiseau: fair was he, goodly, and great, and featly fashioned *Auc. and Nic.* of his body and limbs. His hair was yellow, in little curls, *Lang, p. 4.*

---

[1] *Ch. de Rol.* 426: "Par grant saveir cumencet à parler
    Cume cil hum ki bien faire le set."
[2] "blanches mains, les beles."

his eyes blue and laughing, his face beautiful and shapely, his nose high and well-set, and so richly seen was he in all things good, that in him was none evil at all."

It is said that in England extravagance in dress was due to the example of William II., who would have everything of the highest price. One morning, when putting on a pair of new boots, he asked his chamberlain what they had cost. "Three shillings," was the answer. At which the king burst out, with an abusive epithet, "How long has the king worn boots of so paltry a price? Go, and bring me a pair worth a silver mark." But the chamberlain went out and bought a still cheaper pair, which he told the king had cost the sum named. "Ay," said William, "these are suitable to royal majesty."

Will. of Malm. IV. I.

We leave the knights and turn our attention to the ladies. We see at once that the faces of some of them, and those the more fashionable, are powdered with "blanchet," a kind of wheaten powder, and painted or rouged with "brazil" or "grain of Portugal." Some have evidently thinned their eyebrows, and trimmed or plucked out the hair about their temples to increase their foreheads. Many evidently dye their hair; there are so many heads of a golden hue. We are told that many dye black hair the fashionable yellow; and others wash their hair in wine and other things to change the natural colour. "You are neither to shave your eyebrows, nor yet your foreheads; nor are you ever to put anything save lye upon your hair," says the good Knight of the Tour Landry to his daughters. The practice of tight-lacing is fairly general; waists are pressed unnaturally into small compass; and tight-fitting dresses of gaudy colours are worn to show off the figures thus attained. We hear that the ladies are fond of looking in their mirrors, of clothing themselves in yellow clothes, and of making themselves fair that they may attract men. But there are others, sweet and womanly, who scorn such artifices, and delight the eyes with fresh and natural loveliness. Here is Nicolette, a winsome maid, though certainly somewhat of a fashionable beauty:

O. E. Hom. Morris, *Spec.* I. 25.
Cant. Tales, B. 4648.
Neckam, *De Nat. Rer.* II. 155.
Bk of the Kn. of the Tour Landry, XXI, XXVII, LIII.

"Her locks were yellow and curled, her eyes blue and smiling, her face featly fashioned, with straight brows, the nose high and fairly set, the lips more red than cherry or rose in time of summer, her teeth white and small;...so slim she was in

Auc. and Nic. Lang, pp. 18, 7.

the waist that your two hands might have clipped her, and
the daisy flowers that brake beneath her as she went tip-toe,
and that bent above her instep, seemed black against her feet,
so white was the maiden."

Some are sitting round the hearth, as is customary among
the rich families, especially during the long winter evenings,
telling tales of former days, and conversing upon the eternal
theme of love. One tells a tale of a youth and a maid, *Fl. and Bl.*
Florice and Blaunchefour, whose love commenced in child- Ellis, *Eng.*
hood, and grew as the lovers grew. Difficulties beset their *Met. Rom.*
path ; circumstances sundered them; but their love was all the
stronger, until at last all opposition was overcome by their
constancy. The lover is valiant, the maiden true, but delicacy
is not a prominent feature of the tale. There is also an
overstrained attempt to work upon the feelings of the listeners
which results in bathos. A dying mother looks upon her
babe, and weeps because it reminds her of her murdered
husband. A saucer happens to be near, and the tears fall so
plentifully that it is almost filled. With the contents she
baptises the infant, and then expires.

Now an old man, weary and sad of face, and yet with an
indefinable charm and grace of manner, joins the company
round the hearth; and the ladies implore him to tell them
again a tale they are never tired of hearing. So he begins
the story of Aucassin and Nicolette, now in verse and now
in prose :—

> "Who would list to the good lay,   *Auc. and Nic.*
> Gladness of the captive grey?   Lang, p. 3.
> 'Tis how two young lovers met,
> Aucassin and Nicolette,
> Of the pains the lover bore
> And the sorrows he outwore,
> For the goodness and the grace
> Of his love, so fair of face.
> Sweet the Song, the story sweet,
> There is no man hearkens it,
> No man living 'neath the sun,
> So outwearied, so fordone,
> Sick and woful, worn and sad,
> But is healèd, but is glad
>   'Tis so sweet."

He tells how Aucassin, a great lord's son, was so suddenly
overtaken of love, the great master, that he would neither

be dubbed knight nor take arms, as beseemed a youth of his birth. His father appealed to him to give up his love, a slave girl from a far-off land, and promised that he should have the daughter of the richest man in France if he so desired. But Aucassin averred that his sweet lady would grace the highest place in the world. If she were empress of Constantinople or Germany, if she were queen of France or England, it were little enough for her, so gentle and courteous is she, so *debonaire* and compact of all good qualities. The captain of the town also attempted to dissuade him: "Nay more, what would'st thou deem thee to have gained, had'st thou made her thy leman?...In hell would thy soul have lain while the world endures, and into Paradise would'st thou have entered never." And Aucassin replied hotly: "In Paradise what have I to win? Therein I seek not to enter, but only to have Nicolete, my sweet lady that I love so well. For into Paradise go none but such folk as I shall tell thee now: Thither go these same old priests, and halt old men and maimed, who all day and night cower continually before the altars and in the crypts; and such folk as wear old amices and old clouted frocks, and naked folk and shoeless and covered with sores, perishing of hunger and thirst and of cold, and of little ease. These be they that go into Paradise; with them have I naught to make. But into hell would I fain go; for into hell fare the goodly clerks, and goodly knights that fall in tourneys and great wars, and stout men-at-arms, and all men noble. With these would I liefly go. And thither pass the sweet ladies and courteous that have two lovers, or three, and their lords also thereto. Thither goes the gold and the silver, and cloth of vair, and cloth of gris, and harpers, and makers, and the prince of this world. With these I would gladly go; let me but have with me Nicolete, my sweetest lady." A very quaint and daring theology!

pp. 8 and 9.

pp. 16 and 17.

> "Nicolete thou lily white,
>   My sweet lady, bright of brow,
> Sweeter than the grape art thou,
> Sweeter than sack posset good
> In a cup of maple wood.
>
> .   .   .   .   .   .
>
> Nicolete how fair art thou;
> Sweet thy footfall, sweet thine eyes,

> Sweet the mirth of thy replies,
> Sweet thy laughter, sweet thy face,
> Sweet thy lips and sweet thy brow,
> And the touch of thine embrace."

The lovers were separated and imprisoned; but Nicolette knotted together napkins and sheets, and let herself down from her window. Then, catching up her garments in both hands, because the dew was lying deep upon the grass, she sped through the garden to the postern gate, unbarred it, and passed out into the streets of Biaucaire, keeping always in the shadow, for the moon was shining bright and clear, and so gained the tower where Aucassin lay. There she spoke with him, and the inevitable argument arose as to which loved the other most. "Aucassin," she said, "I trow thou lovest me not p. 20. as much as thou sayest, but I love thee more than thou lovest me." "Ah, fair sweet friend," said Aucassin, "it may not be that thou should'st love me even as I love thee. Woman may not love man as man loves woman, for a woman's love lies in the glance of her eye, and the bud of her breast, and her foot's tip-toe, but the love of man is in his heart planted, whence it can never issue forth and pass away." Finally they escaped together, and "by God's will Who loveth lovers," she healed Aucassin's hurts, and so they rode away.

> "Aucassin the frank, the fair,   p. 34.
> Aucassin of the yellow hair,
> Gentle knight, and true lover,
> From the forest doth he fare,
> Holds his love before him there,
> Kissing cheek, and chin, and eyes,
> But she spake in sober wise,
>   'Aucassin, true love and fair,
> To what land do we repair?'
> 'Sweet my love, I take no care,
> Thou art with me everywhere!'
> So they pass the woods and downs,
> Pass the villages and towns,
> Hills and dales and open land,
> Came at dawn to the sea-sand,
> Lighted down upon the strand,
>   Beside the sea."

The tale has a happy ending, for Aucassin wedded Nicolette,

and made her lady of Biaucaire. And long they lived in gladness and delight, without regret on either side.

p. 46.

"Now my story all is done,
Said and sung."

From their own lips we hear that love has become to these ladies an all-consuming passion, an evil, fatal passion, before which all virtue, all self-control, all true religion, must give way. And there can be no remedy, no hope for change—

Piers Plow.
Pro. 113.

"Till lords and ladies love all truth,
And hate all harlotry, to hear it or to mouth it."

They, and the knights likewise, have caught the fashion of the land of Provence, now for a time part of the royal domains. We are told—

Hand. Synne,
4151, *and of.*
Froissart,
Chron. p. 8.

"That Frenchmen sin in lechery,
And Englishmen in envy."

Light songs of love are upon their lips; light tales in their ears; and they themselves follow the examples set by the unlawful loves of Tristan and Iseult, of Lancelot and

2923.

Guinevere, heroes and heroines whom they hold peerless. It is always the lady, the lover and the husband; or husband, mistress and wife. There is a sorry tale of two ladies

Bk of the Kn.
of the Tour
Land. XVII.

who quarrel jealously over the husband of one of them; they scratch and tear each other, and one breaks the bridge of the other's nose with a stick. The women themselves hold that though for a married man to love another woman may be a false, bad love, yet the married woman may love whom she pleases. And the first of the Laws of Love declares that

Skeat, Sup.
Chaucer,
LXXX.
Neckam, De
Nat. Rer.
II. 155.
Froissart,
Chron. III. 25,
p. 328.

"Marriage cannot be pleaded as an excuse for refusing to love." Neckam (early 13th century) has an exceedingly low opinion of the society and morals of his day. The fact that the Conqueror was himself a bastard had undoubtedly a great influence for evil upon the England of the subsequent period.

M. D'Arth.
VIII. 34.

At the court of King Mark of Cornwall the virtue of the queen and her hundred ladies is tested with a magic horn, and we are amazed to find that we are expected to believe that there are but four who are able to drink clean. Of the knights of

XVI. 3.

Arthur's court but two are proved clean and without spot. Nor does it seem that the gravity of the offence as a deadly sin is ever understood, although death by burning is the extreme penalty which the unchaste wife may be called upon to pay, if her shame become a matter of public knowledge. The age has set itself an ideal far beyond itself. The Knight of the Tour Landry tells us that at one time women of spotted reputations were bidden to withdraw from public assemblies, but adds that for forty years the custom has not been in vogue; instead, they are simply placed below the pure. It is the age of the Courts of Love, with love as a pretext for every licence, and secrecy the only pledge imposed. "He who cannot conceal, cannot love," is the third of the Laws of Love.

Bk of the Kn. of the Tour Landry, CXVI.,CXVIII., and cf. *Anc. Riwle, Cant. Tales,* I. 100, 575. *Hand. Synne,* 8333. *Rom. de la R.* Chaucer, 5030.

> "Know'st thou not well the oldë clerkës saw,
> That who shall give a lover any law,
> Love is a greater law, by my pan[1],
> Than may be given of any earthly man?"

Cant. Tales, A. 1163, and cf. Boethius, *De Cons. Phil.* III. 12.

A knight must put his lady even before truth itself, and must demean himself to any subterfuge for her protection. He must be prepared to swear, outstare and boldly counterfeit a lie to save her honour, must boldly fight for her to uphold her reputation for goodness, virtue and religion. Froissart confirms and emphasises the importance of secrecy when he tells how the duke of Touraine was once displeased with Sir Peter of Craon because the knight disclosed the secretness that was between the duke and a certain lady. "If he did so, he did evil," asserts the chronicler.

Court of Love, 421.

Froissart, Chron. III. 174, p. 405.

One of the ladies has heard of a scandal in a neighbouring castle, where a wife has been led to shame by her lover who had won her by singing both high and low beside her bower. Her husband had discovered her misconduct, and had set traps and snares so that the lover had been caught and, in spite of all entreaties, torn to pieces by wild horses. Another tells of the melancholy of a woman during the absence of her lover. She is sated with the world, even with the things of self. It is no bar to her love that she is already the wife of another. When she and her lover are dead they are buried close together; and from one of the tombs grows a vine, from the other a rose, which creep along the pillows until they meet and intertwine. There is already a touch of pathos in

Marie de Fr., Lai du Laustic, Owl and Night., Neckam.

Trist. and Is.

---

[1] head.

the tales ; and others will tell of those who have withdrawn from the world through disappointed love, to seek seclusion in a convent or hermit cell, where temptation wounds but cannot kill.   There, by continual prayers and tears, fasting and penance, they seek to atone for a sinful past.   Many find the world empty and vain, where nothing serves to excite the senses already satiated with excess.   Even in the days of romance a sense of the dreary commonplace at times creeps in ; from it the poet strives in vain to escape by plunging into wilder and more irrelevant sentiment.

Perhaps the evening's programme may be varied occasionally by the entrance of a jongleur, the singer and popular entertainer of the day.   His first words are a call for refreshment :

Havelok, 13.

"At the beginning of our tale
Fill me a cup of right good ale";

and in the intervals of his entertainment he does not forget to have the cup refilled :

Sir Bevis.

"For the time that God made,
Fill up the cup and make us glad."

King Horn,
1076, 1094.
Auc. and Nic.
p. 42.
Froiss. *Chron.*
III. 153.
Globe ed.
p. 385.

He is not particularly cleanly as to his person, as his face and neck testify, but he is exceedingly clever and very amusing. He is story-teller and mimic, and an imitator of the song of birds, perhaps a tumbler or rope-dancer.   Froissart tells of one who, when it was dark, walked upon a cord stretched above the housetops, with two burning candles in his hands and singing as he went, to the wonder of all who watched his feat.   Perhaps he is also an adept at facial distortions, or he may be a trainer of performing dogs, bears and monkeys.

Neckam,
De Nat. Rer.
II. 129.

Some jongleurs bring in apes mounted upon dogs to mimic the knightly tournaments.   Or perhaps he is a conjurer.   But whatever his forte he must be a musician, and able to play on several kinds of instruments, such as the rote, fiddle, psaltery, sackbut, harp, lute, lyre, rebec, tabor, cymbals, castanets, drum and trumpet.   So we may prepare ourselves for a varied entertainment.   He plays with knives and swords, balancing them in a wonderful fashion with the sharp points upon his tongue, and has a host of tricks.   He places a hat upon a table, and from beneath it produces a curious assort-

ment of objects. Gower uses him as an illustration; and
Chaucer knows him well:

> "There saw I Colle tregetour[1]
> Upon a table of sicamour
> Play an uncouth thing to tell.
> I saw him carry a wind-mell[2]
> Under a walnut shell."

Conf. Amant.
Bk II.
Car. Lib.
p. 121.
Ho. of Fame,
III. 187.

He is a master of illusion—

> "Such as these subtle tregetourës play.
> For oft at feastës have I well heard say
> That tregetours within a hallë large
> Have made come in a water and a barge,
> And in the hallë rowen up and down.
> Sometime hath seemëd come a grim leoun,
> And sometime flourës spring as in a mede,
> Sometime a vine and grapës white and rede;
> Sometime a castle, all of lime and stone,
> And when hem likëd voided it anon."

Cant. Tales,
F. 1141.

When he has sufficiently impressed us with his tricks he
draws a little manuscript from his bag, and chants to us a
romance, perhaps of Alexander and the astonishing wonders
of the East.   He tells us of beings whose lower parts are
those of men, and the upper like barking dogs; of people,
pitch-black in colour, with one eye and one foot, and this foot
they use as a protection against both rain and sun, for it is
large enough to shelter the whole body when they lie upon
their backs; of others with legs eighteen feet long; of yellow
people who are wise and prosperous, and here he strays,
unwittingly, into the truth.   He tells of talking trees, of the
fountain of youth, of the monsters of the deep, of strange
and terrible beasts, of a magic coffin suspended by four
loadstones, and so on.

Ch. de Rol.
Gautier,
p. xxviii.

Alexander,
Mandeville,
etc.

Or, perhaps, he tells us of the deeds of the great Richard
Cœur de Lion, and holds us entranced at the magnificence of
his courage. We hear how Richard gained his title, and are
not impressed by the jongleur's taste; but the recital seems
to please most of the audience. By main force the hero tears
out the lion's heart through its distended jaws, and then

---

[1] conjurer.
[2] wind-mill; a common child's toy carved out of a nut; see Froissart's
Chronicle, III. 153.

proceeds to the great hall where the king of Almaigne and his nobles are dining:

Rich. Cœur de
Lion, Ellis.

> "The saler[1] on the table stood:
> Richard pressed out all the blood,
> And wet the heart in the salt
> (The king and all his men behalt);
> Withouten bread the heart he ate."

We hear of Richard's mighty deeds of valour in the Crusades; but it is not thought to be derogatory to his kingly dignity when, on hearing news which displeases him while eating his Christmas dinner, he kicks over the table in an outburst of rage. Indeed the jongleur calmly informs us that this was his usual method of expressing displeasure. Again, our entertainer would make us laugh, and gives his romance a humorous turn; but it must be confessed that it is a grim and nauseating kind of humour. Saracen ambassadors come to the king with costly presents to arrange the ransom of certain prisoners. With the greatest show of courtesy he invites them to dine with him, but gives orders to slay the prisoners, and to serve up their heads, with names attached, as the first course.

> "An hot head bring me beforn;
> As I were well apayed[2] withall,
> Eat thereof fast I shall,
> As it were a tender chick,
> To see how the others will like."

The ambassadors sit horrified and disgusted while Richard eats greedily, and, with pretended courtesy, insults them with frequent exhortations to be merry. The second course is a feast of dainties, and the king makes a pretence of apologising: he knew not their tastes. At this the audience laugh immoderately. What a situation for the poor Saracen knaves! What a delicious jest! What infinite wit! We think, however, that a people who can possibly find merriment in such a brutal jest must possess an exceedingly grotesque sense of humour; and, when we consider the matter further, we see that in spite of all the precepts of chivalry there must be a corresponding coarseness in habits, and a lack of delicacy and true courtesy towards others, even among the highest classes.

---

[1] salt-cellar.   [2] pleased, satisfied.

A clock strikes; the hour is late; the sleeping cup of wine is brought in; the gathering breaks up, and all retire to rest. Some of the chambers are "marvellously well dight and richly"; some are vaulted, some have bay windows, in some cases protected by stout iron bars set into the stone or into a framework, some are painted, some have pictures on the walls. In some there are fires and chimneys, lamps and candles, with costly tables, curtains and bed-furniture; and soon we shall hear of the use of night-lights. In the larger rooms, where many sleep together, are recesses partially partitioned off to ensure a certain amount of privacy, which is, however, not always regarded as a necessity. Some of the knights sleep fitfully, dreaming of fighting and slaying, and greatly disturbing the rest of others; some are somnambulists. One has a habit of rising in the night and arming himself, and with drawn sword fights all about the house, though he cannot tell with whom, and then goes back to bed again. Next morning, when his servants tell him of it, he says that he knows nothing about it, and that they lie. Some great men have their harper's chamber near to theirs so that they may call upon him when troubled with insomnia.

It often happens that the silence of the night is disturbed by the whisperings of a pair of lovers at the barred windows; and perhaps some errant Romeo will wrench away the iron bars from their sockets in the stone, hoping to replace them before the dawn. It may be, too, that there is the sudden clash of steel which tells of discovery; and then morning breaks upon a dead or wounded knight and a woman taken in her shame. It is strange to hear the words of Lancelot when trapped in the chamber of Guinevere. "Truly," said the queen, "I would, and it might please God, that they would take me and slay me and suffer you to escape." "That shall never be," said Sir Lancelot, "God defend me from such a shame, but Jesu be Thou my shield and mine armour." And elsewhere we read of a wife declaring herself happy to meet a lover "if he believed in God!" We can only believe that these people see no connection whatever between religion and morality.

There was always in the Norman blood a craving which the home life could never satisfy, always the attraction of a roving life, and the inbred love of violent deeds which

M. D'Arth.
XIV. 3, II. 15,
XIX. 5, 6.
Troil. and Cress. III. 671,
1141, IV. 1245.
Gaw. and Gr. Kn. 853.
Ch. de Rol.
2593.
Morte Arth.
Seven Wise Masters.

M. D'Arth.
XIX. 6.

Froiss. *Chron.* III. 27,
p. 334.

Hand. Synne, 4745.

M. D'Arth.
XIX. 6.

X. 24, XX. 3, 4.

Ywonec.

forbade a peaceful, settled life. There was always unrest,
uncertainty, suspicion and jealousy. The king says "My
barons will let me have no rest"; and the barons glance
askance at the encroachments of the king. The story of
Huon of Bordeaux sufficiently reveals the conflicting influences at work within the feudal system, and the weakness
which led to its overthrow.

M. D'Arth.
III. 1.

The lord of the castle we have visited is no exception to
the rule; life's fitful fever urges him. His sons are about
him, and he begins to sigh, recalling the activity of his own
youthful days. His lady notes his mood and questions
wherefore he ponders thus: All is well with him; he has
riches of gold and silver and costly furs; he has falcons and
mules and palfreys; he has subjugated his enemies; and
there is none in all the country round who dares refuse to
come to his side at his call; what further can he desire?
And he tells her that riches consist not of such things as
these, but of kinsmen and friends: "The heart of a man
is worth all the gold in a land[1]." He is hungering for the
old life with the friends who have helped him in his need,
especially for his brother. "Back is bare without a brother
behind it," he says. Besides, there is a famous boar in the
woods to furnish diversion by the way. So he departs
from home; but, being separated from his followers in the
hunt, is attacked by the retainers of an old rival, and slain.
Brother and widow mourn over the body of the dead and his
fatherless children. The brother foresees renewal of strife;
and little Hernaudin, ten years old, passionately laments that
he has not a little hauberk of his own, so that he, too, may
fight with the enemy. And his uncle takes the child in his
arms and kisses him, rejoicing at the brave spirit he shows.
Ever fighting and feud! It is in the blood of the smallest
child. Such is the spirit of a violent, unruly, strenuous age
of licence, idealised and glorified in the literature by a halo
of patriotism and religion.

Garin le
Loherain,
M. P. Paris,
III. 1, p. 218.

Sooner or later comes the day when the young birds, too,
must try their wings. They may have a call to serve their
king at court, to follow him on a Crusade, or to aid him
against his enemies at home. The widow's heart is wrung at
the thought of separation. "Alas! my sweet sons," she says,

M. D'Arth.
XI. 10.

[1] "Li cuers d'un homme vaut tout l'or d'un pais."

"for your sakes I shall lose my liking and my joy, and then wind and weather I may not endure." With tears she delays the day of departure; she cannot lightly lose her boys. But at last they may tarry no longer, and she speaks the parting words of advice: "Serve your sovereign lord well and *Huon of Bord.* truly, as subjects ought to do; be diligent at all times to Steele, pp. 9— serve him truly; and keep company with noble men such as you see that be of good conditions; be not in the place where any ill words be spoken or ill counsel given; fly from the company of them that love not honour and truth; open not your ears to hear liars, or false reporters, or flatterers; be often at church, and give largely for God's sake; be liberal and courteous, and give to poor knights; fly the company of janglers; and all goodness shall follow." So they are well furnished with all things needful to their estate, with rich apparel of silk, and gold and silver, and with an armed retinue for their protection by the way. The last kiss is given, and there is weeping and sobbing in the courtyard as they depart, while the mother, bereaved of her sons, is left swooning in the midst. They go sorely weeping, for it is no unmanly thing to shed tears. Nay, the whole town weeps and prays for them as they pass. It was a serious thing to travel far in those days. The castle is left behind the wood or behind the hill when the hoof-beats of a horse, hard-ridden, are heard. After them comes a squire, in panting *M. D'Arth.* haste, with the mother's last words and something they have XI. 11, XIV. 1. forgotten; and then the last link with home is broken. The mother is never forgotten by her sons; long afterwards, in their sleep, they will dream much of her.

On they ride through the woodland, alert and ready for action. From any copse may come the sun-glint from *Huon of Bord.* helmet or steel-tipped lance.

> "The helms they seyen brightë shine,   *Guy of War.*
> The steeds neighen and together whine,   Ellis.
> 'God!' quoth Guy, 'we ben y-nome[1]!'"

From any ditch or hedge in a narrow way a flight of arrows may descend, breaking vainly upon their armour, but killing *M. D'Arth.* their horses under them, and leaving them helpless, cumbered XIX. 4. with their heavy mail, their ponderous shields and spears,

---

[1] taken.

unable to retaliate upon their light-armed and quick-footed assailants, and completely at their mercy. There is always the possibility of ambush, adventure and peril ; and so, if possible, they join some other company like their own, that their strength may be increased and the risk diminished.

Huon of Bord. They arrive at court, and there are very outspoken, and
etc. bear themselves as gallants should. But they find many of their ideals rudely shattered. The king, it may be, is not the man they have thought him ; his barons are not always good and true ; the Church is not always treated with respect, for the churchmen are, perhaps, not all they ought to be. Men's ideas are constantly changing ; everywhere there are incessant rivalries and jealousies, under currents and cross currents, intrigues and ambuscades. From the *Chanson de Roland* to the earlier part of *Huon of Bordeaux*, perhaps one of the latest of the *chansons*, the change is great indeed.

Ch. de Rol. In the former, Charlemagne is the true emperor, who
3000, 2739. befits the crown he wears[1]; all other kings are children compared with him. He is the majestic conqueror of many
370, 140, 300, realms, a marvellous man ; none can withstand him. His
56, 2740, 530, words are slow and deliberate ; and when he commands all
562. must obey. He is powerful, terrible, implacable ; he fears no man living. All who see and know him say that he is a true baron ; men cannot sufficiently praise him ; he is all honour, all goodness. Who can recount the greatness of his
1733. valour? There will never be his like again[2]. And though already that passionate excitability, which becomes his great weakness in the later literature, cannot always be restrained,
771. it is not supreme, and he has his nobles with him unalienated, for it is for France and them that he feels.

But in *Huon of Bordeaux* he appears in his dotage, and
Huon of Bord. lacks altogether the dignity and self-control which should
Steele. attach to kingship ; while his son, Charlot, is even worse and weaker than himself, a traitor and companion of traitors. Twice in a short period does Charlemagne weakly change his decisions ; once he so far forgets himself as to draw his knife to strike down the object of his anger. He cannot
pp. 35, 50. decide between the innocent and the guilty, and is always ready to listen to the base insinuations of traitors. His peers

---

[1] "E Franceis dient: 'Tels deit porter curune.'"
[2] "N'iert mais tels hum desques à l'Deu juïse."

tell him to his face that he bears himself rather like a child than like a man, that he has become childish, and more like a fool than a wise man. In the earlier *chanson*, Ganelon had indeed told him bluntly that he was speaking childishly, but his words lack the derisive sting of the later development. *Ch. de Rol. 1772.* Hasty, revengeful, changeable, going back upon his plighted word, the tale of his discomfitures seems to afford to the later poet a delight which is almost vindictive.

And this character of Charlemagne creeps from the *chansons* into the romances, where we see Roland refusing to obey him, and receiving from his hand a hasty blow upon the mouth and nose which causes blood to flow. "Traitor, thou shalt abye it[1]," cries Charlemagne in his rage.

> "'Abye,' quoth Roland, 'wole I nought;
> And traitour was I never none,
> By that Lord that me dear hath bought!'
> And brayde[2] out Durindal anon.
> He wolde have smitten the king there,
> Ne hadde the barons run between:
> The king withdrewe him for fear,
> And passed home as it might best been."

Sir Ferumbras, Ellis, and cf. L'Entrée en Espagne (14th cent.).

We know that this is no reflection of the real Charlemagne, but of the kings who followed him, of some who sat upon the English throne. Has Norman kingship fallen so low then as to warrant this caricature?

In the Arthurian cycle there is another illustration of this change. King Mark of Cornwall is taken in treachery by Gaheris: "It were pity," said Sir Gaheris, *M. D'Arth. IX. 39.* "that thou shouldest live any longer." "Save my life," said King Mark, "and I will make amends; and consider that I am a king anointed." "It were the more shame," said Sir Gaheris, "to save thy life; thou art a king anointed with chrism, and therefore thou shouldest hold with all men of worship; and therefore thou art worthy to die." And without more words he lashed at King Mark. Are men's ideas of loyalty changing thus after experiences which show how far the real is removed from the ideal? And shall we not have this fiction translated into history on a grander scale in the Great Civil War? Why does this scoffing spirit, essentially a French trait, make kings the butt for its jeers at

---

[1] suffer for it; pay for it.   [2] drew.

almost its first appearance? And why is it that kings are even more frequently mocked at in the Mystery plays, later still than the romances? The Anglo-Norman once had written that without his king he had no country[1], but now from *chanson* to romance, from romance to Mystery play, in descending scale, men's ideals of kingship are deteriorating. And with this deterioration there is also a corresponding descent in the ideals of knighthood, preparing the way for the burlesques of *Sir Thopas* and the *Tournament of Tottenham.* Why, in the Chester Plays, is the once peerless Sir Lancelot chosen to be the ranting bully who massacres the innocents?

But hear the Brutus of the age, and mark the muttering of the coming storm. "Then alone," says John of Salisbury, "is the whole state healthy when mutual relationships with equal rights exist between superiors and inferiors." If the king be a tyrant to his people, then to kill him is "not only permissible but even just and right." No satire this, but plain speaking, after many warning hints; and the writer dedicates his book to Becket, in itself a straw which shows the set of the wind. Stern things are said of Henry II. by Randulph Niger; and, later still, a lawyer, Henry de Bracton, will tell us that "there is no king where will, and not law, bears rule." And we meet this again in the *Political Songs*: "Therefore, let him who reads know that he cannot reign who does not keep the law." From a later work we take a passage which derives its origin from the popular opinion: "If dignities were good or virtuous they should make wicked men good, and turn their malice, and make them be virtuous. But that they do not, as it is proved, but they cause rancour and debate. Therefore they be not good but utterly bad....The dignity of King John would have destroyed all England." And again in the *Political Songs* the patriot is just as outspoken concerning the misuse of kingship: "If he study to degrade his own people, if he pervert their rank, it is in vain for him to ask why thus deranged they do not obey him; in fact they would be fools if they did."

Life at court has many phases. There are hunting and dicing, feasting and dancing, mimes and minstrels, astrologers

Rom. de Rou.

John of Sal. Polycraticus.

De Leg. Ang.

Pol. Songs, Wright, p. 94.

Test. of Love, II. 6.

Pol. Songs, Wright, p. 121.

John of Sal. Polycraticus.

---

[1] "Kar ja sanz Rei paiz n'averon."

and fortune-tellers in whom all men believe, flatterers and parasites of every description. Thither come actors of indecent farces, whose broad and coarse humour, and obscene gestures, capture the ears and eyes of the courtiers; singers whose songs, even those which they sing in cathedrals and churches, do not tend to edification; place-seeking clergy who spend their days with the hounds, or in pleas and lawsuits, and neglect their cures; and scholars who struggle manfully with the subtleties of quibbling words.

But, possibly, our travellers have been called to join in a Crusade, and soon are again upon the march. Everywhere, from stages in the streets and market-places, from eminences by the wayside, there are fervent monks and priests calling upon men to take up the Cross in the everlasting conflict of East and West, and dispensing absolutions. "Christendom *Ch. de Rol.* is in peril, and needs defenders; for those who die in the 1129. cause there are already mansions prepared in Paradise," they cry. And from the multitudes the shout goes up, "Deus lo vult," "God wills it." Day by day the army *Will. of* grows, and the camp increases with men of every Christian *Malm.* IV. 2. nation. The peasants come from the fields, the workers from the cities, the barons from their castles, till whole countries seem deserted. Some even bring with them their wives and families in great lumbering waggons and carriages. The roads cannot hold the throngs which set forth; the towns cannot harbour them. But many return before the sea is reached; and few of the English peasants travel far.

Many young gentlemen are chosen for knighthood on *Froissart,* the way. It is the custom for them to bathe their bodies, Globe ed., and then to keep watch all night before their arms in a *p. 433.* church. On the morrow, at the time of high mass, they are dubbed with great solemnity, receiving the accolade and the golden spurs. Then there may be a tournament of nation against nation, that the new-made knights may try their swords; or soon, perhaps, there is a quarrel, for not yet have all found their places. "Traitor, thou liest in *Huon of Bord.* thy throat," is heard; and the gage is thrown down to *Flor. and Blanch.* one who has done them insult or wrong. Even the less dangerous joustings may degenerate into hard fighting, in *Chaitivel.* which some are slain, and others severely wounded. But usually, in a tournament, few knights are wilfully slain, the

D.   15

knight's ransom practically insuring his life, since it often meant so much to the victorious soldier of fortune. Indeed we hear that at one time it became no uncommon practice for a knight to abandon a comrade after coming to a secret understanding with his antagonists that he should share the ransom.

Neckam,
De Nat. Rer.
II. 175.

Cant. Tales,
A. 2491.

> "And on the morrow, when the day gan spring
> Of horse and harness noise and clattering
> There was in hostelriës all about,
> And to the palace rode there many a rout
> Of lordës, upon steedës and palfreys.
> There mayest thou see devising of harneys,
> So uncouth and so rich and wrought so weel
> Of goldsmithry, of broidering, and of steel,
> The shieldës bright, head-pieces and trappúres,
> Gold-huëd helmets, hauberks, coat armoúrs;
> Lords in accoutrements on their courseres,
> Knights of retinue, and eke squieres,
> Nailing the spears, and helmets buckling,
> Strapping of shieldës, with layneres[1] lacing,
> There, as need is, they weren nothing idle;
> The foamy steedës on the golden bridle
> Gnawing, and fast the armourers also
> With file and hammer, pricking to and fro;
> Yeomen on foot, and commons many a one
> With shortë stavës, thick as they may goon;
> Pipës, trumpets, nakers, clariouns,
> That in the battle blowen bloody souns.
> The palace full of people, up and down,
> Here three, there ten, holding their questioun,
> Divining of these Theban knightës two,
> Some seyden thus, some said it shall be so,
> Some helden with him with the blakë beard,
> Some with the bald, some with the thikkë haired,
> Some said he lookëd grim and he would fight,
> He hath a sparth[2] of twenty pound of weight."

The lists are prepared; pledges are given on either side; and they proceed to settle their differences with point of lance and edge of sword. If deep guilt is alleged the combat becomes an ordeal by battle, and ill will it go with him who is vanquished. "God knows well what the outcome will be; may He pronounce to-day between us," say the knights; and the superior strength or skill of an antagonist will be

Ch. de Rol.
3872, 3898.

---

[1] straps.   [2] battle-axe.

taken as a proof that he is in the right. "My lord, Sir
Lancelot," says one, "I rede you beware what ye do, for *M. D'Arth.*
though ye are never so good a knight, as ye wot well that ye ^XIX. 7.^
are renowned the best knight of the world, yet should ye be
advised to do battle in a wrong quarrel, for God will have
a stroke in every battle." "As for that," said Sir Lancelot,
"God is to be dread." And yet some knights are known to *x. 14.*
have been slain in a righteous quarrel: "Many men in battle *Test. of Love,*
are discomfited and overcome in a rightful quarrel, that is ^I. 7.^
God's privy judgment in heaven." So, before the ordeal,
each combatant makes his confession, receives absolution and *Ch. de Rol.*
the benediction of the priest, hears mass and takes the com- ^3858.^
munion, and makes offerings to the Church, to strengthen his
heart and purify his soul.

Then they ride through the streets to the lists in grand *Petit Jehan de*
array, with squires bearing their helmets, shields and spears. *Saintré,*
The crowd shouts encouragement to the popular favourite, *Flower and the*
while fair ladies lean out at the windows viewing the *Leaf, 251.*
champions with interest and sympathy, and offering their *Huon of Bord.*
prayers that the one they favour may be successful. The
knight with the fairest face or the comeliest figure has usually
the advantage in this respect. Arrived at the place of
combat, each takes his oath upon sacred relics that his
cause is just; and then nothing remains but for the battle
to decide. Woe is it to him who stumbles in the lists, for
that is a portent of evil. The lists are cleared, the marshals
set; and the heralds cry aloud the grounds of the combat.

> "Then were the gatës shut, and cried was loud,   *Cant. Tales,*
> 'Do now your devoir, youngë knightës proud.'   A. 2597.
> The heralds left their pricking up and down;
> Now ringen trumpets loud and clarioun."

The combatants, despite their weighty armour, leap upon
their horses; and it is a great mark of skill to do so without
touching the stirrup. Their shields are hung about their
necks; they grasp their spears, sharply ground and keen,
in their hands. Sometimes fierce, taunting words are inter-
changed. To call an opponent "a glutton and evil traitor" is a *Huon of Bord.*
very bitter reproach. Spears are couched; the signal is given; *M. D'Arth.*
"Lesses les aler," cry the heralds; the reins drop upon the ^XIX. 9.^
horses' necks; spurs strike deep; and the combatants meet *Ch. de Rol.*
3877.

Cant. Tales,
A. 2602.
at full speed with the roar of a whirlwind and the shock
of a storm.   Lance crashes upon shield, and springs and
shivers into splinters.   The weaker knight is borne from
his horse, and flung violently to the ground, rolling over
M. D'Arth.
X. 44.
VI. 7. and over with the impetus of the stroke, and then lies dazed,
wounded or dying, until his squires come to his assistance
and carry him from the field.   He is often a pitiable sight,
bleeding from nose, ears and mouth, with perhaps a broken
X. 17.
I. 12, X. 18. arm or leg or thigh, or shoulder out of joint.   He is fortunate
if he escape without a broken back or a broken neck.   His horse
may have suffered no less severely than himself, with bleeding
IX. 26, X. 25,
64. knees, or even a broken back.   Occasionally, in his passion,
the victor rides over and over his prostrate foe, mangling him
X. 1. most cruelly.   Sometimes a horse is deliberately killed in the
X. 70. combat ; but the knights held "that it was unknightly done
in a tournament to kill a horse wilfully, but that it had been
Sir Otuel. done in plain battle, life for life."   To kill a horse by
Sir Triamour. accident is a sign of awkwardness and lack of address, and
is always a subject for jesting raillery or bitter taunts,
*Ogier le
Danois.* directed against the unskilful fighter.   Men loved their steeds,
and wept over them as though they were human, while the
horses reciprocated their affection.   When the famous Bayard
*Les Quatre
Fils Aymon.* saw his master Renaut, "he knew him sooner than a wife her
lord."   The fame of a good horse spread as far as that of
a knight, and was just as lasting :

Sir Bevis.
> "God on their souls have now pity,
>   And on Arundel his good steed,
>   If men for horse should sing or read."

M. D'Arth.
X. 74, 75.
VII. 16.
If the combat is more equal, both knights may go down
together, horses and men enveloped in a cloud of dust ; girths
and trappings fly asunder ; saddles give way ; and armour
comes unriveted.   When they recover from the shock, it is a
Cant. Tales,
A. 2561,
A. 2608.
M. D'Arth.
II. 18, X. 19.
Ch. de Rol.
1265, 1615,
3610.
Froissart,
Chron. Globe
ed. pp. 322,
415. matter of sword and shield, of stroke and guard on foot, till
the victory is won, while shouts go up from the spectators as
each stroke is pressed home.   Then hauberks are pierced ;
pieces of mail are shorn away, and through the rents the
naked skin appears ; helms and shields are cloven.   For a
brief space, by mutual consent, the knights may rest to
recover their breath.   They are terribly heated with their
armour ; cases are on record of apoplectic seizures.   But

thoughts of honour and of the ladies who are looking on *M. D'Arth.*
x. 30, nerve each combatant to renewed exertions, and at last one must succumb. Occasionally, in the heat of his rage, or if the fallen refuse to yield and own himself recreant, the conqueror smites off his head, or gives him the "coup de grâce"; but he who refuses mercy to him who asks it is for III. 7, 8. ever dishonoured. Sometimes there is an addition to the *Huon of Bord.*
p. 45. fray when the horses, fired with the spirit of their masters, seize upon each other, and bite and tear and lunge as though they, too, have a difference to settle.

When we come to think of it, an ordeal by battle, or even the less violent tournament, must have been a terrible thing to sit through, especially for the ladies who had husbands or lovers engaged in the fight. Even without such personal interests it could have been for them no light thing, for it *Ch. de Rol.*
3882, 3724. appears that even the men themselves could not always control their feelings. Possibly the ladies of those days, though we hear of them swooning or dying when those they love were lost or dead, were not as yet troubled with what the moderns *Eliduc,* etc. call nerves; or if they were, the romances do not seem to make much of it. The honour and glory of the victor hides all else.

After the combat, some of the ladies, among whom are skilful leeches, search the wounds of their knights, and prepare baths with herbs to rid them of their stiffness and their bruises. After a tournament the evening is spent in ban- *Cant. Tales,*
Pro. 52.
Conf. Amant. queting and making merry, while all rejoice in applauding Bk VIII. the hero of the day, to whom is given the place of honour at p. 415, *Car.*
Lib. table.

But after an ordeal, if great guilt is alleged, terrible scenes may occur. No mercy is shown to the felon knight; and often he who has braved it in all the splendour of costly armour during the day, at nightfall graces the gallows-tree. Cruel and pitiless are the punishments of the time. The traitor is seated astride of a mare or sumpter horse[1], with his *Ch. de Rol.*
481, 1823,
3735. face to its tail, or is placed in a cart and thus driven to the *M. D'Arth.*
XIX. 13. gallows. Despite his wounds, perhaps with broken ribs or *Ipomydon,* a broken limb, he is tightly bound, and, as he writhes in *Alisaunder.* agony, the shouting rabble press upon him, gloating and jeering over his suffering, pelting him with dirt and filth,

---

[1] "sur un malvais sumier."

plucking out his beard and hair, striking him with fists and sticks.

Cant. Tales,
B. 645.

"Have ye not seen sometime a palë face
Among a press, of him that hath been led
Toward his death, whereas he got no grace?
And such a colour in his face hath had,
Men mightë know his face that was bistëd,
Amongës all the faces in that rout."

Ganelon, when captured, is handed over to the kitchen knaves, who pluck out his beard and moustache, strike him with their fists, beat him violently with sticks, drag him along with a chain, "cume un urs" (like a bear), and throw him

Ch. de Rol.
3964.

ignominiously upon a sumpter horse. His end, after the ordeal, is even more terrible. Each of his hands and feet is tied to one of four swift and high-mettled chargers which start away in mad career; the sinews part asunder; his body is torn in four; the blood pours out upon the green grass:

3974.

"It is not right that he who betrays another should boast of it[1]." And the hostages who have stood surety for him are all hanged. The traitor Godard is beaten, "as man doth

Havelok, 2448,
2476, 2504.

bear[2]," and cast upon a foul, scabby, evil-looking mare, with his nose beneath her tail. Then he is flayed alive; a nail is passed through his feet; and thus he is drawn at the mare's tail over rough ground to the gallows, and hanged by the

2511.
Horn, 2820—
30.

neck, no one pitying him because he is a traitor: "Dash it, who cares? He was false!" Godrich, the traitor in the story of *Horn,* is bound fast upon the back of an ass with his face to its tail, and then burned at the stake. Sir Simon

Pol. Songs,
Wright,
pp. 218—221.

Fraser, in the *Political Songs,* is fettered hand and foot, with his legs fastened beneath the belly of his horse, and with a garland of periwinkle set upon his head. Afterwards he is drawn forth upon a bullock's hide, "as was the law of the land," because he is a traitor and false to his lord. Fettered and gyved, and clad in a kirtle of sackcloth, with a garland on his head, he is drawn from the Tower through Cheapside, a large crowd following.

---

[1]   "Guenes est morz cume fel recreant.
          Ki traïst altre, nen est dreiz qu'il s'en vant."
     [2] Evidently the performing bear had a very hard time at the hands of its trainer.

" Many men of Englond
For to see Symond
Thitherward gan leap."

At the gallows he is hanged and then beheaded; his body is opened, the intestines burned, and his trunk is hung up in iron clasps to rot. His head is set up on London Bridge as a spectacle of shame.

That these illustrations are not overdrawn, historical examples will show. About 1096 William de Hou was accused of treason, and, being defeated in the trial by combat, was deprived of sight and manhood. Rhys ap Meredith, a leader of revolted Welsh, captured in 1292, was drawn to the gallows at the mare's tail, and hanged. To these may be added the executions of Sir William Wallace, narrated in Langtoft's *Chronicle*, and of Sir Hugh Spencer and Earl Mortimer, told in detail by Froissart. *(Will. of Malm. IV. 1.)* *(Pol. Songs, p. 321. Froissart, Chron. p. 11, 30.)*

A woman, when her cause was lost, for open unchastity or for witchcraft might be stripped to her smock, and so led to the stake, and there burned. " Such a custom was used in those days, that neither for favour, neither for love, nor affinity, there should be none other but righteous judgment, as well upon a king as upon a knight, and as well upon a queen as upon another poor lady." But far more frequently public scourgings and penance were substituted. *(M. D'Arth. IV. 15, VIII. 34, XIX. 8, 9, XX. 5, 8, XVIII. 6.)*

These revolting details of inherent cruelty will give a truer proportion to our ideas of the later horrors of the Inquisition and the Marian and Elizabethan persecutions.

The march of the Crusaders continues till the coast is reached; and the host prepares to put to sea in great galleys and fighting-ships well furnished for the wars, with top-castles from which bolts and showers of heavy stones may be thrown, and with boats to send ashore for victuals when need requires. They are provisioned with biscuit, wines, flesh, and all other manner of victuals, and furnished with munitions of war, horses and armour, gold and silver, and other riches necessary for the expedition; and there are also cabins where the men may rest. There is a banquet on the eve of departure; disposition is made of property and goods; last farewells are spoken; for they know that many who are setting out so hopefully will never again return. Women weep upon the shoulders of lovers or husbands, and try to *(Rich. Cœur de Lion. Huon of Bord. p. 173.)* *(p. 63.)* *(p. 146.)*

bear themselves as befits the mates of warriors, but they would rather that their lords had stayed at home. In the morning they hoist sail for Palestine, where they hope to see, with their own eyes, the Holy Sepulchre. The route to Jerusalem seems fairly familiar to them ; but of the other parts of the East their knowledge is very vague. Some of them believe that Babylon is in India, to be approached from Jerusalem by way of the Red Sea and the desert, or, alternatively, by way of Damietta and the Nile.

pp. 173, 174.

They land, and in dauntless manner set themselves to overthrow the adversaries of God. No peril is too great, no enterprise too severe, for them. They are engaged in God's work, and in His strength they fight. "God wills it!" is their war-cry. The battle is in His hands, and the right is theirs. If they fall He will give them the crowns and flowers of Paradise, and place them among the saints; no coward ever enters there. Such is the spirit which upholds their courage[1]. They are the friends of God, and will never prove themselves traitors to Him. Some of them are captured by the Saracens, and cast into the dungeons of strong castles ; "but God, who never forgetteth His friends, succoured them"; and this becomes a common saying of theirs. "Above all things God loveth faith and truth when it is in man," they say ; and are not they all faithful and true ? They certainly believe that God cannot possibly fail to give good success to such admirable knights as they, whatever their private faults may be. Their prayers are sure to be favourably answered. They believe that God wills that the heathen shall flee before them like stags before the hounds ; that for them the Almighty will cause the walls of cities to fall down flat, and will bid the sun stand still to prolong their vengeance. He whom God aids does well ; how then can they be discomfited?

Will. of Malm. IV. 2.
Ch. de Rol. 3367, and stanzas CXXIX. CXXX.

Huon of Bord. pp. 102, 189.

Ch. de Rol. 2999, 3625, 1874.
Le Faux Turpin, II., XXV. and *Ch. de Rol.* 3657.

The campaign is carried on in much the same fashion as when the real Charlemagne set out to convert the Saxons of Germany. Great battles are fought in which the heavily-armed knights frequently ride down the lighter Saracens without mercy. "That Saracen seems to me a great heretic," says Turpin ; "I have never loved a coward or cowardice ;

1197, 1225, 1645.

---

[1] The *Chanson de Roland* is undoubtedly animated by the spirit of the age of the First Crusade. See *Ch. de Rol.* Léon Gautier, p. xxiv.

I would rather die than not slay him." Cities are besieged 97, 3661.
and taken by storm; strong towers are overthrown; vast
territories are laid waste and become desert. When victorious
the Crusaders cry aloud that only as many as will receive *Huon of Bord.*
pp. 107, 169,
baptism are to be spared; and so many are christened. 170.
For the rest, they sack, plunder, burn, hang and slay, cutting
to pieces pitilessly all who persist in their errors. Yes, even
the women and children perish with the men, "except such as p. 171.
would be christened," till their blood runs down the streets
like a river. The historian tells us that at Tripolis all the *Hen. of Hunt.*
Bk VII.
waters of the city, even the very cisterns, ran red with
blood.

Again we see the savage uppermost in the Christian
knight as he rushes, with naked sword in hand, through the
streets and palaces of the East. And the irony of it all is
that he believes that thus he is doing God service. Nay, he
even hopes thus to propitiate the Most Merciful, to purge his
own sins with the blood of slaughtered Saracens. A king and *Sir Triamour*,
Ellis.
queen have been denied the blessing of children, and to win
this blessing the king makes a vow to go to the Holy Land,
and there to fight and slay. And we are asked to believe that
the angels rejoice in the butchery of those who have been
taken captive:

> "There they heard angels of heaven; *Rich. Cœur de*
Lion, Ellis.
> They said, 'Seigneures, tuez, tuez[1]!
> Spares hem nought, and beheadeth these!'
> King Richard heard the angels' voice,
> And thanked God and the holy Cross."

Froissart tells how the Saracens marvelled by what right
the Christians came to make war upon them, since they had Froissart,
Chron.
done them no trespass; whereupon the lords of France answered pp. 402, 403.
that Jesus Christ, the Son of God, had been crucified and put
to death by their line and generation, and therefore they
would have amends, and punish the trespass that Saracens
had done long before; and also that the Saracens believed
not in holy baptism, and were ever opposed to their religion,
and believed not in the Virgin Mother of Christ, and therefore
they would revenge the despites that had been done, and
were done daily, to their God and their faith. At which the

---

[1] Slay, Slay!

Saracens did nothing but laugh, saying that it was the Jews, and not they, who put Christ to death. Perhaps one reason for the long continuance of the Crusades, apart from the periodical incitements of religious fervour which led to their beginnings, was that a Crusade occupied the minds of turbulent and wrathful men who would otherwise have troubled the peace at home.

Gower, Praise of Peace, 249.

Under the guise of a Christian zealot the Crusader, when victorious, runs riot in the East. His cruelty, his pride, his lust, are rampant. He is not averse to a lie when it serves his purpose ; and he boasts with glee of the impression he has made upon the Oriental, who is made to say of him : " It is hard for any man to know the craft and subtlety that is in a Frenchman." He revels in all the wealth of the Orient, in gowns garnished with precious stones, and arms and ornaments of exceeding costliness. He plunders palaces with magnificent chambers and halls hung with cloth of gold, furnished with seats of ivory, vessels of gold, and chairs inlaid with gold and precious stones, with beds so rich that their value cannot be appraised, with coverings, curtains and pillows of wondrous beauty, and with the softest carpets on the floors, until the catalogue of all these things becomes fixed and stereotyped in his memory. What a contrast to his own rush-strewn halls at home ! He takes the spoil of the dead Saracen upon the battlefield, and its splendour is beyond his dreams. Nay, such is his greed that at Antioch he even digs up the corpses from the graves, and strips them of their coverings and ornaments. Following the host there is a parasitic horde of camp-followers who batten upon the dead and dying, as, even at home, the custom was. These ghouls are well known : "And so as he went, he saw and hearkened by the moonlight, how the pillers and robbers were come into the field to kill, and to rob many a full noble knight of brooches and beads, of many a good ring, and of many a rich jewel ; and who that were not dead all out, there they slew them for their harness and their riches." Arab steeds of the finest breed[1], with saddles, harness and bridles, fall to his sword ; Arab slaves in the costume of the East are made to wait upon his will ; Arab women minister to his lust. With all this luxury and treasure he at last returns to his ship and re-embarks more like

Huon of Bord. pp. 192, 167.

p. 83, etc.

pp. 115, 147, etc.

Hen. of Hunt. Bk VII.

M. D'Arth. XXI. 4, and cf. *Cant. T.* A. 1005, and Barbour's *Brus,* XIII. 459.

Ch. de Rol. CLXXX. *Hen. of Hunt.* Bk VII.

---

[1] "chevals arrabiz e curanz."

a merchant prince than a Christian knight. Henceforth he will enjoy every luxury to the full; and his fellows at home will envy him his magnificent array when he returns. We may well imagine the influence of all this when introduced into western Europe.

But, sooner or later, the voice of conscience will be heard, and there will be many who see and abhor the evil. To such men as St Bernard and Walter Map they will listen when they tell them that to overcome their own sinful lusts is better than to conquer Jerusalem. Pope Nicholas I. will tell them that the heathen must be convinced of their errors by good advice, by exhortations and by reason, rather than by force. And in 1388 the Council of Placentia will make solemn proclamation, " That the Christian religion ought not to reject Jews and Saracens, because it is agreed that they have in themselves the image of our Creator." Men will be much saner by the end of the 14th century, as Gower shows: *Ch. de Rol.* Léon Gautier, pp. 322, 323, note.

> "And for to slay the heathen all
> I know not what good there might befall,
> So muchel blood though there be shed.
> This find I written how Christ bade
> That no man other shouldë slay.
>
> .   .   .   .
>
> To slay and fighten they us bid
> Them whom they should, as the Book saith,
> Converten unto Christës faith.
>
> .   .   .   .
>
> A Saracen if I slay shall,
> I slay the soulë forth withal,
> And that was never Christës lore."

Conf. Amant. Bk IV. p. 194. *Car. Lib.*

On the voyage homewards, and after his arrival, we may well imagine what tales the knight will tell, and how his fancy will work them up to his own satisfaction. He is not at all without a certain kind of humour; and many of his adventures will appear in no solemn garb. He will tell of a knight disguised as a Saracen in the presence of an eastern prince, and with him twelve French prisoners, comrades whom he dare not recognise. He hears that his leader has died in prison, and would like to vent his grief upon the prince, but dares not. So he finds relief by turning upon his compatriots with his staff, and giving them such strokes that the blood *Huon of Bord.* Steele.

p. 149.

runs down, and yet they are forced to suffer it for fear of the prince, but they curse him in their hearts for the blows. He goes on beating them till they come to their prison, and they go on cursing to themselves. He will tell, too, of a seventeen-foot Saracen giant who tries to win over a Frenchman to his side, offering, as an inducement, the hand of his

p. 164. sister, "who is a foot greater than I am, and as black as a coal"; and of a knight who plays chess with the daughter of a Saracen prince, to lose his head if he lose the game, to win the lady if he win it. He wins, because the lady contrives to lose; but great is her chagrin when he compounds with

p. 203. the prince for a hundred marks in money: "The lady went her way sorrowful, and said to herself, 'Ah! false, faint heart, Mahound confound thee. If I had known that thou wouldest thus have refused my company, I would have mated thee, and then thou hadst lost thy head'." He will think of a certain aged minstrel who was rescued from a Saracen gallows by an

p. 231. opportune sally during a siege. How he ran with his viol about his neck! "He that had seen him fly away could not have kept himself from laughing; he ran so fast that he did not seem to be an old man, but rather of the age of twenty years." He talks of the jests he will play upon those at home. Huon of Bordeaux has Oberon's magic cup from

p. 87. which the wine disappears if anyone in deadly sin presume to drink of it. What a joke it would be to offer it to the old, doting Charlemagne, who weeps piteously when he cannot have what he wants. How the barons would laugh at the old man's discomfiture! Perhaps the emperor would weep again as usual. But it is too bad to plague an old man so,

p. 115. and Huon repents him of the thought. Yet, on the other hand, when we hear, in all seriousness, of a hero striking the

p. 165. heathen gods with his sword, and jousting with the seventeen-foot giant aforesaid so that both their horses fall to the earth, and then stepping a little on one side to give the giant a marvellous stroke upon the helm, which cuts off his ear, we see that the age of Cervantes is not yet.

And, in reply, the home-keeping knight will also tell some

M. D'Arth. marvellous jests: How Dagonet, the fool, was dressed in
x. 12. Sir Modred's armour, and how King Mark turned tail and fled from him while all the knights who were in the secret laughed as though they were mad: how Sir Lancelot dressed

himself in a damsel's array, and overthrew Sir Dinadan; and x. 49.
how the knights took Sir Dinadan into a forest, and stripped
him to his shirt, and put on him a woman's garment, and so
brought him back into the field; and how Queen Guinevere
and all the knights fell down with laughing when he was
brought in among them all. The knights seem to have
loved a practical joke of this kind. A pun, too, came not x. 48.
amiss to them. When Lancelot says, " God forbid that ever
we meet, but if it be at a dish of meat," Guinevere and the
Haut Prince cannot sit for laughing. Perhaps they will *Old Eng.*
remember their parson's famous pun in his homily on Easter *Hom.* "In Die
Day: "Therefore this day is called Easter Day, that is, day Pasche."
of dainties[1], and the dainty is the 'husel[2],' and no man can
say 'hu sel, wu god'[3] it is."

The modern imagination may easily sketch out for itself
the return of the Crusader to his home after an absence of
many years, and little need be said about it. But occasionally his home-coming led to a re-union which was by no
means commonplace. We hear of knights returning, like
Sir Guy of Warwick, in pilgrim's garb unrecognised, that
they may see for themselves what has been happening in
their absence, as Ulysses had done before them. Let us hope
that many had the fortune of Sir Guy who found his fair
Felice engaged in works of charity and pious devotion,
patiently awaiting his return. When it is to a constant
sweetheart, and not to a wife, that the knight returns, we
must imagine for ourselves the fair lady's petition for delay
to make the necessary preparations, perhaps "for to go to *M. D'Arth.*
London, to buy all manner of things that longed unto the XXI. 1.
wedding."

But many a maid was left desolate and forsaken, a sacrifice to the Crusades, from which her lover never returned.
Many such withdrew from the world to the seclusion of a
convent cell. We can almost hear the voice of the preacher
urging on such a one to the love of Christ. Perhaps he tells
her the beautiful parable of the Castle-Lady: How Christ, *Ancren Riwle.*
the fairest, the richest, the wisest, the most courteous of men,
woos the soul, as the earthly knight his love; how He risks
all things, endures all things, gives all things, for her, even to

---

[1] The etymology is, of course, incorrect.
[2] The Sacrament.   [3] "hu sel," *i.e.* "wu god," *i.e.* how good.

the sacrifice of His own life; how He removes all evil and all

grief, and gives instead all love, all happiness. And if we catch the maiden's answer we hear that she chooses Christ for her lover, her bridegroom, and her all.

English maidens were edified, we must believe, by such teaching as that of the *Lives of St Margaret, St Juliana and St Katherine,* of *Holy Maidenhood* and the *Ancren Riwle*[1]:

Maidens delight in thoughts of love; let them learn therefore of the divine love of Christ, and turn aside from the impure and sensual love which is in the world; let them imitate the virtues and the beauties of the holy Virgin; let them strive

against temptations, ghostly and bodily; let them seek for purity of heart and the love of Christ, while practising all the observances which are as a handmaid to the inner rule of the heart. A strong appeal is always made to the natural instincts of womanhood: "Our Lord, when He suffers us to be tempted, plays with us as a mother with her young darling; she flies from him, and hides herself, and lets him sit alone and look yearningly about, and cry, 'Mother! Mother!' and weep awhile. And then with widespread arms she leaps laughing forth, and clips and kisses him, and wipes his eyes. Just so our Lord leaves us alone at times, and withdraws His grace and comfort and favour, so that we find no sweetness nor satisfaction of heart even when we do well. And yet all the time our dear Father loves us never the less, but He does it for the great love that He has unto us."

As a rule, convent life could not have been so very different from that of the world without, nor the nuns so very unlike their more worldly sisters, since the same temptations

seem common to both. Yet "there ought to be a great difference between the lady of a house and a nun." They are especially warned against much speaking. They are to keep no beast except a cat, that their thoughts may not be distracted by worldly cares, and that there may be no loss of dignity through the worries of the same. They are to dress plainly but warmly, with nothing next the skin but coarse linen. Their shoes must be large and warm; in summer they may sit barefoot if they choose. They are not to scourge themselves or to undergo undue austerities. They must not make purses or lace to gain friends for themselves,

[1] "Anchoresses' Rule."

but they may make things for the church and for the poor, as
well as their own clothing. They must not send or receive
letters without leave. Their hair ought to be cut four times
in the year, but they may wash and comb their heads oftener
if they choose. Two maids may be kept to wait upon them
if necessary. They must not speak to men through the
convent windows, and no man may sleep in their house. If
great need cause this rule to be broken they must have an
honest woman with them within both by night and day.

No doubt after the first incitements of religious zeal had
worn away, the nuns thought more and more of the outside
world, and more often sat at their windows to glean news of
it from the passers by. Very often would some old gossip
sit beneath an open window telling tales, and not always
modest tales, to the nuns within. Even choice bits of the
scandal of the neighbourhood in this way reached their ears.
Sometimes, as a knight rode by, a nun would open her
window and enter into conversation with him, perhaps, if he
were a worthy knight and honourable, extending to him an
invitation to dinner, or even giving him shelter for the night.
Serious consequences often resulted from this surreptitious
contact with the world, for such interviews but added fuel to
the natural craving which the nun had set herself to repress.
There is a story of a beautiful sacristan nun who fell in love
with a clerk and found it impossible to live without him. One
day she threw her keys upon the altar, broke her vows, and
joined her lover. But, after five years of roving, the new life
began to pall, and she returned to the convent to find that in
the meantime the Virgin herself had taken her appearance
and performed her duties so that she had never been missed.
The opportunity thus offered, of quietly re-entering the
convent, she gladly embraced. From this we may perhaps
judge that a penitent's return was often made easy for her
without too many inconvenient questions being asked.

The clergy were as their time made them; their fault was
that they were no better. The truly spiritual life seems to
have been lived but by the few; the many were notoriously
corrupt or incapable. The Church "faltered like a humble
and suffering handmaid, and was subjected to many insults;...
her gates were more frequently unlocked by the key of Simon
Magus than by that of St Peter." Many of the priests, con-

Margin notes:

Ailred of Rievaulx. De vita eremetica, III.

M. D'Arth. XIV. 1, XV. 5, 6.

A Selection of Latin stories, No. CVI. Wright, p. 95.

Acts of Stephen, 1.

trary to the ecclesiastical vows, took to themselves wives, which the Church refused to acknowledge as such, though the practice of concubinage seems to have been usually no bar to the sacred office. Hence was given a direct incentive to flagrant

Hen. of Hunt. immorality. Anselm prohibited incontinence, "a thing not
Bk VII. before forbidden," and the historian notes the recognition of the weakness of a celibate system: "Some thought it would greatly promote purity; while others saw danger in a strictness which, requiring a continence above their strength, might lead them to fall into horrible uncleanness, to the great disgrace of Christendom." Credit must certainly be given to

Will. of those who strove for reform. As early as 1095 the Council
Malm. IV. 2. of Clermont had enacted that the Church should be pure in faith and in morals, free from servitude, simony and placeseeking, and that the authorised fasts should be duly observed. It must not be forgotten that there were in the Church such

Jocelyn of men as Samson and Hugh, abbots of Bury, the former a man
Brakelond, eloquent, learned, gifted with inborn common sense, exceed-
Clarke, pp. 51 ingly temperate and industrious, a hater of liars, drunkards
—62, and p. 1. and talkative folk; the latter a kind and pious man, a truly religious monk, unskilled in the wiles of this present world.

But the system itself was corrupt. Of Pope Innocent III. one of his most extreme partisans, Geoffrey de Vinsauf, writes in the following fulsome strain, being led astray by

Nova Poetria, recollections of classical mythology: "Thou art neither God
conclus. nor man but as though between the two, one whom God chooses to be His ally. As such, with thee He rules the world. But he wished not all things for Himself alone. So He willed earth to thee, and heaven to Himself. What could He do better? To whom better than thee could He give it?" And these words are written about the time when Innocent is asserting the papal claims most arrogantly, appointing Stephen Langton to be archbishop of Canterbury in the face of strong opposition, laying England under an interdict, excommunicating King John, and offering the crown to Philip of France. The Englishman will soon speak very differently of this supposed bequest. We see it working out in less important matters when a clerk comes with letters of request seeking a benefice from Samson of Bury. The abbot takes from his desk seven papal mandates with leaden

Joc. of Br. seals attached, and says: "Look at these apostolic writings
p. 84.

whereby divers popes require that certain benefices should be given to divers clerks.   When I shall have quieted those who have come before you I will give you your rent."   Does not Map tell us that the surest method of obtaining office or benefice was to box the pope's ears with a big purse of gold? Pious men lament the scandal, but there seems no remedy as yet; and the true-hearted Grosseteste foresees strife and sterner trouble before the fetters are broken.

De nug. Cur.

The Norman, as has been seen, had always been self-confident in action, and this characteristic now begins to lead him to self-confidence in thought.   He wants to know *why* he should follow blindly the traditions which others have laid down.   There is that within him which is always questioning, always testing, which in spite of precedent is bound to break forth sooner or later.   One in whom reason rules is Berengarius, who begins to test by its light certain doctrines of the Church, among them transubstantiation.   But the state of mind of the majority of men is seen at once.   The most powerful intellect of the day is arrayed against him when Lanfranc takes up the cause of the accepted dogma.   Berengarius is charged with heresy; his life is threatened; and he is imprisoned and compelled to recant.   Happy is he when it is permitted him to withdraw from controversy and take refuge in quiet and prayer.   Such is the age; but it is important that the first signs of the coming change should be noticed.

The most scientific people of the world at this period were the Arabs; and, as the Crusades extended the horizon of the western world, the value of their learning came to be realised.   They had already made great advances in the mathematical and natural sciences, as well as in literature, and from south and east their influence spread.   In the twelfth century, an Englishman, Abelard of Bath, travelled into France in pursuit of knowledge, and thence into Greece and Asia Minor, possibly even to Bagdad itself.   On his return to France he began to teach what he had learned of Arabian science, which was held to be but heathenish doctrine by most of his hearers; so strange, so new, was it; so self-complacent, so bound up in precedent were they. He made translations from the Arabic, and thus threw new light upon the wonders of nature and astronomy.   Especially severe was he upon the undue reverence for authority which prevailed. Free play must be allowed to the faculty of reason; man must think and learn; man must advance. Otherwise there can be no real knowledge. With time his teaching told; and other Anglo-Normans and Norman-Frenchmen, few in numbers but great in enthusiasm, travelled into Spain to sit at the feet of the Arab teachers. By them the *Korân*, in addition to other works, was translated into Latin.

Thus by Berengarius on the side of religion, by Abelard and his followers on the side of learning, were struck the first sturdy blows against the thread-worn principles of mediævalism. What the scholars brought home had its due effect upon the work and thought of Roger Bacon, the first great scientist of the west. A student of Oxford and Paris, and a Franciscan friar, he broke loose, in spite of all opposition, from the trammels of the past, and never ceased his great work of scientific examination, experiment and classification. Such men as he are the teachers of the world. He tells his readers *Opus Majus*, I. plainly that the roots of all ignorance lie in blind reliance upon authority, in the fatuous following of custom, in inexperience, in that little learning which arrogates to itself all wisdom. First free the mind of all prejudice, and then true wisdom may be acquired. So far is he in advance of his age that he knows the powers of the lens and of gunpowder, and *Opera Inedita*, suggests the possibility of the modern steam-boat and horse-Rolls, p. 533. less carriage [1].

And now a new tendency, the spirit of satire, becomes clearly apparent in the Anglo-Norman. He is older and more experienced; the enthusiasms of youth are growing cooler; for him the heroic age is now passing away. He is more sober, more practical, more severe, his thought more mature. With the eye of middle age he looks back upon the rants and conceits, the sins and follies, of youth, and bestows upon them the mocking raillery, the irony, the satire, of the man whose own youthful days are past. Wherever insincerity is discovered, there the lash of the satirist will fall. Hypocrisy is the most despicable of evils, and it is everywhere. Bitter thoughts arise; and yet the rogue can no more be suppressed by argument than by law. But he may be made to writhe under the sharp-pointed jest and the hearty laughter which

[1] "Item currus possunt fieri ut sine animali moveantur impetu inestimabili."

greets his discomfiture.   The erring husband, the fickle wife, the loutish peasant, the unscrupulous merchant, the false churchman, the ambitious noble, the un-royal king, all see themselves in the glass which the satirist holds up so cleverly that their fellows may know them and point at them with the finger of scorn.

Chiefly remarkable, because most subtle and most widely popular, is the *Roman de Renart*, where all in turn are pilloried.   Renart, the type of craft and cunning, is the sly rogue who has ever preyed upon those weaker or simpler than himself; and there are many such.   Oftentimes does it happen, when piteous tales of oppression are brought to court, that Lion, the king, rises in his wrath, and roars and rages at the insult offered to his crown, so that timid and effeminate courtiers fear and tremble.   But it all comes to nothing.   The wily Renart knows how to deal with the royal messengers, who return worsted and mutilated, as did many a king's messenger in those days from the castle of some over-bearing baron.   How impotent one often is when striving to right a wrong!   And yet sometimes it is good to turn our anger into a laugh, and to ridicule what once we should have borne hardly. *Rom. de Renart.*

Fiercer, less humorous, is the cry of the satirist against the clergy.   In the poem on the bishops of the reign of John there is the writing on the wall, "Mene, Mene, Tekel, Upharsin[1]."   The bishops of Bath, Winchester and Norwich are styled "the three insatiables": "'Give,' they say, ' there is not sufficient'"; and the last is directly addressed as "Tu, Norwicensia bestia."   And again, in the series of anonymous poems styled the *Confession of Golias*, Golias is almost a clerical Falstaff, a type of the ribald clerk, a glutton, a wanton, a parasite, and yet a bishop.   In a vision the four beasts of the Apocalypse are seen.   The lion is the pope, who devours; the calf, the bishop, who feeds upon the fattest pastures; the eagle, the archdeacon, who descries his prey from afar; the man, the dean, endued with human guile. The clergy are wanton, and think more of amassing wealth than of their cures.   This one is a trader who goes about *Pol. Songs, Wright, p. 8.* *p. 11.* *p. 10.* *Confessio Goliæ and cf. Pol. Songs, pp. 32, 33.*

---

[1] "Scribentem cerno digitum
Et literis implicitum
Scriptis 'Mane, Tecchel, Phares.'"

from fair to fair; that one is intent upon his farms; and there are those who blaspheme with the wine-cup in their hands. Here is a famous drinking song, evidently meant to be taken as issuing from the lips of a drunken monk:

> "Meum est propositum in taberna mori;
> Vinum sit appositum morientis ori,
> Ut dicant cum venerint angelorum chori:
> Deus sit propitius huic potatori[1]."

The influence of these satires upon the Reformation in later days was enormous. All true Protestants believed their every detail; and every exaggeration was accepted as a literal truth.

Speculum Stultorum, Brit. Mus. I. B. 47056.

Hear now the parable of the ass who wished to be a bishop. Burnellus, a diminutive of brown, is his name. He escapes from his stable, and would rise in the world, and have a tail long and beautiful. Galen, the physician, ridicules him, but sends him off to Salerno to obtain the ingredients of a wonderful elixir which will bring about what he desires. On his way back, the mastiffs of the monk Fromond attack him, and he loses half his tail, while the bottles containing his treasure are broken by his frantic plungings. So his beauty is gone for ever; no longer can he hope to rise by that; and he cannot go back to his stall with only half a tail. What shall he do? He has it! He will go to the University of Paris, the centre of learning. He will be a man of science, a master of arts, a bishop! And all men shall bow to him. He goes, and essays to put his plans into operation. He clips and trims his hair, combs and washes himself, and invests himself in his best tunic. He enters a church, and offers vows and prayers. Then he deliberates which of the schools will best further his purpose. For many reasons he decides to join the English nation. They are subtle in understanding, distinguished in manners, elegant in appearance and speech, able of wit, vigorous of counsel. They are lavish with their money; they shower gifts upon the people; they detest the niggardly. They multiply dishes, and drink without restraint, with "wessail et drincail." He attends lectures;

---

[1] "It is my intention to die in a tavern. May wine be placed to my dying lips, that when the choirs of angels shall come they may say, 'God be merciful to this drinker.'"

he studies; he scourges himself frequently on back and hand and side.   Almost seven years are completed, and still learning will not come to him.   All he can say is, "Ya, Ya."   So farewell to his dream of science and the bishop's throne.   But he can be an abbot and rule in an abbey.   So he tries all the orders in turn, and all in vain.   Then he will have an abbey of his own, the best and most delightful of all abbeys. There shall be no rule of silence with him—there was none at Grandmont; no fasting—they did not fast at Cluny; they shall all dress in good warm clothes—like the Præmonstrants for example; they shall all have their "little women"—like the secular canons.   But now comes the catastrophe.   He meets Galen once more, and is professing to discourse of Church and society, when his Alnaschir-like day-dream is rudely dispelled by a blow from the stick of his old master, Bernard the peasant, who after long seeking has at last found—his ass!

In imitation of Paris, the Universities of Oxford and Cambridge had been founded early in the thirteenth century, but the start was not auspicious.   The students appear to have been as frequently engaged in brawling as in study, for until 1246 it was possible to graduate without examination. Riots were common; north and south, English and Irish, town and gown, were ever in conflict.   In 1214 the townsmen hanged some of the students of Oxford, but were compelled by the pope to make amends.   Sometimes the castle at Oxford was found to be too small to hold the students who were imprisoned.   Some kept "little women" in their lodgings; some held strange orgies in churches.   Even the Fellows had to be warned to live honestly, to refrain from fighting, from holding scurrilous and indecent conversations, from telling immodest tales, and from singing or hearing improper songs.   If the student finished his course at Paris, much the same state of affairs prevailed.   The students were, for the most part, extremely poor and very disorderly, often living in the grossest immorality and crime.   Those who happened to have money were distinguished for their lavish expenditure and excess in every indolent and vicious luxury. In quest of knowledge both teachers and students pursued strange methods of argument and disputation, screaming, threatening, abusing, and even fighting.   And yet from these

Cf. Walsingham, Hist. Ang. I. 278.

Rolls of Parl. II. 76.

Munimenta Acad. I. 60.

Spec. Stult.

seats of learning proceeded such men as Abelard, Roger Bacon, and John of Salisbury—which proves that there is another side to the picture where a willing student was concerned.

Rolls of Parl.
III. 294.

Joc. of Brake.
Clarke, pp. 66, 67.

Many a poor man's son proceeded to the universities, and afterwards entered the Church. The Commons protested in vain against the sons of villeins being sent to Oxford. Samson, the worthy abbot of Bury, was of humble birth, received a free education by the charity of the schoolmaster at Diss, and was afterwards maintained at Paris by a certain chaplain with the proceeds of the sale of holy water. Later he himself provided free education at Bury St Edmunds,

p. 144.

arranging not only for free accommodation for the poor clerks, but also for an annual payment to the schoolmaster in lieu of students' fees. Where such men afterwards occupy the pulpit there will be heard less Latin and French and more English. Samson himself was wont to preach in

p. 62.

English, in his own Norfolk dialect, though he was eloquent in both Latin and French. When a certain monk hesitated to accept the office of prior in the monastery, modestly alleging his lack of learning, Samson reassured him: he could easily read over and commit to memory other men's sermons,

p. 196.

just as others did; and then the abbot proceeded "to condemn rhetorical flourishes and pompous words, and choice sentences, saying that in many churches the sermon is delivered in French, or rather in English, for moral edification, not for literary ostentation." Hence arose among some of the brethren a habit of scoffing at polite learning.

In the purely English mind, slow-working, simple, yet earnest and receptive, the old stock of ideas still lingers beneath the manifold influences and experiences from without. The ancient homilies are still the intellectual food upon which the religious Englishman feeds. The flames and torments of hell, the Judgment, the uncertainties of life, are but relieved as before with the miraculous deeds of martyred saints, and anticipations of the sweetness of heaven. Confession is good for the troubled spirit; and in the *Poema Morale* the Englishman sets forth his sins in detail. But hear a stern-faced English monk as he pours down upon his congregation a fiery denunciation, which shows how closely he has watched them as they assembled before him, and how well he knows the manner of their life; for he is one of them-

selves. He tells them plainly that the devil will get all
fraudulent chapmen; that the cheating brewers and bakers, *Morris, O. E. Misc.* p. 189.
who rob men of their silver with short measure and inferior
quality of ale and bread, are committing sins which will rob
them in their turn of heaven; that the sins of the proud
young men and maidens, who gather together in church and at
market to whisper of secret love, will not go unpunished. They
only come to church because they have made it their meeting
place. The maids think only of looking at their sweethearts,
and leave their rosaries carefully locked up at home; they
care for neither mass nor matins because all their thoughts
are of love and lovers. Very different in spirit and practical
usefulness is this from the sermons in the learned Latin and
the religious love-songs of the Norman-French. The preacher's
words are very apposite, for the Knight of the Tour Landry *Bk of the Kn. of the Tour Landry,* XXVIII.
tells us that there was much frivolity and tittering in church
in his days.

There were many such servants of the Church as this
preacher; and to their numbers were added, in the thirteenth
century, the Dominican and Franciscan friars, the teachers
and workers of the age. Among the students might be found
the Dominican, arguing, expounding, attacking heresy; among
the sick and needy, the Franciscan, nursing, helping, carrying
comfort and consolation, giving up all things for the work's
sake, in obedience to his call. Vowed to poverty, and despising
the world, they enlightened the whole country by their preaching and example. The people flocked to them with all piety
and devotion, hearing, learning, confessing their sins. Among
the poor their work was invaluable; and when their influence
had permeated the lower strata of society it became possible
to say of them that they were the saviours of both the classes
and the masses. But it was this great success of the friars
at the outset which so soon afterwards led to their undoing.

At home, the poor man lived in his rude cottage of mud *Havelok,* 557, 740.
or clay, perhaps as a small peasant farmer growing his corn,
and keeping sheep, cattle, horses, swine, goats, hens, ducks
and geese, providing fodder for his cattle, perhaps hiring a 700.
herdsman or two to watch them and to keep them from
straying and trespassing, if his children were not old enough
to do so. If his cattle strayed they were placed in the pound *Anc. Riwle.*
until all damage they had done was paid for. From time to

time pedlars or chapmen passed from cottage to cottage hawking their wares, and always ready to get the better of a bargain. "The wretched pedlar makes more noise crying his soap than a mercer his precious ware," says the writer of the *Ancren Riwle*. The Englishman was always a good trencherman; and even the poorer classes seem usually to have had a sufficient quantity and variety of food. In Grim's cottage Havelok is promised bread and cheese, butter and milk, pasties and custards or pancakes. Grim, who is the fisherman of Grimsby, hawks his fish in panniers through the neighbouring towns and country places, and returns home with bread and relishes, beans and corn, to supply the wants of his family. When he catches the great lamprey, so well can he sell the delicacy that he returns from Lincoln with wastel-bread[1], sold at a farthing a loaf, simnels, meal, corn, beef, mutton or pork. Yet, when hard times come, the growing youth cannot get enough to eat at home, and must go barefoot, without hose or shoes, to seek his livelihood elsewhere. He comes to a castle, and the cook, noticing his great strength, asks him to enter his service, offering to feed him well in return for his work. "Wilt thou be with me?" asks the cook; "I will gladly feed thee. The cost of thy meat and hire would be well bestowed." "Dear sir," says Havelok, "I ask you no other hire; give me but enough to eat, and I will fetch you fire and water, blow the fire and make it well. I can break and crack sticks, and kindle a fire full well, and make it burn brightly. Full well can I cleave sticks to skin eels[2]. Full well can I wash dishes, and do all that you ever wish." Quoth the cook, "I desire no more. Go thou yonder and sit there, and I will give thee full fair bread, and make thee broth in the pot. Sit now down and eat full eagerly. Dash it! who should refuse thee meat?"

Poor maids entered the service of the well to do, or of the nuns of a convent, where we hear something of their life. They must not gossip, or eat or drink without leave. They must not munch fruit or anything else between meals; nor must they go outside the gate without permission. They must work without grudging, and be always ready and willing. They must speak to no man without leave; they must neither embrace nor kiss a man, nor sport or play with

Havelok, 643.

760.

905.

Anc. Riwle.

---

[1] Fine bread or cake.   [2] By placing the head in the cleft.

him. These probibitions to convent maids seem to suggest
that the average maid was wont to do many of these things.

The poorer and middle classes delighted in games, just as
the knights did in their tournaments. On special occasions   *Havelok*, 2324.
there were jousts and boar-hunts to be seen ; and among
themselves wrestling, putting the stone, archery, and the
baiting of bears and bulls, with harping, piping, dancing,
feasting, singing of gestes and glees, tale-telling, miming and
dicing. At such times much licence was usually permitted :

> "Dances, carols, summer games,   *Hand. Synne,*
> Of many such come many shames."   4681.

And kissing is also set down in the category as giving rise to 8101.
sin. On holy days the people flocked to the church or church-
yard to see the Miracle Plays acted by the clergy and their
assistants ; and later the Mysteries[1], played by the craftsmen's
guilds, were to be seen from points of vantage in the streets.
From the behaviour of the large crowds who gathered to see
them even the Miracle Plays came under suspicion ; and clerks 4637.
in orders were forbidden to take part in them, or to watch them,
because they led to the encouragement of sin. But they might
in the church play the birth of Christ and the resurrection to
make men believe in God. It was sinful if they played on 4651.
the roads or greens. Undoubtedly the playing of Miracles
led to Sunday carols, dances and assemblies of women, and to 985, 8987.
wrestlings and games, in the churchyards; and these gatherings often ended in rioting and bloodshed. Such gatherings
were customary at Bury St Edmunds at Christmas-tide ; and *Joc. of Brake.*
the good abbot at last solemnly excommunicated a number of p. 139.
men for taking part in wrestling and other matches within
the precincts of the churchyard.

The Coventry Plays began at six o'clock on the Sunday *Eng. Mir.*
morning. The Corpus Christi Plays at York commenced *Plays,* Pollard,
  pp. xxxviii.
earlier still, between four and five. An eye-witness of one and xxix.
of the last performances of the Chester Whitsun Plays has p. xxv.
left us an interesting description of what took place: "Every
company had his pageant or part; which pageants were a
high scaffold with two rooms, a higher and a lower, upon
four wheels. In the lower they apparelled themselves, and
in the higher room they played, being all open on the top,

---

[1] M. E. *myster*, a craft, from O. F. *mester, mestier*, occupation, employment ;
Lat. *ministerium*. Hence the name *Mystery* plays.

that all beholders might hear and see them. The places
where they played them were in every street. They began
first at the abbey gates, and when the first pageant was
played it was wheeled to the high cross before the mayor,
and so to every street; and so every street had a pageant
playing before them at one time, till all the pageants for the
day appointed were played. And when one pageant was nearly
ended, word was brought from street to street, so that they
might come in place thereof exceeding orderly, and all the
streets have their pageants before them all at one time
playing together. To see which plays there was great resort,
and also scaffolds and stages were made in the streets in
those places where they determined to play their pageants."
In fact, so great was the resort that the actors and their
assistants were often inconvenienced by the throngs which
pressed about them :

Chester Plays,
Sac. of Isaac,
485.

"Make room, lordings, and give us way,
And let Balak come in and play,
And Balaam that well can say,
To tell you of prophecy.
That Lord that died on Good Friday,
He save you all both night and day!
Farewell, my lordings, I go my way,
I may no longer abide."

A.-S. Laws,
Laws of
Ethelred, 13.
p. 131,
Thorpe.
Joc. of Brake.
p. 202.

Sunday was also, in many places, a market day for open
buying and selling; and it was long before a complete change
could be brought about. Even in the laws of Ethelred an
unsuccessful attempt had been made to break the custom,
when it was ordained that the Sunday festival should be
rightly kept, as was befitting, and that markets and folk-
motes should not take place on the holy day. We learn
that at Bury St Edmunds the change was made in 1201, and
thenceforth the market was held on Monday. The period

O. E. Hom.
In Diebus
Dominicis.
Test. of Love,
11. 9.
Hand. Synne,
846.

of Sabbath rest was held to begin at noon on Saturday
and to continue until Monday's dawn, Saturday afternoon
being the eve of the festival. "Lo! your Sunday begins at
the first hour after noon on the Saturday," says the *Testa-*
ment of Love.

On occasion there was the spectacle of an ordeal by fire
or water. An accused person might be called upon to prove
his innocence by laying his hands upon red-hot irons, sprinkled
with holy water, or by walking barefoot over red-hot plough-

shares similarly prepared. Some poor old woman might be
accused of witchcraft, and tested by being plunged into a
running stream over which prayers had been said. If she
floated she was judged to be guilty; for the water had refused
to receive her. If she sank she was held to be innocent.
More frequently there was the use of the cucking-stool, to *Joc. of Brake.*
which the woman with shrewish tongue, or the user of deceit- p. 79.
ful weights, was fastened and then ducked in the water.

In the popular songs there is a note, ever increasing in
volume, which reveals the depth to which the feelings of
the poor are stirred by the oppression of the rich. There
is much muttering among them, and but half-concealed
hatred, in which both kings and nobles are involved. The
singer seems to have been always on the side of the people.
In the song on the battle of Lewes we hear him rejoicing
over the fall of the court faction, and especially of Richard,
the king's brother:

> "Richard, though thou be ever trichard[1],   *Pol. Songs,*
> Trichen[2] shalt thou never more."   Wright, p. 69.

The people are just beginning to awake, to feel themselves
no longer mere goods and chattels as feudalism would have
had them; and their awakening is seen and feared. Hence
arises much friction. There is a sturdy honesty and worth
about the English peasant which is raising him in the social
scale. Abbot Samson confirms a manor to a villein of English
birth, whose honesty he trusts all the more because he is a *Joc. of Brake.*
good husbandman and cannot speak French.   p. 50.

The poor man, like the rich, might have ambitions; and Neckam,
it was not at all impossible for him to rise in the world. He *De Nat. Rer.*
might, as we have seen, proceed to the university and enter II. 175.
the Church: William of Wykeham, of the next century,
whose motto was "Manners maketh the man," is a notable
example. He might have the gift of composing and singing
songs, and so become a famous minstrel or trouvère with a
court at his feet, like Cercalmon or Marcabru the foundling.
He might amass money by his trade, and take a position of
authority. He might even by his bravery and sterling worth
win for himself a knighthood. "My name is Garnish of the *M. D'Arth.*
Mount," says one, "a poor man's son, but for my prowess and II. 16.

---

[1] Traitor.   [2] Deceive, betray, play the part of traitor.

hardiness a duke hath made me a knight and given me lands;
and his daughter is she that I love, and she me as I deemed."
To balance the power of the greater barons Henry I. raised
men of low degree to high rank and office; and at the
commencement of Stephen's reign, because he pursued the

*Acts of
Stephen*, Bk I.

same policy, the great nobles were estranged, being "disgusted at the pride and pomp of those who, though sprung
from nothing, had been raised above them in rank and
possessions, and exceeded them in power." The jealousy of

M. D'Arth.
x. 61.

the noble makes him say: "Give a churl rule and thereby
he will not be sufficed; for whatsoever he be that is ruled
by a villein born, and the lord of the soil to be a gentleman
born, the same villein shall destroy all the gentlemen about
him; therefore all estates and lords beware whom ye take
about you." But thus a powerful English element was
entering into the nobility and aristocracy to complete with
greater rapidity the blending which was in progress.

With the amelioration of the lot of many who had sprung
from the poorer classes the condition of the whole country
was improving. Despite many drawbacks the wealth of the
nation was increasing. Trade and commerce had begun to
flourish; and already there were many populous and thriving
cities, and many busy ports. And in these centres of industry
the workers were grouping themselves together and drawing
further and further away from the domination of the feudal
lords, to learn what it was to be free and self-governing.
Prosperity made them more and more independent, and
rendered them sufficiently powerful to stand aloof from the
internecine struggles which were already bringing feudalism
to its fall. The knight invested his money in weapons and
armour, in troops of retainers and strong castles, in costly
garments or hoarded treasures, and thus his means were
locked up in those things which could not further increase
his wealth. The merchant invested his profits in larger and
still larger ventures; his capital was always increasing at a
high rate of compound interest, and never was much of it
lying idle. And, in addition, the knight's very necessities, as
well as his luxuries, but added to the merchant's store. In the
large towns there was by the end of the 13th century a new
aristocracy founded upon successful trade, which by its wealth
had begun to rival the older aristocracy of birth. The merchant

had often more money in his purse than the noble; his
dwelling was often more palatial and luxurious; the fur
upon his robe was often more costly. In his mode of life,
in his manners, even in his speech, he had begun to emulate
the followers of the court. He had also developed much
of the Norman keenness, self-assertion and self-assurance;
he was already known as not above driving a hard or
even fraudulent bargain. He would be called "Sire"; and
claimed the respect which is always the gentleman's due.
Here again there is a place where the qualities of the English
and the French may meet.

Neckam,
De Nat. Rer.
II. 177, 178.

It is but a sign of the times when we find the Jews so
numerous in the country. Although hated on account of
their religion, and even more so on account of their wealth,
they had become the financiers, pawnbrokers and armourers
of the nation. "Do not men account him a good fellow who
layeth his pledge in Jewry to release his companion?" asks
the author of the *Ancren Riwle*; and Chaucer mentions

Anc. Riwle.

"a fine hauberk,
Was all y-wrought of Jewës work,
Full strong it was of plate."

Cant. Tales,
B. 2053.

It was all very well for the Englishman to talk of young
Hugh of Lincoln, popularly supposed to have been kidnapped
and murdered by the Jews, and to spread tales of their evil
repute "for foul usury and lucre of villainy," but, at this
period, they were making of him a close and shrewd man
of business. Easy and careless borrowers learned by hard
experience what they would never have learned otherwise.
Benedict, the Jew of Norwich, lent forty marks at interest
to the monks of Bury, and, when the debt amounted to
£100, pressed for payment. As the monks could not pay,
they foolishly borrowed another £100, and gave a bill for
£400, payable at the end of four years. Again they could
not meet the bill; and a deed was drawn up arranging for
the payment of £880 at the rate of £80 a year. On this
and other accounts the monastery was found to be indebted
to this Jew for £1200, beside interest which had accrued.
A sharp lesson to the unbusinesslike sacrist who was responsible for the debt! A little later the abbot himself was
in similar trouble. Wherever he went, creditors, both Jews

B. 1874.
B. 1681.

Joc. of Brake.
pp. 2—4.

p. 48.

and Christians, came about him, demanding payment of their accounts, worrying and importuning him so that he could not sleep. He grew thin and pale, and was often heard to say: "My heart will never rest until I know the extent of my debts." Ever afterwards he took close account of his revenues, and we hear no more of his pecuniary difficulties. But if the Englishman's education in financial and commercial matters was costly he will reap the full benefit of it before a hundred years have passed away. The Jews are making him the greatest merchant-trader in the world.

CHAPTER V.

THE RESULTANT NATION.

OF greatest import in the history of the development of the English nation are the events of the fourteenth century; for then modern life begins. From the great loom in which the threads of life are woven then comes forth a fabric still, for the most part, mediæval in texture and design, and yet containing the beginnings of new strands, which, for centuries to come, will be worked over and around the original texture, to add to the complexity and elaboration, and also, one may hope, to the utility, of the work put forth. Then, as in all such periods, the intelligence of the human race is seen developing most rapidly. Man becomes more critical; his reasonings become more clear; the scales of the past drop from his eyes as he awakens to a fuller sense of his position in the economy of the universe. His leaders preach to him the doctrines of reality and responsibility; and there is that within him which answers to their preaching as he struggles to rid himself of shams and unsympathetic authorities. Then will the value of authority be so much the less, that of the reasoning, working individual so much the more, as authority is judged to be false, unsympathetic or injurious to him who is engaged in the battle of life. And where falsity, hardness or injury appears the cry for reform will be strenuous and unceasing.

With the increasing recognition of the claims of the individual the English middle and lower classes will assert themselves and become a power in the politics of the fatherland. They will know themselves, not as mere dependants upon a despotism or even an aristocracy, but as a nation, of composite structure it may be, but none the less strong and capable, bound together by the closest ties, and for all practical purposes made one and indivisible by virtue of the influence of a popular majority.

As feudalism decays before this new force the balance of power will shift from the class dependent upon tenure of land to the active traders and workers of the towns. Then modern politics will begin; and there will be the problems of town against country, of aristocracy against democracy, of capital against labour, of taxation, of education, of socialism, of foreign immigration and foreign trade. Correlative with these there will be in religion the problems of authority against conscience, of the hierarchy against the ecclesia, of formalism against spirituality, of faith against scepticism, of tradition against reform. And in social life there will be the questions of recreation, of environment, of morality. There will be some organised attempts at a better system of sanitation, and also some slight attempt to grapple with the problem which the parasitic life of the nation involves, reaching from the wretched mendicant or sturdy thief upon the roads to the women who make prostitution their profession. Already the modern love of travel has spread throughout the middle class. And in the crowds which delight in the buffoonery and indecent jesting of the wayside farce the audience of the modern lower class music-hall will be seen in the making.

In the new nation, cut off from the Continent by the silver streak of sea, even the men of Norman blood begin to lose count of their French ancestry, and merge themselves in the mass of their fellow-countrymen. Interests, associations, politics, all preclude allegiance to the shadows of the past, unsubstantial because unprofitable. The victors of Hastings will stand in rank, against a common foe, beside those they vanquished; and the long protracted rivalry of England and France will reach a second phase upon the fields of Cressy and Poictiers. Then we shall see the fathers of modern England working out that lust of conquest and desire for supremacy which have ever been ours. We shall hear them talk of sea power and the importance of the naval problems which their trade and their insular position naturally impose. And we shall see them, now staunchly patriotic to the very extreme of boastfulness, and again, in dubious and darker days, just as pessimistic; though their pessimism will be touched with a spice of that old, grim doggedness which their own forefathers had handed down to them as a national inheritance.

The races have blended; and the fresh virility of the hybrid everywhere appears. But, if language be any test of predominance, the predominant element in the blending is no longer doubtful. Though French is still assumed to be a mark of aristocratic birth and breeding, English is in the ascendant, being borne to supremacy by the rise of the great middle classes, among some of whom the former language, sadly mutilated and ill-pronounced by English lips, is already coming to be regarded as a sign of the parvenu and the toady. "And uplandish men," says Trevisa, "will liken themselves to gentlemen, and strive with great business for to speak French, for to be more accounted of." *Trevisa, Polychronicon, c. 59.*

Early in the fourteenth century the rise of a united English-speaking people is seen in the *Cursor Mundi*, translated, as the author says, into the English tongue for the commons of Merrie England to read and understand, since it is useless to write in French which very few now know, the major part of the nation being of English blood. And a little later Robert Mannyng writes in English, the simple mother-tongue which is easiest in the mouths of simple men, for the laymen who know neither French nor Latin[1]. The English translator of *Richard Cœur de Lion* tells us that not more than one in a hundred of unlearned men can understand French books. And a later writer will say that since the understanding of Englishmen will not stretch to the privy terms of French, however men may boast of their knowledge of a foreign language, the clerk had better indite in Latin for the sake of his learning, and the Frenchman in the quaint terms of his French because it is natural to him, but let the Englishman express his thought in the tongue he learned at his mother's knee. *Cursor Mundi.* *Rob. Man. Chron. 6, 71.* *Rich. C. de L. Ellis, p. 286.* *Test. of Love, Prologue.*

From the middle of the century none of the political songs of the nation are written in French[2]. In 1362 it is ordained that all who plead in the King's Courts, or other Courts of law, shall plead in English, because French is too little known[3]; and in

[1] Mannyng's *Handlyng Synne*, in English, had been written much earlier (1297?); but in his *Chronicle* (1338) he states his purpose plainly.

[2] Political songs and satires in English had begun to appear nearly a century earlier.

[3] It seems, however, that this ordinance was not strictly obeyed for nearly a hundred years afterwards.

the same year Parliament is opened with an English speech. By 1385 we hear the Englishman's opinion that the presence of strange tongues in the country, by intercourse first with the Danes and afterwards with the Normans, has much impaired the language, since some speak with an outlandish pronunciation, "wlaffyng, chyteryng, harryng and garryng, grisbittynge[1]." This is mainly due to the use of French in the schools and castles. But now a change has come to pass, and in all the grammar schools children are leaving off French and are beginning to construe and learn in English, which is an advantage in so far as they learn their grammar quicker than before, but will prove a disadvantage if they travel abroad. For now they know no more French than "their left heel." And gentlemen are ceasing to teach their children French. Even the French still spoken by the gentry is often very far removed from the language of France.

That this change of language betokens a deeper change of sentiment may be seen in the Englishman's growing habit of scoffing at Frenchmen : in one passage there is the taunt that they are very stern and brave when sitting in a tavern and boasting of their deeds, that they fight well with loud words, and hold no man their peer, but they turn tail at once and draw in their horns when put to the proof where strokes are given.

So one of the strongest links with the Continent is broken, and consequently there is a slighter check upon that strong insular spirit which, bearing fruit in manners, customs, life, thought and character, has had so great an influence upon the Englishman of almost every age and class. And this insularity is strongly emphasised, and even localised, by the bad state of the roads and inefficient methods of transit. Everywhere the new-made Englishman has a great idea of his own importance, and is indeed passionately proud of his nationality and country, "flower of lands all about": "England full of play! free men well worthy to play! Free men, free tongues, heart free! Free are all the people; their hand is more free, better than their tongue."

The century opens with the English embarked upon the flood-tide of conquest. The whole of Wales and large portions of Ireland, Scotland and France are in their hands. The new nation has already achieved great things. But see how the manner of its conquests accords with the spirit of

*Trevisa,
Polychronicon,
c. 59.*

*Cant. Tales,
Pro. 124.
Piers Plow.
v. 239.*

*Rich. C. de L.
Ellis, p. 319.*

*Trevisa,
Polychronicon,
c. 41.*

---

[1] "babbling, chattering, growling, harshness of voice and gnashing of teeth."

the age in its savage bravery and pitiless brutality.   Barbour, the Scot, speaks bitterly of the terrible oppression of Edward I., Barbour, *Brus*, I. 115, 100. "that gripped aye without again-giving."   Both Ireland and Wales he holds in such thraldom that those of high degree are made to run on foot like rabble.   The Welsh dare neither ride to battle nor, after even-fall, abide in castle or walled 194. town, on pain of losing life or limb.   In Scotland the conduct of the English is just as grievous.   Right felon, wicked, covetous, haughty, pitiless, do they become.   Scottish wives and daughters are outraged, and if any is wroth thereat they lay wait to find means to bring him to destruction.   The Scots' best possessions, their horses, their hounds and other things, the English take for themselves, and resistance but 215, 275, 455. leads to loss of lands, life or freedom.   Good knights are hanged by the neck, or imprisoned, for little or no cause or reason. When the Scots rise in desperation, only to be defeated at Methven, the king commands that all the prisoners shall be hanged, but happily his orders are not carried out.   In this connection Barbour wrote the famous lines which have ever since been treasured in the hearts of English and Scots alike, for the sentiment is common to both peoples:

> "Ah! freedom is a noble thing!   225.
> Freedom makes man to have liking;
> Freedom all solace to man gives:
> He lives at ease that freely lives!
> A noble heart may have no ease,
> Nor nothing else that may him please,
> If freedom fail; for free liking
> Is yearned for o'er all other thing."

Inspired by this love of freedom the Scots cast down the pride of England at Bannockburn; but the day goes otherwise at Halidon Hill in 1333; and then the English patriot sings triumphantly:

> "Where are ye, Scottës of Saint John's Town?   Minot, II. 7.
> The boast of your banner is beaten all down."

And again:

> "More menacings yet have they makëd,   I. 49.
> Mal gré may they have to meed.
> And many nights, too, have they wakëd
> To harm all England with their deed.
> But, praised be God, the pride is slakëd
> Of them that were so stout on steed,
> And some of them are laid all naked
> Not far from Berwick upon Tweed."

Then the Hundred Years' War with France commences shortly after 1337; and nothing further is needed to show the completeness of the break between the two countries than the utterances of the patriotic poems of the day. However it may drag along afterwards, this war at its commencement is undoubtedly popular. Edward III., "our comely king," has laid claim to the crown of France, and the nation is with him in his attempt to win it. In their opinion he is the rightful heir of that country; and they pray that God will help him to win his heritage. A wave of national enthusiasm leaps into being, swelling to its height when the victories are won against "the caitiffs come out of France," and "the false folk of Normandy." The Conquest of nearly three centuries before still rankles in the English breast; but all are English now who dwell this side the Channel. "Never were men better in fight than English men," the patriot proclaims. Bannockburn has been avenged; and now the stain of Hastings is to be wiped away upon the fields of France.

King, nobles, knights, merchants, artisans, peasants, all have their share in the expedition which is preparing. In merchant ships and great galleys, manned and armed for war, the army is transported across the sea. Above the bulwarks ramparts of woodwork are raised to afford protection to the fighters; some few of the newly invented guns, or military engines, are carried; and thus men-of-war are extemporised, by which sea-fights may be won. Already have these vessels proved their worth against a Flemish pirate of terrible renown, whose ships they captured or destroyed at Dundee in 1332. Now they will destroy the French fleet in the great sea-fight off Sluys (1340); and later at Winchilsea (1350) they will destroy the Spanish fleet which has plundered the English wine-ships in the Bay of Biscay, and even threatens a descent upon the English coast. Already have the English laid claim to the sovereignty of the seas, with so noble and plenteous a shipping in every port and river mouth that all countries hold and call their king "the king of the sea[1]." Thus early do they recognise in naval supremacy the very life and death not only of their trade but of their country

IV. 1, 28, and cf. Froissart, pp. 29, 33, 37.

I. 31, IV. 8.

V. 58.
VII. 72.

III. 111.
II. 1.

X. 14,
Froissart,
p. 77.
Leg. of Gd
Wom. 638.

Rolls of Parl.
A.D. 1372,
Vol. II.
pp. 310, 311.

---

[1] "q̃ touz les pays tenoient & appelloient fire avandit Sr̃ le Roi de la Mier."

itself. In 1372 the fleet, once so powerful, is found to have
been so neglected that it is insufficient for the defence of the
realm; and the Commons point out the great and imminent
peril if an attack should be made by sea, for it often takes
three months or more to fit out the ships for war. Therefore
they ask for a subsidy, " for the salvation of the land," which
is granted them. Possessions over sea are held as outposts
by which the safety of the kingdom is assured and the coasts
guaranteed against attack, and through which the king may
carry war into the heart of a hostile country at his own will
and pleasure, choosing his own opportunity when his preparations are complete. Chaucer's Merchant, who, despite his
debts, wishes to appear as one who has a great stake at
issue upon the sea, is but echoing phrases from the lips of
many bigger men than himself when he professes his great
concern that the sea should be held between Middelburg and
Orwell.

A.D. 1378,
Vol. III. pp. 33
et seq.

Cant. Tales,
Pro. 276.

We follow the English fleet to sea, and soon see them
engaged with the foe. The ships manœuvre for vantage of
wind or sun; trumpets sound; banners and standards float
in the breeze; loud cheers are given by the crews. The
archers begin to shoot; and the guns and engines of war send
forth their missiles. Violently the fleets rush upon each
other, and become locked together. Hooks and grapnels
of iron catch in bulwarks and rigging; great stones, bars of
iron, pieces of timber, and pots of blinding lime are thrown
from the tops upon opposing ships, to the great hurt and
annoyance of the men below; knights and men-at-arms
leap upon the enemy's decks. With pole-axe and spear the
boarders press in among the foe; and many brave deeds are
done, impetuous assailants being taken and rescued again.
Mighty rushes are checked on the points of spears. Now
some flee for safety behind a mast, and out again; some are
driven overboard. Here one rends the sails with a scythe-like
hook; here another pours peas upon the deck to render a
footing insecure; here again, in a breathing space, one brings
the cup for the refreshment of the fighters, and speaks en-
couraging words. So from morn till noon the fight goes on;
and then the way is won to France and further victories on
land, with the great fields of Cressy and Poictiers to follow.

Leg. of Gd
Wom. 633.
Froissart's
Chron. pp. 61,
80.

Hear the patriot exulting over Cressy, the downfall of

the French, the proved superiority of his countrymen and the undiminished might of England:

Minot, VII.
117.

129.

"Away is all thy weal, i-wis,
Frenchë man, with all thy fare;
. . . .
English men shall yet this year
Knock thy pallet[1] ere thou pass,
And make thee polled like a frere;
And yet is England as it was.

Wast thou not, Francis, with thy weapon
Betwixen Cressy and Abuyle?
Where thy fellows lie and gapen,
For all their trickery and their guile."

84.

v. 49, 14, 34.

Listen as he boasts with pride of the English archers by whom Cressy was won: how boldly with broad axes and bent bows they laid low the Frenchmen; how their shooting seemed as though it were snow; and how the pride and boasting of the Normans were abated. How rampant he becomes in his glee! "There Englishmen taught them a new dance." "There men taught the Normans at buckler to play."

I. 15.

"They turned again with sidës sore
And all their pomp not worth a pear,
A pear of price is more some time
Than all the boast of Normandy."

In the personnel of the army which made England great a change has come about, which is itself an index of a greater change in the national life; and this change owes its inauguration to the success of the methods which the Conqueror had introduced at Hastings. That great event, which had led to the foundation of our feudal system, also contained in itself the germ of what was to become one of the causes of its downfall. The skill of the English bowman, and his own knowledge of his powers, went far to establish the rights of the individual, whatever his birth or his wealth might be. There was no more sturdy, more independent, person in the world, none with greater confidence in his own skill and manliness, than the English archer who had bent his bow upon the fields of France. The honour of the archer was well nigh on a par with that of the knight; and to cut the

---

[1] head.

bowstrings of the one was as great an ignominy as to deprive the other of his golden spurs. The English yeomanry
and peasantry will be all the better for these first few years in
France.

No longer is the fortune of battle mainly dependent upon
the shock of the heavily mailed horseman, as in the days of
romance, but much more upon the swift and well-aimed
shooting of the bowman, who at Cressy checked the charge
of the French nobles in mid career, bringing down horse and
man in utter confusion. No longer is the battle "the stour   *Auc. and Nic.*
where knights do smite and are smitten"; no longer are   Lang, p. 11.
droves of ill-armed peasants easily accounted for by a handful
of armoured gentlemen. After Poictiers divers English archers   Froiss. *Chron.*
had four, five or six prisoners each. No longer does the   p. 128.
English king ride to battle followed only by the baronial
levies, but at the head of an array in which are many free
archers, sturdy yeomen, who serve in the ranks for weekly pay,
with their mighty bows and sheaves of arrows, bright and keen
of point, made with goose, swan and peacock feathers. When
Edward III. advanced against the Scots he had some eight   p. 18.
thousand knights and squires, and thirty thousand others
well armed, one half mounted on hackneys, the other half
men on foot sent from the towns and paid their wages, with
twenty-four thousand archers on foot. For the conquest of
Ireland Richard II. led thither four thousand knights and   p. 430.
thirty thousand archers, well paid weekly; and the expense
of the expedition was borne by the merchants and cities
of the realm, who thought the money well bestowed when the
king returned again with honour. The value of the knight
has diminished, that of the archer is increasing. On the field
of battle wealth and birth meant little when the arrow-flight
was "as it were snow," when the long-bows were shooting   p. 43 n.
thrice to the cross-bows once, when chain armour was no
longer impervious, and when the best plate armour, even at a
distance, possessed far too many joints and weak places to
be entirely safe, and might be pierced by direct shooting at
close range[1]. Once down, the knight in his heavy panoply   *Pol. Songs,*
was completely at the mercy of the brown-faced, crop-headed   p. 170.
woodsman, with his broad axe or sword and buckler, and   *Cant. Tales,*
Pro. 113.
sharp, well-harnessed dagger. Besides, the mobility of such   Froiss. *Chron.*
pp. 123,

[1] "Loricam duram possunt penetrare sagittæ."

170, 441, 112. a force was extremely great, for many of the archers were well mounted on strong, wiry nags. In the French wars small detached parties of the English seem to have foraged as they pleased, often at great distances from the main body, and been rarely captured. Chaucer himself may have joined one such party which happened to be an unfortunate exception. All the kings and rulers of Christendom envied the English king his archers, and sometimes enticed them away from him by offers of higher pay. Philip d'Artevelde, the Flemish leader,

pp. 283, 285, 288, 316. had at one time in his host two hundred English archers, and at another sixty, who had deserted from the garrison at Calais, tempted by a higher weekly wage. It was not until other countries were able to train similar bands for themselves that they could hope to meet the English in the field with a fair chance of success.

The archers themselves knew their own value. They knew that the honour of Cressy and Poictiers was theirs; all men acknowledged it. And they were of the people, recruited

Gov. of Eng. from the yeomanry and peasantry. "The might [of England] standeth most upon archers, which be no rich men," writes Sir John Fortescue in the next century. One sees at once the sequel. A new independence, a new manliness, takes up its abode in the humblest farmstead, even in the lowliest swineherd's cot. Has not this man bent his bow at Cressy? Has not that man's son shot at Poictiers? And perhaps near by there is another yeoman or peasant whose son has eclipsed upon the field the fame of his own lord's son, gallantly winning his spurs and a place among the captains. Were there not the

Walsingham, *Hist. Ang.* I. 309. two great free-lances, John Hawkwood, "that distinguished and famous soldier," and William Gold, poor men's sons who had risen from the ranks, with their Free-Companions, upon whom the costliest treasures of the wealthiest cities and castles of Italy and France were poured as the price of their forbearance or support? Do not the English peasants in the

Froiss. *Chron.* p. 258. rising of 1381 speak thus to the brave Sir Robert Sale?—"Sir Robert, ye are a knight and a man greatly beloved in this country and renowned a valiant man; and though ye be thus, yet we know you well, ye be no gentleman born, but son to a villein such as we be. Therefore come you with us and be our master, and we shall make you so great a lord that one quarter of England shall be under your obeisance." Have

not already the French peasants of the Jacquerie begun to p. 136.
assert that the noblemen and gentlemen of France shamed
the realm so that it were better far to destroy them all ; and
do they not proclaim with one voice ?—" Shame have he that
doth not all in his power to destroy all the gentlemen of the
realm !"

Then again, in these wars the mechanic and artisan of the
towns had no small share. As the master gave of his wealth
to provide the war-chest, so the man applied his skill to
furnish the equipment of the forces, an equipment demanding
more and more of ingenuity and technical craftsmanship.
With the necessity for more perfect armour and more complicated appliances for war the cost to the knight was
increasing, while the trade of the master was becoming
more abundant, and the reputation and wages of the trained
craftsman and armourer higher. By his skill was forged the
new artillery, the guns of brass or iron which belched forth   *Sir Triamour*,
Ellis,
an immense cloud of pungent smoke, and fired a great round   *Ho. of Fame*,
stone or swift " pellet," " that smiteth soon a tower to powder." III. 553, II. 28.
Though perhaps to modern ideas this artillery may seem to
have been more terrifying than effective, yet in its own day
such was its fame that Chaucer must needs arm with it the   *Leg. of Gd
Wom.* 635.
fleets which fought at Actium, and Langland could not let
Satan and Lucifer defend the gates of hell against the Christ   *Piers Plow.*
C. xxi.
without providing them with brasen guns, after the orthodox
fashion of the French war.   Henceforth the baron who incurs
the hatred of the people will not feel quite so safe behind the
walls and ramparts of his castle. As the use of the long-bow
had already raised the status of the yeoman, so the use of
cannon and firearms will begin to raise that of the artisan,
and the increased expenditure in war that of the merchant-
trader.   Early in the century the merchant was thought little
of as a soldier. Philip of France once sneered at Sir John of
Hainault, " how that he was a merchant to have his country   Froiss. *Chron.*
burnt"; but a different opinion was formed later when the   p. 58.
burghers of Ghent with an army of five or six thousand men   pp. 272—273.
and three hundred guns defeated the forty thousand armed
men of the earl of Flanders, among whom were many knights
and squires. In England this sharing of the task accounts
for the national enthusiasm, not confined to any one class,
which arose when first the English nation, financed by the

loans of its wealthier middle classes, supported by the votes of its representatives in Parliament, and giving its most stalwart sons to uphold the national welfare and renown, won fame by land and sea in the Scottish and French campaigns.

But in a few years' time, when there are no longer any great victories to boast, and no material advantages to show in return for the great sacrifices endured, while the long-protracted war drags out its weary length from year to year, a great change of opinion rises and grows among the people. War had not yet become an exact science; and the English were unable to reap the real fruits of their successes. Despite the renown of his victories Edward III. found it impossible to conquer all France; and the reason is not far to seek. Though before Cressy the king knelt devoutly at the altar and prayed for a successful issue, and after the victory gave humble thanks to God for it, yet in the battle itself, as had previously been determined, the English gave no quarter and took none to ransom. And later there was the terrible massacre at Limoges, when the English entered the captured city bent upon evil, to plunder and rob, to slay men, women and children, as the Black Prince had commanded them. " It was great pity to see the men, women and children that kneeled down on their knees before the prince for mercy; but he was so inflamed with ire that he took no heed to them, so that none was heard, but all put to death, as they were met withal, and such as were nothing culpable. There was no pity taken of the poor people…for more than three thousand men, women and children were slain and beheaded that day. God have mercy on their souls, for I trow they were martyrs," says Froissart. By such methods was bred a more and more obstinate resistance. And there was also grievous trouble at home, which sapped the strength, and cooled the martial ardour of the nation. In 1349 the terrible Black Death had appeared; and a large proportion of the population, some say one-half, had been swept away. Storm and famine followed, to add to the ravages of the disease, while the war stood still. When respite from affliction came, the best efforts put forth were but as those of one who still feels in body and brain the effects of the wasting and crazing feverishness of the bed of sickness. Though victorious at Poictiers (1356), the army in France became dispirited, and in 1360 suffered greatly from

Cf. *Test. of Love*, Prologue.

Froiss. *Chron.* pp. 102—106.

p. 201.

Piers Plow. III. 188, 205.

hunger and cold. A fearful storm struck terror to the soldiers' v. 14.
hearts; and the king hurriedly signed the Treaty of Brétigny,
with which the people at home were by no means satisfied[1].
Again and again storm, famine and pestilence recurred. The
crops were destroyed, and hunger was prevalent. To drain
the national purse further became a grievous hardship, since
no benefit followed in return. The Commons grudged and
murmured, repudiating their share in what they now say is
the personal quarrel of their king, and not their own. In the
reign of Richard II. they tell him plainly that as it is his war   *Rolls of Parl.*
he ought to pay for it, and that the people ought not to be   A.D. 1378.
taxed further to provide for the occupation of lands and
strongholds beyond the sea.

As early as the reign of Edward I. something of this might
have been foreseen. There was then, to a certain extent,
popular representation in Parliament with control of the
national purse, and we find the king, strong though he was,
confessing that he could not provide for the safety of his
realm without the help of his people; and supplies were
granted him upon conditions. Thus the middle classes began
to assert their power. When Edward II. was crowned, he   Bishop Stubbs,
was required to confirm by oath to the people of England   *Const. Hist.*
the laws, customs and privileges granted by his predecessors.   II. 344.
In the later days of Edward III. the Commons brought
forward their grievances for redress, inquired into the conduct of his officers, and undertook to reform his household.
They even went so far as to denounce his mistress,
Alice Perrers, against whom there was strong feeling in the
country. Though Richard II. claimed to hold the crown by
the gift of God, that was not the opinion of the people, who
welcomed his deposition two years later: "Might of the   *Piers Plow.*
Commons made him to reign." Though the king (*rex*) is   Pro. 113.
said to have his name from his office of ruling (*regere*), he has   140.
the name without what it implies unless he study to keep the   145.
law; and Langland illustrates the popular feeling by the old
fable of the Cat and the Rats. Only the ignorant, who do not
understand what they are saying, repeat parrot-wise: "The
precepts of the king are to us the bonds of law." Langland

---

[1] "Cowardlike thou Conscience counselled'st him thence
   To leave his lordship for a little silver
   That is the richest realm that rain overhangeth."

shows clearly what he and many others with him really
thought. The king may claim to rule the Commons, to be
head of law and they but members, to be above all men and
to take from them what he needs, but conscience asserts that
he may only take in reason what the law gives him, and on
condition that he defends and rules his realm right well and
in truth. And the poem on the deposition of Richard II.
(*Richard the Redeless*) says that rulers of realms were not
created to live as they pleased, but to labour at the law as
the poor man did at his plough. The widespread tendency of
the age is shown in the frequent deposition of rulers during
this century, including Edward II., Richard II., Pope Benedict
(1399) and the Emperor Wenceslas (1400).

"Woe to the land where a boy is king," quotes Langland,
thinking of the evils of the reign of Richard II. We see the
outcome in discontent, insurrection and rebellion, with the
poor against the rich, the nobles against the king, and the
king himself overthrown, and his crown given to another;
"each man for himself, there is none other." Chaucer, bred
as he was at court, seems to have these troubles in his mind
when he writes his famous apostrophe: "O stormy people,
unsettled and ever untrue!..." The world, he thinks, is
turning upside down, from right to wrong, from truth to
fickleness; and all is lost through lack of steadfastness.
Aristocratic Gower goes further still, and sees in the growing
might of the people nothing but a national danger. If the
ferment of democracy be not checked it will suddenly and
unexpectedly break all bonds, and the state will be shattered;
and it must be allowed that, in the circumstances, his words
are very apposite.

In this age the Englishman, like his fellows on the
Continent, stands hesitating upon the threshold of modern
life; the spirit of the Renaissance is already abroad. Everywhere there is upheaval, necessarily involving chaos and
conflict, but opening fresh ground for rapid progress in the
future; and in the new nation, endued with all the freshness
of youth, life is fuller, more vigorous, more pregnant with
splendid possibilities, than ever before. Everywhere there is
the feeling that the traditions of the past are at length, after
centuries of stagnation, completely played out. The spirit of
political liberty, which recognises more fully the claims of the

B. xix. 463.

Pol. Poems,
Wright, I. 405.

Piers Plow.
Pro. 192.

Cant. Tales,
A. 1182.

E. 995.
Lak. of Sted.

Conf. Amant.
Car. Lib.
p. 40.

individual in the social organism, appears and flourishes; and coincident with this there begins to arise a sense of discord springing from the discovery that the older system of despotic authority is no longer working for the best interests of society at large.

This feeling seems to have had its primary origin among the free cities and commonwealths of Italy, and thence to have spread throughout western Europe, not so much by direct contact as by an almost indefinable transmission, much as pollen is carried by the wind or bees to the growths already prepared by nature to receive it. One effect of this transmission, and perhaps it is the most important, may be seen in the literature of the age. Dante had written that true nobility *Convito,* IV. consists in cultivating the virtues with which God has endowed 20. the human character, not in aristocratic descent; and almost simultaneously this teaching is rife in England. Before the commencement of the century Robert Mannyng writes:

> "Unworthily art thou made gentle,   *Hand. Synne,*
>   If thou in words and deeds be ill;   3037.
>
>   .   .   .   .
>
>   Lordings—there are enow of those,   8715.
>   Of gentlemen there are but few."

For, as we read elsewhere, the habit makes not the monk, nor *Test. of Love,* the wearing of gilded spurs the knight. Chaucer echoes Dante, II. II. speaking to those who argue that they are gentle by descent. "Such arrogance is not worth a hen," he says bluntly; he who *Cant. Tales,* is always most virtuous, openly and secretly, he who sets him- D. 1109. self to do what gentle deeds he can, is the greatest gentleman. He who is virtuous, and not outrageous of bearing, though he *Rom. de la* be not gentle born, is truly gentle, because he does the deeds *Rose,* 2191. of a gentleman. Or as William of Wykeham puts it, "Manners maketh the man." Again, in the *Parson's Tale,* Chaucer tells *Cant. Tales,* us that for a man to pride himself upon his birth is great folly, I. 460, and cf. and often destroys his true nobility of soul. Both rich and *Ayenbile of* poor, we are all of one father and mother, all of one nature, *Inwyt,* Morris, and that corrupt. The only kind of gentility to be praised is p. 87. that which endues a man's character with virtues and good I. 760. morals, and makes him the child of Christ. After all, churls spring from the same seed as lords; the churl can be saved just as well as a lord; the same death takes both. Robert

Hand. Synne,
8695.
Mannyng makes a Norfolk bondman reprove the pride of a lord by telling him that God made both earls and churls from the same earth, and to the same earth must both return; the bones of the one will then be indistinguishable from those of the other. Langland advises the rich not to ill-treat the bond-
Piers Plow.
VI. 46.
man. Who knows? perhaps in heaven he may win a worthier seat and greater happiness than oneself; for death is a great leveller, and with him there is no difference between knight and knave. Even Gower writes that all were alike gentle in
Conf. Am.
p. 200.
the beginning. With all this in the air we shall not be surprised, when the insurrection of the peasants takes place, that they sing as they march the words which John Ball quoted on Blackheath :

Walsingham,
Hist. Ang.
II. 32.
> "When Adam delved and Eve span,
> Who was then a gentleman?"

At the other extremity of the social scale we find the same principle at work, completely undermining the older feudal system. Edward III. refuses to render any external mark of homage to the king of France for the duchy of Guienne; and when he appears before the emperor to advance his claim to the French throne, though so far acknowledging the imperial overlordship, refuses to do homage in the usual manner. The French king, cited to appear, simply ignores the summons altogether. The first principle of feudalism has become no more than an empty name.

From Italy, too, comes the quickened sense of appreciation of the beautiful in life, sensuous it may be, but still true to nature. It means much when the Englishman is enabled to break away from the blank and wooden forms of the art of the Middle Ages to tread the path which Giotto has so lately trod before him. He is learning to use his senses, to analyse the life around him, to note the rich beauty of all he sees. The fulness of existence, the joy of living intensely, glows and quickens in his veins. Henceforth he will desire for himself the very best, wherever his interests urge him ; and he will not be so content to satisfy himself with that which lies nearest at hand because it happens to be easiest of attainment. The whole world is opening out before his eyes ; and it is a world of glorious endeavours and magnificent ideals. It is a world of beauty in which harshness and cruelty will by degrees become softened and toned down, that man may less and less frequently, as time rolls on, clash inharmoniously with his surroundings.

It is the age of desire, and satiety seems well-nigh impossible. The Englishman would know all the sciences under the sun, and all the subtle crafts; and in his quest for new ideas he is indefatigable, turning over and over the contents of the Latin, French and Italian literatures, and making their thought his own. He absorbs an enormous amount of learning, often useless, often fearfully inaccurate, but the point is that he is progressing with rapid strides over new ground. Certainly, in his science, we must credit him with being not very far from the true theory of sound waves. We fancy that we have a picture of the typical Renaissance student as we look upon Chaucer toiling away at his books, after his day's reckonings are done, until his brain is almost dazed by the closeness of his application. And this spirit of desire appears in manifold directions leading ever onwards. As it is in literature, art and science, so it is in the national life, in politics, religion and commerce.

Already is England noted for its aptitude for every industry, its specialised trades, its successful operations in foreign parts, its wealth and commerce. Its merchant-traders have risen in social status, until they now form one of the most influential sections of the community. Many of them have seats among the Commons; and their influence in forming the national policy is enormous. London is already a prosperous and thriving port, one of the first trading centres of the world[1]; Sheffield is already noted for its blades; and the English cloth-makers are surpassing the Flemings in their own particular manufacture.

English sailors may be met with in every western port and haven. Some of them are exceedingly adventurous, rough, hard-headed, brown-faced men, sticking at nothing where extra profit or booty lies, men whose consciences go to sleep as soon as they are out upon the open sea. In such the blood of the old sea-rovers still flows freely, and pilfering, piracy and murder are not unknown among them, if we may take Chaucer's Shipman as a type. This sailor tells us that he has drawn many a draught of Bordeaux wine while the chapman was asleep, and he knows of strange and lawless

Piers Plow.
B. xv. 48.

Ho. of Fame,
II. 212 et seq.
II. 139 and cf.
II. 121, and
Leg. of Gd
Wom. Pro. 30.

Cant. Tales,
B. 1210.

A. 3933, Pro.
447.

404.

396.

---

[1] Gottland and Venice were larger ports in the 14th century.

happenings on the high seas when many hapless captives were made to walk the plank. Sometimes, perhaps through such actions as these, perhaps through disputes or jealousy, Englishmen are imprisoned or ill-treated in lands beyond the sea; and then those at home retaliate upon the traders of *L'Envoy a* the offending nation who happen to be in England. Chaucer *Bukton.* speaks of being "taken in Friesland" as though it were one of the worst evils which could befall a man[1].

Piers Plow. Jealousy of the alien frequently appears; for among the *v. 233.* richest of the merchants are the Lombards and Jews, whose *Walsingham,* *Hist. Ang.* methods of accumulating wealth are popularly supposed to be *I. 300.* most unscrupulous. By deceit and fraud they win for them- *Conf. Amant.* *p. 124.* selves the best goods of the land, bringing chaff and taking corn. The Lombards are the slyest of all to make a thing appear very much better than it really is, and so they often make a profitable transaction of what should have been a loss. They are new-comers, and yet they take an influential position in the country. They reap the profit which the Englishman believes should be his, and go free from the burden of the taxation which falls all the more heavily upon him. This allegation may have a very familiar ring to some newspaper-readers of the present day.

Competition is undoubtedly increasing, and often some merchants, with all their show, are hard put to it to make both ends meet. In order to sustain their credit there are *Cant. Tales,* some who live beyond their means, striving to rival in appear- *Pro. 280,* *B. 1210.* ance their more successful brothers, maintaining expensive houses and extravagant wives, and talking with lordly air of non-existent business ventures and profits. But these are, of course, the smaller fry. With some, when at last creditors become too pressing, a pilgrimage sometimes forms a very convenient excuse for keeping out of the way:

B. 1417.
　　"And by that lord that callëd is St Ive,
　　Scarcely amongës twelvë two shall thrive,
　　Continually lasting unto our age.
　　We may well maken cheer and good visage,
　　And drivë forth the world as it may be,
　　And keepen our estate in privity
　　Till we be dead; or ellës that we play
　　A pilgrimage, or go out of the way."

---

[1] In 1396 the English took part in an expedition against Friesland, and, as the Frieslanders refused to ransom their countrymen when captured, no exchange of prisoners was possible.

Of lower degree, but far more stable, are the prosperous master-craftsmen of the guilds in the large towns. Their solid appearance betokens their comfortable circumstances. When they take a holiday, like Chaucer's Haberdasher, Car- Pro. 361. penter, Weaver, Dyer and Tapestry-maker, they go on pilgrimage in fresh and new array, sometimes taking with them their own cook, and always bearing themselves with all the solemn dignity which befits members of a guild like theirs. Each seems well fitted to grace a guildhall dais. There is no pretence about them, no affectation, no tawdry imitations. Stolid, with aldermanic gravity, they are men of few words. Outside their businesses they lack ideas and conversational brilliancy; and this, perhaps, is why Chaucer left it till too late to find fitting tales for them to tell. They are typical well-to-do manufacturers, slow but sure. At home they have left wives whose recognition of the position their money has gained is much keener than their own; as one often sees outside the world of fiction. These good women love to be called "Madame," to take precedence of their less fortunate and envious sisters at vigils[1] and public ceremonies, and to make a brave show of their position with mantles royally borne. And yet, no doubt, if one but knew, even these worthy masters were once frivolous and mischievous, if they were at all like the 'prentices they have left in their shops. But their own 'prentice days must have been so very long ago that it seems scarcely fair to shame their gravity by telling tales of the frolics of their youth.

The London apprentice must have been an exceedingly lively individual, quick at a jest, quick at a quarrel, quick at a bargain; and yet with all the makings of his master in him, to become as grave and respectable as he as soon as a business of his own has laid the responsibilities of wealth and position upon his shoulders. Of him Chaucer tells little that is good, though as the son of a London vintner he must once have known the apprentice in every changeable mood. The one he describes is a stunted little fellow, with black locks daintily A. 4369. combed (even to such small things does heredity condescend), brown-faced as a berry, gay as a goldfinch, a dancer, a lover, a dice-player, a rioter, a wanton, a drinker who loves the tavern better than the shop, a pilferer from his master's till to whom the interior of Newgate is not unknown. Whenever any

[1] wakes.

spectacle is to be seen in Cheapside there will the apprentice be, and his master looks for his return in vain until all the sight is over. But then there is the old story of Whittington to balance this. Perhaps it was the lack of comprehensiveness in the type which caused the poet to leave the picture unfinished.

.One whose work lay in London streets must of necessity have been quick-witted and quick-footed; for the City, even then, was a crowded maze of bustling life, always someone to sell, always someone to buy. Here is part of a countryman's graphic description of his visit to town:

Lydgate,
*London
Lickpenny*.

"Then to the Cheap I began me drawne,
    Where much people I saw for to stand;
One offered me velvet, silk and lawne,
    Another he taketh me by the hand,
'Here is Paris thread, the finest in the land.'
I never was used to such things indeed,
And wanting money I might not speed.

Then went I forth by London stone,
    Throughout all Canwick Street;
Drapers much cloth me offered anon;
    Then comes me one, cried, 'Hot sheeps' feet';
One cried 'Mackerel'; 'Rushes green,' another gan greet;
One bade me buy a hood to cover my head,
But for want of money I might not be sped.

Then fast I hied me into East-Cheap;
    One cries ribs of beef, and many a pie;
Pewter pots they clattered on a heap;
    There was harp, pipe, and minstrelsy.
'Yea, by cock! nay by cock!' some began cry;
Some sang of Jenkin and Julian for their meed;
But for lack of money I might not speed.

Then into Cornhill anon I yode[1]
    Where was much stolen gear among;
I saw where hung my very own hood,
    That I had lost among the throng;
To buy my own hood I thought it wrong,
I knew it as well as I did my creed,
But for lack of money I could not speed."

Piers Plow.
III. 80.

Pol. Songs,
p. 339.

Many hard things are said of the retailers. They do great harm to the poor, who are compelled to buy in small quantities. By retailing they grow rich and buy property with what the poor should live upon; often is their "chaffare[2] all turned to

[1] went.   [2] trading.

treachery." Had they dealt honestly they could not have
built such great houses. Langland's Avarice, a squalid,
miserly, hungry-looking personage, is the type. He had
first been an apprentice, and had learned to lie and weigh
falsely at Weyhill and Winchester fairs. " Had not the grace
of guile gone among my ware it had been unsold this seven
year, so help me God!" he confesses. Then he had been a
draper, and had learned how to stretch and press his cloth
"till ten yards or twelve told out thirteen." His wife was as
bad as himself. She was a weaver who bought from the
spinners, and weighed what she bought with weights that were
a quarter more than they should have been. She also dealt in
ale, and made a great profit by selling an inferior quality to
poor folk, while retailing her best " cup-meal." He had once
gone further still when lodged with a company of merchants,
for he had risen and rifled their packs while they slept. He
had learned among the Lombards and Jews to clip coin which
he lent at exorbitant interest, and on such craftily devised
terms that the pledge was often broken, to his own great
profit. " I have more manors through arrears than through
'miseretur' and 'commodat,'" he tells us. By such trans-
actions a stigma attached to all who lent money at interest;
and we hear that the traders all practised usury. He had sold
goods to lords and ladies, and afterwards bought them back
again, always with great advantage to himself. With Lombards' letters he had carried gold to Rome, and had delivered
there less than had been committed to him. Such is his own
confession.

When Guile is compelled to flee for fear of the king, he
finds a home among the merchants, who put him in their
shop, dressed as an apprentice, to show their wares and serve
the people. Liar likewise finds refuge among the sellers of
spices. All this fraudulent dealing and greed of money is,
men say, the cause of many other sins; the traders keep not
the Church's holy days, and swear by God and their souls,
against conscience, so that they may sell their goods. They
should change their ways and be more charitable, mend bad
roads and broken bridges, take care of wards, poor people and
prisoners, set the young to school or to some craft, and help
religion.

The keenest and most cunning rogues of all were the

Piers Plow, v. 190, 270, and cf. *Pars. Tale,* 780.

v. 214.

Hand. Synne, 5543.

Piers Plow. VII. 20, and cf. *Conf. Am.* p. 444.

VII. 27.

Anc. Riwle. pedlars, who, in the days when shops were unknown outside the towns, passed through the country districts, lustily crying their wares, glibly wheedling or cheating the peasant out of his scanty store of hardly-earned money, and reaping a tremendous profit. All sorts of portable articles were carried in their packs—knives, pins, gloves, lace, wearing apparel, everything that would tempt the countryman and his wife *Piers Plow.* v. 258. to buy. One trick of theirs, we know, was to palm off cats' skins as real furs upon those who knew no better.

Most of the English of this period are extremely susceptible to the cajoleries of the sharper, the cheat and the impostor. Many are still exceedingly credulous, otherwise they would not accept as true such stories as the wonderful *Travels of Mandeville*. Higden remarks upon their curiosity in this respect. They are always ready to listen to the marvels someone has seen or pretends to have seen ; and they are *Cant. Tales,* B. 4541. A. 2958. A. 2960. very superstitious. Friday is thought to be a very unlucky day ; they believe in ghosts, and hold wakes and wake-plays over the dead ; and for possession by evil spirits they have a definite form of exorcism. Nicholas, in the *Miller's Tale,* is thought to be possessed, and the carpenter seizes him by the shoulders, shakes him violently, and cries :

A. 3477.

> "'What Nicholay! what ho! what look adown!
> Awake! and think on Christës passioun!
> I crouchë[1] thee from elvës and from wightes.'
> Therewith the night-spel said he anon-rightes,
> On fourë halvës of the house about,
> And on the threshold of the door without:
> 'Jesu Christ and Saint Benedight
> Bless this house from every wicked wight,
> For nightës verye[2] the whitë Paternoster,
> Where wentest thou, Saint Peter's soster[3]?'"

And elsewhere we hear of a supposedly bewitched child :

Towneley Plays, Secunda Pastorum, Pollard, p. 38.

> "He was taken with an elf,
> I saw it myself.
> When the clock struck twelve
> Was he forshapen."

Cant. Tales, I. 600. We hear also of the practice of various magic arts, and

[1] cross.

[2] guard(?); an uncertain line: Tyrwhitt reads "From the night-mare may the Paternoster defend thee."

[3] sister.

of charms for wounds or sickness.   Of the latter the Parson
thinks that if they have any effect perhaps God suffers such
things to be that more faith and reverence may be given to
His name.   Chaucer seems to be very sceptical in all these
matters, and in the *Nun's Priest's Tale* gives a humorous
turn to the signification of dreams.   Of astrology he seems to
have profound knowledge, as witness numerous references in
his poetry, and his *Treatise on the Astrolabe* ; but when dealing
with ascendants and nativities he says that these are heathen
rites in which he has no faith.   Everyone believes that all
things are governed by the stars and heavenly bodies, and
that there is some natural connection between their courses
and the actions of men.   As to the alchemists Chaucer speaks
of their tricks with that close acquaintance which can hardly
have come from anything but personal experience.   They
dwell in out-of-the-way and secret corners ; and their dupes
are so bewitched with the hope of gold that if they have but
a sheet to wrap themselves in at night and a " brat[1] " to walk
in by day, they will sell all they possess to spend on the craft.

Astrolabe,
II. 165.
Test. of Love,
II. 9.

Cant. Tales,
G. 1159, 1224,
1310, 657,
881.

   But that the best of the English were becoming more
keenly observant, with more ready recognition of the
hypocrisies, the knaveries, the blemishes, the foibles, as well
as the virtues of humanity, the increasing tendency towards
deliberate satire and more subtle humour goes to prove.   They
have become altogether more intellectual and, in times of prosperity, for the most part joyous, light-hearted and out-spoken.
Yet this Norman-French superstructure has for its base all
the seriousness and earnestness of the Teutonic temperament,
which becomes, in its turn, most prominent in days of adversity.
On the whole less dreamy and more practical than of old they
have in them the making of a very useful type.   Though some
accuse them of changeableness and lack of perseverance, said
to be due to the influence of the moon, we ourselves may
better ascribe these characteristics firstly to the blending of
the different elements which went to the making of the
Englishman, and secondly to the extreme youth and inexperience of the new nation.   Their morality was certainly not
all that could be desired, but that again may be set down to
the same causes.   Although in their literature there is much
which savours of deliberate grossness and sensuality, yet there

[1] cloak.

is also a great deal which seems to be rather the expression of an innocent *naïveté*. There is a strain of coarseness deeply ingrained in the blended character, which delights in stories involving licentiousness, scandal and compromising situations.

Pro. 725.
A. 3171,
E. 2350,
B. 80.

But often a deepening sense of propriety appears, and the poet feels constrained to find an excuse or offer an apology for the presence of rude speeches and immoral episodes in his work. All that strangely compounded mixture of good and evil which forms the character of the age may be seen in Chaucer's pages, himself so typically English in his frankness and breezy humanity. If we listen to all that the contemporary literature says we shall find the Englishman at once a gentle-

Ho. of Fame,
177.

man and a savage, honest-hearted and yet a knave, religious and yet immoral, with " more discords and more jealousies... than there be grains of sand."

At first sight it may seem as though, in some respects, many of the ideals of the simpler age are passing away with more mature growth. In the Church lack of spirituality, among the people lack of morality, among the gentles lack of chivalry, among the traders lack of honesty, are all relied upon as proofs. Everywhere there is that great difference between what should be and what is, which places a premium upon hypocrisy, and makes the mask of False-Seeming,

R. de la Rose,
7333.

" right black within and white without," stand out a smooth and smiling horror. Yet surely we can make too much of this. Is it not rather that the spirit of the age is changing from the mediæval to the modern; that the world, while becoming more rational, more practical, more prosaic, is not yet beyond the stage of trial and experiment? There is the want of balance, of comparison, of proportion, which only perfect education and wide experience can give, and which are therefore so rarely found in any age. Against the brightening background of the change the weaknesses which remain stand out with greater vividness. Never before have we had so many poets to satirise the stains upon the garments of humanity; which does not necessarily prove that the stains are deeper, but certainly suggests that the poets are more moral. And when a complaint is correctly diagnosed, a patient has a far better chance of perfect health and strenuous life than when, all unsuspected, an insidious disease is gnawing at his vitals and steadily sapping both mind and body.

Men no longer embark upon a crusade with zealous rashness; and it is better for the world that it should be so. To cleanse their own befouled raiment in the blood of myriads of massacred fellow mortals, heathen though they be, is surely the mistaken aim of cruel minds. Much better will it be when this zeal is applied to reformation at home first of all; when it is recognised that a Saracen has rather a soul to be saved than a body to be slaughtered; when men believe that *Piers Plow.* Christ's call to conversion embraces both Saracens and Jews. B. XI. 114. One doubts at times whether the chivalry of the Mediæval Age, with all its pomp and glare and but half-concealed brutality, ever did so very much for the progress of the world. And our doubt is intensified when we come upon such records as that in Walsingham's *History*, where Sir John Arundel's men *Walsingham,* once threw sixty women overboard in order to lighten their *Hist. Ang.* ships during a storm. One wonders how much of all the pro- I. 423, Rolls. fessed chivalry was real. But now, with the decay of feudalism, its external adornments are slipping away to lay bare the truer, deeper, more universal chivalry which may fire the breast of merchant and tradesman, of peasant and ploughman, as well as that of the highest noble. When the *débris* of the older system is cleared away the new era will begin; kindness and conscience *Piers Plow.* will arise together, and oppression will cease. The warrior III. 297. will find no place in the golden age which is to be, and will have to beat his steel into sickle or scythe, ploughshare or coulter, to toil for his bread, or else perish because of his sloth.

Early in the century an attempt was made to stop tournaments and joustings, which were felt to be but brutalising spectacles of passion and bloodshed; but the decrees were frequently disregarded. Robert Mannyng denounces tourna- *Hand. Synne,* ments as giving occasion for all the deadly sins, pride, envy, 4573, 4605, ire, sloth, covetousness, gluttony and lechery: knights take 4589, 4598. part in them for women's sake, and expend more upon such folly than ever they spend on any deed of mercy; and yet some of them depart from their inns without paying their bills. In the reign of Edward III. tournaments were revived, no doubt in consequence of the martial enthusiasm arising from the French wars, but they soon deteriorated into mere pomp and show of gaudy dresses and trappings, into mere *Cf. The Flower* social functions. There is just this difference between the *and the Leaf,* age painted by the old romances and that of Chaucer. 205 et seq.

Love of dress and personal adornment, such as never was before, is characteristic of the age. Velvets, furs, silks, satins, embroidery and jewels abound, so that Parliament devises sumptuary laws to regulate extravagance. All classes delight in gorgeous colours—a measure of their taste. The fashionable hose and doublets are usually striped or particoloured, white and red, red and black, black and white, white and blue. Garments of fantastic cut, high and wide collars, long pointed shoes with tips linked by chains to the knee, are the mode. Men and women wear either short and tight-fitting attire, revealing the shape of the figure and often so tight that bending is impossible, or else fly to the other extreme of superfluity of clothing, with fanciful trimmings and costly furring, which trails behind them in the mire. And the dress oft proclaims the proud and licentious character of the wearer. Robert Mannyng animadverts upon such artificial and florid extravagance as an outcome of the sin of pride. Robes are often of scarlet of richest texture, decked with "ribbons of red gold," with precious stones, and edged with the finest fur. Head-dresses are made to correspond; and fingers are loaded with elegant rings of gold wire, in which are set rubies, diamonds, sapphires, orientals and beryls. Even the lower middle-class women, when their work is done, delight in dainty array of silk, with purses hanging at their girdles, brooches as broad as the boss of a buckler, and high-laced shoes. The fair wife of one well-to-do carpenter is delicate and small of body, wears a cincture barred with silk, and an apron white as morning milk and thickly gored. Her white smock is embroidered before and behind, and has a collar of coal-black silk. Her cap, too, is white, and its tapes are black to match her collar. Her fillet of silk is broad and set very high. She carefully trims her eyebrows, which are curved and black as a sloe. On holidays her face shines with soap and polishing: "so was it washen when she left her work." On Sundays the Wife of Bath wears fine kerchiefs which Chaucer dare swear must have weighed ten pounds. Her hose, boldly displayed, are of fine scarlet, her shoes moist and new, her hat is as broad as a buckler. Such a woman, endowed with more money than taste, must have been a wonderful sight to behold. And some women, we are told, beneath all their finery, do not possess a smock. It is

Cant. Tales, I. 425.

420.

430.

Hand. Synne, 3449. *Piers Plow.* II. 7.

v. 31.

Cant. Tales, A. 3235.

3309. Pro. 456.

Pol. Songs, p. 153.

interesting to learn that the good Knight of the Tour Landry advises his daughters that for young ladies of their station five robes are sufficient, one long, two short, and two for out of doors. *Bk of the Kn. of the Tour Landry*, ch. L.

The toilet has now become quite an elaborate business. Though to the poor man a bath is almost unknown, the rich man is washed with rose-water, and has his bath scented with herbs. Men curl and adorn their beards and hair, and keep small knives to trim and pare their nails. The women, we see, still practise the arts mentioned in the preceding chapter. The hair of a parish clerk is curled and shines like gold; it spreads out like a great fan; and its dainty parting is quite straight and even. His deportment is meant to correspond. He goes delicately in red hose, with " Paul's window " carved upon his shoes, with points set full fair and thick, and he is clad " full small and properly " in a kirtle of light blue cloth. He can trip and dance in twenty different ways, "after the school of Oxford then." In the higher ranks the same delicacy appears. Chaucer's Squire has locks curled as though they had been laid in a press, and his gown, embroidered with flowers in white and red, is short, with long, wide sleeves. The *Romance of the Rose* gives some interesting advice to a young lover on matters of dress, manners and toilet. He should dress as well as his income will allow, for fine clothing improves a man so much; and his clothes should be fashionably made by the best tailor, with everything to correspond. His boots and shoes should be new and fair, and fit so tightly that the ignorant marvel how they go on and off again. He should wear straight gloves, carry an alms-bag of silk, and be liberal in giving if he is rich. If he has little he should spend the less upon himself. He should always be merry, but not waste his goods; a hat of fresh flowers costs but little. His hands should be washed, and his teeth white; no dirt must be seen upon him; the black must be removed from his nails; and his hair should be well combed. He must not make up his face, for love hates that which is unnatural. *Cant. Tales,* I. 263.

Froiss. *Chron.* p. 333.

Cant. Tales, A. 3318.

Pro. 81.

R. de la Rose, 2254.

Even the clergy must be in the height of fashion; and doctors, lawyers and merchants have, as a rule, fine clothes, though the busy Man of Law, who rides in homely fashion in a parti-coloured habit, girt with a cincture of silk, seems a *Cant. Tales,* Pro. 193, 321.

notable exception. In every rank a close correspondence between dress, manners and character may be seen, all due to the influence of France. The satirist lashes all classes unmercifully, especially the effeminate dandies who are lions in the hall, hares in the field. They look more like gleemen than gentlemen: "Scarcely may men know a glee-man from a knight." Among them are mere boys who think they prove their claims to man's estate by cursing and swearing like their seniors. Even the very grooms and serving men ape their masters in their dress and dissolute lives.

Pol. Songs, pp. 334—336.

Similarly, so scathing are some of the denunciations of the female sex that we are compelled to seek their origin in the strictest monkish austerity of mediævalism. When women become famous in literature the scales will be held more evenly. Let us hear the worst about them first of all. Temper and wiliness are their great failings; and for the former the satirist links together "a wasp, a weasel, and a woman"; for the latter, "a fox, a friar, and a woman." When they quarrel hot and angry words are spoken. "Thou liest," and "Thou liest" in return, leap upon their lips, and they smack each other's cheeks. "Had they had knives," says Langland gravely, "they would have killed each other." The Green Knight asks how a man could escape being deceived by a woman; and the Wife of Bath herself answers: because no man can swear and lie half so boldly as a woman; deceiving, weeping and spinning are theirs by nature. "Men, take heed," says Lydgate, "all is not gold that shineth. They can shave nearer than razors or shears; their gall is hid under a coat of sugar, and as they list the tear is in the eye. Beware therefore; the blind eat many a fly." They are said to be fickle, unreliable, untrustworthy, a mixture of gold and brass, fair to see, but so bad an alloy that they are far more apt to break than to bend. They are talkative and shrewish, ever clapping as a mill, and cannot possibly keep a secret, however important or however frivolous it may be. A witty husband once for a jest told his wife as a great secret that he had laid two eggs. Very soon she is pouring out the wonderful tale to a bosom friend: "Ah! my dearest friend, I will tell you something, but it is to be a terrible secret, and it is not to go beyond us two." And of course the terrible secret is all over the town in the shortest possible space of time.

Cant. Tales, D. 688.

Songs and Carols, Wright. Piers Plow. v. 163.

Gaw. and Gr. Kn.

Cant. Tales, D. 227, 401.

Lydgate, Balade warning men to beware of deceitful women, 22, and cf. Court of Love, 540.

Cant. Tales, E. 1167, 1200, and cf. Chester Plays, Noah's Flood, 105.

Bk of the Kn. of the Tour Landry, ch. LXXIV.

Chaucer, more often than not, speaks very hardly of wives, perhaps, as some have it, being mindful of his own experience, perhaps because the humour of the day requires it of him.   They are mercenary because their extravagance makes *Cant. Tales,* a rich and prosperous husband a necessity.   The simple man ^A. 2681,^ ^B. 1201, and^ must always pay to array them richly for his own reputation's ^cf. *Rom. de la*^ sake, and they have a very delightful time at his expense. ^*Rose,* 9192.^ If he cannot or will not pay, well then someone else must, or lend them money ; and that is perilous.   So declares a merchant's wife.   Another merchant's wife, who causes him "weeping and wailing, care and other sorrow," is said to ^E. 1213.^ overmatch the fiend himself with her "cursedness."   When their husbands die, some widows shriek and swoon and weep ^A. 2821.^ over the corpse, perhaps even fall into a grievous malady and die too.   But Chaucer is cynical about the matter.   It is ^D. 44.^ more their habit, he thinks, to set off in immediate pursuit of another.   "Blessed be God that I have wedded five; welcome the sixth when that ever he shall," proclaims aloud and unabashed the shameless Wife of Bath, who wants to know ^33.^ why men should speak ill of bigamy—or of octogamy for the matter of that !   She tells us herself that when her fourth husband was dead she covered her face with her kerchief, and ^587.^ wept and made pretence of great mourning, " as wives must for it is usage."   But because she had her fifth already in view, she did not weep for long.   Even as the body was borne to the grave she had her eyes upon the fine figure of one of the mourners, a lad of twenty—and she was nearly forty !   Chaucer makes this woman speak candidly of herself, so that he may give us a composite portrait of the vicious woman of her class.   She is a rough, coarse, foul-mouthed gossip, fat and sensual, with bold red face which once was handsome.   She was first married at twelve years old, and every man she married she made miserable, except the one ^384.^ who thrashed her.

> "The bacon was not fetched for them, I trow,   ^217.^
> That some men have in Essex at Dunmow."

Whoever sat at their table she would never spare her biting, ^420.^ wrangling words.   We quite believe her when she says of one ^489.^ of them that she was his Purgatory on earth.   Being headstrong and frivolous she follows all the amusements of her ^455.^

class, dancing to the harp, singing as any nightingale when once she has had a draught of sweet wine. She has been on pilgrimages to all the well-frequented shrines; wakes, processions, preachings, plays, and marriages, complete the list. Woe to the woman who tries to take precedence of her, for her manners are as loud as her dress, and her language as loose as her morals.

556.
Pro. 463.

But about the end of this period a reaction against the constant vilifying of the sex sets in. An early sign of it may be seen in the *Legend of Good Women*; and shortly afterwards Christine de Pisan and Gerson, chancellor of the University of Paris, set themselves to combat the tendency upheld by the influence of Jean de Meung and the latter part of the *Romance of the Rose*. Soon we shall read in English literature that the making of the *Romance of the Rose* was a lewd occupation, that women are not so inconstant as clever clerks pretend, but that they are as women ought to be, staid, constant and pitiful. In this mood Chaucer writes that there are ever a thousand good against one bad, and that there is nothing better than a good woman; and again, with all his jesting humour laid aside, that in truth, though clerks praise women but little, still no man can bear himself so modestly or be half so true. The strongest argument in favour of women is the growing sense of decency and modesty which appears in the literature. In the presence of good women Chaucer must needs confess his rudeness, and apologise for the recital of coarse tales such as befit his coarsest characters. In the presence of the Prioress even the roughest men make some attempt to moderate their language; and all treat her with the deference which her womanly deportment, no less than her position, demands. The old Teutonic reverence for womanhood is certainly beginning to revive. The feeling is increasing that woman is not man's toy, and that triumphs over her are not things to boast about. Sometimes the poet expresses his contempt for the unmanly and immoral creatures with whom the name of woman hangs lightly on the tongue; and satirical contemptuousness is in his tone when he speaks of those who would boast themselves of a fictitious evil reputation in this respect. It is the vile, reprobate man, not the weak woman, who should bear the shame, for his is the fault.

Hoccleve,
*Letter of
Cupid*, 281.

Cant. Tales,
A. 3154,
B. 2295.

E. 934.

2350.
A. 729, 3170.

Ho. of Fame,
III. 650.
*Troilus and
Cressida*,
III. 317.
*Leg. of Gd
Wom.* 1260.

Indeed in the work of Chaucer and his school we often catch a reflection of true and noble womanhood and innocent maidenhood in all its freshness and natural beauty, to which the examples of feminine imperfections are but as foils to enhance further the charm of the type. One heroine is endowed with sweetness, goodness, simplicity, benignity, constancy, truth, surpassing beauty, and womanly mirth and friendliness. The sight of her is a delight to the eyes of man, for in her face there is nothing but what is a sign of good; and her simple word is as true as any bond. Another is modest and retiring, with angel visage, gracious to look upon, root of gentleness and mirror of delight. And another is a true, pitying woman, a comforter of those in trouble, virtuous, staid, demure, of few words, and with nothing mannish in her disposition. *Dethe of Bl.* 480, 482, 916, 933.

Court of Love, 827. Lydgate, *Flower of Courtesy,* 148.

Cressida, before her fall, is sober, simple and wise, goodly of speech, charitable, stately, and tender of heart; "Paradise stood formëd in her eyes." But she is nervous, highly-strung, sensitive, of the plastic, clinging type which refuses to be brought face to face with the stern realities of life and duty. In the flesh she is the outcome of the atmosphere of the Provencal Courts of Love, a woman in love with love; and yet, with all her frailty, how far superior she is to the exotic and sensual southern type from which her creation sprang! The difference is just that between the English ideals of womanhood and those of Italy and Provence. She is told that Troilus loves her; and there is something pleasing and flattering in the proposal which forbids a "No," and something, too, of doubt which stays a "Yes." Furtively she tries to shelve the question for the moment. She will be a sister to him; and writes to tell him so. Later, to another lover, she will profess that love and she are far asunder, and tears will be very near the surface—yet perhaps he may hope; perhaps; at least he may come again to-morrow if he cares; but she will not promise him her love, nor will she say him nay. And after all it is eve before this insistent lover departs, and with him takes her glove. *Tr. and Cress.* v. 817, IV. 1667.

II. 302, 598.

1206.

v. 976.

There is a picture of another pair of lovers in the *Confessio Amantis.* The youth is ever at the side of the maid, proffering service in chamber and hall, watching his opportunity to accompany her to mass and home again. Whatever she bids him do, he does; wherever she bids him go, he goes. When *Conf. Am.* p. 189.

she sits he kneels beside her. When she takes up her weaving or embroidery he sits watching her fingers long and small, now moody, now telling his amorous tale, now singing, now heaving an eloquent sigh. He cannot tear himself away. Even if she has other things to do, and cannot stay to entertain him, he makes excuses to spin out the weary time, now playing with her little hound, now with her birds. If she rides he lifts her into the saddle, and takes her palfrey's bridle; if she drives he rides beside her chariot. Rather an insipid and tiresome lover one would suppose! In the *Romance of the Rose* there is the useful piece of advice that the lover should always strive to gain the favour of the lady's maid by making her handsome presents.

R. de la Rose,
2695.

The bride obtains her trousseau in due season, perhaps from London; and then comes the wedding, preceded by the Holy Sacrament. The priest signs the couple with the sign of the Cross, and they are wedded with full solemnity. After the ceremony follows the feast, with the happy pair seated side by side upon the dais in the hall; and after the feast the company adjourns to the bridal chamber for the quaint old rite of the blessing of the bed by the priest. For three or four days afterwards the bride must keep to her own apartments, and must not eat in hall. Such was the custom in aristocratic circles.

Cant. Tales,
E. 1709.

1818, and cf.
Sir Bevis,
Ellis, p. 268.

1889.

Chaucer, like everybody else, has two opinions concerning marriage; there is all the difference in the world between those founded upon love and those of convenience. One man avers that a wife is wasteful, a servant is more diligent and faithful. "Nay," replies his comrade, "a wife is God's gift verily, man's help and comfort, his Paradise terrestrial.... A wife! Ah! how could any man suffer adversity if he has a wife? Tongue cannot tell, nor heart think, of the bliss between them two. If he be poor, she shares his toil, keeps his goods, and never wastes a bit." She never once says "Nay" when he says "Yea," and is so estimable that every man worth his salt ought, all his life, to go down upon his bare knees, and thank his God for sending him a wife. Robert Mannyng had already anticipated this opinion, saying that a good woman, whose love is steadfast and true, is man's bliss, that there is no solace under heaven which can bring so much happiness as the true love of a good woman.

1310.

1337.

1351.

Hand. Synne,
1907.

On the whole the parental instinct was strong, and the beauty of the innocence of childhood and the charm of motherhood fully recognised.

> "A pretty child is he
> As sitteth on a woman's knee,
> A dillydown perdee,
> To make a man laugh."

Towneley Plays, Pollard, p. 38.

Maternal love forms an essential part of the characters of Griselda and Constance. That of the former is akin to the fatherly love of Abraham for Isaac, capable of regarding the sacrifice of the loved one as the highest test of faith, an ennobling renunciation. Her story was meant to strike a chord of sympathy in every English mother's heart. Desire for the same effect may be seen in the story of the latter, banished from Northumbria, and piteously striving to lull the wailing of the babe in her arms. There is another picture of a mother, a poor widow, watching all night for her little son who has not returned home from school, having been kidnapped by the Jews. At daylight she goes seeking him everywhere, her face pale with anxiety, "with mother's pity in her breast enclosed," and half out of her mind, in every place where she thinks there is a possibility of finding him. Pity for childish suffering, and the awful agony of a parent who must see his children die before his eyes while he is unable to alleviate their misery, is the theme of the story of Hugilino.

Cant. Tales, E. 550.

B. 834.

B. 1783.

> "Alas Fortune! it was great cruelty
> Such birdës for to put in such a cage!"

3603.

In the *Pearl* there is a father who lavishes all his love and care upon his little motherless daughter, but death takes her, too, from him. In the excess of his sorrow he lies upon the little grave, sleeps and dreams. He is in a beautiful garden full of richly tinted and sweet smelling flowers, and he holds in his hand a precious and peerless pearl, which, to his great grief, slips from his grasp, and rolls, and is lost in the grass. Then there is the sound of running water, a brook rippling over shining pebbles ; and the bereaved father looks up and sees across the stream a little white-garbed maid, the pearl that he has mourned and wept for. She speaks to him : " Thou never hadst a pearl, for that thou didst lose was but a rose that flowered and failed as nature bade it, but now, through

The Pearl, Gollancz, st. 65.

st. 25.

Christ, thy rose is proved a precious pearl for ever." And the
father's eyes are blessed, and his heart consoled, with the sight
of his loved and lost one, his peerless lamb, in unspotted
innocence among those who dwell with the Lamb of God in
the New Jerusalem.

st. 101.

"To please the Prince, to make peace with Him,
Is easy, I trow, for the good Christian;
Yea, I found Him, both day and night,
A God, a Lord, a Friend full firm.
O'er that mound befell me this hap,
Prone there for pity of my pearl;
To God committed I then that gem,
In Christ's dear blessing and eke mine own.
    Christ that in form of bread and wine,
    The priest doth show to us each day;
    He grant us to be His servants leal,
    And precious pearls for His pleasance."

Pollard, *Mir. Plays*, pp. 58, 61.
Rolls of Parl. A.D. 1395.
Piers Plow. v. 32.

Boys and girls must have been very much the same at
heart then as now, just as lovable, just as full of roguery and
impish tricks, just as troublesome to manage in their wilder
moments, just as impudent. Langland advises parents not to
spare the rod lest they spoil the child, and not to neglect
proper supervision and training on the plea that they themselves can spare no thought from their labours or pursuit of
money. If little Bet will not work, her mother must cut a bough

Hand. Synne, 4849.

or two. Robert Mannyng says that children must be chastised
but no bones broken. Corporal punishment entered largely
into the discipline of the schools: "With the more sorrow

Test. of Love, II. 11.

that a thing is got, the more he hath joy to keep the same
afterwards; as it fareth by children in school, that for learning
are beaten, when they forget their lesson. Commonly after a
good disciplining with a stick they keep right well the teaching
of their school."

In this age Parliament strove to grapple with the great
problem of public morality. The country swarmed with loose
women, and nothing could put them down; as long as there
were vicious individuals for them to live upon, legislation was

Walsingham, *Hist. Ang.* I. 320, 343.

in vain. And in spite of Parliamentary protests and reforming
measures there was the king's connection with Alice Perrers
as an open example and scandal, which made the problem all
the more difficult. Indeed, a feeling almost of sympathy with
them arose in consequence of the flagrant vices in high quarters.

Chaucer but voices a popular sentiment when he declares that, truly, there is no difference between the lady of high degree and the poor girl, if both go astray, except that the one, because she is of gentle birth, is called " his lady-love," and the other, because she is a poor woman, " his wench " or " his leman." God knows that the sin of the one is the same as that of the other.

Cant. Tales,
H. 212.

The Englishman was still noted for his fondness for the pleasures of the table, for excess in both food and drink, which seem to have been plentiful except in the plague years. Chaucer's Franklin is the typical country gentleman of his day ; and his sanguine complexion shows that he is no stranger to good living. He is a very Epicurean, holding that self-indulgence is perfect felicity. " It snowed in his house with meat and drink." He loves well his morning sop in wine. His bread and ale are always of the best quality ; and there are always baked meats, all manner of dainties, fish and game according to the season. He keeps open house to all and sundry, his "table dormant" standing always ready in his hall.

Pro. 234.

345.

Hospitality towards both rich and poor was the almost universal custom, so that it came to be regarded as a matter of necessity or compulsion rather than a virtue. In the houses of the well-to-do the casual caller would be asked to partake of spice and wine ; and in great mansions it was rare that the weary traveller failed to obtain refreshment according to his degree, if noble or gentle with the lord upon the dais, if of lower rank with his fellows in the body of the hall, which was lighted with torches, and warmed by a fire in winter. There was meat and drink at will, so much so that the Parson complains of the scandalous profusion and ornamentation of dishes, "painted and castled with paper," and of the great display of valuable plate. Only in Lent, "crabbed Lent," was there restraint, when fish and the simpler foods alone were eaten. After the meal all retired early, for lights were supposed to be out by curfew-time ; but sometimes there was a "rear-supper" spread in the lord's own room if he were at all luxurious. An increasing desire for privacy often led the rich man to dine thus in his own private parlour, made comfortable with a chimney-corner by the fire, adorned with tapestries upon the walls, and with

Tr. and Cress.
v. 852,
Pollard, Mir.
Plays, p. 51,
etc.

Cant. Tales,
I. 445.

Gaw. and Gr.
Kn. 502.
Cant. Tales,
A. 3645.

Conf. Am.
p. 324.
Piers Plow.
x. 96.

Hand. Synne,
7259.

glazed windows. This custom gave great offence to the common people; and churchmen looked upon it as an innovation leading to gluttony and other sin.

The guests of high rank might have private bedrooms, or might share the room of the host; the others, when the tables had been cleared away, stretched themselves on beds laid upon the rushes or straw with which the floor of the hall was covered, and in which lay the accumulated refuse of many a past day. Those who slept in the private rooms were much more comfortable, with beds, carpets and many luxuries. Upon the beds, even of the middle classes, were sheets and coverlets of Chalons; and the gentles had feather-beds, sometimes striped with gold, and covered in fine satin, with pillows and pillow-cases of the linen of Rennes. Night-dresses had not yet come into fashion, though night-caps were worn. Rarely even yet, except among the highest, was there absolute privacy in the sleeping apartments; and among the middle and poorer classes it was never looked for. In the *Reeve's Tale,* the two Cambridge students who pass the night at Trumpington Mill sleep in the same bedroom as the family, the man, his wife and daughter, and a little child in its cradle; there was no other accommodation. Such a state of affairs, we can quite understand, was far from being conducive to strict morality.

Cant. Tales,
A. 4140.
Dethe of Bl.
251, 293.
Conf. Am.
pp. 73, 222.
Tr. and Cress.
II. 953—954,
III. 229.
Cant. Tales,
A. 4139.

Travellers such as merchants and packmen often spent the night at wayside inns where several beds were placed in the same room. Fleas were a great pest, and other vermin common. Complaints were often made of the accommodation provided, the food, and the exorbitant charges. Chaucer's Cook is taunted with the stale condition of the fare he provides, but the taunt is apparently undeserved, for his capabilities receive adequate recognition in the *Prologue.* And the Parson says that the folk of low degree who keep hostelries uphold the thieving of their hostlers in many kinds of fraud. But the inn-keeper was often a man of substance, quick-witted, authoritative and prosperous. His wife may often have been all that could be desired, but Harry Bailey's wife, a virago, sharp-tongued and shrewish, did not stand alone. Even her husband was afraid of her, and not without reason. When he beat his serving-men she would bring him the great clubbed staves, and cry, "Slay the dogs, every one; break 'em, back and every bone!"

H. 17.

A. 4347.

Pro. 379.

I. 440.

B. 3110, 3087.

Then there were by the wayside the common taverns where the traveller might obtain refreshment, wine, ale and cake. Over their doors projected the "ale-stake" or "leaf-   C. 321. sel," a long staff tipped with a bundle of branches or leaves,   I. 410. the sign of the trade. Many of these places had already degenerated into mere drinking dens and places of evil resort. Langland has a very realistic description of what went on in them. Glutton, the drunkard, sets off one Friday towards   *Piers Plow.* the church, intending to be shriven and to hear mass; but   V. 303. Bet the brewster and tavern-keeper accosts him; and farewell to all his good resolutions! "I have good ale, gossip," says she, "wilt thou try it? Hast aught in thy purse?" He enters; and we are introduced to the motley company assembled there. Though it is but early morning there are present Ciss, the female cobbler, Wat the warrener and his wife,   314. Tim the tinker and two of his 'prentices, Hike the hackney-man, Hugh the needle-maker, Clarice of Cock's lane and the clerk of the church, Daw the ditcher, Sir Piers of Pridie and Peronelle of Flanders, a rebeck player, a rat-catcher, a scavenger of Cheapside, a rope-maker, a man-at-arms, Rose the dish-maker, and several others. All welcome Glutton with glad cheer, and treat him to the good ale. One puts his own cloak up for auction, another his hood; and so the day is passed with laughing, quarrelling and singing until evensong. Then Glutton has drunk a gallon and a gill. When he tries to leave for home he can neither walk nor stand without his staff, and his gait is staggering. He reaches the door, but his eyes are dim; he stumbles on the threshold, and falls to the earth. One takes him by the waist to raise him up, but only succeeds in getting him upon his knees. To his wife and daughter his conduct brings all the woe of   362. this world. They come to fetch him home, and carry him to bed, where he sleeps off his debauch the Saturday and Sunday through. When at last he wakes, his first words are "Where is the bowl?"; but instead of it he has to hear sharp words from his wife. He becomes ashamed of himself, and confesses his faults. He has sworn "By God's soul!" and "So help me God!" and "Halidom!" nine hundred times where no need was. He has forgotten himself at supper, and has spent most of his time in taverns for love of tales and the drink. It is evidently quite time for him to mend his ways.

We hear a great deal of this drinking in taverns when the day's work was done, and of the brawling, fighting, swearing and gambling which went on there.   Neckam tells us that the fascination of the dice led many to dissipation and debauchery, with oaths, imprecations, accusations, wrangling and fighting; and some who lost played on until they had gambled away their estates and even their clothes.   Some there were who cheated with loaded dice.   The Parson, too, tells us that gambling, with backgammon and raffles, led to deceit, false oaths, chidings, ravenings, blaspheming and denying of God, hate of neighbours, waste of goods, misspending of time, and sometimes manslaughter.   Two gamblers quarrel and swear over the dice, and, with many a profane oath, one threatens to plunge his dagger into the other's heart if he play falsely.   So universal is the habit of swearing that oaths have become almost meaningless, mere expletives, and the use of strong language almost second nature.

As in Chaucer's pages we have the life of the people portrayed, so in Langland's we have the ripening conscience. It is no mere chance or passing whim which makes Chaucer lead his pilgrims forth upon a holiday, mainly upon pleasure bent, and it is not without deep meditation that Langland leads out his in quest of Truth.   Here we have the two great divisions of men and character; the one active, practical, worldly, the other contemplative, introspective, deeply religious.   In Chaucer we see the world as a man of the world actually saw it; and what he saw did not greatly trouble him; better to laugh and jest and mock than to bewail.   In Langland we see it as it appeared to the earnest reformer, who brooded over the wrongs laid bare till he could restrain himself no longer, and was compelled to denounce with righteous indignation those at whose doors the evil lay. And we must not forget that there were many such as he. We see Langland's field full of folk, where Meed, False and Wrong are in the ascendant.   Some are ploughing, setting or sowing, toiling full hard and playing full seldom, while others reap the fruits of their labour only to waste them in luxury and excess.   Among these latter are many of dubious sanctity, steeped in selfishness and lies, and others of open immorality and greed, seducers and oppressors of their kind.   It is the England of the fourteenth century; and so it will continue

Neckam,
De Nat. Rer.
II. 183.

Cant. Tales,
I. 790.

C. 651.

D. 1556, 1628.
I. 590,
Hand. Synne,
669, 769.

Piers Plow.
Pro. 20.

till Conscience speaks, and the pilgrimage in search of Truth begins. Then we shall be in the England of the early Reformation. But the voice of Conscience will not gain a hearing till the nation is brought to its knees, humbled by adversity. In the vein of the Hebrew prophets of old, the poet and seer cries aloud. The wind and storm come, and trees, even great oaks, are levelled with the ground. It is a sign that deadly sin shall destroy them all at Doomsday. Pestilence and famine follow the storm. It is a visitation for their pride. On four occasions the Black Death appears in its greatest virulence—in 1349, 1361, 1369, 1375—and sweeps off half the population, which had been about five millions. Many cities, towns and hamlets are almost entirely depopulated; and there is more to follow.

The rank badness of the sanitary arrangements, and the ignorance of the doctors, may be better imagined from the consequences than described. The condition of the larger towns was deplorable, with their narrow streets and alleys heaped with filth and refuse of every description, with domestic animals running loose in the streets, with high overhanging stories of shops and houses keeping out both fresh air and sun, and rendering the imprisoned atmosphere fetid and corrupt. Worse still, within the houses were the accumulations of straw and rushes which harboured the germs of years, while the situation and condition of the offices was utterly unsatisfactory. No wonder that vermin of all descriptions increased and throve to the still greater increase of infection. After the plagues more notice will be taken of such matters.

The doctors were little fitted to cope with disease, for their methods were antiquated and akin to quackery. Chaucer draws the type whose studies embraced all the medicinal treatises of the ancients together with those of his own time; and the latter were scarcely an improvement upon the former. Astrology was his forte, as many of his patients must have found to their cost. But their bad reputation was spreading widely. Langland says openly that many leeches are murderers, "God amend 'em!", for with their medicines they make men die before their time. The *Political Songs* had already termed them "these false physicians who help men to die." Dieting and nature are the only

Cant. Tales, Pro. 415.

Piers Plow. VI. 274. *Pol. Songs,* p. 333.

Piers Plow.
VI. 270.
trustworthy remedies according to both Langland and Chaucer.

Cant. Tales,
A. 2759.

"And certainly, where nature will not work,
    Farewell, physic! Go bear the man to kirk."

In the times of the epidemics these doctors made great profits; and what they made they usually kept for themselves, being "but easy of dispense." They clothed their dignity in fine robes, scarlet and purple lined with taffeta and sendal, with furred hoods, cloaks of Calabrian fur, and ornaments of gold. There was among them a trait which Chaucer is careful to point out—that of scepticism, or at least indifference in matters of religion; "his study was but little on the Bible," may also be, perhaps, a reflection upon their lack of Christian charity and humility in the midst of the general distress.

Rolls of Parl.
II. pp. 227—
340 *passim*
etc.
Without the towns the distress was just the same. Men became despondent, and let their property go to ruin. The cattle and sheep roamed unchecked over the fields and, because there was no one to tend them, trampled down the crops; many died in the hedges and ditches. Labour could not be obtained for love or money; and in places the crops were left rotting in the fields, while the stricken people were dying of disease and hunger. So the value of the labourer rose to a premium, because the number was small and the need great. Still, higher wages were always to be obtained in the towns; and the life and freedom of the great trading centres tempted the workers. Thus the peasant began to turn artisan; and agriculture and the landowner suffered. The influx to the towns from the country thus commenced; and to legislate to prevent the change by artificial restrictions proved futile, and only added to the number of sturdy rogues and vagabonds upon the countryside.

Piers Plow.
VI. 25.
But there was a feeling abroad that the peasant had his rights as well as his duties, and that he had not been at all well treated. If he must toil and sweat and sow, he must be protected from wasters and wicked men. Wrong was no less wrong when committed by the rich and powerful than when committed by the poor. It was felt that there was

Cant. Tales,
H. 223.
no difference, except in degree, between the wayside robber and petty thief and the tyrant who also robbed and slew,

but on a larger scale. After all thralls are God's people, *Conf. Am.*
and humble folk Christ's friends, as the Parson says; while *p. 170.*
Langland finds his ideal of the truly Christian character in *Cant. Tales,* *I. 760.*
his Ploughman, the type of the honest working-man, upon
whom the well-being of the state depends.

We are introduced to him in the Prologue to the *Canterbury Tales*, where we find him a hard worker, patient, peace-loving, God-fearing, charitable, self-sacrificing, ready at all times, for Christ's sake, to do a good turn to a neighbour in distress. If the English race should never produce a truer working-man than he, its existence will not have been in vain. We are here beginning to touch upon the high-water mark of the early development of the national character. Place this man in true perspective with regard to his whole environment, and I think this view of him will be widely accepted.

> "A truë toiler and a good was he,   *Pro. 531.*
> Living in peace and perfect charity.
> God loved he best, with all his wholë heart,
> At allë timës, though him gamed or smart,
> And then his neighëbour right as himselve.
> He wouldë thrash, and thereto dig and delve,
> For Christës sake, for every poorë wight,
> Withouten hire, if it lay in his might."

We meet him again in the *Plowman's Tale*. He is at *Plow. Tale,* *Pro.*
work in the fields, ploughing with ox and cow, which are
worn to skin and bone. He himself is in no better condition, being thoroughly worn out and sweating with toil. So thin are both his cheeks· that you can almost see through them and mark the place of every molar. His face is tanned with the sun, and the skin is peeling from his nose. His dress marks his poverty; and he has a wife and children to support. Yet, in spite of all, he is sturdily independent. Though he serves God as best he can, he cannot "religiously lout," *23.* and therefore comes great loss to him. In addition to the hard times there is another reason for his poverty, as he *33.* tells us feelingly. Clerks tell him that he should be glad to sweat and toil for their livelihood, though they give him nothing in return to satisfy his hunger. They say that they can, by law, curse and damn him to the brink of hell; and so they distress him with their "candles quaint and bellës

clink." They make him and his fellows thralls at their
pleasure; and say that he cannot otherwise be saved. They
take the corn and leave him the dust; and if any protests
thereat they tell him that he raves.

God Speed the Plough.

One who walked through the fields and saw the ploughman
at his task prayed aloud that God might speed the plough.
"Yes," said the ploughman bitterly, "there is need to pray
that prayer, for we work hard all the year to maintain the
whole world. The parson comes to us for his tithe of the
sheaves. The king's purveyors come for wheat and oats,
beef and mutton, butter and poultry, and we have to deliver
them at court, and be paid for our trouble with blows. We
have to pay the 'fifteenth' and the 'greenwax[1]' besides the
rent of our land. All men come to us; prisoners, clerks,
friars, preachers, summoners, priests, scholars of Oxford, tip-
staves, minstrels, beggars and women; all want something.
And our man of law must not be forgotten, but must have
money every quarter. Yes, indeed! I pray to God, speed
well the plough!"

P. Plow. Crede, 421.

Yet again we meet him in *Pierce the Ploughman's Creed.*
The times are very hard now, and his fortunes at their lowest
ebb. He is still at work in the fields, good, simple-hearted
fellow, hanging over his plough. His coat is a tattered rag
of coarse material. His hood is full of holes through which
his unkempt hair makes its way. His knobbed shoes are
clouted thick with patches, and yet as he walks his toes peep
out. His hose, daubed with the mire of the furrow in which
he walks ankle-deep, hang down over his gaiters. Upon his
hands are two scanty mittens, made of rags, and covered
with mire, with the fingers worn away with toil. Four feeble
heifers draw his plough; one can count their every rib, in
such miserable condition are they. His wife labours with
him, urging with long goad his pitiable team. She wears
a coat or skirt cut very high, so scanty in fact that she has
to wrap herself in a winnowing sheet to keep out the bitter
cold; for there is ice upon the ground, and where her bare
feet tread she leaves tracks of blood behind her. At one
end of the field there is a little bowl, usually kept for collect-

440.

ing scraps, and in it is a babe, wrapped in rags. Two others,
twins, about two years of age, are beside it: "And they all

[1] hundred rate.

sang one song that was pitiful to hear; they all cried one cry, a careful note." The husband and father sighs sore as he tries to still their wailing. It is a touching picture of deplorable poverty in mediæval England, that heart-breaking poverty which followed the plague years and the wars, which neither toil nor foresight could overcome. Is it possible that the Ploughman can so continue, day after day, month after month, and keep unstrained his faith in God and charity to man? Such is the test by which we try him. And yet, as this book, too, tells us, he is an honest and good Christian, ready to share even the little he has with others still more unfortunate than himself.

From the early years of the century the cry of the poor has risen up to heaven. The people bear the king's taxes very hardly. What with the "fifteenth" and the "wool-tax" *Pol. Songs,* they are compelled to sell their cattle, their vessels, and their p. 183. clothes; and what makes it all the harder to bear is that half the tax extorted from them does not reach the king. "Surely he might have taxed the rich and spared the poor." It is p. 149. hard to lose where there is but little, and many to share that little. All seem against the peasant. He must not even take the fallen boughs to make his fire. He never has money, never has rest, but is robbed on every side, while in sweat and toil he wastes away. The proud array in which the horseman rides is pillaged from the poor. Whether the harvest be good or bad he must pay the taxes for the wars, even if he has to sell his grain while it is yet green. His horse, even his seed, and all his year's savings, must go to satisfy the demands made upon him. And the rich care not a jot for it all. "Might is right, light is night, and fight is p. 254. flight."

Langland shows Peace pleading before Parliament against *Piers Plow.* Wrong, his oppressor, who has robbed him of his wife, sent IV. 48. underlings to take his geese and young pigs, and borrowed his horse and never returned it, nor paid a farthing for it, however much the man pleaded for his own. Wrong maintains retainers who murder his hinds, seize upon his produce before it ever reaches the fair, and fight in his market. He breaks down his barn door, bears away his wheat, and gives him but a tally, or a beating, for ten quarters of oats. "I dare not for fear of him fight or chide," pleads Peace; "I

scarcely dare look on account of him." It is no wonder that
Pol. Songs,
p. 186.
the rising of the peasantry was anticipated long before it
came to pass. If they had had a leader they would have
risen long before[1].

And yet poor men's sons, in spite of all this hardship,
probably because of it, rose in the world, to the great disgust
of the well-born. "Now must every cobbler set his son to
*P. Plow.
Crede,* 744,
and cf. *Test. of
Love,* II. 2.
school, and every beggar's brat learn on the book, become a
secretary and dwell with a lord, or become a false friar to
serve the fiend, so that the beggar's brat becomes a bishop
and sits among the peers, and knights and lords' sons bow
low before him. And his sire is a cobbler, soiled with grease,
with teeth tattered as a saw through biting his leather!"
Not always are such beloved even by their kin:

Plow. Tale,
156.
> "For to lords they will be like,
> A harlot's son, not worth a haw!"

They have sometimes more power in the land than the king
and all his law; and yet their fathers never rode aught but
Shanks's mare, and travailed sore for what they ate, suffering
drought and wet, hunger, thirst and cold. Had they themselves been "out of religion" they must have hung upon the
plough, and thrashed and digged from town to town, with
sorry meat and not half enough.

The poor man had little reverence for the law, since it
seemed to take little thought for him. On the slightest
suspicion or for a very small offence he might be condemned
to death or imprisonment, the latter punishment being perhaps even more terrible than the former, for men and women
were left in miserable filth and disease, till their bodies
putrefied and their limbs rotted away. Justice was in a very
crude condition, and mainly itinerant, passing through the
shires and boroughs twice in the year. Manifold abuses
Piers Plow.
III. 135.
existed, and bribery was far from uncommon, causing men
to lose their lands and their lives, and setting prisoners
free for gold. The false went free, while the true, who
had done no wrong, were taken and hanged. For the poor
the law was an incomprehensible maze, in which they could
never find redress, though they should plead for ever, unless
they gave presents and money. Thus it was that the

---

[1] "Je me doute, s'ils ussent chief, quod vellent levare."

servants of the law got for themselves their furred robes
and great riches. The *Political Songs* are very outspoken
on the matter; while Robert Mannyng asks what will be the
lot of those robbers, earls, knights, barons, justices, sheriffs   *Hand. Synne,*
and bailiffs, who strip the poor people bare while the rich pay   6789.
what they will. As for the counsellors of lords, wicked lawyers and false accountants, who take no heed of right, and
advise wicked laws so that poor men may not live,

> "Therefore shall they and their counsail   5413.
> Go to hell both top and tail."

Numbers of the peasantry, innocent as well as guilty, took
to the woods when the law threatened them, for there was
the only safe abiding place when once the hue and cry was
raised.   So their hand turned against every man, because   *Percy's*
every man's hand was against them.   *Reliques,*
                                                                 I. 270.
Of course there are always at least two sides to every   *Nut-Brown*
question.   Not all the poor were honest and hard-working;   *Maid.*
and for the lazy and dissolute the hard times were not without a profitable lesson.   Not all the peasants were like the
Ploughman.   There is the Miller, a stout churl, big and
brawny, who always bears away the ram, the prize of the   *Cant. Tales,*
wrestling match.   He is a coarse-mannered rascal, rough of   A. 3120,
                                                                 Pro. 545.
tongue, who cries aloud in "Pilate's voice," and swears.   He
will remove neither hood nor hat for any man, and shows
courtesy to none ; a very boor.   As he rides he can scarcely
sit his horse, for he is very drunk and his face is pale with
excess.   It is not with him an occasional lapse, for he knows
quite well that he is drunk by the sound of his own voice.
Morality and he hold no fellowship.   There is the Reeve, or
bailiff, long and lean, a hot-tempered fellow, as coarse as the
miller, yet suspicious and cowardly.   He has won money
for himself by fleecing a trusting master.   And there is the
Cook, another coarse drunkard, so drunk that he falls from
his horse.

Some peasants worked well, but others preferred to sit
together singing over their ale a drunken catch, or telling   *Piers Plow.*
idle tales.   There were others, impostors, pretending to be   VI. 110,
                                                                 v. 398,
blind or lame, who really deserved neither help nor pity;   VI. 117,
and others who were wastrels and braggarts, who would live   VI. 167,
                                                                 v. 398.
by violence if they could, caring nothing for authority or

right: "I was never wont to work, and now will I not begin," says one; and another: "Though I should die this day I should not care to look up." Famine alone was capable of setting such as these to work; and sometimes it did its work so thoroughly that some were lantern-jawed and lean for the remainder of their lives. They were glad enough then to eat with the hogs, or to get beans and bran baked together, or milk and poor ale. The impostors were at once seen working with flails from morn till eve for the farmer's potful of peas, or they seized spades and shovels to dig and delve. Those professedly blind and bedrid soon were well again, and glad to toil for beans and the food of horses and hounds. Hunger came even to the worker. He could no longer afford pullets, geese, pigs, salt bacon or collops; he had but cheese, curds, cream, oatcake, loaves made of bran and beans, parsley, leeks, cauliflowers, peascods, beans, baked apples, onions, chervils or cherries, and lived in hope of the next harvest. If that were good, everyone became very independent again, and fed of the best, with good ale to drink. The wastrels again refused to work and recommenced their wandering. The very beggars refused to eat bean bread any longer, only wheaten bread of the best quality. They would drink no halfpenny ale, but only the best and brownest. The labourer was not satisfied with penny ale and bacon, and vegetables of the day before, but desired to have fresh meat, or fish fried or baked. He held out for high wages, and began to mouth his discontent that he was ever born a workman. He had a grievance against God, a grudge against reason. He cursed the king and all his council, who made laws to grieve him; he became violent, seditious, rebellious. Langland, whose testimony is corroborated by Gower in his *Vox Clamantis*, adds a solemn warning: "But I warn you workmen, work while you can, for hunger is hastening fast hitherwards, and flood, famine and storm shall come upon you, and the fruits shall fail. Then shall death take you, and dearth shall judge you, for such as you shall die of hunger unless God of His goodness grant us a truce."

The rebellion came in 1381, and threatened to overthrow the whole social order. At last the peasantry have grown strong enough to form a united group among the people, resolved to attain by joint action what individual effort could

Margin notes:

VI. 188.

Piers Plow.
VI. 321.

Froissart,
Chron.
pp. 250—262.

never hope for. They said that in the beginning there were
no bondmen, and why then should they be kept under like
beasts? If they worked for their lords they would have
wages for their labour as well as other men. The priest,
John Ball, shaped their thoughts into words: "Ah! ye good
people, the matters goeth not well to pass in England, nor
shall not do till everything be common, and that there be
no villeins nor gentlemen, but that we may be all united
together....We be all come from one father and one mother,
Adam and Eve; whereby can they say or show that they be
greater lords than we be?...They dwell in fair houses, and
we have the pain and travail, rain and wind in the fields."
Naturally, again, lack of experience led to gross excess; and
some ignorant extremists acted as though they were not so
much drunk as mad.   Gower, land-owner and aristocrat,
sees with dismay the danger threatening his own order, sees
the brutal passions of men triumphing over their humanity:
"May such a day never come again in our age!" He pictures
the curse of God falling upon the people, changing them to
beasts, wild monstrosities of passion, who in their madness
snarl and fight even against each other, from whose cavernous
mouths sulphurous flames dart forth. In this terrible vision
of anarchy asses refuse to bear their burdens any longer,
desiring to be as horses; oxen refuse the yoke, and will no
longer eat straw; swine are possessed with the devil; dogs
prowl in search of prey; beasts, birds and insects destroy the
land; while Wat the Jay[1] harangues the strange assembly,
preaching rebellion, revolution, anarchy: "O wretched slaves,
now comes the day in which the peasant shall drive out the
lord; let honour, law and virtue perish, and let our court
rule."   Stirred by his words their passions rage; and Ball,
himself devil-taught, teaches them as a prophet.

The peasants advance upon London, their hate blazing
most violently against the merchants of alien birth. Those
they seize are ruthlessly butchered. They shout and cry as
loud "as though all the devils of hell had been among them."
They go from street to street slaying all the Flemings they
can find in church or other place; none are respited; and so
with the Lombards. Tyler demands that all connected in
any way with the law shall also be beheaded. They have the

Walsingham, *Hist. Ang.* I. 457.

Vox Clam. I. 8, I. 1.

I. 2.

I. 3, 4.

I. 5—8.

I. 9.

I. 10, 11.

Froiss. *Chron.* p. 256, and cf. *Cant. Tales,* B. 4583.

[1] Wat Tyler.

Walsingham,
Hist. Ang.
I. 464, 461.
City at their mercy; they sack the Tower; they butcher Sudbury, archbishop of Canterbury, mangling him brutally with eight strokes of the axe before he dies. The spirit of revolution is abroad, demanding blood, too much blood, in expiation of wrong. Yet there is devotion to a cause to urge them on, something of the glory of a new-born freedom to light

I. 457.
up here and there the dark places of the struggle. The Savoy is destroyed; its vessels of gold and silver, its draperies of gold and silk, are broken or torn in pieces, and then thrown into the Thames. Anyone who keeps aught for himself is to lose his life; for the whole nation must understand that there is a principle involved, that avarice is not their motive. Rudely armed with whatsoever is nearest to their hands, with clubs, staves and rusty swords, with bows blackened by smoke and age, and arrows ill-trimmed, they have the country at their feet. King and nobles are powerless against their united front. One of them, Grindecobbe by name, is·captured, and then set free on condition that he persuades his followers to

II. 27.
surrender. "Fellow countrymen, whom even now some little freedom has relieved from long oppression, stand now while you may, and fear not for me. If now it is my lot to fall, I shall die in the cause of freedom won, thinking myself happy to finish my life with such a martyrdom. Act now as you would have done had I been beheaded at Hertford yesterday," is the message he delivers before returning to meet his fate.

On Blackheath, before two hundred thousand men, John Ball, the rebel priest, makes his famous speech, its text

II. 32.
> "When Adam delved and Eve span,
> Who was then a gentleman?"

II. 33.
He emphasises the natural equality of mankind: "equal liberty, the same nobility, like dignity, similar power" are the great free-rights of man. In the beginning all men were created equal; slavery was the invention of wicked men, and not of God, to oppress the poor. If slavery were of God He would have created master and slave. Thus does the wheel turn when the spirit of liberty animates the majority, poor and oppressed as they are. And Walsingham, like Gower a strong partisan of the aristocracy, styles the tenets Ball proclaims "absurdities," "ravings[1]," and says "he taught

---

[1] "deliramenta."

also the perverse dogmas of the perfidious John Wycliffe and II. 33, 32.
the opinions and false insanities which he held."

But Walworth's steel pricked the tumour; and the poor, deluded peasants proved more by their disastrous end than by their early successes how just in principle their cause had been. The promises of redress made by their terror-stricken, conscience-smitten opponents, which led them to lay aside their arms and to disband, were all forgotten or disregarded; and their ringleaders, with a great host of the rank and file, were put to the sword.

How far the direct teaching of Wycliffe had formed the minds of the rebel leaders can scarcely be decided; though it seems certain that what the Wycliffites were putting forth as a spiritual theory the insurgents were attempting to carry out into political practice. All men equal in the sight of God, personal fitness, spiritual as well as temporal, the sole qualification for rule, this Wycliffe had preached long before; and the insurgent leaders made the most of his arguments. Among many mistakes, terrible excesses, much that was horrible and bloody, modern socialism thus made its first great fight in England; and its practice ruined its theory for a time. Certain it is that the decline of Wycliffism was almost coincident with the overthrow of the peasants in 1381.

Many obstacles the peasantry had had to face; some they had surmounted; and one of the greatest of the latter was the ineffective means of transit and communication. It took much in those days to make a popular movement general throughout the country. The roads, even the high-ways, were always in a sorry state, so that travelling was always a hardship, and intercourse of district with district very restricted. Hence rustic dulness and ignorance of all but a very little of the world remained almost without change for centuries. Holes and bogs were everywhere; *Cant. Tales,*
vehicles stuck in the mire, and it often involved much D. 1541.
thwacking and many oaths before they were free. Even B. 3987.
H. 63.
the horseman had to ride very carefully at times to keep *Piers Plow.*
his steed from falling in the slough. To repair bad roads VII. 26.
was therefore regarded as a work of charity. All sorts and conditions of men passed slowly and painfully along the highways; the wealthy in their lumbering, yet luxuriously furnished, carriages and horse-litters, the well-to-do on

horseback, the poor on foot with staff in hand and wallet on back. In the fields and by-lanes lurked a host of sus- *Cant. Tales,* G. 658. picious characters, the waifs and strays of mediævalism, who were a pest to the peaceable wayfarer. The legal restric- tions upon labour and wages put forth from time to time after the plague years, together with the hunting down of the fugitive insurgents, filled the countryside with reckless, roving vagabonds who lived and robbed as they chose. Many attempts were made to check their depredations, one pre- caution being to clear the undergrowth on either side of the public highway. But the pest long continued ; and it would seem that the sturdy robber often had the public sympathy upon his side. At least he was a bold man although a Fortescue, *De Dom. Reg. et Pol.* criminal. "It hath been oftentimes seen in England that three or four thieves for poverty have set upon six or seven true men and robbed them all," says Fortescue, some ninety years later, assuming that the number and daring of the thieves is a signal proof of the superiority of the national courage. " There be therefore more men hanged in England in a year for robbery and manslaughter than there be hanged in France for such manner of crime in seven years." It was "lack of heart, and cowardice," he thinks, which kept the French peasantry from rising in a body like their English brethren.

Strange customs were in evidence upon the roads. There might be seen the criminal, or suspected criminal, fleeing for sanctuary, and the outlaw and banished man, bare-footed, bare-headed, clad only in his shirt, carrying always a wooden cross in his hands, and hastening to take ship at the nearest port. If the cross were laid aside, the man's life was at the mercy of any who cared to take it. *Test. of Cress.* 341. There was the leper with cup and clapper, for whom the road was cleared with haste, even where the throngs were thickest. There was the special messenger hastening with *Piers Plow.* C. XIV. 39. his news, carrying no coin and enjoying certain privileges, extending even to short cuts across the wheat or mowing grass. There, too, was the student begging his way to university or school. And there was the wandering min- strel, leisurely in his movements, carrying songs and tales II. 227. both false and true, in days of revolt sowing sedition and making endless trouble among the peasantry. By the wayside the latter was already bringing great disrepute upon his ancient profession, sinking to the level of a common buffoon, behaving with a disgusting indecency which pleased the coarse tastes of lewd men; and this grossness was also spreading to the drama.   Already the growing evil had been recognised and classed among the deadly sins by Robert Mannyng; and in the sixteenth century the downward progress of the minstrels will be attested by Stubbes in his *Anatomy of Abuses* when he speaks of their notorious drunkenness and obscenity.   Already the audience of the lowest class music-hall was in process of formation. C. XVI. 205.

Stubbes, *Anat. of Abuses*, ed. Furnivall, p. 171.

If the poets are to be believed, the free, open-air life in the fields had the greatest attraction for every Englishman. The dawn of spring tempted him forth with the manifold delights of the countryside, its birds and flowers, its warm slopes and merry-sounding brooks.   To deprive him of the simple and healthy pleasures for which his natural impulses taught him to crave was to take from him the best part of his life.   He could fully sympathise with the imprisoned bird : although its cage of gold be never so gay, and it be fed with every dainty that one can think of, it had twenty thousand times rather live free in a forest rude and cold, and eat worms and such like things. *Cant. Tales,* H. 163.

It was in the springtime that the freshness of nature's beauties filled the roads with crowds of pilgrims, bent on combining religion with recreation and gaiety.   Sometimes mounted, and dressed in their best, with holiday air, but sometimes naked to the shirt or barefoot if penance so demanded, they passed to the shrines of popular saints.   Even the poor Ploughman got out his clouted clothes, his gaiters and cuffs, and set out with a seed-basket instead of a scrip.   To the middle-class women, such as the Wife of Bath, pilgrimages were a delight only to be equalled by the spectacle of a Miracle Play or a wedding.   Shiploads of pilgrims passed over sea, and hurried everywhere, trying to see everything, and listening with credulous wonder to all the tales their guides chose to tell them.   It is no wonder that pilgrims soon achieved a reputation for marvellous inventions of lying tales. We have a picture of one just returned, with bowl and bag, a hundred "ampulles[1]" in his hat, signs of Sinai, shells and Pro.

Piers Plow. VI. 60.

Pro. 46.

---

[1] small phials.

v. 520.

crosses, keys of Rome, and a vernicle. He tells us that he comes from Sinai and the Holy Sepulchre, that he has been in Bethlehem and Babylon, in Armenia, Alexandria and many other places, as the signs in his hat testify, that he has walked far and wide in wet and dry to seek good saints for his soul's health. But he is nonplussed by a question which is meant to contain a subtle element of irony : " Knowest thou at all a saint whom men call Truth ? couldest thou show us the way to the place where he dwelleth ? " " Nay, so help me God," he replies, " I never before now saw palmer with staff or scrip ask after him." So the pilgrim sometimes did as much harm as good to the cause of religion, for it was soon perceived by his fellows that he was not always improved by the journeys he had made and the life he had led. The reformer was of the opinion that a man was better employed at home about his business.

In out of the way places in the woods and fields lived many who secluded themselves in the hermit's cell, and sought thus, like Richard Rolle of Hampole, to escape the many temptations of the world, the flesh and the devil. Others, more practical, but perhaps less fervent, applied themselves to pious works, dwelling in more populous neighbourhoods to receive the alms of passers-by. But the parasitic tribe soon perceived an opening for profitable imposture ; and as the hermits increased in number their reputation decreased till they became nothing more than mere professional beggars, cloaked in the most degraded hypocrisy. Langland has much to say of such as dwell by the highways, and in towns among the brewers, and beg in churches. They are vicious, entirely destitute of morality, and lazy, making pretence of humility to win alms, so that in the evening they may stretch themselves at their ease by the warm fire. They drink deep before they retire to bed, and do not rise in the morning until it suits their pleasure. Then their only endeavour during the day is to get food and money without working for it. Sheer laziness and nothing else makes them profess themselves hermits. But we are now upon the threshhold of a Reformation which will remove these stumbling blocks to the cause of religion.

Piers Plow.
Pro. 53.
C. I. 30.
C. X. 40.

At this period a large proportion of mankind may be grouped into three classes—fanatics, hypocrites, sceptics.

The fanatics were stirred by morbid zeal to the very extremes of self-torture; the overwhelming sense of the presence of evil in the world and in the soul tending to disturb the balance of their minds, and to lead them panic-stricken to the very excess of self-abasement. Such were the Flagellants, drawn from every class, who sought to expiate their sins by scourging their naked bodies, until the blood flowed, with knotted cords through which nails were passed, accompanying the scourgings with hymns and prayers. Of the hypocrites the satirists will tell us more hereafter. Of the sceptics we have mention of many who, in an age of developing reason, were driven by the two former classes to the other extreme, believing in neither the redemption of mankind, nor the immortality of the soul, nor the existence of God. The cause of the evil times was by many asserted to be the sin of the unbelieving lords, some of whom said that there was no God, that the sacrament of the altar was nothing, that there was no resurrection after death, but that as died the beast of burden so also ended man himself. But, perhaps, when we probe the matter to its depths, the existence of such free-thinkers may be taken to imply the massing of the forces for an immediate movement towards reform.

> Walsingham,
> *Hist. Ang.*
> I. 275.

> Will. of Shore.
> *Seven Sac.*

> Walsingham,
> *Hist. Ang.*
> II. 12.

With the reformer's eye we are permitted to examine the condition of the religious mind of this age; and he waxes exceedingly satirical as he penetrates beneath the hollow shams and mockeries of religion which are on every side of him. What he cannot overthrow by direct assault he will undermine with the sharpness of his tongue; and in proportion as he is filled with enthusiasm for purity and inspired with a passionate zeal for truth, so much the sharper his tongue will be. His burning indignation will blaze forth against the deceiving servants of Rome; and his scathing denunciations will never be forgotten. Ask him why he speaks so bitterly of men's sins, and he will answer at once, "To amend 'em, in good faith, if God will give me any grace." The leaven is working till even the man of the world, Chaucer for example, will laugh the hypocrite out of countenance, and hold up his imposture to derision. With the passing of the age of the Crusades, men can now attend more closely to their own spiritual condition; and to many the revelation of self will come as a violent shock, until in time

> *Plow. Tale,*
> 1289.

the growing habit of introspection will sow the seeds of Puritanism and reform.

Piers Plow.
1. 3, 7², 75.

Holy Church, the mother, is still the great ideal: "a lady, lovely of countenance, clothed in linen," who reveals the wise words of Holy Writ. It is her hireling ministers, the rogues who drape themselves in her vestments for silver, that befoul her reputation and impair her work. She herself is beyond reproach. Suspicion is aroused on every side of her, for there is ever a false ring in the speech of her servants, and it is hard to know what to believe; but it never touches her holy person. She at least is true. In their perplexity men cling despairingly about her knees praying for guidance and light.

79.

> "Then I bowed on my knees, and cried her for grace,
> And prayed her piteously pray for my sins,
> And also teach me kindly on Christ to believe,
> That I might work His will Who wrought me to man,
> Teach me to no treasure, but tell me this same,
> How I may save my soul."

It is a repetition of Adam's cry in the *Genesis*, the very essence of many a Puritan prayer. And Holy Church replies again and again that truth, for which the reformers

85, 205, 133.

are striving, is the precious jewel to be desired. "When all treasures are tried, truth is the best"; yet few there be that

v. 537.

find it. Truth itself, to be effective, must be no mere form upon the tongue; formalism, by itself, is empty and vain. Though a man be true of his tongue, and true of his work, though he be chaste as a child crying at the font, there is no

1. 178.

virtue in masses and hours unless he have true love in his heart, and care for the poor.

How far the Church had striven to influence men's minds may be seen in all the religious poems of the age. The foundations of faith, and the expression of them, are not changed from those of the Old English days. The ten commandments, the twelve articles of faith, the seven sacraments, the seven deadly sins, good and evil, death and the Judgment, heaven and hell, are all embraced in dogma, unchangeable and inviolable. Of the general observance of the ordinances of the Church there are traces everywhere. The mass is sung daily; and tran-

substantiation is regularly taught, though Wycliffe arises to
confute it :

> "And in the Sacrament also that soothfast God in is,
> Fully His Flesh and His Blood Who for us death endured,

   · · · · · · · · · · ·

> Because Christ said it is so, so must it needs be.
> Therefore study thou not thereon, nor stir thy wits,
> It is His blessed Body, so bade He us believe."

P. Plow.
Crede, 822.

828, and cf.
Hand. Synne,
9949.

But these lines the reformers afterwards suppressed. Sin
always has its punishment; no one knows whom God will
smite, or how the worm of conscience will strike with remorse.
Fasts and penances are imposed, though sometimes they
lie heavily upon the simple-minded. In Lent fish and the
plainer foods alone are eaten. We hear the peasant lamenting
that because he does not know his creed the priest will
enjoin upon him as a penance abstinence from flesh-meat the
length of a Lenten after Easter, and on every Wednesday
also. Celibacy is imposed upon monks and nuns, but the
ordinance is never very popular even among the people
generally, who are beginning to understand the social question
which is involved. "If I were pope," says the Host to the
Monk,

Cant. Tales,
C. 277.

P. Plow.
Crede, 8.

> "Not only thou, but every mighty man,
> Though he were shorn full high upon his pan[1],
> Should have a wife."

Cant. Tales,
B. 3140.

The evil consequences of the system are thought altogether
to outweigh the good ; human nature cannot long endure the
unnatural restraint :

> "See how they cry and wring their handës white
> For they so soon went to religiön!
> And eke the nuns, with veil and wimple plight,
> There thought that they be in confusiön:
> 'Alas,' they say, 'we feign perfectiön
> In clothës wide, and lack our liberty;
> But all the sin must on our friendës be'."

Court of Love,
1100.

    The religious thought of the age contains an admixture
of many classical and Teutonic elements. Thus we have
Chaucer, whose theological opinions may be taken as those
of the educated English layman of his day, now discoursing,
on orthodox lines, upon predestination, free-will and Provi-

Tr. and Cress.
IV. 961.
Boethius, etc.

[1] head.

dence, the great theological problem of the Middle Ages; now putting forward the views of the Stoics handed down by Boethius: "Make virtue of necessity; be patient, and think that he is Fortune's lord who recks not of her, and she daunteth no one but a wretch"; and again showing the influence of the fatalism of his Teutonic ancestors, speaking of the shaping of the Wyrds and the dooms of the Fatal Sisters. And yet again we find him, as an intelligent man of the world, joining in the regularly organised attack, at once rationalistic, intellectual and critical, as springing from the Renaissance spirit, which was directed against the weaknesses of the churchmen and the abuses of the age.

Tr. and Cress. IV. 1586.
Leg. of Gd Wom. 2580, 2628.

The burning question of the day, on which the Reformation turned, concerned the temporal authority of the pope. Again and again were legal measures taken to prohibit appeals to Rome, and the bestowal of English benefices upon papal nominees, frequently foreigners who never saw their parishioners. Great was the indignation of the independent Englishman at the extortion of Peter's Pence and tribute from those who found it hard to pay. By 1366 this tribute had not been paid for over thirty years, and after that date regular application for it ceased to be made. The Great Schism and the wicked lives imputed to the popes went far to confirm the Englishman in his opinions. "The pope has no pity on the Church, and, claiming to govern all men, governs not himself," says Langland. "Into the sword the Church's key is turned, and holy prayer into cursing," says Gower. So much that was done in the name of religion was so utterly shameless that Rome had become altogether distrusted by every class—its influence seemed to be always making for evil; there was so great a difference between its precept and its practice. The Ploughman tells us that some of the servants of Rome would sell both heaven and hell to put pennies in their purse, and asks, "What does a tiller at the plough know of the pope? His creed is enough for him." His view of the origin of the temporal power of the papacy is that once upon a time the emperor gave the pope such high lordship about him, that at last, poor innocent fool, the proud pope put him out of office. "They say that to Peter was given the key of heaven and hell; but I know that Peter took no money for the sins he sold. These so-

Piers Plow. V. 51.

Conf. Amant. P. 37.

P. 39.

Plow. Tale, 167, 453, 693.

365.

called successors are too keen about money, while their
conscience is blunted. Foul befall all such deceivers! Peter
was never so great a fool as to leave his key with such a
rascal."

Pope Holy, Romanism personified, had become the
very symbol of the hypocrite and impostor; in secret never
eschewing a wicked deed when men were unsuspecting,
while outwardly appearing precious, with pale and piteous
visage, a simple creature. There was no evil which she could
not conceive in her heart, and but faint were the prayers she
offered to God and His saints. She made herself look thin,
weary, and lean of face, wore a hair-shirt, and professed to be
occupied in good works, but it was all profession, to gain the
praise of men. And for such vain glory she lost the kingdom
of God. "May the gate of Paradise, that blissful place, ever
be refused her!"

Rom. de la Rose, 413, 426, et seq.

With hypocrisy, simony and bribery went hand in hand, so
that the false enjoyed what was meant for the true. They had
"poisoned popes and impaired Holy Church," and filled the
country with a degraded brotherhood. Clerks were covetous;
the religious orders ceased from prayer; preachers did not
frame their lives to accord with their preaching; bishops,
priests and monks kept horses and hounds, instead of providing for the poor, thinking more of riding and hunting than
of their Church, and saying within themselves, "The life is
sweet." They busied themselves more with chancellorships
and the king's treasuries than with their spiritual cures.
Parsons and parish priests complained of their poverty by
reason of the plagues, and obtained licences from their
bishops to dwell in London and "sing there for simony, for
silver is sweet." They served lords and ladies as stewards,
and neglected their parishes. To all "the heaven is far, the
world is nigh"; and the satirist gave them the title "The
Order of Fair Ease[1]." There is one who confesses that he
has been priest and parson for over thirty years, and yet can
neither sol-fa nor sing, nor read lives of saints; that he can
find a hare in a field better than he can construe one clause
in "beatus vir" or in "beati omnes" and teach it to his
parishioners; that he can hold love-days[2] and hear a reeve's
reckoning, but in canon or decretal cannot read a line. He

Piers Plow.
III. 127, 146,
IV. 119,
III. 311.
Cant. Tales,
Pro. 165.
Plow. Tale,
133, 181, 1005.
Conf. Amant.
p. 239.
Piers Plow.
Pro. 60.

83.

Conf. Amant.
p. 37.
Pol. Songs,
p. 137.

Piers Plow.
v. 420.

---

[1] "C'est le ordre de Bel-Eyse."   [2] days for settling disputes.

acknowledges that he repudiates his agreements, delays to pay his servants' wages, and treats them with wicked will and wrath; that he knows not what either gratitude or courtesy means, for he has the manners of a hawk. They lived vicious lives, sufficient to corrupt a whole parish or country, and made presents to their bishops to wink at their misdeeds. They disputed for his wealth at the bedside of the dying, while the poor passed away unshriven and uncared for. With their ill-gotten gains they aped the fashions and display of the knights. There is a certain parson who has gathered to himself much wealth; and his daughter has married a rich miller who received with her " many a pan of brass." She had been brought up in a nunnery; and her airs and graces as the daughter of a rich parson are overwhelming. She is as proud and pert as a magpie, and thinks herself very superior because of her kindred and upbringing. But she is as repellant as ditch-water, full of abusiveness and disdain. Her father has ambitious aims for his daughter's daughter whom he intends to marry into an old family, and to whom he purposes to leave his wealth.

Cant. Tales, I. 895.

A. 3944, and cf. *Hand. Synne.* 6173. A. 3966.

> "For Holy Church's good must be expended
> On Holy Church's blood that is descended;
> Therefore he would his holy blood honoúr,
> Though that he Holy Churchë should devour."

A. 3981.

Chaucer's Monk is one who knows more of the pleasures of the world than of study or toil; and his person is that of a man who knows more of feasts than fasts, for he is very fat, and his face shines as though it had been anointed. He is the ecclesiastical product of Merrie England. There is a Nun's Priest who has fared no worse than his monastic brother, for he has great brawns and neck, a massive chest and ruddy face, with eyes keen as a hawk. And there is a friar, fit companion for these two, lolling lazily on a bench. He is a churl, great and grim, grown like a tun, with a face as fat as a distended bladder, hanging like a bag on both his cheeks, with quivering double chin, large as a goose-egg, grown all of grease; all his flesh quakes like a quick-mire. He is warmly dressed in a clean cope of double worsted reaching down to his heels, with a white kirtle of fine material.

Pro. 165. 206.

B. 4645.

P. Plow. Crede, 220.

The mendicant friars, who had formerly been the strength of the Church, have now become a source of weakness, though there were still among them some good men and true who lived and toiled in accordance with their vows. Some of them, too, were bound by the strongest ties to the poor among whom they laboured, and with whom they sided in the rebellion, preaching the doctrines of socialism, even to community of goods. But of good friars the reformer has no need to tell, though he prays that God, of His good grace, may save all friars who live faithfully, and amend those who are false. At first the orders were founded "fully on truth," as "pure and perfect priests to live in penance, in love, in humility, in preventing of pride, and grounded on the Gospel as God Himself bade." But now they are all lies and flattering tales, and are accursed of Christ. One says that the devil himself brought in the friars, "painted without," to deceive the Church, that Satan sent them from hell to cumber men with their craft and to ruin Christendom. Others, Wycliffe among them, ascribe their paternity to Cain, and prove it thus: *851.* *506.* *480.*

> "Now see the truth whether it be so.
> That friars Carmes come of a K,
> The friars Austins come of A,
> Friars Jacobynes of I,
> Of M come the friars Minors;
> Thus grounded Caim these four orders
> That fill the world full of errors
> And of hypocrisy."

Pol. Poems,
Wright, I. 266.

Langland calls them "children of Judas" and "servants of Lucifer." Apparently no name is too bad for them. And this vituperation spreads until it involves the whole Roman Church; while the pope himself does not escape the name "Antichrist." The hot hate and disgust in the reformer's heart are plainly seen.   *Piers Plow.*
Pro. 35, 39.

But see now the base friar and his methods. He is a wanton, merry fellow, popular with the rich, for his penance is always easy if money be forthcoming. With them no one could be pleasanter, more courteous, more lowly of service, more seemingly virtuous. But with the sick poor he is an altogether different being. To have acquaintance with such lazars does not befit such a worthy man as he, does not   *Cant. Tales,*
Pro. 208.
D. 1709.
Rom. de la
Rose, 6295—
7126.

6855.

accord with the dignity of his order; it is not honest; it may not advance! "Where findest thou a toiling labourer have me for his confessor?" asks one of them. Yet he goes from house to house begging food or clothes or money; and stoops to win even the smallest coin from a widow well-nigh destitute. He comes to the house of a bedrid peasant who has a little money, and settles himself in a comfortable corner. In the course of conversation he does not forget to throw out hints about the negligence of the curate, and to exalt himself in comparison. The good wife, who seems especially anxious to please him, asks if he will dine. He would not mind a capon's liver with a thin slice of her soft bread, and a roasted pig's head to follow. He is a man of little sustenance; the Bible is his food! The invalid husband is by no means a believer in him. In a few years he has spent many a pound upon the friars; the gold is gone, and he is none the better for it. "Ah," says the friar, "that comes of your inconstancy. Had you held to me and my convent it would have been very different; but it is always so much to this convent and so much to that, so that what you give is dispersed in many directions. You would have our work for nothing; and God Himself said that the workman was worthy of his hire." But his cajoleries are unsuccessful, and in the end he leaves the house in a rage.

Pol. Poems,
I. 264, 265.
Songs and
Carols, p. 76.
Cant. Tales,
D. 865.

P. Plow.
Crede, 50, 82.

762.

Many friars go about like pedlars, combining the two professions, sometimes for profit, sometimes for a less honourable purpose, carrying purses, pins, knives, girdles, gloves, silks, furs, spices, and even small hounds for the women. They betray wives and maids, beguile them of their goods with flattering words, and therewith provide the means for their licentiousness. With stout staves in hand they roam about to the places where their lemans lie lurking in the towns. And these women can afford to dress in the height of fashion, with great head-dresses, and ornaments beside their eyes. These, the friars say, are their sisters; and so they go about deceiving the people. "Would to God they were made to live in a wilderness and forbidden fair ladies' chambers," says the author of *Pierce the Ploughman's Crede.* "If lords but knew their craft they would not have them made so comfortable in their houses at night. They would shut their heads in the straw to sharpen their wits. They ought to be made to dig and delve and eat plain fare, beans and bacon, rather than partridges, plovers and peacocks, with dainty drinks; for this high living is but a cause of their immorality." The Englishman is so very bitter in his accusations that our suspicions as to his veracity would be aroused if there were not so many to bear corroborating testimony, and if we did not know what the times were.

By their rule the friars had devoted themselves to poverty; they were to receive neither money nor houses nor land, and were to live upon alms as humble workers and pilgrims. But now they are often followed by a stout varlet carrying on his back a sack containing the fruits of their house-to-house visitations. So far from leaving all worldly delights they roam about haunting wrestling matches, fairs, wakes, merry-makings, markets and taverns. They leave matins and *Plow. Tale,* masses, and invent vain interpretations of Scripture to please *868.* *Piers Plow.* the people, in order to get money "to pay for the drink," and *Pro.* 58. *P. Plow.* to dress as they desire. When the barns are full "then come *Crede,* 591, 72. cursed friars and crouch full low" to receive their portion. There is scarcely a house where they do not receive something. Some of them have greater possessions than ten knights put together; they have more money hidden away than the wool merchants; and yet offer one of them privately a penny for a mass, and "if his knave be not ready to take it, *282.* put out my eye." And so they buy themselves bishoprics with bags of gold; they become counsellors of kings, with *360.* whom they curry favour. They raise magnificent monasteries with high walls, orchards and gardens, and secret *118.* posterns leading to the fields; with lofty chambers in which are fire-places and chimneys, wide windows with glass glittering like the sun, arches, pillars and quaint carvings, painted and polished, adorned with shields, statues, tombs of knights in alabaster, and figures of ladies in gilded garments; and there are kitchens and dormitories which must have cost an enormous amount. Yet the builders will beg a basket of wheat from a peasant who finds it hard to pay half his rent in a year. "These buildings seem to turn bread into stones," says Wycliffe. If one will give them something, they promise that he shall be shown kneeling before the Christ in the middle of one of their stained glass windows, that St Francis *126.* himself shall fold him in his cope, present him to the Trinity, and pray for his sins. Another friar offers absolution for a cartload of wheat, and then says that his order is putting in an expensive window. If the man will pay for it, and have his name graven upon it, his soul will be secure of heaven.

Piers Plow.
III. 48.
P. Plow.
Crede, 29, 404.

They give it out that the coffers of Christendom and the keys of heaven are in their hands. And yet the poor man who goes to learn from them is told that he cannot have either their pardon or their prayers without pay, and that he must not waste their time : a housewife is dying who has left them ten pounds in her will, and perhaps they may get something more; when she has given it them the sooner she dies the better. The man is mad to expect to learn from them.

Piers Plow.
II. 210, 229,
V. 136, 144.
Walsingham,
Hist. Ang.
II. 13.
P. Plow.
Crede, 542,
554, 744, 648,
282.

Langland says that they are false, lying, wrathful, depraved. "Thou liest!" springs readily to their lips. "He is a friar, therefore a liar," is a common saying. Their pride is as great as their wealth; they lour and are jealous if they have not the first place at feasts; they suffer neither sovereign nor subject. No wasp in the world will more wilfully sting than a stinking friar, if one should step on his toe. They are ever deceitful, professing to follow fully the rule of St Francis, but they are far more comfortably clad than ever he was. Under their copes they wear coats of fur, cut off at the knee so as not to be seen. In cold weather they wear hose cut off at the ankle for the same reason; instead of going barefoot, as he bade,

303.

they have buckled shoes. And in their purses they carry spices for their delight. "Oh! if men but knew their trickery and cunning words they would pay them little reverence, and see them as they are, images of hypocrisy grafted upon fiends."

622.

There is a horrible scandal connected with the end of these men. They are said to fare in proportion to their success. Those who cannot beg go about in clouted shoes and worn-out clothes, and are well-nigh starved, while their more fortunate fellows have every luxury. The rich friar will not lend a poor brother a penny to save his life. When they become old and feeble, or are maimed or diseased, so that begging is no longer possible, a terrible fate awaits them. It is whispered that some are laid in a secret chamber with close-fitting earthenware pots drawn over their heads, and thus in a little while are asphyxiated.

Closely allied in practice to the friars were the pardoners, who were not necessarily friars or priests, but whose functions were supposed to be derived directly from the pope himself, though their credentials were often forgeries. They, too, are brim-full of lying tales, and mean, smooth and oily. With their atrocious stock in trade of manufactured relics, assisted by flattering and deceitful tongues, they get more money in a day than the parish priest can get in two months. With these they make the parson and his people their apes; which does not say much for the perspicacity of either the parson or his people. But then they are simple folk, and for them the halo of Rome is still about the men. In church they put on such an air of dignity, and preach with such fluent and haughty speech, showing their bulls and seals, their relics of rag and bone, that the credulous are always deceived by their hypocrisy. And thus some of them earn as much as a hundred marks a year. "Do you think that as long as I can get gold and silver by preaching that I shall live in poverty, or work for my living?" asks one of them. Their craft succeeds so well and thriftily that at times they almost forget that dissembling is necessary, as they flaunt their wares with but half-veiled impudence. Then the Englishman, as the light of reason dawns upon him, begins to see more and more clearly how basely he is being duped, and gives the impostor a sharp rebuff, couched in pretty plain terms, which cannot always be fully reproduced.

Piers Plow. II. 219, V. 647, Pro. 68. *Ho. of Fame,* III. 1037. *Cant. Tales,* Pro. 669. C. 320, 329, 421, 369, 439, 946.

We can quite understand the indignation of the plain-speaking reformers at all they saw and heard; and just as clearly can we see what the Englishman is beginning to expect from his priests. These satires give a double reflection of the character of the age, the primary of the satirised, the secondary of the satirist. Undoubtedly the orders and officials of the Roman Church must previously have been a great power for good, or they would never have obtained such a hold upon the people. But their day was now approaching its end, and already many refused to attach any degree of holiness whatever to anything they did. At the Judgment Day all their pardons, letters and indulgences would be as nothing: "Unless Do-well help you I set your patents and your pardons at one pie-crust," says Langland; which reminds us of Wycliffe's answer when he was asked what was the use of these things: "By such reason think many

Piers Plow. VII. 191.

men that these letters may do good for to cover mustard pots."

When we consider the manner of the young clerk's training, his education, and the university life in which his most impressionable years were spent, we are not altogether surprised that in after years he was not always what he should have been. He learned very little that was of any practical value; and that little, more often than not, made him but a clever juggler with words, which aided him, if he were so bent, to deceive still more cleverly. At Oxford we find a poor scholar who has taken his course in Arts, but all his fantasy is to learn astrology. And to this bent he adds a certain nicety and voluptuousness which do not promise well for the future. At the head of his bed, instead of books, there lies a gay psaltery, on which he is wont to make melody by night. At Cambridge there are two young students frolicsome and ready for any escapade, inclined to fall into any temptation. Remove these youths to an atmosphere still further vitiated, and how shall they escape the deeper contamination? One parson confesses that he ran about in youth and made no effort to learn, and so ever since has been a beggar through his foul sloth.

But there is the very best material in such clerks as Chaucer's Clerk of Oxford. With hollow face and deliberate speech, riding quietly and modestly upon a sorry jade, with threadbare garments and but little gold to help him on, he is the very type of striving and deserving poverty. On such as he the future of Church and State depends. All his thought is centred upon his books and his desire to become a priest, so that he passes by opportunities of worldly office which might provide him with a competence. He would rather have at the head of his bed twenty books of Aristotle and his philosophy than rich robes or fiddle or psaltery. All the money he gets goes in learning and books. He bids fair to become a true and faithful servant of the Church, but even in his case there is a flaw in his upbringing. He is poor and dependent upon others, and so is of necessity, after the fashion of the time, accustomed to beg before he takes up his work in the Church. Had he been of less worthy character he would have been already an adept in the art of living upon others. If he afterwards turn friar this training will be greatly to his

Cf. *Conf. Am.* Bk VII

Cant. Tales, A. 3190.

A. 4002.

Piers Plow. V. 444.

Cant. Tales, Pro. 290.

material advantage. But we fancy that even now he has his mission, and that in the years to come many a poor soul will thank God for the guidance of both his preaching and example.

The scales are falling from the Englishman's eyes, and the wrongs he sees sit heavily upon his soul. By these facts we may gauge the progress of his development. At last he has reached the point where he can perceive, and strive to remove, the evils of his race. Destructive criticism must always precede the age of new construction; and here, amid the *débris* of the old, carefully pondering over the plans and ideals of the new, we must leave him to his work. We see him in the tall, gaunt figure of Langland, passing through the jostling crowds of London streets to pray for rich men's souls, and yet living his life in a world apart, a world of ideals of what ought to be, where rank, fine clothes and jewels go for nothing, where even theology, as then understood, is a vain help. He stands the harbinger of the Reformation to come; and yet he is but a fool, a madman, to those who look only upon externals, and fail to see the light of truth within. But before his work is done there will be many upon whose hearts such burning thoughts as his have stamped indelible impressions. The Englishman has never been so completely idealistic as to stay long in the midst of dreams, and now the awakening has come, and with it the Reformation is known to be at hand.

First among the workers was Wycliffe, scholar, theologian and priest, a plain-spoken Yorkshireman with all the keen and independent spirit of the north, with that rugged firmness which would be called obstinacy in a weaker cause. He took upon his shoulders the mantle of Richard Rolle of Hampole, also a Yorkshireman, but blended with his ecstatic fervour the ideas of Marsiglio of Padua, the English Ockham, author of the dialogue between Knight and Clerk, and Richard of Armagh, author of *De pauperie Salvatoris*. With powerful argument he stripped religion of the outer casing of temporal authority which had grown around it, and referred back all dominion to God, seeing in man but the instrument of the divine working, worthy or unworthy to rule as he fulfils or does not fulfil the part divinely assigned to him. By this standard must even the pope himself be judged; on this

Cf. Walsing-ham, *Hisi. Ang.* I. 324—363.

Summa in Theologia.

principle alone must his authority stand. If the pope did not fulfil the will of Christ, then he was but the servant of Antichrist, and his ordinances were therefore not binding upon the members of the true Church of God. Admirably cogent is the logic of Wycliffe's reasoning; and it stands to the credit of the Englishman that he was one of the first fully to comprehend the force of it. Freedom to live in accordance with the dictates of conscience, instead of following blind tradition, is henceforth his desire. And the working out of the ideal commenced when Wycliffe and his helpers translated the Scriptures into the vulgar tongue, and sent forth preachers to present a plain, unvarnished tale of truth. If the time had been more fitting, if there had been no rising of the peasantry, and if the Wycliffites had not been, rightly or wrongly, connected in the popular idea with the insurgents of 1381, the fruits of his labours might have been gathered without the lapse of years which actually occurred. But somehow or other an element of suspicion attached to those who followed him; and "Lollardy" came to savour only too often, among the general public, of rant, excess, heresy and revolution. When Wycliffe came into conflict with the friars and the papal authority, the main force of his movement expended itself in the excessive strife stirred up, in combating the attacks of opponents and persecutors who styled him heretic[1]. It was to the peasantry that his appeal was chiefly made, and they took him to their hearts with gladness, for he taught the alleviation of their lot; hence the tendency towards excess; hence the confusion of ideas; hence the suspicion of the wealthier classes. No one denounces more strongly than Gower the evils present in the Church, but, like many others, Lollardy he cannot away with; for it appears to him to subvert so much that had come to be considered an integral part of Catholic doctrine. He says that the saints of old ought better to be believed than those whom men know to be not holy.

As Chaucer's pilgrims ride on their way to Canterbury there is one who rebukes the ready oath from profane lips,

P. Plow.
Crede, 528.

Conf. Am.
p. 238.

---

[1] "Witness on Wycliffe who warned them with truth;
For he in goodness of ghost straightly them warned
To wave their wickedness and works of sin.
How soon these sorry men pursued his soul,
And over all 'lollered' him with heretics' works!"

only to be contemptuously called Lollard for his pains. It is *Cant. Tales,*
B. 1171.
the poor Parson who is thus roughly repressed ; and in him
we have, in one clear glance, the Englishman's ideal. Here at
last is the constructive process ; here the mark to which the
Englishman is pressing on, attracted because the man is
English like himself, and true, representing that for which
good men crave. Some such priests must have been well
known in England, or the character would never have been
drawn. But it is not so much the recognition of the existence
of such a type, as the person—the courtly Chaucer, the broad-
minded man of the world of the richer middle class—by whom
the type is set forth, which shows how high and true the
English ideals are becoming. At last we are looking upon
the Englishman's definite ideal of perfection, as far as he can
apprehend it. There are, I think, but few characters in our
literature equal to Chaucer's Poor Parson of a Town, and
none superior. This picture of the parish priest does Chaucer,
and those for whom he wrote, infinite credit.

He is a good, simple man, learned and devout, "not Pro. 477.
I. 57.
textual " he says modestly, though his sermon would seem
to prove otherwise, rich only in holy thought and work,
patient in adversity, wonderfully diligent and benign. Loath
is he to enforce payment of his tithes from his hard-pressed
parishioners, rather would he give of his own, and deny
himself: he could in little have sufficiency. For from his
birth he himself has known the cares and pains of poverty.
His parish is wide and scattered, but neither sickness nor
stormy weather stays him from visiting the farthest, small
and great, upon his feet with staff in hand, ever placing Pro. 496, 527.
example before precept[1]. He never leaves his flock while
seeking advancement for himself elsewhere: "He was a
shepherd and not a mercenary." And though himself of
holy life and work he has pity in his heart for the sinner,
to whom he is never hard or haughty in speech, but always 519.
discreet and kind. To draw his folk to heaven by fairness

---

[1] "This noble example to his sheep he gave
  That first he wrought and afterward he taught.
  Out of the Gospel he these wordës caught;
  And this figure he added eke thereto,
  That if gold rustë what shall iron do?
  For if a priest be foul on whom we trust,
  No wonder is a lewëd man to rust."

and good example is his aim. Yet when duty requires he can sharply chide the obstinate whether of high or low degree. He thinks nothing of pomp and dignity, and his conscience is no pliable thing, admitting the pleasures of the world at convenience. For his recreation we find him riding on pilgrimage to Canterbury; and in the motley crowd of pilgrims he is not at all at ease. There is nothing in common to him and the lordly monk, the lady prioress, and the other ecclesiastics. He is but the poor parson, the ploughman's brother. And he must have been just as ill at ease with the secular members of the company, when two of them get shamefully drunk, and some are vying with each other in telling tales of doubtful decency with the usual accompaniment of coarse oaths. At last he can stand it no longer when the

B. 1166.　Host calls for his tale "for God's bones!" and "by God's dignity!" and he makes his protest, only to meet with derision. It is no wonder that his speech seems awkward and his views restrained in a company where worldly men hold sway, where

B. 3155, 3980.　even the monk is made to know and keep his place, and take all patiently. But the good man is bent upon improving the time. When Canterbury is almost reached his turn comes to tell his tale. The ribald talk is hushed, the pilgrims become more subdued, as the towers of England's holy city come in sight; and he strikes an entirely new note: why should he sow worthless stuff out of his fist when, if he list, he may sow good seed? So, if they now care to hear, he will tell some moral and virtuous matter. Thus he leads the minds of his hearers from their own journey to the great pilgrimage of life, en- compassed on every side with temptation, sin and death, and

I. 48.　yet a progress towards a celestial city where the tired
1075.　pilgrim finds rest after toil. There, after its long striving with the world within and the world without, imperfect humanity, once foul and dark, frail and mortal, shall become clearer than the sun, immortal, and so strong and whole that nothing may ever impair it; and the soul shall be replenished with the sight and perfect knowledge of God.

CONCLUSION.

HERE, with the conclusion of the *Canterbury Tales*, we may leave the Englishman upon the threshold of modern life, face to face with the ideals of his future. For him the days of headstrong youth are over, and he is preparing for the great work of his early manhood. We have seen him as nature made him, healthy, vigorous and masterful. We have watched his conversion, and noted his passionate love for God and the difference which Christianity made in him. We have seen him in trouble and distress, learning the hard lessons of adversity, and coming from them chastened and subdued. We have seen him sitting at the feet of keener, more practical men than himself, humbly gathering in that which the foreigner taught. And at last he has re-asserted himself, a pupil wiser than his teachers, because he learned carefully and with perseverance. Through it all he has never lost his own individuality, though becoming more and more imbued with all the influences from without. He has always been English at heart, simple, rugged, patient, dogged, but he is now far more intellectual, and will become far more stable. We have found the meaning of the scornful words upon his lips, of the bitter disdain he pours upon the hypocrisies and shams which degenerates had imposed upon his inexperience. After long trial he is at last beginning to find them out, to lay them side by side with truth in a comparison not at all to their advantage ; and so we may look forward with greater confidence to his future. Now more experienced, a complex reasoning creature, his conscience fully awakened, his errors clearly seen, we can leave him to his work of construction and further development, of which even to-day the end is not in sight.

Lydgate, Skeat's *Supplementary Chaucer*, p. 408.

"Go forth, king, rule thee by sapience;
Bishop, be able to minister doctrine;
Lord, to true counsel give audience;
Womanhood, to chastity ever incline;
Knight, let thy deeds worship determine;
Be righteous, judge, in saving thy name;
Rich, give alms, lest thou lose bliss with shame.

People, obey your king and the law;
Age, be thou ruled by good religion;
True servant, be dreadful, and keep thee under awe;
And thou, poor man, fie on presumption;
Disobedience to youth is utter destruction;
Remember you how God hath set you, lo!
And do your part, as ye be ordained to."

INDEX.

For EU product safety concerns, contact us at Calle de José Abascal, 56–1°,
28003 Madrid, Spain or eugpsr@cambridge.org.

www.ingramcontent.com/pod-product-compliance
Ingram Content Group UK Ltd.
Pitfield, Milton Keynes, MK11 3LW, UK
UKHW042146130625

459647UK00011B/1202